PRAISE FOR
THE COMMONWEALTH OF SELF-INTEREST

"Paul's must-read book brings together key concepts fundamental to customer engagement in a post-digital world. Trust is the ultimate currency. In a commonwealth of self-interest, organizations and individuals will live and die by how well they uphold the mission and purpose of their brand. This dynamic of experiential engagement transforms the future of the customer and disrupts digital business forever."

—RAY WANG, CEO Constellation Research, author of *Disrupting Digital Business: Create an Authentic Experience in the Peer-to-Peer Economy*

"Paul once again has taken on a challenging topic of Customer Engagement. The future of every business is fully understanding how, when, where, and with what channels to engage your customers. This book is critical to understanding the principles behind engagement and why it is important."

—BOB STUTZ, CEO Salesforce Marketing Cloud

"Understanding the voice of the customer and engaging customers on their terms is foundational to long-term business success. Paul delivers great clarity and practical advice any executive should embrace to effectively compete in today's hyper-driven digital economy."

—ANDRES REINER, CEO PROS

The

COMMONWEALTH

of

SELF-INTEREST

The
COMMONWEALTH
of
SELF-INTEREST

BUSINESS SUCCESS THROUGH
CUSTOMER ENGAGEMENT

PAUL GREENBERG

56G Press
Manassas, Virginia

To my always amazing, wonderful wife Yvonne, love of my life, my spirit walker, my dreamcatcher.

It is not from the benevolence of the butcher, the brewer or the baker that we expect our dinner, but from their regard to their own self-interest.

—ADAM SMITH

CONTENTS

ACKNOWLEDGMENTS

I love acknowledgments—and I hate them. I love them because I get to thank whoever I feel like thanking. They are always the ones who either directly or indirectly helped me with the whatever it took to get this book done, and they deserve more credit than I can possibly give in a written acknowledgment. (Unfortunately, I can't make a video to be inserted in this book.) I hate them because I inevitably forget one or two or more people and feel like a jerk for not remembering them. So, this time, I'm organizing my acknowledgments so that you can see who it took, over the years, to put this all together, and who made a difference in my life in general or in the book and, thus, we have what I hope is a happy compendium of gratitude for people willing to be a help and a force in my life.

First, I want to thank my family. You saw the dedication to my wife Yvonne, so I won't repeat it here, but her continued encouragement was instrumental in my finishing this book—and, take my word for it, "instrumental" is an understatement. Orchestral is probably a better way to put it. She was my conductor, my woodwinds, brass, and drums, oh, and my vocals.

My brother Bob was there for me always, and I not only thank him for that but for being my brother—which has made my life so much easier and better—because he's my brother and I know he always has my back no matter what. And, of course, I have his. He is a rock and a rock star in business and as a dad, husband, and, of course, brother.

I also want to acknowledge the gods of comedy and satire for their role in putting together this book. Somebody not long ago asked me why I was in the CRM and customer engagement world and I told them the following. "I wanted to be a standup comedian but realized that if I told a bad joke, my career could be over. If I was a CRM guy and told a bad joke, then they'd say, "Oh, he's a CRM guy. Of course, his jokes suck." So, I'm a CRM guy and, now, a customer-engagement guy who is beholden to the Marx Brothers, S.J. Perelman, Steve Martin, and Saturday Night Live, and all that they all stand (up) for. I hope that, as you read the book, you find enough humor, snarkiness (Microsoft Word wants to correct this to "smarminess" or "shakiness." Hmmm...), and maybe even a good enough joke or two to remind you that, while I may be talking about customer engagement, life is too short to not be happy and laugh out loud at least once a day—and hopefully more. You can't get any more engaged with your own soul than that.

There is one guy who keeps showing up in my life—my book life—as a mentor—and the rest of my life—as a friend—and that's Roger Stewart. First, he took a chance on me years ago when he was an Editorial Director for McGraw-Hill and I was an unknown in the world of CRM. If it weren't for him, my book *CRM at the Speed of Light* wouldn't have happened, and my career wouldn't have been my career. Back then I needed to be validated by a third party, and Roger Stewart's taking that shot with me—which I did not throw away—was just what I needed. Now, since I am grateful to say I no longer need validation, I can produce this book on my own and I expect it will do well enough, thank you. And, once again, Roger is there to guide me through the process by being my editor and making me sound better, and my guidance counselor on things like book formatting, cover design, publishing and distribution. Once again, I couldn't do it without him. Thank you for everything from the beginning to now, Roger. I am just happy I get to know you and even once in a great while hang out with you. Heinold's First and Last Chance Saloon, Jack London's hangout in Oakland, CA, here we come.

Even though there were many contributors to this book who I am going to thank, I want to single out a few who were instrumental beyond their contribution: Brent Leary, my CRM Playaz partner, who provided solid support every day with a kindness that I didn't deserve; Esteban Kolsky, who would check in on me at the exact right moments when I needed him to check in on me; and Denis Pombriant, also an author, always a friend, and someone who stirred my intellectual juices, giving me a bit more clarity than I had before talking to him. I'd also like to thank Marc Benioff, who has written the foreword for my last three books. Given his schedule and how many demands there are on him, I'm deeply grateful he was gracious enough to do it again. Also, thank you Bruce Culbert, who has been there for me as a member of my non-blood family for more than a decade and wrote a helluva piece for this book, too.

I'd like to also give a special shout out to Ray Wang, a major influencer in the technology world I inhabit, for his support over the years and his knowledge of the industry I live in—making my job (and life) easier. This book wouldn't exist without Ray. He's been a great friend.

One more special thanks to Phil Venville, SVP of Strategy at Thunderhead, who is a true friend and thinker par excellence. Many hours of conversation about this book helped me beyond even reasonableness to frame customer engagement the way it deserves to be framed. For all that and for introducing me to a flat white, Phil, thank you.

Also, thank you to Karl Wabst, Silvana Buljan, Barry Trailer, Joe Hughes, Brian Solis, Scott Rogers, Marta Federici, Charlie Shin, Bruce Temkin, Brian Curran, David Myron, Michael Wu, Alan Berkson, Rachel Happe, and Ray Gerber for helping me out with contributions to this book. They are all luminaries in their own right, and, oh, how they shine!

Lauren Vargas, John Hurley, and Srikrishnan Ganesan contributed their knowledge so that I had someone smarter than me who could briefly talk to the subjects that readers needed to hear about. Thank you, thank you, thank you.

I could go on and on with the actual influences on my life and those friends by the dozens, and special friends by the ones, who stood by me while I attempted to make this a tour de force of a tome. But I don't have the room here. Suffice to say, though, thank you so much for everything.

Finally, I want to thank the universe for having me. I have loved this ride and hope this is a great way to return the thanks. Let's trust that the rest of the ride is as good as it has been so far.

FOREWORD

When Paul asked me to write this foreword for *The Commonwealth of Self-Interest*, I thought about the massive changes that have occurred since Salesforce was founded nearly 20 years ago. We started with the simple idea that business software could be delivered via the internet in the same way that people could buy books on Amazon. That concept evolved into a company built on three groundbreaking ideas: a new technology model based in the cloud, a new pay-as-you-go, subscription business model, and a new integrated corporate philanthropy model. Underlying those three ideas is a total focus on the customer and being the best example ourselves of exceptional customer relationship management.

I've known Paul since the beginnings of Salesforce, and over the years I've relied on his wisdom as we've made Salesforce into the fastest growing top-five software company in the world and the global leader in CRM. Paul has been an astute observer of the CRM industry as it's evolved and a staunch advocate for companies to develop more customer-engaged cultures. And, he has inspired me as we've evolved our thinking and products.

Today, we are living in the single most innovative era in history. Expanding access to the internet, the explosion of data, increased computing power, and advances in artificial intelligence (AI) are reshaping the way every company across every industry engages with its customers.

It's truly the Age of the Customer.

All companies today are undergoing a digital transformation, and they are doing it first around their customers. In this Age of the Customer, it's imperative that business leaders put their customer at the center of everything they do if they want to succeed. And the definition of customer is expanding as the Internet of Things (IoT) grows from billions to trillions of connected devices. The reality is that, behind every app and every device—from jet engines and lightbulbs to thermostats and cars—is a customer. This is an internet of customers, where every industry—transportation, construction, supply chains, agriculture, medicine, retail, energy, entertainment, and more—is getting smarter and more efficient.

Over the last few decades, we have built systems of engagement on top of systems of record. And, now, we are adding on systems of intelligence that leverage AI to create even more highly personalized, one-to-one customer experiences. Companies like Amazon, Airbnb, Netflix, and Uber now offer highly personalized, intelligent customer experiences that the older companies in their respective industries are racing to duplicate.

When I meet with companies to talk about a vision for the future of their businesses, it's not just about the cloud, AI, mobile, and other game-changing technologies—it's about the customer experience. This is a huge cultural shift. The leading companies understand that they need to shift focus from selling products to providing intelligent customer experiences that lead to deeper customer engagement.

Customers are on a more even footing with the companies they engage with than ever. Half of the workforce today is made up the millennial and younger generations, for whom internet-connected devices are an extension of their being. They have an expectation of frictionless, real-time interactions with brands. They also have an expectation that companies they do business with have a commitment to making the world a better place, and, in Paul's words, are trustworthy, empathetic, believable, and respectful.

At Salesforce, our nearly 30,000 people are guided by four core values to keep us on the path to customer success: Trust, Growth, Innovation, and Equality.

Nothing is more important than building trusted, transparent relationships with customers. It is the foundation of customer relationship management.

Every company depends on growth to succeed, and in this Age of the Customer the vital currency is customer relationships. CRM is the fastest-growing enterprise software category, and its growth reflects the increasing importance of customer engagement as a catalyst for growth.

The desire to grow and build deeper customer relationships can't happen without a culture of innovation. Harnessing technology advancements, which are maturing at an increasingly rapid pace, is essential to enabling world-class customer experiences. The entire history of Salesforce is one of continuous innovation, applying the cloud, mobile, social, IoT, and now AI technologies to help more than 150,000 companies grow and succeed.

Finally, people want to do business with companies that also aspire to a higher purpose. Companies that support equality, social justice and environmental issues are more likely to be trusted by customers and earn customer and employee loyalty. As businesses, we can be financially successful and, at the same time, make the world a better place for everyone. We don't just serve our shareholders, but all of our stakeholders—customers, employees, partners, communities we live in, and the environment. And advocating for equality— equal rights, pay, opportunity, and advancement—as well as improving public education and healthcare systems and creating a more sustainable planet, are in the interest of all stakeholders.

Giving back is also part of having equality as a core value. In 1999, we transformed corporate philanthropy with our 1-1-1 integrated philanthropy model, which leverages the resources of Salesforce for public good: donating 1% of Salesforce's product, 1% of Salesforce's equity, and 1% of employees' time to help nonprofits achieve their missions. As of the first half of 2017, we had given more that $160 million in grants and over 2.2 million hours of Salesforce employee volunteer time, and we've supplied more than 31,000 nonprofits and NGOs with free or heavily discounted software. More than 2,000 companies across 50 countries have signed up for Pledge 1%, a global movement to create a new normal where giving back is baked into the DNA of companies from the very beginning.

This is my story, and, as I have experienced, your story. The way you think about your business and how to engage customers at deeper levels will be improved by absorbing the content of *The Commonwealth of Self-Interest*. Paul asks how you can satisfy the self-interest of each of the customers so that their experience is exceptional enough for them to want to continue to do business with you. This book will give you the guidance and insights to rise to the occasion with every single customer.

Mahalo,
MARC BENIOFF
CEO, Salesforce

INTRODUCTION

S igh. Every time I finish a book, I vow never to write another one. They are so hard. But then, within two to four years, the book is almost obsolete because a sea change of some kind comes along and makes dramatic alterations to institutional thinking, approaches, systems, technologies, and cultures that stirs my blood and makes me get back into it again.

So, probably sounding a bit more arrogant than I mean to, I see a significant change going on right now that needs to be identified, defined, clarified, reported, distributed, and consumed—and, in lieu of something better coming along, I've taken on the project to do just that.

"Okay, Paul," you are probably saying, "Enough with the self-congratulation poorly disguised as humility. What are you talking about?" I'm so glad that you asked. Oh, and thanks for calling me by my first name.

This time around, I'm writing about customer engagement.

Starting around 2014, customer engagement became a top-of-mind concern for businesses and governments (although it's called "constituent engagement" in the latter case). This is occurring for all kinds of reasons, but if I told them to you here I'd really have no purpose for writing the book, now, would I? So, go to Chapter 1 whenever you're ready, and you'll find out the broad brushstroke reasons. At least what I think they are.

"Ah," you say, "Isn't it the case that every business has always been thinking about engaging customers?" To some extent, that would be true. All businesses that I run across in my travels as a CRM guy are interested in either acquiring new customers or keeping existing customers or both. Of course, to do that, customers and/or prospects have to interact with you, i.e., engage.

But, while all that is true, what is different is that customers have changed pretty significantly over the last decade in terms of their character, behaviors, demands, expectations, and experiences. So, what it takes to have those interactions begin and then continue is very different than it was just a few years ago.

If you read the fourth (and, I swear, the final) edition of my earlier book, *CRM at the Speed of Light*—my 800-plus-page tome—you may remember that

I closed it with a simple formulation. "If customers like you and continue to like you, they will continue to do business with you, and if they don't, they won't." That is about as simple a definition of what it takes when it comes to customers interacting with you. They have to like you—and want to communicate—for whatever reason. They also have to trust you—meaning that they believe you operate not only in your own interests, but in their interests as a customer, too. You will hear me repeat this formulation several times throughout the book. It is that important.

But what isn't so simple is that what customers demand in order to continue to like, trust, and communicate with you isn't easy to fulfill. Customers are considerably more demanding than they were a decade ago. In fact, they can be so demanding, and, even, at times, entitled, in the somewhat nasty sense of the word, that it becomes a genuine issue for businesses to figure out, not just exactly what these customers are demanding, but what those businesses have to do to meet the demands without bankrupting themselves in the process.

Yeah, but isn't the customer the king (or queen)? The answer to that is a not-very-simple "no." They are partners, not clients, if you are doing what you need to do; but they have a radically different idea of what value is to them than you have as a business. That difference has to be considered, and the customer's itch scratched; but they don't have to have personal back scratchers. What you each (and both) get out of the interactions and transactions is paramount to business success, but the key word is "both," not just the customer.

Don't get me wrong. I'm a customer advocate. Always have been. I'm a former union organizer and 60s radical who has been on the side of justice for my entire life. When I was young, it was the proletariat; now, as I approach my dotage, it's the customer. But I also recognize that businesses are just that—businesses—and, unless they are specifically charities or non-profits with a different, perhaps more social, purpose, then they are in business to make money, not just to serve customers. They serve customers to make money. But smart businesses realize that the value must be mutual, not one-sided.

This goes to the heart of customer engagement and why it's so important to understand. Value exchange is the core of all business relationships with customers. As we will see throughout the book, a fully engaged customer provides considerably greater value to a company than one who isn't. That means it is in the interest of a business to provide that customer with what he or she needs to be fully engaged—but not at the expense of losing the possible benefits that will be accrued from the customer in return. *The Commonwealth of Self-Interest* shows how to ensure that mutual benefit is the order of the day and that your customers feel no sense of violation as your business accumulates its benefits in whatever form they take.

So, what does that mean that businesses have to do . . . or, at least, what they need to be thinking about?

CUSTOMER CENTRICITY? NAH. CUSTOMER-ENGAGED

The solution to handling customers that's been posited for the last decade has become a revered cliché. The company has to be customer-centric. Customer-centric definitions range from "creating a positive consumer experience at the point of sale and post-sale" (Business Dictionary.com) to "placing the customer at the center of a company's marketing effort, focusing on customers rather than sales," (Dictionary.com), to a more radical "looking at a customer's lifetime value and focusing marketing efforts squarely on that real-world, high-value customer segment to drive profit" (Dr. Peter Fader, *Customer Centricity,* 2013). The latter definition apparently offended enough customer advocates to create another category called "customer-focused," which means, more or less, "give customers what they want." At the time, Dr. Fader was absolutely right about what he was saying and far more definitive than anyone else.

Times changed. And a third approach became necessary. In the course of this book, I am going to establish that third area which will encompass and supersede both customer-centric and customer-focused. That will be to define the idea of a "customer-engaged" company that is both providing value to and receiving value from customers. In the course of that, I will also be looking at what defines a "high-value" customer, and, trust me, it isn't just the amount of money their household is worth to a company over their estimated lifetime as a customer. Chapter 16 should, let us say, make your notion of measuring customer value considerably more expansive.

If I've done the job I fully intend to do, you will also, by the end of the ride, have seen the big picture and know why customer engagement is so important. You'll know the approaches, the programs, the strategies, the processes, the technologies, and the culture necessary to build a company that can at least aspire to fully engage its customers with a chance of success. You will have heard stories from experts and companies on how they went about doing this—successes and failures—and you will have more than just me vying for your attention. I also hope (and, if I can be mildly egotistical here, expect) you will have enjoyed yourself along the way. These things are a lot of fun, not just valuable. This isn't a stuffy book. Not on my watch. Or with my "pen."

WHAT ARE YOU IN FOR?

To do this, I've arranged the book so that it's as easy to consume as ice cream with high butterfat content (unless you are lactose intolerant—then come up with your own food metaphor).

The initial chapter sets the stage. It's about a universe far, far away and a long time ago. It identifies the larger forces at play. We've all heard about business transformation, digital transformation, customer experience, customer engagement, digital media, and social media ad nauseum. Even though we have probably gotten sick of each and all of those over-hyped phrases, all of them represent valid concepts that are impacting business in a way that we may never have seen before. They have transformed how businesses need to run in the 21st century. So, we can't discount their power, despite our desire play whack-a-mole on those phrases each time we hear them uttered.

Following the first chapter, the next several chapters are spent identifying and structuring a customer-engagement framework. What is customer engagement, and who are the customers that customer engagement is targeting? How are they thinking? To that end, I'll be introducing the concept of the "commonwealth of self-interest," a phrase with a sort of retro catchiness, but one that is central to how to think about dealing with contemporary customers. Given that, how does engagement differ with and integrate with customer experience in a meaningful, rather than merely literary, way? Which companies get this?

Once we establish the framework, the next order of business is defining customer-engagement strategies. What do we have to plan for to fully engage, and also proactively prevent complete disengagement of, our targeted customer base? What do we have to know about customers to develop these strategies? How do we get this information? (Big hint: customer journeys are mega-important here.) What are the operational requirements we need to consider to execute the strategy?

Okay, when we get to that point, definition clear? Check. Framework established? Check. Strategies defined? Check.

Then, we'll start drilling down into the programs that are required and possible when it comes to customer engagement. What specific programs work under what circumstances? How do you set goals and objectives for the outcomes you want from the programs? What are examples of programs that work?

Do we rest on our laurels at this point? Nope. We drill even more deeply into the customer-facing components, marketing, sales, and customer service, and look at how they've changed in the age of digital transformation. For example, how has marketing become not just a messaging and positioning pro-cedure but the first and second lines of engagement? What does that mean in practical terms, given the outcomes that are needed from the effort? Who is doing this well, who is doing it not so well? Add sales and customer service, along with their respective transformations, and you will get an idea of how a business has to realign and rethink its contemporary customer-facing work.

We move from this to the contemporary technologies available that fall under the umbrella of customer engagement. It is a vastly bigger universe than CRM. What is a system of engagement versus a system of record? What about the use of data and analytics tools to help define personalization and engage-ment strategies? What kind of technology ecosystem would be ideal when it comes to customer engagement? Is it even possible to achieve?

Next up—outcomes. Optimally, we'd love to see advocates and, minimally, loyal customers. How do we get there? What kind of customer-desired out-comes are asked and answered?

The last section is about something that vexes practitioners all the time. How do we measure all this? The idea of customer value has changed rather dramatically with the rise of consumer and business influence and peer trust. How do you quantify that? Look, honestly, I'm not the guy to do the math. I'm far too right-brained. But I'm smart enough to know when someone is onto something. In this section, I'll be examining the work of Dr. V. Kumar. More on him when the time comes.

All right, all right. The real last section is the very brief summation of the book and my spin, err, thinking on where customer engagement will be going at the time you are reading this. (That would be now.)

WAIT! I FORGOT TO TELL YOU THE FORMAT

Much as I love writing books, I'm not stupid enough to think I know every-thing. Therefore, I'm going to make sure that you don't just have to rely on only what I'm saying, but, instead, I'll bring in experts and tell you their stories.

Several chapters will include a lengthy and substantial case study to show you that it can and has been done. All chapters will give you examples of suc-cess and, sometimes, failures when it comes to the approach to customer engagement that the chapter is focused on.

Many chapters, though not all, will have, in addition to me, one or two expert advisers who will provide you with some best practices and great advice on how to take your engagement initiatives forward. On occasion, because they are more expert than I am, the advisers will have an actual section in the chapter. They may not agree with me all the time. That's what makes this such an exciting and important area. We all are exploring what we have to do to satisfy the needs of our customers and our businesses simultaneously—and there is no uniform agreement on what that is. You get the benefit of the most significant, current thinking on the subject.

WAIT AGAIN! A GENERAL POINT

One thing that becomes apparent as you read this book is that the subject is big and rather all-encompassing. Thus, some of the topics that are addressed in one chapter could just as well be addressed in another, or in a third. For example, I address churn management in the section on data and analytics (Chapter 13) in a case study of how churn-reduction was effected at Telenor, a Norwegian telco, using predictive analytics. I could just as well have used the same case study in Chapter 12 to discuss customer service, but I chose to use it to show you an incredibly valuable use of predictive analytics and an approach to the analytics framework. If you don't like that, sue me. Not really. Just kidding. I can't afford the payments. But please realize that there is no point complaining about where I put things in the book. I put it where I put it for a reason. Besides, the book is already published, so I can't really move it. Feel free to not be happy with my choices, but at least try to understand why I did what I did.

I'M AVAILABLE

Not that way. I've been happily married to Yvonne Greenberg for well over thirty years. I'm not that great of a catch anyway. Trust me on that.

But I am available to communicate with you if you so desire. I am a baby boomer who is immature and, thus, embraces millennial communications methods—so there are many ways to reach me. You'll see discussions of omni-channel in this book. I am omni-channel.

- My website is www.the56group.com—one of the best ways to interact with me.
- My email address is paul-greenberg3@the56group.com.
- My Twitter handle is @pgreenbe
- My Facebook name is pgreenbe
- My LinkedIn name is pgreenbe

- My Skype name is pgreenbe (Seeing a pattern? Not my password, hackers!)

- My office phone: 703-551-2337

- My mobile phone: 703-338-0232

- My ZDNet Blog, Social CRM: The Conversation, is at www.zdnet .com/blog/crm/

There are a few dozen other social sites (Tumblr, About.me, YouTube, Medium, etc.) that I participate in, but you'll be doing fine with what I'm providing you. Please feel free to contact me, and I'll return the communication as soon as I am able. I promise.

I also run a competition every year for more established companies, the CRM Watchlist, based on a company's market impact. It is considered a significant industry award for reasons I cannot fathom but that I am eternally grateful for. Feel free to ask me about it, and I will respond, although there is a chance that, by the time you ask, I'll no longer be doing the Watchlist. Nothing is forever, though I'd love that to be the case.

But enough about contacting me. We have something to do now—and that's talk about customer engagement. I will do everything in my power to keep you fully engaged. That's what this is all about anyway, right?

SECTION ONE
Overview

The journey begins here. What's it all about? Why bother to talk about customer engagement? How will we walk or bike or ride on the pathways through this book?

Chapter 1 drops the flag, and the race begins.

CHAPTER 1

Nature, Nurture?—
Digital Customer, Digital Business

I t's not often that I start a book with a truism. Actually, it's not often that I start a book at all, really. But this time around, a truism it is.

The world has changed. Changes in the world are irrevocable. To make these irrevocable changes good ones, with benefits to you as a businessperson, rather than damaging ones with disaster in the offing, *you* have to change, too.

That's the truism. Given the nature of truisms, of course, you already know that.

But here is something you might *not* know, or at least that you might have the wrong idea about.

You probably think that we've had a business revolution over the past decade or so.

If so, you'd be wrong.

What we've undergone is not a business revolution but a communications revolution that has transformed how we communicate, with whom we communicate, who we trust when it comes to communication, what we expect of communications, and what we use to communicate with. It has also transformed how we create, distribute, and consume information. It has affected not just businesses but almost every institution and individual on the planet.

A COMMUNICATIONS REVOLUTION

This is why business transformation, especially digital transformation, is at the top of business agendas across the globe. At a minimum, it means companies are trying to figure out how to address specific concerns that involve their newly empowered and often entitled customers who have unprecedented access to information and to each other. At the other end of the scale, it can lead to a dramatic re-invention of business because, once again, the customers and the employees are demanding much more personalized relationships than at any previous point in human history. Either way, changing your business to meet the demands of empowered customers will be essential to keeping those customers engaged. It is of paramount importance to every business.

So, let's begin our journey with a short trip to the outlands. I'm going to take you to Australia. Why? Because, in 2015, Australia established a government Digital Transformation Office.

Digital Transformation Goes Mainstream

Since we are at the outset of this book, you might be asking, "Why would that be important?" Even though transformed communications are mainstream, neither public nor private institutions implementing the right programs are.

What Australia is doing is an appropriate way to begin this book because it highlights the fact that digital transformation and engagement are real and are in progress. An entire country is committed to making the shifts in communication and information distribution work at scale, all to better their citizens' relationship to them.

When they announced the Digital Transformation Office (DTO) on January 23, 2015, part of their press release stated:

> *The DTO will comprise a small team of developers, designers, researchers and content specialists working across government to develop and coordinate the delivery of digital services. The DTO will operate more like a start-up than a traditional government agency, focusing on end-user needs in developing digital services.*
>
> *The DTO will use technology to make services simpler, clearer and faster for Australian families and businesses.*

To get to the point that an entire government commits to the institutionalization of a digital transformation program as a matter of policy, something had to have happened long enough ago to make this viable to these normally conservative, slow-moving institutions in the public sector.

That would be the communications revolution.

The DTO is clearly focused on engaging Australian citizens. The contemporary digital customer requires engagement as a condition of involvement with an organization, and it's a requirement for the engagement to continue.

Those expectations are due to a communications revolution, not a business revolution, that has been taking place for more than a decade now.

To understand this revolution, we need to look at how we communicate now and how we create, distribute, and consume information.

How We Communicate

We communicate differently now than we did even a decade ago. The types of communications devices we use, the context that the communications occur in, and the expectations of the individual regarding communications over time are drastically different. This transformation has created a new set of protocols for dealing with different communications media and channels, and it has empowered people to demand responsiveness in ways that were unthinkable less than a generation ago.

While we've heard repeatedly that millennials are the prime "digerati" who are communicating differently, that isn't strictly the case. To be fair to them, as a generation, they did spark the communications transformation; but we've now gone well beyond the time when the individual customer's age made a difference. While I'm not saying there are no generational differences at all, the data tells us that all generations are becoming increasingly wedded to their smart devices as the prime receivers and purveyors of communications and information.

In April 2015, the Pew Research Center, one of the best agnostic research bodies in the world, did a study called "U.S. Smartphone Use, 2015," based on first-quarter 2015 usage, and found that 64 percent of Americans owned a smartphone, while 54 percent of the 50–64 age segment owned one. By January 2017, these numbers had leapt to 77 percent and 74 percent respectively. The only segment that lags a bit is the 65+ age group, which was at 27 percent in 2015 but had reached a more respectable 42 percent by 2017. ComScore, in their MobiLens' and Mobile Metrix' reports, set the number, as of January 2015, at 188.6 million smartphones in the U.S., which they say is an even greater 76.9 percent market penetration than Pew Research indicated. Regardless of which number is right, there is something telling in this data. It means that a significant majority of Americans of all generations (except the very oldest) own smartphones. In other words, it's not just millennials who are attached to their smartphones, oh you purveyors of urban myth. To add to this, when we consider other smart devices, 53 percent of smartphone owners also own a tablet. There are 156 million tablet owners in the U.S. Though if you eliminate *me*, that number probably drops down to 154 million tablets.

Here is something even more telling. It's not just that 2.4 billion people have them; it's what they do with them, which tells us that there is a new kind of customer. A digital customer dominates the business world now and, as we shall see later, controls the conversation. Let that statement sink in, and leave it alone for a while. We'll get into it more later.

What do these digital customers do with their smartphones, besides drop them and crack the screen glass? (Or is that just me?)

Let's investigate.

Information Creation, Distribution, Consumption

What makes this so fascinating is how mundane it is. We are using these *extraordinary* devices to carry out the most basic functions and activities, *ordinary* things that we do every day.

Smartphones are used to carry out everyday activities like:

- Looking up a health condition—62 percent

- Doing online banking—57 percent

- Looking up real estate listings when trying to find a place to live—44 percent

- Looking up job information—43 percent

- Taking a class—30 percent

(Source: "U.S. Smartphone Use, 2015," Pew Research Center, Aaron Smith and Dana Page)

Not lost in this data is an almost automatic trust that what you are doing is secure (e.g., banking) and reliable (e.g., looking up health information). We'll be looking more deeply at trust in Chapters 9 and 15 because it is the foundation for the changes in behavior that we are seeing among customers, and it's fundamental to what a business needs to not just retain 21st century customers but turn them into advocates or, at least, to garner their loyalty.

The lesson here is that the ordinary things we do in life are increasingly being done via channels that didn't even exist a decade ago. Not only that, but they are becoming the norm. We talk about millennials being digital natives, having grown up with these channels, but baby boomers and Gen Xers use them naturally now, too, even though the devices were not part of their childhood culture. This phenomenon has changed the behaviors of human beings in ways that are profound and sticky. But it's more than just communications. We consume information very differently than we did not that long ago.

The implication is that businesses must create and distribute information in new ways. I'll be discussing this throughout the book, so I'm not detailing it here, but suffice it to say that the information has to be based on currency and relevancy. It needs to be up to date and, for me as a customer, it has to be what I want to see. It has to be distributed so that I can see it when I want to, and it has to be presented in the format that I want to see it in. "Format," in this context, means three things: the device that I want to receive it on, such as a smartphone, tablet, computer, or physical object (e.g., a magazine); the type of medium I want to experience, such as digital text, print, video, or audio; and the channel I want to receive it in, such as web pages, email, text messages, social networks, or video platforms.

The Digital Customer

Industry pundits for the last few years have called these communications-heavy, information-swallowing consumers "digital customers." But, as the data above shows, they are now so ubiquitous we might as well just call them "customers." Why not? The bulk of customers, regardless of generation, are using smart devices and digital tools habitually for communication and information-gathering to make their purchasing decisions.

With the widespread use of smart devices and the incredible amount of information now visible to consumers that may previously have only been available internally if at all, the expectations of customers have changed. Being a customer is only one of the hats that a person wears every day of his life. Parent, employee, driver, friend, reader, TV watcher, volunteer . . . all are hats we wear each day, and these roles drive the interactions we have with institutions and other individuals. In the course of a day, we use our smart devices to enhance or support the interactions we have either through communications media or information gathering. Because of these devices, we have developed a new set of expectations. We can get information about anything on demand. We can get a service response within minutes or hours. We can watch a movie at high resolution via streaming services. We can text our best friend and hear back in seconds or minutes. We are rewarded for our loyalty to a brand. All of these, even if initially they were how a customer interacted with a single company, have become universal expectations. As customers, we expect to get all of this in the format and time that we want. We also expect that the service level we get from a company will be no less than the best they provide. Most importantly, as customers, we expect that the company we are dealing with knows enough about us to value us as individuals, and that they will provide us with the types of choices that make sense to us and give us the kind of control over our experience with them that we want. Anything less is #FAIL.

Let me tell you a personal story.

Several years ago, I signed up for a site called GetGlue. This was basically a site that gave you data like, "9,218 people are watching NCIS. What are you watching?" The only information they had about me at the time was my email address. I was trawling around the site when I did something that unlocked a Radiohead badge.

I can't stand Radiohead. Don't get me wrong. While I'm a baby boomer, I'm not one of the "only classic rock is great" crowd. Contemporary performers like Imagine Dragons, Lumineers, and Drake are all favorites of mine. But I never could stand Radiohead's music. Ever. So, I was immediately turned off and never went back to the site again.

Given that all GetGlue knew about me was my email address, they didn't exactly have enough knowledge to give me a particularly satisfying response, did they? But they could have something that, more than likely, would have kept me coming back to the site. Any guesses?

They could have given me a choice. What if, instead of telling me I got a Radiohead badge, they had told me I'd get a selection of badges (e.g., Jimi Hendrix Experience, Aerosmith, Lumineers, Coldplay, Radiohead)? That would have made all the difference in the world. I'd choose one I like, and they'd get a data point about me. Win. Win.

Even though I'm a baby boomer, I'm a classic digital customer, too. I want a choice. I have expectations of a personalized experience because I can get one from other companies who do similar other things. And, thus, the standard is set.

A lot of what I am saying here you may consider old hat. Stats on the new ways we communicate and on customer expectations are flooding the digital plain. But what is becoming clear about the digital customer is that they demand more, they expect those demands to be met, and a big part of what they demand is a *meaningful* response. "Meaningful," in this case, means personalized. It means a response that indicates that you, as a company, know enough about them to make relevant offers and give them consequential choices about the ways they can communicate and interact with your company.

There is a lot more to know about this digital customer, but I'm going to wait until Chapters 2–4 to get into it. Consider this a taste of things to come. This is the 20,000-foot overview of what the book is all about. Because this chapter is the pacesetter for the rest of the book, I'm also about to introduce something that you will see peppered throughout. I'm going to introduce you to thought leaders who will tell you what they think, in their own words, and maybe what *you* should be thinking about when it comes to customer engagement.

The esteemed Ray Wang gets to start the series.

THOUGHT LEADER: RAY WANG

Technology industry analyst, CEO, and thought leader Ray Wang is a longtime dear friend of mine and one of the most influential people on the planet Earth. (I don't doubt his likely influence on the moon and Mars either.) He is the author of the book *Disrupting Digital Business* (2015). His day job is CEO of the highly respected Constellation Research, a boutique market-research and analyst firm whose influence far exceeds its size. Ray has been highly outspoken on the value of digital disruption and what is and isn't hype. Here is his take on why digital business is the business of customer engagement.

Ray, here's the mic.

⚬ ⚬ ⚬ ⚬ ⚬

We are at the beginning of the digital revolution. As the pace of change accelerates, few rules seem to apply. In the case of digital business, these models have progressed over the past 20 years. However, non-traditional competitors have each exploited a few patterns with massive success. As the models evolved, winners realized there are more than a handful of patterns, tweaks to the business model, and the application of a new technology.

In fact, the impact is significant and now quantifiable with 52 percent of the Fortune 500 gone since 2000 and the average age of the S&P 500 Company, since 1960, down from 60 years to a little more than 12 years. That 500 percent compression has changed the market landscape forever in almost every industry.

In this digital age, we live in a post-sale, on-demand, attention economy. "Post-sale" shows how the value exchange after the sale is worth more than the initial sale. "On-demand" refers to our need to access outcomes and experiences in smaller but faster increments. "Attention economy" reflects on how brands and organizations compete for saving time or capturing one's attention.

So how do leaders competing with brands and organizations born in the digital age succeed? As brands and organizations determine how to react, they realize this is more than a quarterly initiative or special project. The change must come from within. Leaders must seriously consider how they will transform business models and determine how they engage with not only people but also things around us.

To succeed, we can't just look at the latest cool set of technologies of the day. We have to think bolder about transforming business models. This means understanding the one or two key metrics that businesses must measure to ensure their success.

For airlines, the key metric is revenue per passenger per kilometer, not safety, customer satisfaction, or on-time performance. For professional services firms, the key metric is profit per employee, not average deal sizes or certified professionals.

This shift to understanding the business model is the heart of digital transformation. Success requires leaders to move beyond incremental innovation, however, which is what organizations normally do to push the next set of product improvements. Transformational business models require out-of-the-box thinking and the creative destruction of multiple business models. I often use the iPhone as an example of a device that destroyed 27 business models. These industries that will never recover from $400 digital-camera makers include one-hour photo development, camcorders, record stores, book stores, navigation GPS devices, thermometer manufacturers, watches, and, yes, even the flashlight.

Related to this business-model shift is the move from selling products and services to keeping brand promises in an attention economy. Product companies such as mobile phone operators give products away for services contract revenue. Services-based companies use freemium to drive services revenue in premium experiences. Experience-based companies give away experiences for business models.

As we move along this value chain, the brand promise serves as a paramount principle of the organization's mission. Once you realize that we live in an attention economy, you realize that the goal is to capture someone's time or reduce the time to get something done. The battle for time is paramount in delivering a brand promise. Digital winners know they can succeed by keeping true to the brand promise.

A successful approach is to imagine the smallest unit of a product and service you can sell or provide access to. What happens when we go from buying a case of coke to paying for a sip of coke? Imagine a $50 pass for all you can sip at any Coca Cola freestyle machine. Understanding unit-cost pricing models enables a transformation of the experience.

Successful organizations know that data is the foundation of digital businesses. Every touch point, every click, every atom of digital exhaust provides relevant insight. As data aligns with business processes, we gain better information. We then take this information and analyze it for patterns. The goal is to ask questions of the data and then surface patterns that augment our ability to make better decisions.

Why do sweatshirts sell better in September than December? Why do blue sweaters sell well in Ann Arbor, Michigan, rather than green sweaters? College sports aficionados would know this is related to the sales of team merchandise. With this insight, stores would make better decisions and change when they order and what colors they stock. More importantly, we can use this insight to construct new service offerings, broker the insight for benchmarking data, or create new market places.

The new winners of the digital era have built business models that aggregate the distinct components of network economies. They bring content (the product or service value), networks (sourcing and distribution), and the arms dealer (technology advantage) together.

Prior to the digital age, most organizations chose one of these components as the primary business model and partnered with the others to create a network economy. However, over time, organizations realized they needed to build business models that included two or even all three of these components.

In fact, successful winners of the digital era have created an asymmetrical advantage by taking over all three components. For example, in the consumer world, four companies have the ability to deliver on these network economies: Apple, Amazon, Google, and Microsoft. These companies have the content, the network, and the arms-dealer capabilities to monetize on trust and identity.

As brands and organizations seek digital scale, they strip out friction in the network and lower transactional costs. By removing the intermediary and going direct, organizations can reduce non-value-added interactions. Where there are networks to participate in, however, there must be a good exchange of value.

By tapping into peer-to-peer (P2P) networks, selfish value-exchange creates trust and transparency in the network. In some cases, the solution to stripping out friction and transaction costs is to create your own platform. Organizations who open up their platform to spur innovation can find themselves gaining digital scale adoption.

The shift from analog to digital systems represents a continued march to delivering on mass personalized systems. These systems over the next 20 years will start with a design point of being intention driven, solving the issue of massive individual scale, and enabling personalized experiences. As these systems traverse the space-time continuum and tap into P2P networks, what we learn from these systems is that they do not replace their predecessors. In fact, with each wave, the new systems abstract information from the older systems to create new paradigms.

Delivering on these customer-segments-of-one will require a few foundational concepts.

Choose-your-own-adventure type of journeys—With no real beginning or end, expect these systems to work like a *Choose Your Own Adventure* book. Funnels fall aside as customers, partners, employees, and vendors jump across processes, make their own decisions, and create their own experiences on their terms. Journey maps must account for infinite journeys and support customer-centric points of view.

Continuity of experience—A customer may start an experience on a mobile device, carry it with them to a car, jump into the office, and then come back to the home. Regardless of channel, device, platform, or situation, context is carried. Experiences are delivered with massive context and personalization. While customers do not expect a disruption in the experience, they do expect relevancy regardless of the context.

Intention-driven design—Currently the fashionable approach is predictive. Predictive modeling does a great job of using history to predict future patterns. Intention-driven design tests for shifts in patterns by setting up hypotheses and awaiting the results. If we know a person always gets a specific type of coffee at the same time every day, that's predictive. An intention-driven system will test to see what type of coffee is purchased based on time of day, weather, relationships, location, and even sentiment gathered from heart rate or actions. The test comes from an offer or studying shifts in patterns and behaviors. These self-learning and -adjusting capabilities are powered by cognitive computing approaches.

So far, we've spent most of our time talking about business models and strategy. We now turn to humanizing digital. Why? Digital, by nature, can seem hard and cold. With digital, we need the best math as we have entered a war of algorithms. These algorithms will drive our ability to automate, predict, and augment decision-making.

We also need the best design. Having the best math may lead to great spreadsheets and tons of numbers without context. Pairing the best math with the best design means we consider the human component. So, where we often hire for science, technology, engineering, and math, we need to also account for anthropology, ethnography, design thinking, user experience, and storytelling. The goal: bring right-brain and left-brain capabilities together.

At an individual level, few folks possess the mastery of both right-brain and left-brain thinking. Hence, the secret to success requires an understanding of how each individual fits into a team of digital artisans. Successful organizations show each team member how their interactions contribute to the overall success of the organization and why each team member must be equally valued.

* * * * *

Ray, that rocked. Thank you!

I hope that you now have the overview you need to dive into customer engagement. If not, I would recommend that you reread this chapter and then keep moving. At the end of this journey, you'll have a good idea of how to approach the strategy, program, and implementation of customer engagement, both at the small end and at scale.

SECTION TWO

The Framework

N ow we have to put customer engagement in context by creating a framework to use throughout the book and, hopefully, for you to use for the rest of your wonderful life. That means providing definitions and showing how customer engagement, CRM, and customer experience all interact. What are the differences? And, spoiler alert, we explain what "The Commonwealth of Self-Interest" is—and, no, it's not Massachusetts.

CHAPTER 2

Customer Engagement . . . Definitely

We've established the larger reasons for the boardroom's interest in customer engagement—the core of that interest being the communications revolution that has transformed us. By "us" I mean all human beings, not a particular category of humans. What we expect of communications and how we see information have now been altered irrevocably.

But, after all, this is a business book. So, we are going to focus on a particular role that humans play—customer—and a particular set of institutions—businesses—and examine how the communications revolution has forced companies to rethink how they deal with their now *digital* customers.

To frame the definition of engagement, I'm going to tell you something here that I will repeat several times throughout the book. The fundamental premise of business, the one that supersedes all else, is very simple.

> *If a customer likes you and continues to like you, they will continue to do business with you. If they don't, they won't.*

As a business, you have to be aware of your own limitations in getting that customer to continue to like you. And you have to figure out how to do it without breaking the bank.

The other part of the framework needed to define engagement is what I believe to be perhaps the most obvious business premise ever. Businesses are looking for two key outcomes. The first is to acquire customers, the second to retain customers. That has been the nature of the relationship between customers and businesses from the time Hammurabi set down his first code of laws to the present day.

Your job is to get consumers to like you enough to let you acquire them as customers and then continue to like you enough to keep them as customers.

That seems simple—but it is far from simple to actually do. To understand why, we have to examine what customer engagement is and how it resonates in the thinking of progressive companies.

Let me give you an idea of what I mean by "far from simple" by using an example.

I love sports—baseball, football, pro and college basketball—pro mostly, some college (go Northwestern Wildcats!) and hockey. I also love New York teams, from passionately to somewhat less than that, in this order: Yankees, Giants, Rangers, and Knicks. I have soft spots for teams like the Green Bay Packers because of one of my closest buds, Wayne Hintz, and the Los Angeles Rams due to one of my other closest buds, Brent Leary (who you will hear from later in the book). I also like the Norwich City Canaries football (aka soccer) team due to my connection to them back in the early 2000s via their then CIO Mario Zambas.

Why do I love the Yankees? Because of my baby-boomer childhood on Long Island, growing up with Mickey Mantle, the Yankees Hall of Fame player who was a hero to most New York kids in the late 50s and early 60s, me among them. Because they represent winners. Because they are part of the city that I grew up with, love, and identify with—my civic pride. Because of several indefinable things, too. I have a complex emotional bond to the team that I can't possibly assume is governed by reason in any way.

You're probably thinking, "Wait, I want my money back! I paid for a book on customer engagement and got a book on sports, or a personal memoir, or . . . something."

Hold up, right there. This is all about engagement.

Think not? Then think about something related to a business you care about. Maybe it's the sports teams that you identify with and live and die for. Maybe it's not a sports team. Maybe it's a clothing store like Nordstrom's or a shoe line like Christian Louboutin or a big box retail monster like Tesco. It could be your all-time favorite restaurant. Maybe it's some musical icon that you've been in love with since you were a little kid. Maybe you're an Apple fan.

What each of these examples represents is an existing engagement with an entity—mostly a brand. It is something that you have had enough of a positive experience with over time that you want to continue to associate with that "thing" because—and what I'm about to say is scientific—it makes you happy to do so.

But what it also represents is the complexity of engagement. Take a look at all the reasons that I'm a Yankees fan—civic pride, childhood nostalgia, and association with a winner. Add the fact that they once had an early hero of mine, too. Those characteristics might be pretty widespread among a large portion of the older Yankees fan base. But what about the younger fan base? All those things still hold true (except there is no Mickey Mantle). Other factors might include the fact that their dads and moms are fans of the team, or that they like hanging out at the stadium the same way they might think about hanging out at the mall. Maybe they just think the logo is a great fashion statement. (That isn't so farfetched. The Yankees logo is the most recognized sports logo in the world.)

But, now, add the expectations I have as a fan. Yankees fans expect to at least go to the playoffs every year—so the pressure to deliver is even greater than the norm. Given that they aren't going to the playoffs every year as we, sadly, have recently seen far too often, how can the Yankees retain my interest and desire to be involved emotionally with the team when they aren't meeting my annual and immediate expectations?

I'm also a New York Giants football fan. I also like other teams, though not as much, like the Green Bay Packers and Los Angeles Rams, because of those close to me who root for them. Even with all this passion and all these likes (and unnamed dislikes) according to the demographic and social data that rounds out my profile, I'm not a great candidate for a Yankees or Giants season ticket because I currently live in the Washington, D.C., area. I could be a good candidate for merchandise, though, and one or two or possibly a few more games when I get to New York—as well as something else that I'll be talking about in just a minute.

But wait! There's more. I also love Broadway, and I'm a foodie. All those dollars I want to spend when I'm in New York on plays and restaurants and the Yankees are discretionary and not limitless. How will I allocate the funds on my next visit? Do I have a consistent pattern of spending that shows the Yankees that I'm even worth pursuing to buy a few higher-priced tickets to a few games each year? Or am I clearly spending the money elsewhere? It's reasonably possible they can find out, given my activity on social networks.

What this means is that the transactions associated with purchases that might be related to the Yankees aren't dollars that might go to other sports teams, necessarily. They are discretionary dollars, which makes this even more complicated. That means they might go to Broadway, to seeing *Hamilton* or *Come From Away*. Or to eating at a great restaurant like Daniel or Le Bernardin. Or maybe I'll just stay in DC and go to a movie, make a purchase on Amazon, or buy a bottle of top-shelf liquor—given the price of Yankees tickets, Johnny Walker Red isn't what they compete with. Or, if times are tough or it's a rainy Sunday, maybe I'll save my money and stay inside watching the game on TV and doing nothing else.

See what I mean? Even if you had no data beyond my interest in the Yankees, for me to spend money with the Yankees they still have to keep me engaged—if they choose to. But from the enormous amount of data I've just given you about myself, you see that they are also competing with the diverse interests I have when it comes to how I spend my discretionary dollars. And they're also competing with inertia—staying home and watching the game on TV is a lot easier than getting to a ballpark, whether I live in New York or not. Plus, the reasons that I love the Yankees are not just complex but complicated.

The question becomes, am I a customer worth retaining? The Yankees have to first decide that. For the sake of this example, let's assume they do the numbers (we'll get into that later) and then let's assume they say, "We'll keep him." Then there are multiple decisions to be made, some which require my (the customer's) involvement and some that don't.

Of all the data that I just provided—transactional, social, brand-specific, emotional, interests general and specific—which is the most important to the Yankees for providing what they need to know to make a decision about me? The second, third, and fourth most important? The *least* important?

If they've determined which data is important to them, run the analysis, and decided, "We'll keep him," what do they think is the optimal possible transactional relationship I might have with them? Season ticket holder? Several games a year in higher-priced seats? Merchandise? Lots of food purchases at the stadium? Combinations of the above?

What other kinds of interactions might they seek? Do they, with the data they have, see that I might be a great advocate for them on social networks, in front of crowds, in written works? Do I influence purchases? More specifically, can I influence people who have a greater propensity to purchase season tickets, merchandise, etc., given the networks I travel in and the wider influence I have?

How have I interacted with them and *about* them with others? That has a lot of bearing on my value to the team given what the 21st century customer requires and how they act—privately and socially.

Given that, what are the outcomes that they need from me to get to their goal for me? How do they provide me with what I need to achieve those outcomes?

Think about it for one minute. Then remember that I'm just one customer. Imagine this scaled to millions of customers. How does a business handle the needs and desires of this demanding, even at times entitled customer when they have to do it for millions of them—each of whom is demanding a personalized (not personal) response, and each of whom has some amount of disregard for the other millions of customers?

Luckily, as you will see throughout the book, the tools, the programs, the strategies, and the measurements are all there to make this something more than guesswork—a combination of art and science that is actually reproducible.

To begin to master this, we begin by defining what customer engagement is. Because of the plethora of definitions that have been put forward, sorting this out isn't as easy as it sounds. But it is doable.

WHAT IS CUSTOMER ENGAGEMENT?

To understand customer engagement, it's necessary to figure out what customers are looking for and how they want to look for it. Customers aren't looking for just products and services any longer. They are looking for the products, services, tools, and consumable experiences that provide them with a more complete set of capabilities to judge how they want to interact and transact with the company over time. The customer is also looking for the feeling that the vendor "knows" them well enough to make it a personalized set of products, services, tools, and consumable experiences. These offerings should be "good enough" (not delightful) to make that customer want to continue their interactions with the vendor. But, unto itself, these combined characteristics aren't the definition for customer engagement—they are merely the guide to unlocking the mysteries (though, for you U.S. TV fans, not of Laura). In later chapters, we will be looking more closely at the relevant products, services, tools, and consumable experiences, but for now let's just go on faith. Everything will be clear once you have gotten through the book.

To begin to define customer engagement we have to see what it isn't.

What *Isn't* Customer Engagement?

What is customer engagement *not?* One school of thinking identifies engagement with intense involvement with a brand. In other words, imagine you are on the phone being, let's just say, "passionate" with a customer-service person or a sales person or with your friends and involved in all things related to a particular product or service. While that may seem a bit freakish, just think of Apple fans who love all-things-Apple and hate Microsoft because it's Microsoft, aka, not-Apple. I once wrote a post praising Microsoft for something they did, and Apple fans went at me like I was the Prime Evil in *Diablo 3*. It was nasty. All because I was nice to Microsoft. God help me if I ever *criticize* Apple. I'll be turned to stone.

These fans are often walking Apple product fashion statements. They don't just use Apple products, they figuratively, and, with the Apple Watch, now literally wear them—showing them off as accessories. Especially if they have the bucks to buy the Apple Watch Edition ($10,000–$17,000 per—yikes!). But, regardless of their, sometimes, overbearing intolerance, Apple fans are fully engaged customers of a company. That is the kind of customer engagement that has given Apple the largest market cap in the entire world.

But that passion isn't the only kind of engagement there is. You can be engaged casually and be satisfied as well. Engagement is *not* characterized by the intensity of the interaction. It isn't characterized by the frequency of the interaction. It isn't driven by the emotional state of the communication. It isn't driven by the loyalty and/or advocacy of the customer—though the advocacy or loyalty is driven by interactions over time and is reflected by their nature.

Let me give you another example. In 2007, my wife Yvonne and I remodeled our kitchen. We put in a new KitchenAid refrigerator (since replaced in 2014 by a GE Monogram because the KitchenAid turned out to be, let's just say, less than stellar) that used water filters. They provided one with the fridge, but I had to find out how to replace those water filters.

I found a site called Fridgefilters.com.

I ordered two filters to be safe—though I probably shouldn't have—and then the site asked if I'd like to set up a notification. I said yes, and with a couple of clicks arranged to be notified to buy two filters every six months. Thus, every six months since 2007, I've gotten an email that notifies me it's time to buy two filters. I click on a link that takes me to the filters, and then I click on a link that allows me to pay, and . . . boom! I'm done. The only other thing I see is an email message telling me the filters have shipped.

Simple, casual, easy, utilitarian. I *love* this company!

Why? Because they give me exactly what I want from them. Not a delightful, intense, emotionally stirring experience, but a simple, utilitarian interaction that is good enough to satisfy my desires when it comes to this company. It speaks to me in exactly the way I want it.

Think about it. I'm so happy with this company and my ongoing communications and transactions with it that I'm telling all of you about it, as I have tens of thousands if not hundreds of thousands of people in audiences I've addressed. You can't do better than that! My interactions with the company are entirely casual and occasional; yet I'm an advocate—and a nonstop one at that.

That's what I mean. The key to customer engagement isn't the intensity of the interactions but that the interactions occur at the level of emotional involvement the customer wants and gives the customer the results they want.

There are many other things customer engagement *isn't*, but I'll only mention two more. It isn't loyalty or advocacy. As we will see in Chapter 15, it can lead to loyalty and/or advocacy, a good thing, and can be measured by them, too; but it isn't the same thing as either loyalty or advocacy and doesn't necessarily involve either in the interaction. Loyalty and advocacy are outcomes devoutly to be wished but not drivers per se of customer engagement.

The question remains then, if it isn't any of these things, what is it?

The Definition of Engagement

Since almost everything in the universe related to definitions seems to start with Wikipedia, we'll see what Wikipedia offers. Maybe it'll be great and make my job easy.

> *Customer engagement (CE) is the engagement of customers with one another, with a company or a brand. The initiative for engagement can be either consumer- or company-led and the medium of engagement can be on or offline.*

Nope. The Wikipedia definition of customer engagement is pretty much useless. I mean, "customer engagement is the engagement of customers?" That's like me saying a human being is a being that is human. Give me a break.

So, let's leave that one behind and move on to the next one.

Don Peppers and Martha Rogers—that incredible business duo who turned business on its head in the early 90s with their approach to one-to-one marketing which is iconic today—define engagement as "proactive involvement."

Accurate, neat, and simple. The definition probably needs a bit more detail than that, though, to flesh it out.

How about the definition by Richard Sedley, who, at the time he defined it (2007), was the Director of the Customer Engagement unit at Cscape, the noted design agency.

> *Repeated interactions that strengthen the emotional, psychological or physical investment a customer has in a brand.*

Not bad, really, but it doesn't take into account the company's side of the engagement.

Finally, let's view the one that Eric Peterson, a noted web analytics expert, has for online engagement:

> *[Online engagement] is an estimate of the degree and depth of visitor interaction on the site against a clearly defined set of goals.*

In part true, as least as far as both online engagement and measurement of that goes. But still not quite enough—and it doesn't take "offline" physical engagement or the hybrid nature of engagement into account.

All of them (except the stupid Wikipedia definition) contain elements of truth, but I think I have a definition that goes to the heart of customer engagement and implies what is needed to accomplish it successfully—all of which will be made explicit in these pages.

Here goes:

Customer engagement is the ongoing interaction between company and customer—offered by the company, chosen by the customer.

That is a lot in a single sentence. Let's break it down a bit, though. (Again, the whole book is about breaking this down.) But, first, allow me to introduce a few stage-setters at this juncture.

The Characteristics of Engagement for the Company

One thing that we have to be crystal clear about for companies when it comes dealing with customers is that they start with constraints. Among them:

Financial constraints—Only so much money can be allocated to supporting a customer's immediate interactions with the company and the experience of that customer with a company over time. This is particularly true as you scale up to, say, the level of Citigroup, which has roughly 200 million customers to deal with.

Time constraints—There are limits to how much time staff, even full-time staff, can devote to customers, as a group and as individuals. Again, scale up, and the time allocations become smaller and smaller per customer.

Personnel constraints—A company can only hire so many people who are devoted to customers. This may *seem* boundless to some extent since, for example, customer service is going to hire people, marketing is going to hire people, the sales group is going to hire people, and so on. In some companies, people are hired to be management or practitioners devoted to customer experience. United Airlines for example, has a Vice President of Customer Experience with a wide range of responsibilities. Here's the description by him on LinkedIn of what his duties are:

...currently driving a service and hospitality-centric approach across our 120,000 employees and contractors; overhauling every aspect of the ~50 United Clubs worldwide; redefining key aspects of the customer

journey including during disruption events; and driving a step-change evolution in deriving customer insights and driving improvements across the enterprise to enhance customer satisfaction.

If United were fully staffed to do all that, how many staff members do you think it would take? Whatever number they have, it isn't enough. There are only so many people that a company can devote to a specific capability, despite their best intentions.

Regulatory/compliance constraints—This is arguably the most perfidious set of constraints because the company can do nothing *but* be constrained by them. The regulations the company is subject to and the compliance necessary are not only elements that hamstring their ability to act but sometimes prevent them from providing the optimal level of engagement or overarching experience the customer is looking for. The most obvious ones are privacy concerns and regulations. To provide the optimal opportunity to engage with the customer, a lot of data about that customer has to be considered. Often, privacy laws and regulations prevent the use of the kind of data that has to be captured and considered in developing the customer profile. You can do little to nothing about that unless you want to change the law. In fact, starting May 25, 2018, the General Data Protection Regulation (GDPR) went into effect in the European Union, creating the strictest privacy-protection laws in history—so immense in scope and punishment that they will force businesses worldwide to change how they handle data.

Customer constraints—This one may seem odd, but it isn't. The customer wants certain things and doesn't want other things. The company needs certain things and doesn't need other things. The company has to figure out the balance between what they need and what will get the customer angry if they take what they need. For example, if a customer needs their package on Wednesday and paid you a premium to see that it got there that day, you have to be ready with the means to get it there—which means the courier service relationship, the processes, the business rules, and the protocols all have to be in place. And you also have to be ready with the answers if it doesn't look like it's going to get there in time despite the customer's needing it that day or if it actually didn't get there on time without any warning. Those protocols have to be in place to deal with success or failure—and they have to be there even with a 100 percent rate of success over years. The cost, time required, training involved, and labor that has to be expended to be prepared to deal with the issue are constraints because they are necessary preparations in anticipation of a problem rather than a simple *ad hoc* reaction to the problem after the fact.

Operational constraints—The business rules, business processes, and internal procedures of a company can operate as a brake on the effort to engage customers the way that they want to be engaged. The easiest example? Think of the legal department that has to approve a blog post before it's posted, or has to review a document or agreement that needs immediate action. Does the legal department actually care about that immediate action? No. They care about protecting the interests of the company no matter what kind of stoppage it creates. In their defense, protecting the company is their job. But legal departments have to change, too. While their history has been fire prevention, we are now in a world where they also have to be able to put out fires after the fact. So, for example, concerning the blog post, they must set out the legal strictures before any posts go out. Then, they let them go out without legal review in each case—and, if there is a problem, well, solving those problems is one of the things that lawyers get paid to do. It's a different approach for a different, more demanding, era of business.

Of course, the biggest point is that there are limitations imposed on a company before they start thinking about how to best engage their customers in a way that provides value to both. Those limitations have to be accounted for—and they are—in the part of the definition that says "offered by the company," which we will get to later.

CHARACTERISTICS OF ENGAGEMENT FOR THE CUSTOMER

You know the expression, "The heart wants what the heart wants." Well, to a large extent, that is the key driver of customer behavior. It starts from a simple premise. All human beings are self-interested and, in a given time and context, want whatever it is that makes them happy. The chapter called the "Commonwealth of Self Interest" (which is also the title of the book, in case you didn't happen to notice) will cover that in detail, but for the purposes of this definition the best way to understand "chosen by the customer" is to know a few basic things.

All humans are self-interested—We want what we want, not what someone *like* us wants. (In that lies a story to be told . . . soon.) As Paul Greenberg, I want not what born-in-New York, Jewish baby boomers who root for the Yankees want, but what *Paul Greenberg* wants. I also don't care about the others who are associated with me as customers of the same company. I want to have *my* needs met.

Give me choices that I can control, and I'm happy—If the choices offered consist of things that interest me, then, at the least, I'm going to be happy because I'm going to have chosen what I want to do and how I want to do it from a group of things that seem to speak to me. (Remember the GetGlue example last chapter.)

The idea of value that I have as a customer is very different than the idea of value that a company has—A company believes that value is derived from revenue, profitability, shareholder, or, more enlightened, stakeholder value, and perhaps customer satisfaction or Net Promoter Score measures. A customer's idea of value is to *feel valued*. A lot of data is available to support both sides of the equation, as you will see later.

At a High Level Then, What Does the Definition Mean?

So, to set the stage for the rest of the book, I'm going to give you a one-step-deeper look at the definition—let's call it the 15,000-foot rather than the 20,000-foot view.

Please allow me to reiterate the definition.

Customer engagement is the ongoing interaction between company and customer—offered by the company, chosen by the customer.

To provide successful customer engagement, a company has to work with what it can, given all the constraints that it operates under, including the business planning for the current year and immediate future years that it's already done, the budgets that are available to it for an engagement strategy and program, and contingencies to be prepared to deal with the pressures of providing something that works for a customer base that could number in the millions or even hundreds of millions of customers. What that means is that the company has to figure out how to provide, to each individual customer, those products, services, tools, and consumable experiences that allow the customer to choose which ones he or she wants to use to further the interactions and enhance and support their positive feelings due to the continuing success of those interactions. That means the customer gets to feel as if the company values them, while the company gets the customer, and possibly those that the customer directly and indirectly impacts, to continue not just to interact but to transact with the company. A value is provided by one to the other that is sufficient for both.

Of course, the customer's need to feel valued is very different than the company's desire for revenue and profit. Both are legitimate objectives, however, and appropriate to the particular party that wants them. How to translate them into something commonly beneficial—in other words, to provide value to both parties while the quite different protocols and mindsets of each are met—is one of the conundrums facing the science and art of customer engagement. (I'll take care of solving those conundrums by the time you're done reading this book.)

Now we have an overarching definition of customer engagement. Some seriously cool organizations have done big-picture engagement strategies and programs successfully. And, you, lucky peeps you, I'm going to tell you about one that is particularly cool and very effective. It is a pro-sports example, and who doesn't love that? You don't? Oh. Well . . . I'm still telling the story.

CASE STUDY: THE PHILADELPHIA FLYERS— ENGAGEMENT AT *SO* MANY LEVELS

I want to be clear before we begin: I'm a diehard NY Rangers fan. But, honestly, while I'm hardcore when it comes to the events on the ice, I must admit the Rangers don't even come close to the Philadelphia Flyers as far as having a complete and effective customer-engagement program is concerned. Not even close. Though, at least in 2017, they had a better team. Not a small comfort.

Anyway, here's the overview.

Sports teams, despite the clinically insane amounts of money that they give to the athletes on their teams, are mid-sized businesses. Not only are they mid-sized businesses, but to make it worse, they are cash-strapped mid-sized businesses with small-business-sized staffs. Because they give so much money to their professional athletes, they are hard-pressed to support a fully staffed office. There are franchises whose financials qualify them as enterprises according to *Forbes* magazine's annual sports franchise review of the Dallas Cowboys ($4 billion), my beloved Yankees ($3.4 billion), Real Madrid ($3 billion), and Manchester United ($3 billion). Even the biggest ones still sit on the low end. In other words, they are smaller businesses than you probably thought.

But they have the aura of large-enterprise endeavors with tons of money and resources. This myth has credence because, as noted, they give so much money to their professional athletes. Regardless of the reason, it impacts the expectations of fans everywhere. The aura of expectations is usually a lot larger than the reality of the performance possible. Realistically, you are looking at a mid-sized business with a small-business-sized staff that has fans who expect enterprise-sized response. When the glow of diehard advocacy/fandom starts to wear off, which happens when there are more than a few losing seasons, the seats empty and the fans start, shall we say, spending their discretionary dollars elsewhere.

Thus, the most important thing a team can do is try to keep the fans engaged, even with the limitations of their size and budgets competing with the outsized expectations of the fans.

The Philadelphia Flyers National Hockey League (NHL) franchise manages to do that exceptionally well.

The Goal

Getting fans in seats at a game is a team's number-one priority. Even if fans go to just one or two games a year, they are a huge benefit to the team. Not only does the individual fan buy tickets, merchandise, and food, they are also the recruiting ground for season ticket holders. It's in the interest of the team to make sure that the environment at the stadium is conducive to the fans and that the existing season ticket holders feel the commitment they have made to the team is worth extending. That means that the fan experience over time has to be one that makes them think, "I'm coming back again this year," even if it is a miserable losing season.

The lifeblood of any professional sports team is not the solo fan at a single game but the season ticket holder. These are the fans dedicated to the team to the extent they are willing to spend thousands of dollars per year, often year after year, to pay for seats at a large number of games, many of which they might not even attend.

The value of the season ticket holder is immeasurable—metaphorically of course. You can, after all, easily measure the value in how much they spend and when and where they spend it. They not only are clearly identifiable large chunks of ticket revenue, but they are tied to food, drink, and memorabilia. They are also tied to a secondary ticket market by putting other fans in their seats, who can be considerable additional sources of revenue for the team. They are the fans who provide repeat revenue.

Optimally, a season ticket holder will renew early. The benefit to the team of their doing so is straightforward.

- More revenue in the coffers sooner

- Reduced cost in getting the renewal since it happens earlier than expected/planned

- Time that would have been spent on the effort can be allocated to something else (e.g., acquiring new season ticket holders or planning for the next season)

- Emotional relief—"Okay, we're good with him/her for another year."

All in all, an early renewal is immensely beneficial.

The Flyers understand all of this: how to provide the individual fan with the best possible experience at the stadium or wherever they were engaged with the staff, and the value of getting season ticket holders' early renewals. To do both takes a lot of planning and execution. It also takes a willing and engaged/enabled/empowered staff.

The Philosophy

While a winning drives great fan response, it doesn't happen every single season. Consequently, the Flyers understand that they have to gear their efforts to see that they are focused on how to keep the fans fully engaged continually in a manner good enough to make the fans want to continue to support the team in good times and bad. But that's a complex thing. Think of the example of my passion for the Yankees back in the early days of this chapter. The Flyers not only understand it but embrace it in a way that makes that commitment to the fan complete and fully intertwined with everything the organization does, from its players to its executives to its staff.

Listen to Sean Tilger, the SVP of Operations wax eloquently on this.

The "How You Doin'?" program is the culture of this organization. We are always making sure that we aren't just implementing software, but are embedding the philosophy and outlook into everything we do internally and externally.

So how can this be more than just marketing?

The Strategy

What characterizes the Flyers as special is that they have a clear-cut strategy that is fully aligned with the philosophy and a program aligned with the strategy. The entire idea, from beginning to end, is outcomes-based, i.e., focused on results that are related to a return they are trying to effect. It is *customer-engaged*—a new term I'm introducing for a company and its culture. The bulk of what that means is better left for Chapter 9, but for our purposes here it means that the company proactively communicates with the customers and gets them involved in activities ranging from simple feedback or loyalty/advocacy programs to co-creation of products and services. The engagement of the fans is ongoing, proactive, and as close to real-time as possible. It also means that the employees are fully empowered to interact with customers as a priority of their work day and that the culture and incentives are there to support that effort. The Flyers are a customer-engaged company because they:

- Engage the fans in all ways, with multiple programs that address different types of fans
- Know each fan's individual lifestyles and customize accordingly as best they can
- Measure always and keep learning
- Use all channels but focus on the interaction, not the channel
- Involve the customer in the lifeblood of the company
- Incentivize the staff to make sure that the interactions with the fans are always the best possible, regardless of circumstance

Big bold claims. How do they do this? The two programs they've created to accomplish their ends are the "How You Doin'?" program for the game-bound fan and the "Early Bird" program for the season ticket holder.

How You Doin'?

You can thank *Friends* for this one. I know you all watched it, but for those few of you who didn't, "How you doin'?" was an expression used by the character Joey, who is Matt LeBlanc in real life (or maybe, just maybe, it's the other way around). The Flyers adopted this moniker for their program aimed at providing the best possible levels of engagement with the fans and the staff at Wells Fargo Arena (the Flyers' home ice) or even at the corporate headquarters.

The way it works is brilliant in its simplicity. Every fan who comes through the gates is greeted by a staff member and asked if there is anything that they can do for them. If there isn't, nonetheless, an interaction with the fan has occurred—they have been greeted. If there is, the staff member, whoever it is, is empowered to leave their station and go take care of the problem or query, whatever its nature. The idea is to not come back until the problem is solved or the question answered. The fan may or may not accompany that staff member. If they don't, they are asked to wait or to go to their seat and give the staff member the seat number. One way or the other, the staff member resolves the query and then informs the fan of the results.

The staff member then gives the fan a card that asks how they did. The card rates them with 1–5 stars, and, if the fan cares to, they can nominate the staff member by name. There are convenient boxes all over the stadium to drop the card off.

Now, it gets even more interesting because the staff is incentivized. If they are nominated enough times, there are substantial bonuses and even a vacation for a much-lauded staff member. Look, they are human beings. While we all like to think we do everything out of our altruistic good natures, that isn't the case. People like to be rewarded for being good—again it goes to the heart of what I briefly said earlier. All people want to feel valued. To get a reward for being a great staff member goes to the heart. You are being recognized as a valuable, good, and important person. Nothing wrong with that. You may be an altruist too, but it doesn't hurt to be seen by others as one of the good ones. The Flyers, understanding human nature, do just that—reward the good ones because of their highly successful interactions with the fans.

HOW YOU DOIN'?—THE RESULTS

Having a great story is something, but results are needed to validate the great story. In the case of the "How You Doin'?" program, they wanted the fans to feel valued at their venues—which would encourage them to come back, see more games, eat and drink more, buy merchandise, and maybe even become season ticket holders.

The numbers speak for themselves. Over the three seasons from 2010–2012, 87 percent of all the fans were greeted. On a scale of 1–5, with five stars being the best response, amazingly, 97 percent of the fans gave the effort 5 stars. Good start.

But even with this easy, engaging environment, this friendly ambiance, the Flyers don't lose sight of the fact that their target is the season ticket holder. Thus, "Early Bird" was born.

EARLY BIRD

The idea behind the "Early Bird" program was simple: get season ticket holders to renew early. That simple effort, if successful, was potentially worth hundreds of thousands, if not millions, of dollars in revenue to the Flyers. To restate, the goal of the program isn't to get someone to *become* a season ticket holder or even to up their commitment—it is simply to get current ticket holders to renew early.

To do that took a lot of revamping of the client-development work. To begin with, they had to form a client-development department. They had to do the basic blocking and tackling of getting sales reps to become account reps, with each assigned hundreds of accounts to handle and then refocus toward getting early renewals.

While they had tried some cool/cutesy social media and web initiatives in the past to lure the season's ticket holders, they had little to no success with them. But what they did have, via social media, their systems, transactions, and Ticketmaster, was a lot of data on each season ticket holder. They aggregated all that data and sent it over to Turnkey Sports and Entertainment to analyze the propensity of each season ticket holder to renew early. Ten proprietary criteria were identified as indicative. Turnkey came back with a complete map of all their targets, with a rating system of 1 to 5 stars, with 1 star being least likely to renew early to 5 stars being most likely to renew early. Remember, the goal is to get them to renew *early*, not just renew.

Once they had this data, they developed several programs. To keep their focus laser-like, they put aside the 1-star results and simply hoped for their early renewal due to the momentum around them. But they developed specific programs for the 2–3-star and the 4–5-star folks.

The 2–3-star season's ticket holders were reached at games and asked to come to the Hall of Fame room, a room at Wells Fargo, that has dozens of plaques and photos that outline and reflect the team's great history, especially in the late 70s, when the Broad Street Bullies, led by Bobby Clarke, reigned supreme in the NHL. Once they gathered in that room, ice cream, wine, beer, and snacks were handed out while the value of early renewal was preached, bruthah, to the 2–3-star "stars."

That might not sound like much, but think about it. Surrounded by the history of a very successful team while eating comfort food and drinking "comfort" liquids makes you feel good. I have this mantra, "You don't have to have luxury, you just have to *feel* luxurious." Same deal, this environment makes you feel good. That is all it has to do. You'll see the results in a minute.

For the 4–5-star holders, you got a postcard in the mail. Yes, a postcard. That postcard said, "If you renew early," you have can choose from a variety of gifts. My favorite one by far: if you have a child between 6–14, they get to go on the ice at the beginning of a real game and high-five the team as it comes out. OMG! Why in the name of whoever wouldn't you renew early? It's worth it just to see the look on your kid's face, isn't it? I guess if you were cold and heartless—or didn't have kids—you could choose one of the others, such as attending a team press conference.

Additionally, you could be entered into a drawing that would be for several one-off prizes. For example, lunch with the Broad Street Bullies at the Broad Street Bullies Grill.

One other thing, if you entered the Wells Fargo Arena at the season ticket holder gates, you got a card telling you how to renew early and that you would have access to a barbecue if you did. That would be the team barbecue. Can I get another "OMG!" here, please?

You get all of this not for shelling out more money, but the same money early. Who wouldn't?

EARLY BIRD—THE RESULT

Apparently, no one wouldn't. Everyone wanted in on the action. Even for those season ticket holders designated a single star—meaning lowest propensity to renew early—the results were superb. From 2010–2012, the percentages of early renewals were (based on projected propensity ratings):

- One Star—83.7 percent
- Two Stars—87.5 percent
- Three Stars—84.3 percent
- Four Stars—89.1 percent
- Five Stars—92.0 percent

Not only that, but each year from 2010–2012, roughly one thousand more than the prior year renewed early. Spectacular results due to a strong, fully engaged organization with a clear plan.

Lessons Learned

What are the takeaways from this amazing customer-engaged franchise's efforts?

- Make sure that, before you do anything else, you know what your goals are and the outcomes that are needed to achieve the goals.
- Build a culture that will sustain whatever efforts you make—and that includes incentivizing the employees beyond just a pat on the back to support that effort.
- Develop the appropriate programs.
- Know all that you can about each customer.
- Use all resources available to you—whatever the channels.
- Execute continuously.
- Measure and learn.
- Keep doing it.

Great story, huh?

While the story of the Flyers may end here, the story of what customer engagement is and isn't doesn't end here, nor does the sports theme of this chapter.

Ladies and gentlemen, I give you Charlie Shin.

THOUGHT LEADER: CHARLIE SHIN

I've known Charlie Shin for several years now, and he very well might be the most ardent and curious and innovative executive when it comes to CRM in professional sports. He runs the fan engagement and CRM initiatives for Major League Soccer, and the results of his (and his team's) efforts show, with a huge uptick in both interest and involvement in professional soccer in the United States over the past several years. The title he gets for that is Vice President of Fan Engagement, Major League Soccer. What makes Charlie both a practitioner and a thought leader is his ability to not just understand and drive innovation but to articulate it to a larger crowd than his immediate audience. Take a look at what he is working on with MLS to drive customer engagement and how he is thinking about it, and what I've just said will be crystal clear.

Time to step onto the field, Charlie. It's your game.

*   *   *   *   *

The evolution of digital transformation and the introduction of new technologies have shifted traditional marketing power from brands to customers. This isn't any different in the professional sports industry. Sports fans are more likely to be digitally connected with the means to find information at their fingertips, and this trend has forced many sports marketers to rethink how they engage with their fans.

In order to accommodate today's ever-changing digital landscape, professional sports organizations need to better understand the overall fan journey (how one becomes a fan and engages with the team) and provide a personalized experience to maximize the engagements. Traditionally, fan engagements were represented as in-stadium attendance or TV viewership at home, hence the reason so many professional sports organizations placed a great deal of importance on these factors. Now, whether it be digital, mobile, social, or gaming, fan engagements are represented in many different forms. By providing the most relevant and exciting content, sports organizations have an opportunity to engage with their audiences like never before.

Let's say there's a live soccer game taking place with a sold-out crowd of 25,000 fans at the stadium and 400,000 average viewers watching the game on ESPN2. In addition, there are over 150,000 Twitter users posting, reading, and sharing comments about the game. After the game, a highlight video was viewed by 55,000 users on Facebook and the club's website. In addition, one of the celebrities that attended the game posted a video of the winning goal on his Twitter account that reached over 3 million followers. Next morning, the club pushes out a short documentary video of the homegrown player who scored the winning goal from last night to their one million mobile app subscribers. Finally, 250,000 fans who play the EA FIFA game select your club to replicate last night's bicycle kick.

As you can see from this example, digital transformation has not only impacted the nature of fan engagement, it has also impacted how the sport and its content are created, distributed, and consumed by fans. As a marketer, imagine if you can have a single view of every fan interaction indicated above at your fingertips. Now imagine how you can leverage that rich data to create a differentiated and seamless fan experience. These are just a few areas that many sports marketers will need to think about to establish a proper CRM strategy and the technology infrastructures to enhance their overall CRM capabilities.

At MLS, an internal study found that an EA FIFA video game was identified as one of the key drivers behind fan interest in MLS. In collaboration with EA SPORTS, MLS developed a pilot program to drive greater video game plays and a performance model to measure the impact on club engagements using the game-play data. The pilot program included a variety of interactive engagements between the fans and MLS clubs through offline and online platforms. Fans would see the EA FIFA video version of the MLS player goal celebration in-stadium during a live game or be asked to play the MLS rivalry match scheduled for the weekend within the EA FIFA game for a chance to win special game packs. The pilot campaign resulted in very active digital and social engagements among EA FIFA gamers with its participating clubs. In addition, the campaign drove greater game plays, which helped drive greater interest in MLS clubs.

The pilot program is an illustration of digital disruption and its impact on fan engagement well beyond the game and its players inside the white line. It also illustrates why marketers need to understand and recognize the importance of becoming a customer-centric organization. Advances in technology and communication, combined with the explosive growth in data and information, have given rise to a more empowered global consumer. A clear understanding of customer needs and behaviors across the organization will help drive profitable growth strategies.

The journey to customer centricity will not be an easy endeavor. In building a strong foundation for the future, marketers will need to focus on a new set of core principles to redefine consumer engagements. Here are five simple steps for getting started.

- **Turn your customer data into insights**—Define your target customers and their needs.

- **Identify your customer journey**—Identify and generate customer engagement across their life cycle.

- **Build an integrated value proposition**—What will it take to deliver whatever customers need and want at the right price, right time, and right channel?

- **Develop customer driven KPIs (Key Performance Indicators)**—Build an actionable scorecard that keeps your customer strategy aligned across the organization.

- **Establish a customer-centric culture**—Only genuine, customer-centric innovation that is embedded into the organization will produce significant growth and deliver competitive advantage.

Achieving customer centricity is not about implementing a grand vision but rather a journey that adjusts to changing market and consumer dynamics to meet their expectations.

Thank you, Charlie.

This chapter is defining and, thus, merits *two* thought leaders rather than one. So, now I'm going to introduce you to Phil Venville.

THOUGHT LEADER: PHIL VENVILLE

Phil is the SVP of Strategy at Thunderhead, a technology company that specializes in customer-journey tracking. But, more than that, he is also a thought leader and one of the only guys in the technology-company world who has developed an intellectual framework for customer engagement. It's called EngageOne. What makes EngageOne so compelling is that it has a solid theoretical foundation to support the actual material efforts that the framework suggests. That isn't an easy thing to do, but he did it. Which shows you how big a deal Phil really is. And he's a truly good person too. What a combination!

So, Phil, the stage is yours to explain your take on customer engagement and the framework you've defined. Its slightly different than mine, but we are definitely aligned.

You've read this far into the book and are, hopefully, getting the idea that customer engagement is pretty important. In fact, over the last five years or so it has attracted a lot of attention among practitioners and academics alike. Engagement is a concept based on a solid theoretical foundation that delivers insights and valuable explanations about consumer behavior. I'm going to provide in a nutshell some insights into the key foundational principles of customer engagement and why they're important.

So why now? Interest in the idea of engagement was originally driven by the inability of traditional metrics to adequately explain consumer behavior. That failure has been amplified as technology has added further complexity to the ways in which businesses and consumers interact. The real-time context in which the work of the digital economy is done has forced engagement to the forefront, shaped by service thinking (the Service-Dominant Logic that is inextricably linked to the engagement concept) and new ideas about value.

Over the last few years, a tremendous amount of important work has been done by researchers in marketing and service disciplines to develop a theoretical framework for customer engagement based on foundational principles and common definitions (see my notes on the book's website for references). Based on this work, I've outlined below a number of key principles that underpin the concept of customer engagement.

Engagement reflects a psychological state

First and foremost, engagement reflects a psychological or motivational state on the part of the customer within specific relationships, for example with a business, brand, or product. The use of the term "engagement" in this sense has its origin in the social sciences, where it is a well-established concept that has been in use for decades.

Engagement is based on experiences but is different from experiences

Engagement is not the same as experience. Engagement is driven by experiences, but it is a multi-dimensional state that is fundamentally different from experience. The important takeaway is that engagement is the end-game, and any attempt to "manage" customer experiences has to be seen from the perspective of engagement, i.e., the flow of experiences across the customer journey rather than one-off disconnected experiences.

Engagement occurs over time

Engagement is built over time. The essential point is that engagement builds over iterative, dynamic cycles of interaction—the non-linear flow of experiences. It's difficult to overemphasize just how important the dimension of time is to engagement, and it is the reason why the ability to manage the threads of customer interactions and journeys is so critical to building engagement.

Engagement is driven by the needs, wishes, and preferences of the customer

This is a fundamental point discussed widely in the book (and germane to its "commonwealth of self-interest" theme). Only the customer can decide what has value, not the business. What the business must do is offer the best propositions (within the current context) to enable the customer to derive value. Of course, the business must derive value too.

Engagement is driven by a flow of interactions that are value-driven, where the value (and the form it takes) at each step is determined and co-created by the customer, according to their needs and wishes.

Engagement is not the same thing as involvement

This is a common misunderstanding. Engagement does not necessarily require a high level of task involvement—think about the Fridgefilters.com example earlier in this chapter. The reverse is also true—a high level of task involvement does not necessarily mean a high level of engagement (e.g., filling out a web form). It is not necessarily about active behavior either—engagement can result from persuasive content or empathy with a story (that is, being mentally transported into a narrative).

Engagement is a multi-dimensional concept

The key point to understand here is that there are many different facets to engagement, including cognitive, behavioral, sensory, and emotional, to mention a few. This is a caution against taking simplistic approaches to engagement that focus on just one element (e.g., emotional triggers or gamification) in what is a complex mix of factors. This impacts metrics, too. Because it is multidimensional, engagement is hard to quantify, and the focus should be on measuring the outcomes of engagement rather than on trying to quantify engagement itself.

WHY DOES IT MATTER IN THE REAL WORLD (AS OPPOSED TO ACADEMIA)?

The concept of customer engagement provides a framework for making sense of the complications and complexities of relationships between a business and its customers. A transformative shift from transactions to relationships is taking place, and a robust theoretical foundation for customer engagement is absolutely critical to navigating this new reality.

Engagement emphasizes the importance of time and the flow of experiences, an insight that underpins the need to be able to sense and guide the complete customer journey. It provides a coherent foundation for designing and managing customer interactions in today's context-driven, omnichannel world. Furthermore, it provides a touchstone for rethinking strategies for digital marketing and advertising.

Understanding engagement is the key to building stronger and more profitable customer relationships and highlighting the metrics that really matter. It's central to understanding customer behavior and managing customer retention; and it provides an explanation as to why engaged customers are so valuable, not just in direct financial terms, but in advocacy and influence. These fundamentals become even more important with the growth of the subscription economy and the increasing interest in the valuation of the customer franchise as a business asset.

Finally, the impact for technology and innovation: the concept of engagement, impacting as it does on every consumer touchpoint, inverts the role applications play, subsuming them to the engagement context. The CRM applications market is the largest and most dynamic segment in the enterprise application software market. Adding in the other elements of marketing, ecommerce, and the broader digital advertising ecosystem, we can see that the economic impact of engagement as a concept is as broad as it is deep. Consequently, it provides tremendous opportunities for innovation.

◦ ◦ ◦ ◦ ◦

That's a wrap. Thank you, Phil.

So that's customer engagement defined, practically and theoretically, and set up as a framework for your thinking ahead to strategy and programs, to planning and execution. But so many people are talking about customer experience—and, honestly, aren't customer engagement and customer experience the same thing? You've probably figured out that I don't think so, or I wouldn't have even asked the question. Chapter 3 is just a page turn away, and in that we'll figure out the difference and the symbiosis between the two.

CHAPTER 3

It's a Matter of the Experience, Right?

I told you it was just a page-turn away. I'm assuming that, if you've gotten this far, you're now good with customer engagement's definition. Before we get on to the definition of customer experience and its synergies with engagement, let's recap where we are.

First, we know that we are in the midst of a maturing digital-communications revolution that has transformed how we communicate, how we trust, what we use to communicate, our expectations of the communications, and how we create, distribute, and consume information.

Second, we know that, given the nature of this communications revolution, customers are expecting to be able to engage with us as businesses in the way that they care to engage—which is engagement under *their* control—and, in return, they give us their loyalty and their hard-earned dollars (or other appropriate currencies).

Among the questions that need to be answered next are the following. How does this impact customer experience? Is customer experience different than engagement? Does knowing the difference (which of course, gives it away—the answer is "yes, they are different") mean anything in the real world? Or is it something for academicians alone to argue over? What are those differences? How do we approach them when it comes to customer experience? Will the Yankees make the playoffs this year? Okay, not the last one. Though . . . will they?

CUSTOMER EXPERIENCE VERSUS CUSTOMER ENGAGEMENT

Arguably—and I am argumentative, but only in the nicest way—the "versus" in this header shouldn't be there. They aren't really opposed to each other in any way. But, in the world of customer strategy, they are often used interchangeably, and they shouldn't be. What they are is interwoven.

To start it off, let's make a something of a blanket, and somewhat obvious, statement.

> *Successful engagement with a customer over time can lead to a potentially great customer experience. And if the customer experience is positive, the engagements are likely to be more positive than they otherwise would have been and the customers more forgiving of negative interactions than they otherwise would have been.*

The success of this singular engagement over time, or its failure, leads to what most consider "the" customer experience. (As we will see, there are other kinds of customer experience, but for the moment I'm going to table that.)

The broad idea of customer experience is what Bruce Temkin, the thought leader and adviser I consider the world's leading customer experience analyst, defines as,

> *"The perception that customers have of their interactions with an organization."*

Along those same lines, I see it as,

> *"How a customer feels about a company over time."*

That feeling can change, but, make no mistake about it, it is how they *feel*. How engaged a customer is with a company is often determined by how they are feeling at a specific moment in time about a company and about the actual ongoing interaction. Customer engagement is based on the success or failure of interactions, and emotion plays a huge role in that success or failure. Customer behavior is key to either anticipating how they are going to interact or understanding how they interacted and why in that particular way. The customer's history with the company and their feelings about the company have a significant impact on the results.

How, then, to think about the customer experience when mapping a strategy for engagement? Well, each year Bruce Temkin gets roughly 10,000 actual customers to rate their experience with individual brands in multiple industries. His resulting rankings are based on three things, all of which can be considered planning guidelines for your company's engagement strategy. They are:

- The success customers had with recent interactions with the company. Did the customers accomplish what they set out to accomplish?

- The ease of their recent interactions with the company.

- Based on those recent interactions with the company, how did the customers feel about the company?

Embedded in these criteria is something that can't be overlooked, much as we'd like to do just that. It isn't the actual experience the customer has with the company, but their *perception* of the experience that matters most. Halt! What does that mean?

It's Not What You Think . . . Or Is It?

While I'd love to be generous and say that what companies provide is what customers really and truly get, it is actually what customers *think* they are getting and how they *feel* about it that matters. Whether what they actually get is important to them is another matter.

Before you make me into a demon who is devaluing authenticity and transparency, let me explain.

As important as needing to be authentic and transparent is to a relationship with a customer, one other thing that governs the relationship of the company and customer is the willingness of the customer to engage or disengage with their feelings about the company, which are framed by their long-term experience.

For example, if you look at Bruce's "2018 Temkin Experience Ratings," you see that Comcast is one of the bottom feeders—as they always seem to be. They are rated as providing among the worst experiences of all. Out of 318 total companies that were rated (each with at least 100 respondents from the survey), Comcast ranked 314th. What makes these pathetic numbers even more sad is that this is an *improvement* over 2017! This has been Comcast's pattern for many years.

What that says historically is that, as customers interacted with Comcast, they were left with a bad taste in their mouths over the experience, which leads to a continued negative feeling about the company. The anecdotal evidence to support this is overwhelming. It got to the point that, in early 2015, a story hit the news that a Comcast customer claimed she had a heart attack due to an anxiety-producing, stress-inducing, customer service interaction with Comcast. Whether it was true or not, the dislike of Comcast was so great it went viral because people wanted to believe that about Comcast. If they were customers, they had enough bad experiences to lend that story credibility, or at least to provide an anchor for their desire to think badly of Comcast. This desire to think poorly of Comcast extended even to individuals who weren't customers because they had heard so much cumulatively bad stuff over the years that this was merely more fuel to the always-burning flame.

I was a Comcast customer for 16 years. I would say that the bulk of my service interactions with Comcast as an ISP—I use DirecTV for my TV provider—were horrible. Due to being a customer and due to their overarching bad reputation, which kept my professional interest piqued, I had a terrible taste in my mouth about them.

But did you see what I said? I stayed a Comcast customer for 16 years! Why did I stick it out so long even though my service interactions were continuously horrible—and I kept *hearing* horrible things?

In my case, there were three interlaced factors, and these are factors that notably impact customer relationships with companies generally. First, the technology that I had access to with Comcast was, despite their horrible behavior as a company, reliable enough and fast enough to meet my basic needs. The number of interactions I had with Comcast, either physically or digitally, weren't all that many. The reputation of Verizon, their chief competitor when it came to local FIOS service, was mixed, with some saying they had a very good experience and others saying they had a poor experience. Together these led to the second reason: inertia. The cost of switching remained high enough, the volume of interactions low enough, and the uncertainties about what I was getting into with Verizon real enough to make it seem like too much of a pain the neck to switch. The single biggest cause of inertia, however, was the third factor: thinking about the amount of time it would take to switch an email address that ended in comcast.net to one that ended in verizon.net. That would likely be months. And in the end, it *was* months.

In fact, the only reason I finally switched, despite my disdain for Comcast, was that an email offer was sent to me, accepted by me, withdrawn by Comcast, and then sent to me again! That triggered a boiling over of the accumulated bad will, and the next day I terminated my contract with Comcast.

Comcast Lessons

So, how does this help us understand engagement vs. experience, or how experience impacts the customer's relationship to the company?

The framework is quite simple. Comcast knew nothing about me as a customer other than as a set of transactions and service calls. So, they have no idea why I left; nor did they ask.

If you look at it closely, you see the following.

- 16 years of bad service interactions

- The overall reputation of Comcast as a horrible customer-service company, which was reinforced by my personal experience

- Their absolute lack of knowledge of me as an individual customer, and their apparent lack of interest in getting to know me, which led to the next item

- My perception that they didn't care about their most loyal customers, all of which led to the final action

- An event trigger—an actual attempt at engagement on their part—that took all four of the above and exacerbated the total effect, leading to enough of a jolt to move me from my inertia to cancellation

An event triggered it, but it was my overall experience with Comcast that framed the departure. If I had experienced a great history with them, I would have chalked the event up as a problem to be solved, though I was otherwise happy. But a bad overall customer experience over many years led to full disengagement. The customer's experience is intimately tied to how they feel over time about you. Thus, the amount of importance placed on the results of a particular interaction will vary, as will the decision on how to respond to the results, based on how you are feeling about the company overall at the time. Again, a good long-term experience would have meant that I most likely would have stayed with Comcast and let the problem go as a glitch, but a horrible overall experience meant bye, bye Comcast.

To really think about a customer's experience requires thinking about the context and the framework of the customer's relationship to the company, not just the sum of the interactions, because each interaction at a given moment is impacted by how the customer feels about the company as a whole at that moment in time—which effects the outcome that the interaction produces. That means not only having the knowledge of individual customer's transactions but their interactions with the company and their conversations about the brand. It also means that, as you amalgamate and analyze all that information to gain some individual insight, you must also find the common elements needed to define the programs that will make the customer's involvement over their time with you relatively frictionless and possibly even enjoyable. All this must be done while satisfying the purpose for which they engaged with you in the first place, whether the reasons were utilitarian—convenience, price, availability, services—or more emotional—love of the brand or status. What you offer them, in combination with the results derived from their interactions with you, will drive their feelings toward your company. In later chapters, I'll look at, among other things, designing experiences and systems of engagement as part of an overall engagement program so that this isn't left as a general mystery to you.

The Hudson Hotel and the Margin of Utility

The impact of a single set of engagements with a company can't be underestimated when it comes to the memory of the experience. If your engagement added up to something that was subpar, the customer experience, as short term as it was, and, thus, as short on emotional data, can still impact your overall feeling about a company.

Many years ago, I was speaking at the Asia Society in New York on a subject that I honestly don't remember, and I was put up in the Hudson Hotel. This was in 2008, and the recession was present in all its very spare finery.

The hotel seemed to have a lot going for it on the surface: a minimalist building designed by master designer/architect prodigy Phillipe Starck, a super-trendy, very bright white-colored bar with drinks running $20–$25 a cocktail, and it was packed on the weekends. It fell under an *au courant* trend called "Euro Retro," which was designed to have inexpensive rooms that were, in theory "smallish" but well-appointed, with, perhaps, Hans Grohe fixtures, and lobbies with high ceilings that were dark. It sounded very cool.

But, once I walked into the room, well, "smallish" might have been the understatement of the century.

Here are some of the room's "characteristics."

- If you laid on the bed and turned to the right, you'd bang your nose on the wall; turn to the left, you'd bang your nose on the wall. I don't think there was room to drop a dime between the bed and the wall. I know I couldn't put a suitcase down on the floor near the bed.

- You want to work? Fine. There was a desk of sorts. But to sit at it, you had to sit at the edge of the bed.

- The TV was mounted high, like a hospital TV, so it wouldn't take up any precious space on the ground real estate.

- Worst of all, there was no wall between the "bedroom," if you can call it that, and the bathroom—just a translucent curtain. So, you could, if you were with someone, see into the bathroom. Gross was perhaps the only word for that.

That's how bad it was.

While the Hudson Hotel may have been chic, and super-cool, it did one thing very, very wrong. Measured against all hotels I have ever stayed at, it failed to meet the fundamental expectation I have of *any* hotel: a place where I can sleep, rest, and work comfortably. That is the basic utilitarian function that any hotel has to meet before being *très chic* kicks in as an enhancement to an overall experience.

Now, if I were to take the rest of the experience at the Hudson and simply eliminate the failed utility of the room—i.e., the main product— it was a truly chic, trendy, utterly cool, though a bit insincere (elevators called "lifts," aka Eurofake) experience. It would have been awesome if I weren't staying there. But the simple fact that I couldn't roll over in bed without banging my head on the wall, and that I could see the well-appointed fixtures of the bathroom through a curtain from my desk, which was pretty much up against the foot of the bed, made the room a big #FAIL for me.

My purpose for being at the hotel wasn't to go to the bar, as trendy as it may have been. For me, the primary use of this "product" was to sleep in my room.

Keep in mind, sleeping on the bed is *the* most ordinary of the functions that are associated with the overall hotel experience. As you will hear me say in several contexts, one of the most important things that you can do as you engage customers and build their experience is to keep the ordinary, ordinary. That means that baseline expectations must be met without friction.

> *When the ordinary fails, the impact is greater on the results of the experience than when the extraordinary or luxurious fails. Because there is no expectation that failure is even possible when it comes to the ordinary.*

The Hudson Hotel failed at keeping the ordinary, ordinary; and it crossed the boundary by providing me with a dysfunctional product for an ordinary expectation. They failed to meet a standard that I'm calling the "margin of utility."

The margin of utility is that part of the customer experience which involves the functional reason for the customer's interest in the company. It could be what a product does or what a service provides. It is the result of its "use." It has little to do with the ambiance or additional accoutrements that go into the totality of the experience. But it has a significant impact on the experience.

Keeping the ordinary entirely ordinary is the foundation of a customer experience, and the failure to do that despite the success of the other components usually will mean that the overall experience will be a frustrating failure to the customer. No one cares about feeling luxurious if they can't go to the bathroom—metaphorically speaking, of course.

Because of this I will never go back to the Hudson Hotel. I don't even know if it is still in business. My experience with the hotel due to that one seminal stay makes me not really care either.

Customer experience at this universal level cannot be enabled by technology nor can it be governed by automation. You cannot enable feelings, and that's what this is—a feeling. Remember: "how a customer feels about a company over time." If the experience is long-term, like Comcast, or short-term, like the Hudson Hotel, it is the sum of my feelings at the present moment about companies that I am dealing with or have dealt with, and all the technology in the world won't trigger anything different.

There is a kind of customer experience, however, that can be created and/or engineered and modified, often with the use of technology. It is a modular "experience" that is designed to be consumed as a service related to a product, or something in between. I call them consumable experiences. Others call them whatever they want.

CONSUMABLE EXPERIENCES

Back in 1999, Joe Pine II and his co-author James Gilmore wrote a seminal book called *The Experience Economy*, which was updated in 2011. In this pioneering book, Joe and James took mass customization (see Chapter 4) and expanded upon the idea with modular experiences. These are experiences that are created, designed, and implemented for consumption. The implementation, which Pine and Gilmore call a "staging," is typically monetized and is as much a set of engagement interactions as a designed and staged experience. The very first line of the book was, "Goods and services are no longer enough." As they make the case in the updated version from 2011, they say businesses still haven't done enough and are still stuck in the goods-and-services-only mire. That holds true in 2018 and will hold true in the near future, though more and more businesses are getting smart about the provision of experiences. I think it needs to go a step further to foster strong, positive engagement. In Joe and James's bright eyes, it's goods, services, and staged experiences. In mine, businesses in the 21st century need to provide products, services, consumable experiences, *and* tools, to succeed, or, minimally, to differentiate themselves from the pack. We'll talk about tools in Chapter 14. For now, let's stick with what these consumable experiences are.

CASE STUDY: CONSUMABLE EXPERIENCES—AMERICAN GIRL

The best way to understand consumable experiences is to hear about one. Mattel's American Girl division has been more successful over its life than even Barbie when it comes to attracting contemporary audiences. For those of you not acquainted with them, the American Girl doll is a doll with a theme. It can be historical, like Felicity, who lived in 1774 and is a horse lover and patriot spy, or contemporary, like Tenney, "who writes songs and plays guitar." Associated with each of the dolls are a storyline and dozens of accessories ranging from furniture to clothes to a book about the doll. But that's only the beginning. The base doll costs from US $60 to $115. The accessories go for even more—up to $275 for a diner, for example. But the true premium is wrapped around immersion with the doll at the American Girl stores.

American Girl has stores all over the country, usually at major malls. When you take your child there with their doll, you can not only accessorize the doll and learn more about its story, you can let your child have lunch with the doll, get their hair cut with the doll, and even watch a play with the doll. All in all, your child and that doll have a great day, which probably makes you roughly $400 lighter than when you came in.

In many of my speaking engagements for the last several years, I've asked the following questions of my audiences:

- How many of you have taken your child to the American Girl store?

- How many would do it again?

A surprisingly large percentage of these relatively affluent audiences have done so—more dads and daughters than any other combination. All but one person in my entire experience said they would take their daughter back.

Think about it, the doll has no idea that its eating lunch, getting its hair cut, or watching a play. It's a doll, for Pete's sake! But your child . . . just look at the smile on their face and the connection to the doll via the experience at the store. I know that many of you reading this are smiling now, thinking about when you've taken your child there. Do any of you regret spending that kind of money for the experience that your little one had? (The child, I mean, not the doll.)

THE AMERICAN GIRL EXPERIENCE BRIEFLY DECONSTRUCTED

This is an almost paradigmatic example of how to design and monetize a consumable experience. Consider the primary two characteristics:

The design is modular—What is in the store are the products and services that are needed to present an interwoven narrative and to provide a set of interactions that immerse the customer in the story.

The design is customizable—The customers can choose the elements that speak to them as individuals. If my doll is Tenney (though I don't play with dolls, I swear), then I am going to choose a set of actions and accessories that are different than if my doll is Felicia. But the broad set of products—accessories that support each doll and experiences that apply to all dolls equally, such as the haircut, lunch, and theater—are made available. The customer gets the choice of which of them they want to consume, thus designing their own version of the narrative that is being provided to them within the constraints of the offering. For example, what is not being offered at American Girl stores is a Barbie or Ken doll or anything that goes with those dolls, even though they are owned by Mattel, too. An overall narrative is associated with the design of this set of consumable experiences.

What is extraordinary about the American Girl "experience" is the design itself—the target audience for the experience is the child, but the target audience for gaining the revenue is the parent. This transaction is dependent on the bond between parent and child, specifically the delight the parent feels despite the heavy cost because they see their child light up.

The reason that this is an interesting example is because the "target child" is physically dragging their personal data into the store by bringing their doll in with them. A smart store employee has the cues for conversation and upsell and cross-sell literally right in the hands of the child. The actual consumable experience of American Girl is implemented via the services and goods offered as accompaniments to the doll that was brought to the store—the theater, the lunch, and the hair dresser cutting their hair. The accessories that are purchased at the store are those that are associated with the doll that the child brought to the store. All of this is immediate, in the moment, easily consumed, a wonderful premium-priced experience for the child, paid for by the parent(s).

But there is another way to provide experiences that are also created, engineered, and consumable—the brand experience.

CONSUMABLE BRAND EXPERIENCE

What if you are trying to create a brand experience—one that is more for framing what the brand is to the customer, whether they are in the store or at home or at another institution—rather than just selling them consumable items. That's a bit of a dilemma because the monetary reward isn't necessarily as immediate; but the long-term results in terms of both perception *and* financial gain are mission critical. How do you do this in a way that has the impact that you are shooting for at scale? What is the thinking that's behind this?

To show you that, I'll tell you another story—the story of the Teeling Whiskey Distillery, the first new Irish whiskey distillery in Dublin, Ireland, in 125 years.

Teeling Brothers: Top o' the Experience to Ya!

Irish Whiskey is the fastest growing spirits category in the world. Where it was invisible about 10 years ago, and had been declining for decades, it's now, according to the International Wine and Spirits Research data, growing at the rate of 11.2 percent per year, 200 bottles being sold every minute, more than 104 million bottles exported in 2016. It also tastes really, really good. This growth has sparked a major interest in the distilleries, and, along with the charm of Ireland itself, has driven a booming tourist trade around distillery visits in the country—with nearly 2 million tourists hitting the various distilleries (the biggest one being Midleton, home of Jameson) and other significant brands that traverse the price and taste spectrum from end to end.

As a result of this boom, dozens of new Irish whiskey brands have been appearing over the past several years, vying for a piece of this fast-growing market. Of all of them, the most distinctive and the most successful has been Teeling Whiskey, the crown jewel of that long-time iconic Irish whiskey family . . . who else?... The Teelings—Jack and Stephen. They had the good sense to hire Alex Chasko, an American from Portland, Oregon, who has been the creative force behind the company as its master distiller.

The results at Teeling speak for themselves, with the establishment of a global brand that's worked its way into hearts, minds, and wallets, and established itself as a category leader in a very short time.

Without going into a lot of detail, I met Alex in 2014 in Dublin at a private whiskey tasting that he conducted with me and four friends from my client company, Thunderhead, arranged by the Fitzwilliam Hotel. Let's just say that we shut the bar down around 3am. Alex and I stayed in touch via LinkedIn and Facebook and, since I had become a huge Teeling fan due to the tasting in 2014, I got some data on the Teeling Distillery. What caught my eye is that in their first year of operation, 2016, as the first new distillery in Dublin in 125 years, 150,000 people passed through their portals to see this new upstart competing with the likes of Jameson and Bushmills. So, vacationing in Ireland in 2017, I paid a visit to the distillery to find out about the experience, and here's what I discovered, in addition to the fact that there were two more Teeling expressions I loved.

The Teeling Distillery experience is a brand experience. It is designed to make sure that when you think of Teeling, you think of it not—the way Jameson presents in their experience—as a venerated brand, but, instead, as a contemporary brand of Irish whiskey that is discovering new vistas and breaking new ground and is, thus, *exciting* to be around. When you walk into the modest building on Newcastle, you see to your right a small café where you can enjoy a sandwich or a salad and sit around and chat. The front desk there advertises three types of tour, which really means three levels of whiskey tasting—ranging from 15 euros to 30 euros—and the more you pay the higher up the whiskey line you get. The basic tour gets you the trinity of their most widely distributed whiskeys—the Small Batch, the Single Malt, and the Single Grain. But it is the distillery itself that truly creates the experience and paints the brand with the brush it wants to be painted with. What starts to distinguish the tour here from other distilleries is the Exhibition Hall, which you are led into at the start of the tour. You start it deliberately without a tour guide, so you will have time to look around and absorb the history of the whiskey trade in Ireland and Dublin. It is presented in a fun way, with bottles and stock certificates and photos that involve both current and long-dead distilleries. This is important, and having no guide is important. Why? Because your experience with the history—which lasts about ten minutes before a guide shows up to start the guided tour—is meant to be self-learned. That way, in effect, history is out of the way. Then you are led into a room where there is a short video of perhaps three minutes in which Jack and Stephen Teeling welcome you to the distillery. Then comes the real deal: the tour of the distillery. Before I get to it, though, I want to explain why the preliminaries are done this way.

Teeling's brand image is meant to be progressive. As Alex Chasko, the aforementioned master distiller put it, "We are a new generation of whiskey making. We start with the next chapter in Irish whiskey." So, the history of Irish whiskey making and the welcome video are not dwelled on. You find your own version of the history by wandering the Exhibition Hall in whatever way you want for ten minutes or so, and then the welcome video you see on the way in is around three minutes, because they want to get you quickly to the meat, or maybe, the mead of the matter—how they make whiskey.

When you actually see the distillery, there are several things that strike you besides three incredibly large (15,000, 10,000, and 10,000 gallon) copper pot stills. The distillery is spotless, *and* there are a helluva lot of viewing windows in the various pieces of equipment.

Remember, we are dealing with an experience created to produce a specific feeling around a brand image. For Teeling, that means a new-generation distillery that is focused on producing contemporary and "generally personalized" expressions of whiskey that are targeted for specific groups and specific markets.

Thus, the primary focus of the experience is the distilling process. What makes this a truly interesting story is that Teeling actually thought of something that I never would have figured on. When they built the distillery, they built it with the idea that tourists would be going through it in large numbers. So, for example, the distillery equipment has clear glass windows, the floors are spotless, the guides are multi-lingual, and the tours are designed to have about 10–15 people come through at any given time in any given tour, with a guide so that the flow remains steady and non-intrusive. The actual pot stills, for example, though they handle between 10,000 and 15,000 gallons, are also built for their aesthetics. The distillery, the backbone of their actual work, is designed not only to optimize the creation of the whiskey, but to provide a unique experience for various groups of people.

The distillery and the tour are crafted to also provide a sensory experience. In the course of the tour, you will see and hear the distillery and smell and taste the whiskey—a sensory experience related explicitly to Teeling's offerings and their workplace and no other. It is very unlike the Jameson experience, for example, which is far more focused on the history of the distillery and its current brands, and is highly compartmentalized into segments like history, how to drink whiskey, etc., in equal measure.

Teeling is a distillery built from the customer's point of view. But what makes this even more compelling is that this is the way that the whiskey is made. "We're making whiskey we like to drink," says Chasko, and, "because we know our audiences and what they are likely to like, we are right more often than wrong."

The Exhibition Hall itself has the display exhibits built on roller wheels. The reason? That way, companies can hold dinners and local food fairs can ply their wares in the hall, so it gets to serve a dual purpose. Though not sexy, it is an important part of the overall experience.

What can we learn from an experience designed to define a brand?

- Knowing what you want your brand to be seen as before you design the experience certainly helps a great deal. Do you want it to be traditional and historic? Do you want it to be next-generation? Do you want it to be seen as small and creative? Larger and expansive? Teeling obviously defined itself as the "next generation in Irish whiskey making," and the core reflection of that is the creativity in the expressions of the whiskey and in the contemporary distilling equipment and process.

- At what touchpoints do you want the customers fully engaged? Partially engaged? Engaged only because they need to be, so they can be fully engaged next time? The strategy of Teeling was to fully engage customers via their deep dive into the "behind the scenes" of the distilling process, use the welcome video as a short gateway to that, and de-emphasize the history so that they could keep the focus on "the next generation" as the brand's theme.

- What are the instruments of the experience? In the case of Teeling, it's the actual "look inside" the distillery—directly into the equipment, but also walking the floors to see how it's all put together.

- How does the experience get integrated into the ecosystem that the brand participates in or is the centerpiece? In the case of Teeling, it's the Newmarket community they reside in. The Exhibition Hall is designed via exhibits on rollers to be cleared for business luncheons/dinners and food fairs from the surrounding local community.

- Rather than focus on the touchpoints only, what about the ambiance—the look and especially the feel? With a café available to you as soon as you get in so you can take it easy while you wait or contemplate your visit—a comfortable, long tasting table—the feel of the place is "relaxed" and, while not "fun" *per se*, it makes you "feel good" about being there.

These are all general points on the crafting of a brand experience. In this case, Teeling's design of their brand experience puts a stake in the ground that defines how they want to be seen and expresses how they are different than Jameson/Midleton or Cooley. That way, when a customer or an industry publication thinks about Teeling, they see a company that is creative and progressive and masters of their craft, which is the art and science of contemporary distillation. That's what Teeling is going for—and that's what Teeling gets. They've won 116 awards through mid-2017, in four years. It's hard to argue with that kind of success. Why bother arguing in fact? Drink up!

I'm thinking that maybe your experience with me this chapter is not enough to convince you that I'm right. Okay, then. If you don't believe anything I've told you so far, then maybe you'll believe my next guest—Scott Rogers, one of the most seasoned and thoughtful practitioners I've known when it comes to customer experience. He's been there, done that. Scott, convince them I'm not lying, please.

THOUGHT LEADER: SCOTT ROGERS

Scott Rogers is most recently VP/Market Intelligence at Digitas/LBi. He has more than 30 years of experience in consumer and customer insights, analytics, etc., primarily in retail on the client side, but also the consultant and agency sides, in both B2B and B2C. He is a longstanding practitioner and thought leader, as well as a great friend. His knowledge of customer experience and the idea of how to go about providing that long-term excellent feeling about a company is nearly unparalleled. He has had experience at companies like David's Bridal and American Credit Union, among others, in creating the environment—internally and externally—to help customers feel that they are continually valued, which helps them stay engaged. He is a living incarnation of that, by the way, being a fundamentally good human being who instinctually makes people feel valuable. His power is that he can take that art and make it a science.

The stage is yours, Scott.

* * * * *

Growth and profitability are mission-critical to companies. Acquisition, retention, share of wallet, etc., are the strategies employed to accomplish growth. However, the customer environment today, with its turbulent confidence and trust, social media exploding "word of mouth," and a few companies like Amazon, Disney, etc., setting consumer expectations for every company, shows that external conditions are increasingly impacting efforts and driving the importance of customer-focused strategies and objectives to survive and thrive. Hence, the rise in terms like "customer experience" in the past decade.

Customer experience? Wikipedia defines it as "the sum of all experiences . . . a *customer* has with a *supplier*. . .over the duration of their *relationship* with that supplier." And the more-than-a-decade-old 80/8 research is still true, that "80% of companies believe they deliver a 'superior experience,' while only 8% of their customers think they do." Clearly, those companies' perception of reality is not the same as their customers'.

Most companies, and most advice, focus on the experience a customer has during interactions with the company, from investigation to purchase and support. However, to the customer, the use of the product and/or service over its lifetime is just as much a part of their experience. Their value journey starts with the job(s) to be done that creates the need and ends with the use of your product/service as solution to their need. From the customer's standpoint, their "experience" is not only their interaction with your company, but also their perception of how well your solution met and exceeded the need they had. Their willingness to recommend, satisfaction, and loyalty are impacted by every point of their journey.

Understanding the customer from the customer's perspective is critical. It's their wants, needs, likes, and dislikes that are the foundation for growth. According to Forrester Research, "If the customer is your boss, the voice of the customer is your performance review." The explosion in data and tools to capture and analyze it has made listening to the voice of the customer incredibly easy. The biggest challenge is making sense of it, as illustrated by the IBM survey of CEOs stating their "companies are data rich, but insight poor." Do you know why customers shop and buy from you, and why they continue to?

A few real examples will help illustrate the points. The first is from David's Bridal. A little context is necessary. David's Bridal is a U.S.-based retailer selling female apparel and related items, primarily for weddings. Founded in 1991, by 2001 it had a 20% share of the wedding-gown market, and almost 40% of all brides in the U.S. shopped at a David's store for their wedding, making it one of the largest. Its growth target was 40% market share.

Our research showed that the number-one reason a bride shops at any bridal shop is word of mouth, and her willingness to recommend was highly correlated with her rating of "service," despite David's core strengths of price and selection. 74% of those rating the service as "excellent" said they would recommend David's, versus only 3% who rated the service as "poor."

A common internal myth was that the wedding was a once-in-a-lifetime event, the bride was the "decider," and bridesmaids were told what to wear. (Picture Katherine Heigel's character in the movie *27 Dresses*.) This myth fostered a culture and behavior that focused on the bride. The average wedding had 4 bridesmaids, 3 of which were single. (Now picture Malthusian theory.) Achieving growth plans meant getting those single bridesmaids to return to shop for *their* weddings, and further research showed that prior experience clearly mattered. Growth (and survival) meant every customer, not just the bride, mattered.

This research prompted a long and arduous culture change to be truly customer-centric, even instituting a customer advisory committee where we recruited a woman who started the Facebook group "I'd rather be single than plan a wedding with David's Bridal."

Our first step was a customer-journey mapping project to understand the customer experience from their viewpoint. Three critical points to keep in mind: 1) choose a representative sample of customers that mirrors your customer base, not just your best customers; 2) engage senior management to participate; and 3) start the conversations with customers by listening and not leading. Open-ended conversations tap into their memories, and, whether true or not, their memories are the stories they tell and impact their future behaviors.

This project resulted in several epiphanies in senior management. Avoiding a multi-million-dollar project that had a high priority internally but no importance to customers was great, but the subsequent impact on the words and actions throughout the company was priceless.

The last story comes from Kay-Bee Toys, an egregious example of listening but failing to understand. Based on a study to find out what customers wanted, the CEO began an initiative to redesign the stores, implementing as many of the customers' top ten desires as possible.

Several of these were experience-related. Two of the top three were "wider aisles (to permit two strollers to pass)" and "lower shelf heights (to reduce a claustrophobic feeling and fear of things falling)." Implementing these, however, meant reducing total shelf space, and thus, total inventory. But the merchants were addressing this by focusing on top desire No. 5: "selection of the hottest toys."

The result? Sales dropped by the same amount that the inventory was reduced in all but a few stores. What the initiative ignored was the number-one desire of customers: that stores "have the toy they were looking for." The company failed to understand the impact of competing priorities.

Experiences matter. Our memories (true or false) drive our future behaviors, consciously and/or unconsciously. Yes, sometimes we do things we hate, such as continue to do business with a company even though we dislike them. Most of us bail, however, at the first opportunity an acceptable alternative comes along. Frequency is not the same as loyalty.

Truly understanding your customers, their wants, needs, likes, and dislikes, what they value, their journey and the importance of your part in that journey, can drive strategic initiatives that have greater impacts.

Don't be complacent with good satisfaction or Net Promoter Scores, though. The credit union industry is a great example. Scores in this industry greatly exceed those of banks. 30% of people in the U.S. are members of a credit union. However, the credit union industry has less than a 7% market share, exemplifying a clear disconnect between attitudes and behavior.

As Clayton Christensen states in his book *The Innovator's Solution,* "Competitiveness is far more about doing what the customers value than doing what you think you are good at." Focusing on the experiences that drive behavior and value to the customer is paramount.

. . . . .

Scott, thank you so much for this. Your "experience" over the years shows.

We take it to our next speaker, Bruce Temkin, so that you can get it from the perspective of an analyst and thought leader who has been the number-one person in the customer experience world for many years.

THOUGHT LEADER: BRUCE TEMKIN

There is no one, I repeat, *no one*, who is more respected when it comes to customer experience than Bruce Temkin. This guy, a former Forrester analyst and now the founder and CEO of his own research and advisory firm, Temkin Group (now an SAP company), is the world's foremost thinker when it comes to the strategies and the programs, the processes and the methodologies that help institutions improve their long-term efforts to keep customers happy. But even beyond that, he's shaped the customer-experience world with his thinking, his research, and his creation of the Customer Experience Professionals Association—an organization that amalgamates the best and the brightest in customer-experience thinking, planning, and execution. What he's got to say, you've got to hear. Titles don't do him justice, but his are Managing Partner, Temkin Group; Chairman Emeritus Customer Experience Professionals Association.

Take the mic, Bruce

⋆ ⋆ ⋆ ⋆ ⋆

THE BASICS: WHAT IS CUSTOMER EXPERIENCE?

Customer experience seems like a simple concept, but people interpret it in many ways. As a first step, it's critical to develop a shared view of what it is. Let's start with a basic definition of customer experience:

> The perception that customers have of their interactions with your organization.

The word "perception" is critical because customer experience is in the eyes of the beholder. It's not what you do as a company, or how your employees think about what they do. It's how your customers *think and feel* about what you do.

"Interactions" is plural for a reason. It's not about just one interaction or a single type of interaction like customer service or sales. Customer experience encompasses all of the interactions with your organization, and it includes everything from TV ads to monthly billing statements to reviewing your offerings on a mobile device.

Customers perceive these "interactions" along three dimensions: success, effort, and emotion. They perceive *success* based on whether they are able to achieve what they want to do. They perceive *effort* based on how easy or hard it is for them to do what they want to do. And their *emotion* is altered based on how the interactions make them feel.

Emotion: The Missing Link of Experiences

While customers perceive experiences through three dimensions, organizations frequently neglect one of them: *emotion*. How many times have you been in a meeting when you discussed customer emotions? Probably not very many. Ignoring emotions, however, does not make them go away.

This turns out to be a severe problem. Not only is emotion a critical element of a customer's experience, but it turns out to be the one that most significantly drives loyalty. In studies of tens of thousands of consumers, Temkin Group has found that emotion has the highest correlation with consumers' desire to buy more from a company, forgive a company if it makes a mistake, try new products from the company, and recommend the company to a friend or relative.

To begin focusing on emotion, you first need to understand what it is.

People are inherently emotional beings and every interaction customers have with you will make them feel a certain way—whether you intend it to or not. It turns out that experiences influence emotions in two ways.

The first is *stimulation*, which is how an experience influences their internal state. The second way is through *identification*, which is how people view themselves within the context of other people. If you're having an ice cream cone, then the joy you get from the great taste is *stimulation*. How silly you feel when people see the ice cream dripping from your face is *identification*.

Instead of ignoring customer emotions, start talking about them.

To help the dialogue, Temkin Group created what it calls the *Five A's of an Emotional Response*. Every time a customer interacts with your organization, they are left feeling one of these emotions: *Angry, Agitated, Ambivalent, Appreciative,* or *Adoring*. These emotions can become very powerful if you start using them in your organization's vocabulary.

When you're discussing experiences of customers, be explicit about which of the *Five A's* describes how the interaction made them feel. And when you're developing new experiences, discuss how you want customers to feel about the interactions and identify ways to measure and ensure they feel that way.

In front-line environments, such as contact centers or retail sales, you can use the *Five A's* to elicit employee empathy. After completing an interaction with a customer, have employees identify which of the *Five A's* they felt best describes the customer's emotion. This list can be used as a coaching tool to discuss why the employee selected that emotion and what they could have done to create a different emotional response.

Using a common language for emotion is a great way to start focusing your organization on this critical element of customer experience.

Design Experiences for Real People

Now that we're finally talking about emotions, let's examine how you can design experiences that create lasting emotional impressions. Why is this important? Because people don't remember experiences the way that they actually happen.

Our memory is not like a video recorder; it does not record every moment, placing equal emphasis on each second. Instead, it is like a camera, taking snapshots at certain crucial moments of the experience and then retroactively judging the experience based on those key snapshots. And our loyalty is based on how we remember those experiences, not on how they actually occurred.

There are several strategies you can follow to capitalize on how people remember experience. To begin with, make sure that experiences end well. It turns out that the end of an experience has a disproportionate effect on how customers remember the overall encounter. If you're examining phone-based tech support interactions, for instance, make sure that your technicians close out their calls in a way that make customers truly feel cared-for. Sometimes a genuine *"is there anything else that I can help you with today"* can go a long way.

You should also recover as quickly as possible from any service miscues. It turns out that people remember the most extreme level of their emotion. So, when something goes wrong, it's not a good idea to let the negative emotions fester, as customers will often become more upset over time when they have a problem that is not being addressed.

Also, it's a good idea to create pleasant surprises. When customers are presented with a good experience that they aren't expecting, it can provide a strong positive spike in their emotion. It turns out that people tend to remember these types of rapid emotional shifts.

And finally, remember that your customers are not typically looking to interact with your organization. They are trying to accomplish something that is causing them to connect with you. If someone is booking a flight with an airline, it's not because they have a desire to interact with the airline, buy a ticket, or even get on a plane. The contact with the airline is just a necessary part of a journey that they really care about, such as delivering value to an out-of-town client event or having a great vacation with their family. To best meet customers' emotional needs, you must focus on their overall journey, and not on your individual interactions.

❀ ❀ ❀ ❀ ❀

Thank you, sir. Number one indeed.

Hopefully, you've now got a grasp of how customer engagement and customer experience are twins, though not identical by any means. How the customer feels about the company over time has a symbiotic impact on every single interaction over the short-, mid- and long-term that your customers have with you, and vice versa. What makes this so complex is that the interactions themselves are expected by the customer to be personalized, and that ain't easy. But, fear not, dear reader, we'll take that on in the next chapter. Take a break, get something to eat, watch some TV, text someone, and then get on to Chapter 4. There's so much yet to come.

CHAPTER 4

The Commonwealth of Self-Interest

What a weird phrase, huh? It seems a bit abstract and yet dense at the same time, which means that maybe it isn't the greatest title for a book; but once you get it, you *really* get it. And then it makes a lot of sense. Though maybe still not the greatest title for a book.

Density and abstraction aside, the commonwealth of self-interest (COSI) is the way to define your business in an era where personalization of an individual's overall experience and specific interactions are part of what you need to offer. You also have to figure out how to do this at scale as your customer base grows to the point that you can't tailor an individual offer to a single customer without significant cost. Yet, you still need to make that individual offer even if you have thousands, or even millions, of customers. The problem facing you is that each of them doesn't care that you are constrained, nor do they care about each of the other customers you have. They care about the interactions they have with you and whether they get the kind of outcomes they are looking for from you, as well as getting the value they want from those outcomes and from their overall experience.

Like it or not, the basic truth that drives your customers not only in their interactions with you but all their actions in life is that, because they are human beings, they are self-interested. Your recognizing that and planning for it can make the difference between success or failure, or at least between the growth or the stagnation of your business.

When trying to engage customers, then, there is no getting around the need to work with and on their self-interestedness. Given that the communications tools available to customers are powerful and easy to use, businesses must take heed strategically, not just as a response to a problem or as a way to push a program. On the glass half full side, however, the business benefit in recognizing their self-interest strategically is substantial and even, potentially, enormous.

You can engage customers successfully around their self-interest without bankrupting yourself. Hell, that's the whole idea of this book. In the next section, I'll start helping you think about engagement strategy; but first we need to set up a final piece to complete the engagement *framework*. If we are successful at doing that, the rest flows and the valuable congress of company/customer interactions over time can be planned and implemented. One of the ways I'm going to try to convince you I'm right is by presenting a really long case study at the end of this chapter to show you the commonwealth of self-interest at work in real life, so you'll know it's not a pipe dream. Is it perfect? No. Is it convincing? You tell me.

But, as with most things, we need to start at the beginning, with the meaning of self-interest.

SELF-INTERESTED DOES *NOT* MEAN SELFISH

According to the most recent United Nations estimates as of the end of 2018, there are approximately 7.7 billion human beings on this planet. While it might be self-evident, I'll say it anyway: each of those human beings is unique in most ways. They have different hopes, dreams, stresses, desires, paths in life, and relationships—and they each think with a set of different metaphors. But there is one thing that *all* of us have in common—we want to be happy. What it takes to make us happy is different, how we get to what we consider happiness is different, and what happens when we get there is different. But what we all have in common is that we want to have a good life and be happy. Additionally, we don't want to be miserable as we take our journeys toward happiness. We want to be happy on the journey, too, and having as much control over it as humanly possible is one of the things that makes us happy. Ultimately, in the grand scheme of things and at the atomic level, that's what life is about.

This isn't a fact unknown or speculation from some cheerful, overly optimistic guy. The *World Happiness Report Update 2016* (yes, there really is an annual report on what makes us happy), established the broad criteria for subjective well-being: happiness, smiling or laughter, enjoyment, feeling safe at night, feeling well-rested, and feeling interested. The negatives they noted were anger, worry, sadness, depression, stress, and pain. A social "theme" emerged from the previous year's report:

> At both the individual and national levels, all measures of well-being, including emotions and life evaluations, are strongly influenced by the quality of the surrounding social norms and institutions. These include family and friendships at the individual level, the presence of trust and

empathy at the neighborhood and community levels, and power and quality of the over-arching social norms that determine the quality of life within and among nations and generations.

That's all great, and, personally, I'm happy and the report proves it. But the question remains: how does this translate into a business that, by its very nature, depends on interactions and transactions with people? Not so cocksure anymore are you?

Let's start with the simple value proposition that I introduced at the beginning of the book. It takes the essence of customer relationships down to its most naked.

If a customer likes you and continues to like you, they will continue to do business with you. If they don't, they won't.

As basic as that statement is, a deeply complex problem that each business must solve is associated with it: satisfying the self-interests of its *individual* customers without breaking the bank.

Even at the level of a few customers, that isn't so easy to do. It's why, in countless tomes about CRM, customer experience, customer engagement, or *anything* that uses customer as an adjective, the paradigmatic example you continually see is the writer's memory of the mom-and-pop-shop owner who gave them the sugary thing they liked when they were little each time they came to the store. For whatever reason, we all have memories of things like that (yeah, I know you do) which not only give us fodder for explaining archetypal personalized customer engagement, but also gave us tooth decay. The problem we face now with examples like that is it's not the 1960s or '70s or '80s or '90s any more. Even though that example might be accurate in explaining the feeling you *want* your customers to have about you, the paradigms for engaging customers, as well as the requirements for doing so, have dramatically changed in the new millennium.

Additionally, you probably aren't dealing with three customers or thirty customers; it's probably more like three million or thirty million, each with their own self-interested agenda. We are now talking about personalized interactions, great engagement, interesting experiences, and a good-enough overall customer experience at *scale*.

The fundamental questions a business should ask itself are:

How do I satisfy the self-interest of each of my (fill in the number) customers so that their experience with me is good enough to make them want to continue to do business with me?

and

What does that mean to an organization already constrained (see Chapter 2) by multiple factors?

Before we go further, let's dive a little deeper into the idea of self-interest. Despite my allegation that self-interestedness is not selfishness, I can hear you asking, "But *isn't* self-interest selfish?" No, it isn't. What, then, is it?

Adam Smith, who I have some differences with, did understand self-interest. In *The Wealth of Nations* he wrote, "It is not from the benevolence of the butcher, the brewer or the baker that we expect our dinner, but from their regard to their own self-interest."

What he was saying is a matter of fact when it comes to people generally. They tend to act in the way that is most personally beneficial—that is, in a way that makes them the happiest they can be under whatever circumstances surround them (also known in 21st-century buzzwords-with-substance terms as "in context"). In the instances of the butcher, brewer, and baker, they each chose the livelihood they chose because it was one that gave them some satisfaction and earned them a living. They sold meat, made beer, and cooked baked goods because they knew that, to make money, they had to. It satisfied their self-interests in multiple ways. We can also make a reasonable assumption they liked what they did.

The translation to contemporary businesses is straightforward. Do those things that you do for those self-interested individual customers that make the relationship valuable to them. A little at a time, make those things habitual—which, in technological terms, means automate them—and you will have customers who are happy masters of themselves who will continue to interact with you.

But, to get to that point, self-interest needs to be more clearly defined because it's not as simple as pure *economic* self-interest. If it were, we could leave things at the level of transactions.

Enlightened Self-Interest vs. Just Plain Ol' Self-Interest

This is the world of Mother Teresa, and that's not a flip statement. While she didn't create the concept, she lived a life of "enlightened self-interest." What is that, and are most people practitioners?

The answer to the second part of the question is . . . kinda, sorta, maybe.

For example, the *Millennial Impact Report: 2014* revealed some interesting numbers on what motivates millennials to work at a particular company. Look at the breakdown from 1,500 respondents.

- A company's involvement with causes influenced 55 percent of millennials to accept a job.

- Once in a position, the main factor in determining whether they remained at their company (beyond compensation and benefits) was having their passions used and fulfilled (53 percent).

- Following behind was a belief in the company's mission and purpose (20 percent).

- Bonds with co-workers (20 percent).

What drives millennials (and many members of other generations) to work at a company is the company's commitment to social good, also known as corporate social responsibility. But keep in mind that this is what is in the millennials' self-interest. Not only must the company doing good, but, as the survey says, they stay at the company if they are having their "passions used and fulfilled."

Self-interest, when it comes to businesses and work, goes beyond just making sure that companies satisfy customers with the right products and services.

To highlight the importance of understanding what the idea of self-interest means both individually and at scale, ladies and gentlemen, I enter into the record the *2015 Cone Communications/Ebiquity Global CSR Study*. For those of you not aware of what CSR means in this case, it is the abbreviation for "corporate social responsibility," not "customer service representative." In other words, it refers to what the company is doing to support the world, or at least the community, that it resides in. The data Cone gathered shows how much deeper self-interest truly goes when it comes to engagement with customers. Here are some of the more meaningful numbers.

Companies that support social and environmental issues

- have a more positive image to consumers (93 percent)

- are more likely to be trusted by consumers (90 percent)

- engender more customer loyalty (88 percent) than companies that don't

This has a direct impact on the company's bottom and top lines. The study found that customers would be

- more likely to pay more for an environmentally and/or socially responsible product (71 percent)

- willing to reward a socially/environmentally responsible company by buying its products over others and/or speaking about it positively to others (31 percent)

- willing to punish a company that was clearly operating counter to environmentally/socially responsible efforts (19 percent)

- willing to buy a product from a relatively unknown company if it were shown to be operating socially/environmentally responsibly (80 percent)

In 2017, Forrester Research, in their *Forrester Data Consumer Technographics, North American Omnibus Survey,* found that 52 percent of all customers evaluate company values when making a purchase—up a whopping 21 percent over the prior year.

I can go on with significantly more data supporting the obvious here, that self-interest goes beyond economic need, and, thus, that there is a lot more to how customers consider engagement from their own perspective. You are responsible as a business to understand the customer's self-interest to a point and to develop a customer-engaged culture that supports the customer's self-interest in conjunction with a recognition of your own constraints, whatever they may be.

Ultimately, self-interest is tied to happiness in all areas for a person. When they are customers, certain business criteria should be met that foster that happiness. One of the most important of those criteria is providing the customer with the gift of choice.

SELF-INTEREST, CHOICE, AND YOU

Perhaps the most important part of the journey to happiness we are all traveling on is that we get to control as much of how it's going to go as we possibly can without impinging on anyone *else's* journey. That means, as individuals and as customers, we get to make the choices as to how and with whom and why and with what we engage. We get to choose our own paths.

The Choice of Choice

We've often said—okay, *I've* often said, but there is safety in numbers—that what humans crave is choice. Urban mythology says the more choices we have the happier we are. Another urban myth says that too much choice, i.e., "overchoice," makes us unhappy. Which, if either, of these is more than just a myth? Let's take a close look because a permutation of this question matters a great deal to how you engage the 21st century digital customer.

The amount of happiness or the distress an individual feels isn't determined by generalized choice or the amount of choices available. But three factors related to choice *should* be considered when planning an engagement strategy that goes to the heart of human thinking, feeling, and behavior. They are the amount of choice and the quality of choice in the context of *control* of choice.

Amount of Choice

One of the stickier myths is that the amount of choices is what makes people happy. The more choices they have, the more they feel that they can get what they want. But it isn't that at all. In fact, too much choice is confusing and, according to Barry Schwartz in his famous 2004 book *The Paradox of Choice*, causes paralysis when trying to choose. In effect, I have so many options I can't just pick one. I don't know what to do. What makes people happy is the control they have over the choices they make. The more control they have, the better the experience is for them because they get to control the tone, tenor, level, and cadence of the engagement, which translates into control over the interactions they are having with the company. Too much choice leads to confusion and to either a feeling of helplessness or a desire to stay inert (in other words, to not do anything).

This May Be the Start of Something . . . Personalized

Offering a high percentage of appealing options is important to customer engagement because it implies that the company knows enough about the individual customer to give them an array of options that are meaningful. As we will see throughout the book, this makes the customer feel as if they are valued. The single most important thing a company can to do retain that customer and keep them engaged is to make them feel continuously valued. To do that, the response, the basket of options, should be one that has relevancy to the customer—meaning they know the company has done enough homework on them and tracked them enough to provide them with a customized set of options. What makes this even more delicious is that they get to make their own choices.

Giving the customer control of the choices they make provides immense value to the business.

Several years ago, Disney Destinations became aware that their customers were getting tired of the complexity of dealing with travel agents, and this was impacting their business negatively. Disney, if nothing else, is always innovating, and they came up with the idea, which was not entirely novel at the time, of providing tools on the Disney Destinations site that would enable potential travelers to arrange their vacations without the "aid" of a travel agent. Not only could they pick and choose the components of the vacation they wanted, they could save the vacation in mid-stream and come back to it when they wanted. And, when they came back to it, a recommendation engine monitoring their choices and the choices of many like them would provide other options, notifications of price changes, and other valuable information to support them in their vacation choices, thus eliminating the need for a travel agent.

Do you know what the single most important piece of the toolset was? No?

It was the save button because that gave the vacationer a sense of being able to control how to proceed with the vacation. They were no longer reliant on anyone but themselves. Control of choice.

All of that is great but the implication of providing customers with the quality choices they need to make the options feel as if they are personalized is that you need a fair amount of data when it comes to "knowing" something about the individual customer. How do you handle this at scale? What if, for instance, you are financial services giant Citigroup with 200 million customers, each of whom wants something different, to some degree, when it comes to how they interact with the company. The customers are aware that Citigroup is operating within constraints—maybe—but, even if they are aware, individually none of them really cares. They are probably also aware that lots of other customers want things from Citigroup simultaneously . . . and they don't care about that either. They want what *they* want.

Yet Citigroup, or whoever you want to imagine in their place, realizes that they must make as many of these customers as they can feel valued, or else those customers may take their business elsewhere. In the world of consumer banks, due to regulatory constraints among other things, there are limits on the product differentiation they can offer since interest rates are not determined by the banks. Services and service levels, then, are where the differentiation comes in. Yet each of Citigroup's customers has a different portfolio, a different life, and a different set of requirements and expectations. What's a bank to do?

Earlier, we saw that a key component for successful engagement is control of choice—not choice itself. That means that the customer commands how and when they want to interact with the company, and the company provides them with the options to do just that.

But how does the company provide those individual customers with the right choices to begin with—and do that when they have to scale—without going bankrupt in the process?

ENTER THE COMMONWEALTH OF SELF-INTEREST

As peculiar as the phrase may sound, the "commonwealth of self-interest" means that, after the necessary customer research has been done and the feedback analyzed, a group of tools, products, services, and consumable experiences are being delivered in real time, or nearly so, that are meeting the perceived personalized needs of the individual customers. The commonwealth of self-interest starts from the idea that all human beings are self-interested and need to have that self-interest recognized by being made to feel valued as individuals. Businesses can't provide each individual with products, services, tools, or consumable experiences produced only for them, but they can provide a set of each of those that satisfies many of the personal requirements needed to fulfill the self-interest of many of the individuals engaged with them. Some customers will fall away, but the majority will perceive this as their being valued if it's done right. It is personalization at scale.

So that we can start from a clear understanding, here is the working definition for the commonwealth of self-interest:

> *The commonwealth of self-interest is a framework for the ecosystem of products, services, consumable experiences, and tools, supported by the strategies, programs, culture, processes, and technology systems needed to provide personalized choices to customers. It is a partnership between the company and customer with an endgame of mutual value exchange.*

The commonwealth of self-interest (COSI) has its roots in the mid to late 1980s, predating the current communications revolution, when it became apparent to some of the most progressive thinkers of the era that customers were going to need more than generically produced goods and services to satisfy their increasing demands. A lot was driven by the manufacturing technologies of the era—mass production and computer aided design—which allowed for customized products at low unit cost. Plus, the 1980s were a time of affluence, and the desire for goods that were customized to the pleasure of the buyer was high. This was the era of yuppies, the so-called "me generation," and credit was easily available, as were credit cards. So, the moment was ripe. In 1987, in his work, *Future Perfect*, Stan Davis identified mass customization, the ancestor of personalization, for the first time. The concept was simple— developing enough of a variety of goods and services in an affordable way, at scale, so that "nearly everybody finds exactly what they want." It was characterized by the production of low-cost but high-quality goods and services, short production cycles, and even shorter product life cycles. It required customer participation in the form of feedback so that the services and goods produced were aligned with customer needs or at least interests.

What made this work was the modularity of the goods and services. The company was able to produce those things that could be combined potentially in a nearly infinite number of ways—at least one of which could satisfy the desires of every customer who was interested in the products/services. That could be twenty customers or twenty million customers. It ultimately didn't matter because the lust for the product/service was satiated by the offering or a combination of offerings. The customer had some control of the choice of how they combined the parts that the company was willing to offer to them. Because the product offerings were limited, the manufacturing and distribution costs were kept in check.

But, while that was an important breakthrough, evolution became necessary when the demands of customers for emotionally satisfying interactions became a "thing." Personalization is now how you deal with digital customers and their demands.

PERSONALIZATION

Don't worry. I'm not jumping into personalization and leaving something called "mass customization," which seems to resemble personalization, sitting there unacknowledged. I'm sure you're wondering, "Is there a difference between mass customization and personalization?"

Oddly, that's a difficult question to answer because everyone, including me, who's attempted to answer it for the last roughly ten years has a different answer, even when there is agreement that there is a difference.

Why the need to distinguish?

Mass customization has been around since 1987—or at least it reached popular literature via Stan Davis at that time. From the 1980s to now, it has served as a process for building products that fit the needs of individual customers, as they identified those needs for the manufacturer.

By the beginning of this millennium, however, customer demand radically altered and became nearly entitlement. Customers figured out that if companies don't give them what they want—even beyond goods and services—then they can easily go elsewhere because digital commerce takes away inconvenience as a brake on switching. That means, with the rise of courier services and ecommerce marketplaces like Amazon, the big box retailers who had been able to beat mom-and-pops on cost and convenience, and on supply-chain efficiencies, no longer had locations (convenience) as much of an advantage. Courier services got the package to the customer in 2–4 days, whether it was sent by a big-box retailer or a tiny one-person show. As time went on and Amazon became a marketplace for those one- and two-person shops that did online business by using Amazon's services, the playing field almost completely leveled.

The market began to shift away from the original intent of mass customization, which was a process designed to get products and services of value produced at efficient cost into the hands of groups of customers. Tools became available to the customer that would enable them to sculpt their own experience, and thus to create and personalize their own products and services from the "raw" materials of those options that the company wanted to make available to the customer. The customer still didn't control the process of production, but they controlled the results. The availability of digital tools increased the control the customer had over their engagement and thereby played a role in potentially increasing their commitment to engagement with brands. Customers' control of their own choices became increasingly easy. Tracking all this with CRM systems and creating communications with systems of engagement gave the companies the ability to track customer data—their activities and transactions, their search habits, their conversations about the brand, and their social profiles, which included their hobbies, interests, styles, concerns, and brand sentiments among many other things. That meant that with the right tools and services, they were able to gain more insight into more customers' commitments to the brand, and thus the means to address each customer's concerns and demands. While mass customization remained an option, control of personalized experiences and outcomes began to pass into the hands of the customer.

Mass customization and personalization at scale both provide what customers want—a highly individualized engagement and experience with a company—if they care about the company enough to want it.

THE COMMONWEALTH OF SELF-INTEREST: PERSONALIZATION PLUS

So, that leads us to our world as it is today—a business world increasingly subject to the needs, desires, demands, and sometimes entitlements of customers. While this historic pendulum swing seems unfair to business, there is no point in passing judgment. It is what it is. Customers now control the conversation about the brand (and many other things), and, as a result, businesses have to not only respond with programs that support that control and the customer's demands but embrace the concept that their customer has moved from being part of a herd of cud-chewing bovine objects of a sale (in the eyes of business, not me) to a full-fledged partner who is collaborating on providing value to and getting value from the company. The company has to satisfy this "condition" at scale.

Think about it.

- As human beings, we are all self-interested. Check.

- Because we are self-interested, when it comes to demands on companies, as customers, we want what we want—a sufficient set of options, be they tools, experiences, products and/or services, that indicate the company knows something about me, is offering me things that make sense to me, and providing me with choices. Check.

- Then we want control of how we choose, what we choose, the channels we choose on, and the way and when we want it delivered. Check.

- We want those choices delivered to us quickly, and often in real time. Check.

- To the extent it makes sense in terms of our time and the company's requirements, we would like some say in how the company produces products and services for us and provides tools and experiences to us. Check.

- We want it to be relevant enough to us as individuals to foster that mutual value exchange. Check.

- The company wants its customers to be happy, so those cheerful souls can impact revenue positively, directly and indirectly, in an ongoing way. Check.

- Period. Check.

To make all these dreams come true requires substantial work, risk, and a willingness to put the necessary time, effort, and money behind it. The COSI framework is the dreamcatcher.

But you, as a once-again skeptical reader, say, "That is all great in theory and a wonderful fantasy, but as a business person I live in the real world; and the real world says this is a gigantic, idealistic fantasy."

I am going to show you that it is already a dream-come-true in the real world. The PC and video games industry has provided us with a model to emulate. Let's close this puppy out by telling their story and extracting the elements that make this a truly great model for the commonwealth of self-interest. Are you game? Heh. Heh.

CASE STUDY: THE PC AND VIDEO GAMING INDUSTRY

The electronic games industry is one of the world's largest entertainment segments. According to a variety of market research studies, the industry is expected to reach a total of around $120 billion by 2021. What they define currently as "the industry" consists of PC games, video console games, and smart-device (i.e., mobile) games, as well as some in-game advertising. The largest percentage of game players, 56 percent, use a PC, 53 percent use a console, and several other devices are used, with the fastest growing segment being mobile games. E-sports—those watching competitive video gamers playing for large cash and other prizes—is also a growing segment. Professional e-sports competitors play games like Overwatch and League of Legends to gigantic high-energy crowds both in person and via the web and TV. For example, in the e-sports Intel Extreme Masters 2017 World Championship finale in Katowice, Poland, in 2017, live attendance hit 173,000, and there was a total viewership online of more than 46 million. Staggering numbers which even dwarf the Superbowl.

The other part of this market, often neglected in discussions, is the hardware it takes to run these complex and power-hungry games, cloud or no cloud. Despite declining PC sales worldwide over the last several years, the one segment that is growing dramatically is the PC gaming-enthusiast segment—which, as of 2017, exceeded $32 billion. This includes pre-built systems, but, also, because PC gamers are also strongly attracted to custom build-your-own (DIY) systems, it includes the component parts, too. This market segment is growing roughly at the rate of 26 percent per year. Add that to the $121.78 billion in 2017 games sales, a growth rate that is expected to bring the market to $180 billion by 2021, according to newzoo who covers this sort of thing, and you are talking about a very high-stakes market that is aimed at customers who have enthusiast-level emotional ties to the products, services, tools, and experiences—and to the lifestyle—that comes with all this.

This market segment isn't, as popular belief might have you think, millennials who grew up gaming, or who, as every comedy in the theaters that incorporates millennials might have you think, are mindless, dorky kids geeking out in front of their TV with their gaming console. The distribution of gamers is surprisingly even-handed when it comes to age. According to the Entertainment Software Association (ESA) 2017 annual report, the age distribution of gamers is:

1. Male

    a. Under 18 years old: 18 percent

    b. 18–35: 17 percent

    c. 36–49: 11 percent

    d. 50+: 13 percent

2. Female

    a. Under 18 years old: 11 percent

    b. 18–35: 10 percent

    c. 36–49: 8 percent

    d. 50+: 13 percent

In other words, it is remarkably evenly distributed across generations and gender, which is notable when it comes to revenue, marketing, and market potential. Full disclosure here: I am an avid PC gamer. So, I am vested and invested in this model in both a professional, here's-how-it's-done way, and a personal, I-love-this-stuff, way.

This level of success is not surprising for more reasons than I can cover here. There are dozens of studies on the success of this market segment that cover the economics, the sociology, the psychology, and the anthropology. For me, and for customer engagement, this is the perfect storm when it comes to the commonwealth of self-interest—perhaps the best possible example of how the commonwealth of self-interest can work in practice. The gaming industry, for more than a dozen years, has focused on providing products, services, tools, and consumable experiences to create highly personalized relationships. While many of the PC and console games that are released each year are games that provide some customization options, a significant amount of these games is equally as much platforms for customization, so you can use the game you purchased as a base and rebuild it any way you want. (This is called "modding.") Now, we are starting to see data plays, i.e., the use of real-life activities interspersed with game activities, to not just gather data for marketing purposes but to customize the individual gamer's experiences and do it in real time, though we are still at the cutting-edge with the latter.

Back in 2005, at a Gartner Group Customer 360 CRM event, I spoke about the PC and video gaming world as the prototype of a new business model that could be adapted to the business world universally. I'm proud to say that I was right about that, and what I'm going to do now is tell you the story of PC and video gaming and the world of modding to draw out the lessons you need to put into practice. The commonwealth of self-interest isn't just a cool but almost unfathomable term, it's an actual business model that has been put into practice. Make no mistake about it—this is no longer a prototype, but a mature, proof-of-concept business model.

It's time to tell the story, so gather 'round, men and women, and warm your hands at the fire.

We begin this tale in 1983, with the Apple II release of *Castle Wolfenstein*, an early first-person shooter. In the original game, you starred as an Allied spy who shot it out with Nazi bad guys. A fan of the game took the original actors and text from the game and replaced it with new text and new characters all based on the Smurfs. Thus, not only was *Castle Smurfenstein* born, but the world of modding was born along with it. This changed the landscape by making the game a platform, providing tools for the gamers to modify the platform, and passing control to those gamers to play the game that they wanted to play.

That was, however, only the first instance of modding and, thus, worthy of the modders' Hall of Fame and important to the story, but it is not the heart of the tale. The true story of the electronic gaming industry as a commonwealth of self-interest began in 1990 with the release of another Hall-of-Fame classic, *Duke Nukem,* by Apogee software. Fans began to modify not only the characters in the game but also the different levels, and, since they had no tools to do that, they created "level editors" that they began to publicly distribute so that other fans could modify the games, too.

This was noticed by legendary game publishers John Carmack and John Romero. In 1992, as co-jefés of id Software, they acquired the rights to *Castle Wolfenstein* and created a game based on it called *Wolfenstein 3D*—an even more violent shooter than its predecessor. They established a new business model for PC games and, eventually, even for software, with the first "freemium" model. The first few levels of *Wolfenstein 3D* were free of charge to play, and you could do just that by downloading and installing the game. If you wanted to continue to play after you beat those free levels, though, you would need to buy a registered version. In the meantime, because the initial distribution was typically the freeware version, fans began to modify the base game by providing free additional content on a larger scale, including weaponry and other game extenders.

Thus, two elements of the commonwealth of self-interest were put in place.

Element #1—A business model that drove interest with a new form of distribution.

Element #2—The ability of the fans/customers to co-create, with the tools to help drive the model and the media to help distribute it.

By 1993, with the release of one of the most famous games of all time, *Doom,* id Software's CEO John Carmack had incorporated the ability to modify and create new content into the DNA of the game itself. The only "ask" that id had was that the modifications be done and distributed with the registered version.

Most of the modders complied, and, in fact, in many cases, the modifications were coded so that they could only be used in the registered version.

Element #3—The customers were partners of the company, not just consumers of its products.

This was so successful that, in 1997, Carmack released the source code of *Doom*, thus increasing the velocity of modifications to the game and, in fact, making Doom a platform, not just a game with tools. Something that customers had done in an *ad hoc* way was now being institutionalized by the company so that the partnership could evolve. In fact, there had been a hint of it the year before with id Software's retail release of *Final Doom*, a product that was a compilation of fan-made levels of the game. The revenues from this were shared with the creators of the mods.

Element #4—There was a mutual value exchange.

Over the next twenty years, modding became an integral part of the value of the game, extending it well beyond whatever its plain-vanilla state had been. It was the foundation for what I now consider the proof-of-concept of the commonwealth of self-interest.

One exceptional mod is indicative of how well the COSI concept can work in practice. Sega has a series of wildly popular games called *Total War*. This series, with titles like *Rome: Total War, Medieval: Total War, Total War: Attila*, and, more recently, *Total War: Warhammer I* and *Total War: Warhammer II*, has sold more than 20 million copies since its founding in 2000 with *Shogun: Total War*. Its popularity skyrocketed with the release of *Rome: Total War* in 2004. The game sold extremely well and was a lot of fun to play, trust me, but there were continuous complaints by its devotees about the historical inaccuracies of the game. A group of roughly 30 developers, graphics artists, writers, etc., from multiple locations, banded together in 2005 and announced a team that would create an historically accurate version of *Rome: Total War* with the tools that were provided by the game company. They called it *Rome: Total Realism* (RTR). What made this a remarkable effort is that it was done entirely digitally; and the community, though more limited than at its peak, still exists to improve the mod (which is now in beta for its eighth iteration).

Element #5—Customers (via communities in this case) actively participate in the evolution of the products, services, and tools.

A look at their site back in 2005–2006 now shows that this 30-odd-member team wasn't just a ragtag gang of hackers or developers, but an organized entity. It consisted of writers, 3D designers, graphic artists, a public relations person, and historians among others. If you look at their current site, you'll see that this is what the team is made up of: historians, researchers, administrators, community and forum moderators, web infrastructure specialists, IT managers, a public relations person, coders, graphic artists, and a mapping specialist. They have freelance support for writing, art, beta testing, and design. They have social media specialists and YouTube influencers who helped them with promotion. That's just the (unpaid) staff. The fans of their mods have supported the betas by building out highly specific technical assets for the mod. Some examples would be unit textures, "campaign pine trees," and original accurate maps.

What this tells you is how phenomenal the level of active engagement is. There are even mods built by gamers on top of the RTR mod. Sub-mods?

The forums' topics range across the standard software stuff you always see, such as bug reporting, feature suggestions, and so forth, but also include historical discussions that, over the years, have ranged from the size of the epaulets worn by a specific phalanx in the Roman Republic to the economic state of the Gauls or Visigoths at the time of the fall of the Republic. And these get heated.

Element #6—Advocates actively participating in the "commonwealth" due to their own self-interest.

Keep in mind this isn't a "company." It's a group of modders who communicate digitally, have never met, and whose homes span the globe. This mod has been done for free for all the years from 2005–2018. This is not a for-profit project. In fact, a plea that is still up on their website from 2015 says they know it's been a while since they asked for money, but it costs $120 a year to maintain the site and they are dependent on contributions to do so. $120. That shows what value is to the customer-producers in this case—the love of the game itself, the pleasure they derive from playing it, and the visceral value of the feeling they get as a crew that this RTR mod is doing something to drive the pleasure of the game for the community. When the first edition of the mod came out in 2005, it was nearly a gigabyte. Despite the lower Internet bandwidth and download speeds of the time, they still had 800,000 downloads the first week. That's an indication of the value they created for Sega and for the game's fan communities. The value continues more than a decade later.

Element #7—Broad, deep, and varied levels of engagement driven by the level of personal interest to the gamers.

The value of modding can't be overestimated. This kind of user-created content was the subject of a study done by two University of Haifa researchers in

February 2017 called "Placing a Value on Community's Co-creation: A Study of Video Game 'Modding' Community." It was a comprehensive study, but the net result is that, with the adoption of open platforms by game companies that allow for mods in some way, even with license restrictions that allow the game companies to control distribution at some level, there is a direct impact on the bottom line. The study found that:

> *... when the firm supports the modding community, the average increase in sales per game (selling at 97,000 units) would be in the sum of roughly 15,000 units ... Thus, the value proposition for supporting the modding community is a 15% increase in sales.*

This isn't lost on the game companies. Blizzard, a game maker known for several iconic games (e.g., *StarCraft, Diablo*) brought modders to BlizzardCon, their annual gamers' conference, to get their feedback on future games and future releases of existing games, providing the gamers with what had historically been highly protected information. Sites began to spring up to support mods of specific games, as did sites that aggregated mods. The world's biggest mod aggregation site is Nexus (nexusmods.com). This is a paid-membership site with varying plans, including a £49.99 lifetime membership. Here are their stats as of late 2018 to give you an idea of both their scope and the level of interest of the modding community in the personalization of their gaming.

> *We host 265,632 files for 625 games from 85,854 authors serving 15,809,168 members with 2,915,704,888 downloads to date.*

You see that correctly. More than 15 million members and nearly 3 *billion* downloads to date.

Element #8—Monetization works both ways, for company and customer. Mutual exchange of value takes place at a transactional level.

Modding is a very powerful addition to the gaming world's business model because most interactions occur in communities and user forums, providing the means to scale the discussion. Aggregators like Nexus support individual mod sub-forums so that, as an individual gamer, you can provide inputs that are not only monitored by the creators of the mod but also by the game companies themselves. These are coupled with the sites like *Rome: Total Realism* where the same sort of engagement goes on but focused around a single mod and its adherents, developers, and users. One byproduct of this engagement has been that some of the mod developers end up with full-time jobs from the company that produced the game they built the mod for.

Element #9—The creation of an ecosystem of companies and customers. The recognition of value derived from each side begins to blur the lines between the company and customer in a good way. They are integrated parts of a whole ecosystem.

But the satiation of demand for personalized content doesn't stop with mods or the communities built around the customization of games. The increased availability of personal data is now part of how game companies and other entertainment entities work together to provide gamers with an optimal gaming experience that is based in individual gaming preferences.

Do you remember what Charlie Shin said in Chapter 2 about the relationship between Major League Soccer and the game company EA Sports? Here's a brief recap if you don't.

At MLS, an internal study found that an EA FIFA video game was identified as one of the key drivers behind fan interest in MLS. In collaboration with EA SPORTS, MLS developed a pilot program to drive greater video game plays and a performance model to measure the impact on club engagements using the game-play data. The pilot program included a variety of interactive engagements between the fans and MLS clubs through offline and online platforms. Fans would see the EA FIFA video version of the MLS player goal celebration in-stadium during a live game or be asked to play the MLS rivalry match scheduled for the weekend within the EA FIFA game for a chance to win special game packs. The pilot campaign resulted in very active digital and social engagements among EA FIFA gamers with its participating clubs. In addition, the campaign drove greater game plays, which helped drive greater interest in MLS clubs.

The pilot program is an illustration of digital disruption and its impact on fan engagement well beyond the game and its players inside the white line. It also illustrates why marketers need to understand and recognize the importance of becoming a customer-centric organization. Advances in technology and communication, combined with the explosive growth in data and information, have given rise to a more empowered global consumer. A clear understanding of customer needs and behaviors across the organization will help drive profitable growth strategies.

Element #10—Highly personalized data-driven experience and engagement.

As time marched on, so did the gaming industry. The business models began to transition with the evolution of new forms of gaming via mobile and now professional e-sports.

But it doesn't stop here, even though, if the above were all that there was to the model, it would be enough to prove the validity of the COSI as constituted. It is a symbiotic relationship between the gamers and their gaming companies that leads to mutual value. The gamers get not only a highly personalized experience and the means to continually engage via multiple platforms and media, but they are also able to provide feedback that is listened to and develop a product that isn't just to their liking but often can be monetized and widely distributed. The companies are not only able to monetize the engagements with a variety of pricing models, they are able to collaborate with their customers to improve the experience they are having all the time by having those customers provide enormous quantities of highly relevant data about their game-playing behavior, as well as personal likes and dislikes. That is how you satisfy millions of customers—if that's how many you have—but let them retain control over the engagement and make them feel valued.

This vertical industry has had time to mature and, with that maturity, evolve in a way that scales its value, shows you what a more mature COSI-like framework brings to the table, and exposes some of the possible warts that come with age. Gaming has aged well and rather dramatically, but not necessarily elegantly. This is, however, by no means the end of the story.

Steam Rises

One thing that makes communities part of a viable business customer engagement program is that, when the business offers them, they can be managed from behind the firewall and still provide the benefits that community brings. Products like Lithium, Salesforce Community Cloud, and others provide mature companies with the technology needed to build and maintain communities and measure results.

Valve, the creator of one of the most popular games in history, *Half-Life 2*, and a mod that still remains a revenue monster, *Counterstrike*, started a service called Steam in 2002. I'd like to say that they understood the organic forces that were driving the gaming world and also understood that there was a huge opportunity if they could capture all this electric activity, reproduce the relationships, and take the *ad hoc* and fragmented character of it all and aggregate and institutionalize it. I'd also like to be able to say that they knew that to do that they'd have to create and own the ecosystem that drove all of this. But that wasn't the case at all. Steam, which is now the largest gaming ecosystem, and, in fact, one of the largest business ecosystems of any kind, was started by Valve because they thought that it would be a good idea to have a platform that could update games automatically and also protect against piracy.

But what it has evolved into is so much more than that. I'm not going to spend the time needed to run through its actual evolution, but I am going to give you an idea of what it has become.

DIGITAL DISTRIBUTION PLATFORM FOR BOTH VALVE AND THIRD-PARTY GAME COMPANIES

As of mid-2018, Steam had 21,406 different games that were available for purchase. Almost 3 billion copies of games have been sold on Steam since its inception. In 2017 alone, this generated $4.3 billion for Valve in purchases, royalties, and fees. It had more than 15 percent of the total number of games sold in the world. Steam allows members to pay for games and for download-able content (DLC) that requires the game to use it. Additionally, because the Steam platform resides in the cloud, games can be downloaded multiple times to multiple devices without additional fees, a huge advantage to the members. They also allow games being sold through third parties such as Humble Bundle or Fanatical to be downloaded through Steam with a product key.

LARGEST ACTIVE-GAMING COMMUNITY IN THE WORLD

Steam announced that, by the end of 2017, they had over 125 million active accounts and more than 67 million active users per month, with around 291 million players. They allow sharing of games at no extra charge with family members and close friends. Interactions related to an individual game—ranging from community discussions to updates from the game developers to special deals to solving technical issues—are carried on via game hubs.

USER-CREATED CONTENT

User-created content and feedback is the centerpiece of the Steam ecosystem. It creates ongoing interaction among developers, publishers, end users, and the overall actual Steam community. Steam's platform provides for user-created content in multiple ways.

First there is the Steam Workshop, which is both a toolset and a distribution platform for mods. Adding the functionality to monetize the mods in 2015 caused a bit of a hiccup. Even though several big shot modders were in favor of it, the Steam team, to their credit, saw 130,000 signatures on a petition opposing it, and thus the functionality was removed. The value of mods isn't in monetization but in their ability to build community and provide customized content to satisfy individual gamer needs.

You could still monetize content on the Steam platform. Independent developers are given the opportunity to develop and sell games to Steam's community. Originally, in 2012, they launched Steam Greenlight, where independent game developers could showcase their games. Whether or not Steam would allow them into the supply chain was dependent on the votes of the community. This didn't work as well as they had hoped because the platform became rife with people gaming the system. Game makers also complained of uncertainty and unreliability. In early June 2017, despite 90 million votes on thousands of indie candidates, Steam Greenlight was shut down. A week after it was shut down, it was replaced by Steam Direct, which involved a more traditional approval process—Steam decided directly on whether the game was greenlit. But the opportunity for monetization remained. If you were an indie developer with a good game and you got it approved, you could dream about a best seller.

FEEDBACK LOOP

In a lot of ways, it still all depends on the gamers themselves. Gamer recommendations are a key to game purchases. Not only are their mass recommendations on the microsite for each game—e.g., "Very Positive last two weeks (855), Mostly Positive overall (31,211)—but they have super-fans called "Curators" who apply and are selected to review games, often before others get the opportunity. Even the mass recommendations can be drilled into to view the individual recommendations in as much minute detail as you care to see. Additionally, because of the game hubs, community comments are aggregated to the individual game microsite, adding additional color and more content for decision-making. The community conversation has room for recommendations for specific improvements to the game that are addressed to the developers. So, the Steam community of 125 million has the opportunity to reach the developers and the publishers and to directly provide input with the backup of the implied power of 125 million possible "listeners" to the conversations. This Amazon-like review system is word-of-mouth institutionalized. It allows the potential game purchaser to see what thousands think (quantitative) and what individuals think (qualitative) and what selected curators think (expert opinion). This is data that a potential consumer can use to help them decide on the transaction.

In addition, you can always see not just what the Curator thinks but what is popular among those friends in the Steam community that you're connected to with a simple pull-down menu item click.

Algorithms are constantly running in the background, cataloging your entire journey across the Steam universe. If you purchase a game, the algorithm notices; if you read reviews of a game, it notices; if you rate and review a game, it notices. Steam generates game queues, i.e., games that the engine recommends based on the tag frequencies in your journey. Within the queue, as you go through the personalized set of recommendations, you can add a recommended game to your wishlist, follow it to keep abreast of news and developments, and either buy it or say that you aren't interested. More recently, you can customize the tags that you want the algorithm to stop considering. For example, I eliminated "gore" as one of the tags that showed up in a few of the games that I had tracked. Please, no judgment. I'm not that violent, even when I'm playing a game. I swear. The algorithms are constantly refining my likes and dislikes to provide me with a highly personalized experience across the entire ecosystem, which, of course, enhances my engagement with Steam.

REVENUE MODEL MONETIZES ECOSYSTEM— COMMUNITY-DRIVEN ECONOMY

Needless to say, Steam isn't a charity, nor is it a community whose sole purpose is for its users to be happy. It is a business that sells games and all the accompaniments to games. Because of its focus on its customers/members, the revenue model that they've built is organized, with some occasional hiccups, around making sure that both Valve and the members gain real benefit from what made Valve $4.3 billion in 2017.

The revenue model has multiple levels. The most obvious is game activations. Steam had more than 370 million game activations in 2016, most which were purchased, although there were a significant number of "free to play" activations. Additionally, tied directly to many of the individual games were the fees for DLC developed by the game companies, which ordinarily range from $0.99 to $19.99, depending on what kind of content is added to the game. Valve's own "free to play" games, like the wildly popular multiplayer Dota 2, rely on in-game micro-purchases ranging from strictly cosmetic items (new outfits or hats) that have no impact on gameplay but are designed to provide a highly personalized in-game experiences, to new, more powerful weapons that can help you win the game.

Parts of this model benefit Steam Community members. You earn items to trade or sell based on in-game achievements or transactions. Those in-game items (trading cards in a manner of speaking) can be sold in the Steam Community Market. The money is placed in your Steam Wallet, which is a credit holder that provides you with money to spend on Steam games—Steam Community-only cash. Because these sales are real money, Valve takes 5 percent of the sale—and the users who sell the item have to use the cash to buy Steam games. Think of it: the customers have sold items they earned as extras for doing something in the Steam Community or in a game. They now own credits with which to buy games, and Valve is also making something from the sale—in their case, real cash, not Steam credit.

The developers are also rewarded. If Steam Direct greenlights their game, they can put it up in the Steam Store even as an "early access game." That means that the game could still be in alpha—which is a very early stage of development—and not only can it be purchased, usually at a good pre-release discount, but the customers can give feedback to help the game get from alpha to beta to release. Meanwhile, the game developer and Valve make money on the journey.

This multilayered, somewhat complex, revenue model provides value to both the user and to Steam. It rewards

- the user for success in the games and for community activity

- the developer for creation of the games

- the company with sales, subscription fees, transaction fees, and distribution fees

Win-win all around the ecosystem.

It's not perfect. Customer service tends to be a recurring problem with Steam. But all in all, this is further proof of the validity of the commonwealth of self-interest, with an entire industry committed to the approach.

Lessons to Be Learned

I want to start with the lessons from this case study that you should *not* learn. Interpretations of the incredible success of the electronic games industry are often narrow and stultified. "What we learn from PC and video games is that we need to make things more fun! More competitive!" Thus, we saw the brief flare up in popularity of gamification. There is nothing wrong with making things more fun, and even more competitive, so customers have a better experience. But the most powerful lessons to be learned here don't come from the games; they come from the gaming industry. The industry's *business model* is transformative—engaging customers in the most advanced way, treating them as your partners, and realizing a mutual value exchange. This is the business model driven by a commonwealth of self-interest. What are the universal lessons—the ones that will ultimately be elaborated on in the rest of this book—that you can learn from the PC and video gaming industry? Here are a few that might make a big difference to you.

- The commonwealth of self-interest is characterized, first and foremost, by a mutual value exchange between the company and the customer.

In this case, the gamer gets to participate as a partner in conjunction with the game company to build the kind of game they want to see as individuals, to interact at whatever level they choose to interact, and to be supported at no matter what that is.

- The engagement of the customer and their experience over time are highly personalized, even when dealing with millions of customers. This is the signature of the PC and video gaming industry. Make the gaming experience and all the interactions associated with it "yours," in the form you want, from entirely new games to cosmetic in-game changes to existing games with skins for the interface to clothing for avatars. This is now enhanced by the rich data available about the journeys, the personal likes and dislikes, and the conversations among the gamers.

- To reach that state at scale, the business has to provide the necessary products, services, tools, and consumable experiences and place them at the customers' disposal. The industry institutionalized the customization opportunities for gamers by providing them with the tools, after the gamers themselves created their own tools to modify games in the earlier stages of evolution.

- The culture of the business has to be customer-engaged not just customer-centric, meaning the DNA of the company has to be focused on providing what the customer needs to be good enough to keep them engaged—even when it means leaving things that are ordinarily in the control of the business in the hands of the customer instead. Steam is focused on making sure that the gamer's experience is the paramount concern of the company, even with the customer-service warts. This engagement model is more the industry standard than not.

- The revenue model should be one that benefits all hands if at all possible. This means that if there is a way for the customer to gain something from the transactions, they should be given the opportunity to do so. One caution here: this can't always be the case. Steam has been in the forefront of seeing that gamers are rewarded with community currency and real currency, as well as providing the distribution network for independent game developers and publishers in addition to more traditional commercial firms.

- To build the commonwealth of self-interest takes both a platform and an ecosystem. This is not either/or. Steam provides tools to both the game developers and the gamers themselves and a deep community that allows them to interact and exchange value with the company and amongst themselves.

If everything in the world was beautiful, all our businesses would have the COSI framework that I'm suggesting here. The PC and video games industry has the most advanced DNA in this regard, and Steam is the most mature reflection of something approaching a genuine practical commonwealth of self-interest. Is it possible to have that in other industries or at other companies? Sure. The rest of this book is devoted to showing you the strategies, programs, culture, policies, technologies, and systems that will help you start thinking this customer-engagement thing through—and, even if you don't fully evolve the COSI framework, successful customer engagement with direct and indirect impact on your business is definitely a possibility.

Let's *do* this.

SECTION THREE

The Details: General

How to develop a customer engagement strategy, design the programs, and create the culture. How to map the customer's journey so that you not only know what you're talking about but who you are talking about and what they are doing—right now. First, the general game plan . . .

CHAPTER 5

Developing an Ecosystem: Designing a Strategy

I've spent Sections One and Two setting the framework and definitions for thinking about customer engagement. Effectively, they are the "how to describe it" sections. They set the stage for what Section Three is all about—getting down to how to start doing things at your company to make customer engagement work. We just built the frame. Now we are going to find the right canvas, and then we will start to paint.

That is a very arcane way of saying, "Now that we've got the framework, it's time to develop the strategy."

WHY A STRATEGY FIRST?

Why *wouldn't* we begin with strategy? We need to identify what we already have and what we need to do, and then we need to figure out how to go about implementing what's needed. That's our strategy—our vision and our mission plan for executing programs that will engage our customers. We need to plan before we build the programs, not exactly an out-of-the box solution.

But a business strategy can be a more complex endeavor than it was in the past because, as a well-known former presidential candidate once said, "It takes a village." In business terms, this translates to "it takes an ecosystem" to please a digital customer. Identifying the ecosystem you have and building the ecosystem that your customers require are critical parts of both strategic thinking and user-experience design that you would be wise to not ignore.

THE ART OF THE ECOSYSTEM

Business ecosystems are nothing new. In fact, even though I've been talking about ecosystems for years, unbeknownst to me until I did research for this book, for many years before I was talking about them, James Moore was.

Moore defined it back in 1993, in an article in the *Harvard Business Review* (HBR) entitled "Predators and Prey: A New Ecology of Competition." He came up with a long but accurate definition of what we all now call a business ecosystem.

> *An economic community supported by a foundation of interacting organizations and individuals—the organisms of the business world. The economic community produces goods and services of value to customers who are themselves members of the ecosystem. The member organizations also include suppliers, lead producers, competitors and other stakeholders. Over time, they coevolve their capabilities and roles and tend to align themselves with the directions set by one or more central companies. These companies holding leadership roles may change over time, but the function of ecosystem leader is valued by the community because it enables members to move toward shared visions to align their investments and to find mutually supportive roles.*

As long winded as this definition is, I can get on board with the bulk of it. The broader ecosystems are part of an extended value chain that most companies have wrapped around them to provide some additive capabilities that support their vision, mission, and reach.

I am going to concentrate on a particular kind of ecosystem in this chapter and the thinking around it, and that is the customer ecosystem. Generically, everything that Moore said in 1993 makes perfect sense—but in a world where customer engagement is king, a customer-focused ecosystem is the kingmaker. First, though, let's talk about the enterprise value chain—the institutions and people who constitute the building blocks that are necessary for a business to run successfully.

ENTERPRISE VALUE CHAIN

Each business has a set of capabilities it provides that define it as a business. This is its core business. It could be anything, really—and that core business can change. For example, for the first 95 years of its existence, Pitney Bowes' core business was to provide machine-produced postage to companies regardless of size. Even though that remains a cash cow for the company, currently they are focused on what their Vice President of Product Management, Clarence Hempfield, calls "Connected Commerce." No longer just producing machines to dispense postage, they have a software-solutions business which encompasses data, location intelligence, analytics, and customer engagement through personalized video. They've got a strong e-commerce business, a sophisticated business-technology solution that has some of the largest consumer brands as its customers. All in all, their current core business is far, far away from what the company was known for in its first 95 years.

But, despite changes over time in what the core business might be, the constant is that all businesses have a core set of capabilities that drive how they approach customers, sell to those potential clients, run their operations, build and manage their products, and are perceived in the market. This is the unwavering centerpiece that is administered by employees—both management and staff—and direct suppliers to and distributors of core business products and services.

Beyond the core business, but also including it and certainly supporting it, are business partners, external agencies (e.g., a government regulatory agency), direct customers, suppliers that are not supporting the core business but are supporting other corporate functions (e.g., the office supplies company), influencer networks, and investors/other stakeholders. This is what I call the enterprise value chain. It is an internal business ecosystem that in its totality drives a single company's efforts to succeed in the marketplace.

Each day, customers are interacting with that enterprise value chain. For instance, when a customer traverses Amazon's website and then purchases something, the number of actions that are triggered with that purchase is enormous. First, Amazon has to identify what kind of customer it is—an Amazon Prime member or not. Based on that knowledge and the options that the customer has chosen for delivery, Amazon has to make a shipping decision. It is conceivable that there was a promotion—perhaps a discount or a small credit to the Amazon account of that individual—associated with the purchase. Amazon's marketing systems, accounting systems, supply chain and logistics systems, etc., all have to do something to the transaction—record it or take another action on it. Each system captures it so that it can either use it later (e.g., process a return), analyze it later (e.g., optimize an offer based on buying patterns), or perhaps produce the record (e.g., a federal requirement for filing taxes). I'm merely showing you a few of the things that might be involved in a single transaction, and I'm barely touching the surface. Then the shipment has to be prepared. An inventory management system figures out the optimal warehouse to ship the product from given inventory availability and the customer's ship-to location. The product must be shipped based on the analysis made, the customer's status and their selection of shipping option, and the shipping company's availability in the geographical area where the customer lives. All this is triggered by a single transaction. The product is shipped and, one hopes, successfully delivered within the timeframe chosen by the customer, whether a specific choice is made or a default is set by the service-level agreement associated with the customer's status (i.e., free second-day delivery for Amazon Prime customers).

But here's what makes that interesting. The customer doesn't give a crap about all of that. They don't care which shipping company ultimately gets jurisdiction to deliver the product. They don't care what warehouse it came from or which systems were used to get it going. They simply ordered the product and want it delivered per their expectations. Twenty systems and five companies besides Amazon might have been involved in the ultimate delivery (e.g., the warehousing company if it's externally sourced, the shipping company, etc.) but the customer simply wants their product delivered in a timely way.

Amazon, as the parent of the ecosystem, with its own specific enterprise value chain at the center of this, is seen, rightly, as the responsible party. Think about it. I presume most of you have shopped on Amazon and a very significant amount of you are Amazon Prime members. If your package doesn't come in the two days promised, who do you call? The shipping company? I doubt you even know who that is until the product arrives. You contact Amazon, even though it wasn't their fault that the package was late. It was the shipping company's problem. But, as the owner of the ecosystem, it was Amazon's responsibility.

To companies that think in terms of ecosystems, as Amazon does, that is an obvious premise. Once they are aware of the late arrival, Amazon deals with it by penalizing themselves and rewarding the aggrieved customer with an apology and an extra month of Prime if the customer asks for it. If Amazon were not thinking about the ecosystem, then they would fob off responsibility to the shipping company and not be thinking about how to handle the customer's aggravation. Instead, they compensate the customer for failing to meet expectations.

What makes this so important is how central the customer is to all that Amazon thinks and plans. The supply chain, the entirety of the enterprise value chain, is organized around customer concerns and desires. But to know what the customer's concerns and expectations are, and to understand what a customer wants of a business and sees in an ecosystem, we should understand what the customer-engaged ecosystem is all about.

THE CUSTOMER-ENGAGED ECOSYSTEM

The enterprise value chain that we just described is how a business runs from the inside out, and, you'll note, it includes direct customers as part of its matrix. But the customer-engaged ecosystem is working from the outside in. It is a business that is defining its strategy around the idea that the customers of the company need to be engaged with that company and trust that company and, most importantly for the purposes of thinking around an ecosystem, get what they think they need from that company, even if the company doesn't produce the products or services directly that the customer is seeking.

I say that with a major caveat, though. The model has constraints. The most important one is that no one company can provide everything that a customer thinks they need. No ecosystem built around customer needs is built around all of them but, instead, is built around what the company that parents the ecosystem believes that they can provide—when it comes to both the resources and the company's narrative. More on the latter, later.

WHAT DOES AN ECOSYSTEM LOOK LIKE?

The customer-engaged ecosystem starts from the premise that the customer is seeking both direct and, if possible, related value from the brand they are interacting with. Is that an ironclad premise? No. A company needs to work with their customers to find out what the customer expects or, if not expects, would like from the company.

Let me give you an example. Several years ago, David's Bridal, at the time, the largest purveyor of wedding apparel in the world, as Scott Rogers pointed out in Chapter 3, began to rethink how they viewed their customer. Originally, they saw what you might think is the obvious. The customer was the bride, and the focal point of the bride was the wedding. Given that they sell wedding apparel, this made sense—bridal gowns, bridesmaids outfits, etc., were the meat and potatoes of their revenue. But they also realized in the earlier stages of their self-examination that the weddings that their customers revolved around had considerably more than looking wonderful at the ceremony involved, if you thought very slightly out of the box. For example, during the wedding, flowers to decorate the venue were important. This was potentially an additional revenue opportunity, but one not directly related to what David's Bridal sold. Post wedding, the newly married couple was likely to take a honeymoon. Here was another opportunity beyond the actual event, but one that could be included as part of a total "bridal experience." What if they could partner with companies who provide flowers or who can support a honeymoon trip? These are things that the bride, the associated families, and the wedding planners could take advantage of that David's Bridal didn't produce. So, they partnered with florists, cruise lines, and others who could provide products and services that added to the experience that immediately surrounded and were part of the wedding. For example, the couple could get a 10 percent discount on a honeymoon cruise if they contacted a cruise line via the David's Bridal website or used a coupon provided by David's Bridal when they paid for their wedding gowns and accessories. David's Bridal became not just a wedding apparel provider but the purveyor of a "bridal experience." There were issues in how they went to market with it, but the idea was spot on—and a great business opportunity for David's Bridal.

What David's Bridal did at the time was to identify an opportunity based on broadly defined potential customer interests to impact the overall experience that their customers had. That example is drawn from a business-to-consumer (B2C) environment—where the business is taking the needs of an individual into consideration. But what about in a business-to-business (B2B) environment—where businesses need to think through the extended needs of another business? That must be different, right? In principal, actually, not—as we shall see shortly. In practice, somewhat.

Time for the story of Project Unite.

PROJECT UNITE

Let's start with some words from Matt Bray, who, at the time of this interview, was the director of Strategic Alliances for sales compensation vendor, Xactly, but is now a vice president at Salestrip.

> *Early in 2015, over an Old Speckled Hen ale (or two), I chewed the fat with my good friend Richard Goodall (founder of InvoiceIT, which was acquired by SteelBrick and is now part of Salesforce CPQ, et al). Our debate: how to accelerate lead/quote-to-cash digital transformation to empower sales. We were both perplexed that some off-platform digital suppliers were offering independent applications—including contract management, CPQ, ICM, quota management, etc.—and spinning a one-size-fits-all, "best-in-class" lead/quote-to-cash-branded message.*

Matt and Richard were perplexed.

> *Why would customers want to take a broad mix of digital applications across lead/quote-to-cash, confined to the development dollars of one*

supplier, off-platform with an inability to integrate or scale? It made no sense.

This conversation was the origin of what the participating companies call "Project Unite."

Conceptually, Project Unite is what I call a mini-ecosystem: a smaller, go-to-market alliance of companies that provide complementary products and services that align with the needs of a similar, overlapping, but not identical, customer base.

Due to the considerable effort that it takes to create an institutionalized ecosystem, there should be a good reason for its existence. In this case, it made sense to look at a consortium of strategic partners that could provide end-to-end sales-process-enabling technology. The Project Unite specific goals were to:

- leverage the Salesforce platform

- build a scalable ecosystem that delivered

- integrate platinum-certified independent applications from digital suppliers who shared the wider lead/quote-to-cash vision

- "supercharge" (Xactly's word) shared customers and sales people

While their target market in that lead/quote-to-cash range is broad, they have a specific segment in mind: disconnected on-premise, hybrid, off-platform, single-supplier solutions.

The selection of partners in a smaller ecosystem is somewhat different than in a larger ecosystem that is dominated by the platform or applications provider it is being built around.

For example, if you are part of Microsoft's ecosystem, it isn't a matter of making sure that you have a relationship among equals with Microsoft and all its partners, given the vastness of their network. What would be the ideal opportunity for becoming part of their ecosystem would be a horizontal opportunity that allows them to go to market with you across different industries or applications groups. For example, Thunderhead, the provider of customer-journey orchestration technology has that kind of relationship with Salesforce. They are fully integrated into the Salesforce Marketing Cloud as the real-time interaction management layer of the platform (Salesforce calls it Interaction Studio). Veeva and Vlocity build specific versions of Salesforce for different industries and are Salesforce's ecosystem partners. Yet, there is no partnership between Veeva, Vlocity, and Thunderhead. They are, however, all part of the same overall partner ecosystem—each fulfilling specific customer needs that Salesforce doesn't natively fill.

In the smaller mini-ecosystems, it is much more a partnership of equals, even though the effort tends to be galvanized by one company. Selecting partners is quite tricky because it isn't just a matter of finding complementary applications, services, or features and functions. There must be synergies in culture and a willingness to foster the ecosystem as a whole—and, thus, each other company within it. That means strategic, go-to-market relationships must be shared among the partners, which are governed by a joint vision and mission for the ecosystem.

In the case of Project Unite, the companies that are part of the alliance are Xactly, Spring CM, NewVoiceMedia, Sage, DocuSign, SteelBrick (later acquired by Salesforce as their CPQ solution) and CloudSocius.

Their first step in the creation of this mini-ecosystem was to set goals that they could align with concerning how they would sell and what they could sell, how they could jointly market, and the rules and governance that were necessary to make the ecosystem work. That meant sales, marketing, and even legal departments of the participating companies met and came up with a common set of objectives and agreements on how things would be done, then setting responsibilities for making sure those things got done. Because this is a tightly knit ecosystem, they had to find common ground when it came to definitions of customer success, how they were going to handle accounts jointly or individually without damage to their individual company's efforts, how lead generation was going to be defined, the processes for handoffs from marketing to sales, and who's salespeople were going to handle what. And that was just the very tip of the pyramid.

Additionally, most of the partners in this ecosystem were solutions providers, not systems integrators. So, they partnered with systems integrator Cloud Socius, who was willing to create a practice to sell the joint Project Unite offering, not just the individual offering of each of the partners.

Project Unite is a representative example of a cohesive, well-structured partner ecosystem. Your company ecosystem, whether fully institutionalized or not, also requires thinking about design, production, and implementation. Doing that provides you with the means to start thinking about customer-engagement strategies (next up) in a digitally connected world of expected personalized interaction.

MAPPING THE ECOSYSTEM

The steps to mapping an ecosystem and then building it are straightforward.

1. Decide who your customers are and what their overall experience in relation to you is. Are they what you have historically been focused on,

or are they more broadly engaged in complementary activities that you haven't accounted for in the past? Are you targeting a new market and thus a new set of customers? What would their overall experience be like in their day-to-day activities? (To be clear, this is not the same as the customer-journey mapping which we will directly address in the next chapter.)

2. Speak to your customers via feedback and advisory boards to find out what it is they would, if all were possible, want from you end-to-end. Remember the David's Bridal example of providing, not just wedding apparel, but flowers and honeymoons. Project Unite was not just Xactly compensation solutions but lead-to-cash process enablement.

3. Once you have that data, decide what you can already natively offer, what you want to build, and what you need to find partners for.

4. Find the partners who should be a good cultural as well as product-and-services fit. Minimally, they should be a "not-bad" cultural fit. For example, David's Bridal could strike multiple cruise-line deals and not have a huge amount of interaction with the varying cruise lines, so the need for a good cultural fit was a bit less imperative since it was a bit more of a utilitarian partnership. But all the companies at Project Unite were going to market and selling together, so the culture fit had to be exceptional.

5. Once you find the partners, start working on aligning the effort—that means governance, common definitions for things like leads and customer success, how you are going to handle accounts, who has access to what data that is gathered from the customers and the transactions, etc., plus, of course, revenue recognition and revenue-sharing accords.

6. Start making sure that the selected sales people are trained in ecosystem offerings and the marketing folks are up to speed on how to get the word out. So, for example, Microsoft will work with their Dynamics CRM salespeople and its partner network to train them in selling Adobe Experience Cloud.

The fifth item on this list—alignment—must be complete and satisfactory to everyone before you launch to minimize the risks that are inherent in a model that has multiple partners operating at a peer level. The rewards, potentially, are immense in the level and size of the sales, but also in the value that the customer feels the company is bringing to them with the ecosystem.

The thinking that is required in identifying customer needs/wants from end to end is still paramount to success when defining your strategy, as expansive or as limited as it may be. The epitome of customer engagement is your company's ability to be the customer's trusted adviser and go-to resource for all things that they feel that they need from you. It isn't always feasible to create an ecosystem, despite the need to think that way. Nonetheless, you do need a customer-engagement strategy before you start thinking about the programs you want to effect for your customers. Delimiting the strategy to an area of focus is perfectly fine and, in fact, can often be more beneficial than an ecosystem, given the limitations of your resources.

WORKING STRATEGIES FOR ENGAGEMENT

The obvious foundation for a customer-engagement strategy consists of the customers you have and that you are looking to acquire. Too often in my discussions with practitioners I hear, "We do what our customers ask of us." That's fine . . . to a point. If your strategy is focused solely around keeping the customers you already have, however, you are limiting yourself severely. They are going to tell you what *they* want. But as for the wants, desire, and needs of groups you don't know or who don't know you—well, they aren't them. You also need to be aware of the expectations and the behaviors of the customers you are looking to acquire. That means not only designing your strategy around engagement for the sake of retention, but engagement for acquisition. Needless to say—but I'll say it anyway since I'm happy to state the obvious— the relative weight you place on retention versus acquisition is up to you and is often determined by factors you have no control over. For example, an industry truism says the cost of customer acquisition is far greater than the cost of customer retention—up to five times as costly depending on who you believe. Additionally, a 5 percent increase in customer retention means a 25 percent to 95 percent increase in profit, according to studies done by Fred Reichheld in his 2001 article, "Prescription for Cutting Costs." Even today, these numbers hold up. What that suggests is that, in tough economic times, or when your company is going through a rough patch, the customer-engagement strategy will lean toward how to retain your existing customer base and less on acquisition, which, for example, on a meta-macro scale, means you might not invest very much in mass marketing in traditional ways or in much marketing at all. Lots of factors determine how you define your strategy, though a full exposition is well beyond the scope of this book. I'm going to assume you know how you are leaning and provide you with some examples of customer engagement strategies that may fall short of an ecosystem but that are nonetheless viable strategies for deciding how you are going to approach your customers. Even though I am placing these steps in serial order, please realize they often are done in parallel. For example, you may be defining your objectives *and* the measurement of those objectives at the same time.

STEP 1: DEFINE YOUR OBJECTIVES

To leave your customer engagement strategy at the level of "we need to be more customer-centric" or "we need to engage our customers more" is a big mistake. They are so broad as objectives as to be meaningless. Why do you want to engage your customers? What is a problem you are trying to fix or an improvement you are trying to make? What level of innovation are you trying to achieve? Each company should have a specific idea of what kind of results they are looking for and what kind of outcomes lead to those results. So, for example, a standard reason for an engagement strategy is that there is a high churn rate at your company and you are looking to reduce churn. Another reason might be that you are trying to increase retention (different than reducing churn), and you are looking to do that by expanding your loyalty program—providing more benefit to your loyal customers in return for their increased purchases with you. Two advanced strategies that you might be considering are getting a segment of your more feedback-oriented customers involved in several product/service co-creation projects. That means that your objective is to get a small group of your customers to help you innovate. Another advanced project, but one that is a true marker of the difference between a customer-centric and a customer-engaged company (more on that in Chapter 9) is that you might be aiming at creating customer advocates who will help you evangelize the brand (or perhaps recruiting influencers who are already brand supporters). Finally, your strategy could be as simple as increasing revenue for the company, or for certain products, by a specific percentage. But you need to define the return that you are looking for.

For example, Australia and New Zealand Banking Group (ANZ) is Australia's biggest bank ($20 billion AU) and a customer of SAP Customer Experience. Their engagement strategy had a simple objective. They understood that their customers didn't like to spend time banking. Their objective was to reduce the time that their customers spent banking and keep them fully engaged in the time that they *were* banking. The results of a successful execution of that strategy led them to receiving 10 percent fewer complaints and increased customer satisfaction to 83 percent. All in the name of an objective that was to make the customer's day easier.

STEP 2: DEFINE YOUR MEASUREMENTS

The time honored "must do" when it comes to customer engagement or any real business strategy, is the design and definition of the metrics necessary to measure the success (or failure) of the strategy. That means:

Return on Investment (ROI)—In more thoughtful environments, the broad criteria of ROI are more focused on what Peppers and Rogers called Return on Customer (ROC) in their seminal work on that subject. ROC is calculated as the firm's current-period cash flow from its customers, plus any changes in the underlying customer equity, divided by the total customer equity at the beginning of the period. Customer equity is like the idea of customer lifetime value, which is the total amount of net present value generated by a customer and their immediate household over what is calculated to be their lifetime as a customer with that company. In Chapter 16, we'll look at the contemporary metrics in more detail, based on the work around the value of customer engagement done by Dr. V. Kumar. But, ultimately, the idea of the return you are looking for—be it increases in revenue, reduction in churn, greater spend from your loyal customers—can, as often as not, be quantified, though not always. For example, it's hard to quantify advocacy, but some results of advocacy are measurable. You can try to increase the number of your advocates, the quality of their efforts via measuring their engagement in social channels, or the amount of traffic they drive to your community. Ultimately, you need to identify the result(s) you want to get from your engagement strategy.

Benchmarks—Once you know what return you're looking for, you also know that to get those results certain things should happen. The outcomes that lead to the desired results have to be superior, meaning that they need to meet or exceed some standard that is both appropriate to what you want to achieve and are bringing to the table in terms of resources and are something that has had measurable results that are verifiable and available. These are the benchmarks you want to set. For example, if you have three steps that, if done well, will lead to the return you are seeking, you need to know what "done well" is. That means the generally available historic data—both internal and external—should give you enough information to find what reasonable number will serve as your benchmark. IGD, a not-for-profit UK-based training and research organization focused on the food and grocery industry, did a case study on a global personal-care-products company whose objective was to expand its European footprint and engage customers with best-in-class standards. IGD, via their research arm IGD Academy, started this project by sending out a capabilities survey to 50 members of the personal-care-products company's team to get a feel for what this company did when it came to "the state of trading relationships between manufacturers and retailers' expectations of supplier capabilities." Once they got the results, they benchmarked them against 100 branded suppliers who had completed IGD's annual engagement survey and against results they had from other sources in 15 European marketing companies. They then could benchmark against what the internal results were and, thus, identify strengths and weaknesses. The key here is that they set the benchmarks they were looking for and then did the surveys to get the data they needed to provide the results they needed to get.

Key Performance Indicators (KPIs)—Once you've established the results you want and the outcomes needed to get those results, you need to be able to quantify the progress you make toward achieving the goals. Those are called "key performance indicators." How are you doing as you traverse the path to succeeding in accomplishing your strategy? What are the markers along the path and how do you measure against those? The idea is quantifiable along the lines of "we need to reach this number by this date." Responsibility for achieving those numbers is typically assigned to an actual person or team. Compensation is tied to the achievement of the KPIs, frequently along the lines of, "if you meet the objective by the date, you (all) keep your jobs;" "if you beat the timeline, you (all) get some reward;" "if you don't make it, uh oh." The KPIs, of course, are milestones that vary. For example, if the engagement strategy is tied to what is called customer success, then the customer health score at a certain juncture is the marker. If it is tied to customer service and contact centers, then increasing the first-contact resolution rates may be a KPI worth achieving.

STEP 3: KNOW YOUR CUSTOMERS

Once you've established your objectives and defined your paths and markers on those paths, it's time to start finding out who your customers are, who your potential customers are, and what they are looking for from you as a company. That means, in line with the thinking about customer ecosystems, you have an idea of not only what segments your current customer base represents, but their likes and dislikes and, most importantly, what their expectations are of you. Find out what they are realistically expecting and what they would like to have in an optimal environment.

Multiple mechanisms are available for you to find out what you need to about your customers, and they are exceptionally straightforward. They take time and effort and some money but are not excessively expensive and will not tie you up so badly that you decide to not have children in the interests of work. Some that you might consider:

Customer Advisory Boards—These take significant effort and can be expensive, but they are a source of ongoing information about your customers' likes and dislikes, complaints, and suggestions for improvement. There are broad and narrow versions of advisory boards. You can create an online advisory board that periodically surveys the customers on it. To be honest, that's more of a name for an identified specific group of customers who you survey in a continual fashion and in return report back to them on the results and how they are being used. The more elaborate and, for mature companies, more substantial option is a small—ten is a good number—group of handpicked customers who are given a greater level of access to the company's plans and thinking and asked to collaborate with the company in the design of the customer-engagement strategy. Not only are the advisory board meetings conducted regularly online and via conference call or on any digital platform but, typically, there is a quarterly or twice-annual or even once-a-year meeting with the board in person that is all-expenses-paid by the company—and a really good dinner somewhere—for presentations and discussions with the group. Keep in mind, these advisory boards can be somewhat time consuming if you think you are starting from scratch. A good resource for templates and best practices related to building these CABs is customeradvisoryboard.org.

Surveys—These can be invaluable for understanding customer needs. Unlike the "online" advisory board, survey customers aren't necessary identified, nor are they surveyed on a repeat basis. They are a representative valid sampling of the customer base of the company conducting the survey or a representative sample of the type of customers that the company is interested in attracting.

Listening—This is simply using social-listening technology to capture the conversations about your brand—good and bad—to provide you with insights into what the public is thinking about your company.

Data analytics (transactional and interaction)—Even at this early stage, data analytics can play a role if you care to invest the time and money into the supporting technology. There are offerings from SAS, SAP, Oracle, Salesforce, Microsoft, Tableau, and others designed to understand customer behaviors.

(A lot more on the data and technology tools can be found in Chapters 13 and 14.) Transactional data is available within your CRM system. Most likely, as you gain experience with the system, you will find there is enough data to give you some insight into how your customers behave as a group, what their likes and dislikes might be, and even their individual behaviors.

Customer Journey Mapping—This is the subject of Chapter 6 but, briefly, the customer's journey is a sloppy one. It isn't an orderly romp through the steps that the sellers wish it could be. Mapping that journey at scale and down to the individual is imperative to knowledge of the customer. But I'll hold a lot of that for Chapter 6.

STEP 4: KNOW THYSELF

If you've been doing the work, you have a clear picture of what you want to accomplish, the road to its accomplishment, and what customers are expecting. While it seems ever so customer-centric of you to do the requirements-gathering from customers, so you know what they need and what their hearts' desires are, one other paramount factor should be considered when you are architecting your strategy. Your business needs to be successful, and you are subject to the constraints that I ran by you in Chapter 2. Consequently, not only is the factor defined by the statement "know thyself," but also by "to thine own self be true." That means you should decide what you can provide to the customer given

- their needs
- your budget
- your staff and labor time
- the return you are looking to get
- the outcomes you need to achieve the return

These are going to vary widely, obviously, but these factors—the constraints, the needs of the customers against your constraints, and the ability to accomplish the objectives—will impact how you allocate resources to this effort.

STEP 5: DEFINE HOW YOU WANT TO THINK ABOUT YOUR CUSTOMER STRATEGY: RETENTION OR ACQUISITION OR...

This is not as obvious as it sounds. In this case, we are looking at both acquiring and retaining customers unless your strategy calls for something different. Invesp, a marketing science organization, did some studies that, if you put them in real-world terms, are head-scratching but true—and anecdotal evidence supports these conclusions. To summarize, even though they found that the probability of selling to an existing customer is 60–70 percent and to a new customer is 5–20 percent, even though the existing customers spend 31 percent more than new customers, even though an increase in customer retention by 5 percent means an increase in profitability by between 25 percent and 95 percent, and *70 percent know that it's cheaper to retain than to acquire customers*, 44 percent of the companies queried still spend more time focused on customer acquisition, while only 18 percent focus on customer retention, and only 40 percent of the companies try to balance the two. See what I mean? Head scratching. Nonetheless, reality is what it is. You should figure out how you presently and for the near future want to weigh these scales, with at-least anticipation of your immediate future so that you can define how you want to focus your energy, time, and money.

If you are focused on acquisition, then clearly your marketing spend is going to be higher than if you were not because you are attempting to reach larger shares of audience and engage them. It isn't a matter of just spending marketing money. It's where you put your efforts and what kind of institutional "buckets" you can provide to keep their attention once they are initially engaged. What makes acquisition far more difficult than it used to be is that it is no longer a matter of competitors competing for the initial eyes of the prospect, it is a matter of capturing the attention of that prospect when they are getting bombarded by up to 3,000 messages a day, among them . . . yours. That means, to get their attention, you must be thinking of how to personalize the message you send them—making it meaningful to the individual without ever having met them. Once you do accomplish this, it also means being able to maintain the relationship and keep their attention on an ongoing basis. So, you might combine social media interactions to capture their attention and have an online community to keep their attention once you've captured it. Or you might be a moth-to-a-flame kind of institution—drawing attention because of the value of the information that the community provides. For example, Sephora has an online community called "Beauty Talk." It provides a place for Sephora customers, or anyone interested in learning about beauty and beauty products, a place that aggregates and organizes deep content on those very subjects. They provide access to beauty "insiders" to help community members with tips and ways of thinking about the application of their products. They have a "lounge" where community members can chat with each other about the products. A rich library of content is available that explains, among other things, the foundations of . . . foundation. They have the requisite celebrity endorsements and discussions, of course. All in a community organized for acquisition and retention.

Lithium, the community platform provider who built the Sephora Beauty Talks community found, in running analytics, that there are super fans who are prone to buy ten times more than a regular community member (who, in turn, is inclined to buy twice as much as non-community members). But it wasn't the arch-communicators who were super fans, it was the lurkers who spent hours a week trolling for content and actually possibly never even interacting once. They were committed to the Beauty Talk content, not to talking about beauty. So, recruit a new customer to the community and they had a shot at becoming a person who contributed 20X more than the non-member to Sephora's bottom line.

Sephora Beauty was geared toward both acquisition—luring new customers with rich content—and retention by keeping the conversation going and the information interesting and relevant. However, if your strategy leans heavily to retention, then you want advocacy and loyalty programs, personalized special offers optimized to be interesting to the target individuals, and tools that make their communications with you frictionless or at least simpler/easier. Additionally, you can develop content personalized to their interests and made available on multiple channels.

A balance might call for some from each side or a permutation not mentioned.

STEP 6: THINK THROUGH THE COMMUNICATIONS MEDIA WITH WHICH YOU WANT TO CONVERSE WITH CUSTOMERS

If you travel back in time around a decade or so ago, the hottest communications strategy was "multichannel." What this meant was that you gathered enough data on an individual customer to ascertain the channel they preferred and then optimized accordingly. However, while that may have been the case a decade ago (and the jury is still out), it is no longer preferable as a communications strategy. We now think "omnichannel." What that means is that individuals don't think about which channel they use but use multiple channels at any given time for the sake of convenience or preference (or how they communicate with someone else), so the idea of optimizing a single channel is no longer appropriate or advisable. For example, think about the device that you are probably carrying in your pocket or have attached to your ear or frontal lobe. How many channels reside on that device? Natively: text, phone, and video chat. Otherwise, as many as you want as long as there is an app for it. That could mean Skype, email, Facebook, Twitter, LinkedIn, and dozens of other social communications media. At a given time, you could be conversing with multiple people via multiple channels. You could have linked one channel to another. Several years ago, I had my Facebook and Twitter accounts linked to each other. During the 2009 World Series, I was on Twitter and Facebook (while watching the Yankees clinch the World Series sitting in a hotel room in Bogota, Colombia). When I tweeted something, that, of course, also showed up on my Facebook feed and generated 94 comments. That's what I'm talkin' about. While omnichannel is a terrible term for what it means, it is de jure what we use. ("Channeless" is probably better since we aren't thinking about the channel that we are using, we are just transmitting and/or receiving a conversation or comment.) The evidence of the value of omnichannel is indisputable and prolific. Nowhere is this more evident than in the retail world. In a study of 46,000 customers done by Medallia and Rice University and published in the *Harvard Business Review* (January 17, 2017), the value of making an omnichannel effort with retail customers was incontrovertible. Omnichannel customers' average spend was 4 percent greater than other customers in the store and averaged 10 percent more online. The more channels they used, the more they spent. If they used 4 or more channels in the store, the purchases were 9 percent higher than the average single-channel user. Even more intriguing was the commitment that the omnichannel customers had to the retailer. By comparison to the single-channel user, the omnichannel customer, within six months after their latest omnichannel experience had logged 23 percent more shopping trips to the retailers' stores and were more likely to recommend that retailer. It not only engendered greater share of wallet but greater loyalty.

STEP 7: BUILD THE PROGRAMS

Chapter 8 is devoted to building the programs, so I'm not dwelling on it here, but it needs to be referenced since it is a major part of your strategy (i.e., the execution of it). The value of building the right programs—meaning the ones that get you the results you are aiming for—couldn't be more obvious. But the work in making sure that they are the right programs can be painstaking, the rate of failure high, and the need to make changes on the fly frequent. The mindset that needs to be present is the willingness to fail and to be agile (aka, flexible). Luckily, an enormous body of existing work encompassing successes and failures is available for you to draw from—some in every industry—so, whatever you do, you are more than likely able to find a vast body of literature to help you design and develop the elements you need for your programs. For example, the utilities industry is deeply involved in the creation of programs, mostly geared to feedback, for engagement of their customers. Scottish Water, the Scottish water company (duh), gives complete transparency into their strategic planning and insights into customer engagement, largely driven by their November 2012–February 2013 national feedback "consultation" on the future of water services in Scotland. It was called "Your Views Count" and led to a substantial document, the updated version, Part 2 of which was released in 2015 with plans to be the strategy going forward to 2021. That same year, they created a customer forum for continual interaction with their customers so that the surveys weren't the end of the story. That was all incorporated into their "Strategic Projects Plan 2015–2021," which is available to all that are interested. This document is available at

scottishwater.co.uk/assets/about%20us/images/contact%20us/listening toourcustomersphase2v15.pdf

The surveys, in conjunction with the regulatory and financial constraints on the other side of the equation, helped drive not only the programs for engagement, but the forum for ongoing engagement to help improve the programs for water purity, sewage disposal, and so on.

STEP 8: INFORMATION TECHNOLOGY (IT) STRATEGY

The final step, once you have all the above taken care of, is to develop your IT strategy. The irony here is that in almost every single instance that I have heard or seen, IT is rarely the last consideration, but, in fact, is much further up the chain in the planning stages. Often, IT is the driver rather than the enabler of the strategies and programs that are being discussed. The extreme it can reach was reflected in a call I received about ten years ago from a small consultancy run by friends of mine who had a client—a fairly large and sophisticated one—who called them and said, "Hey, we've just bought $5 million of PeopleSoft CRM software. What should we do with it?" While my memory of the exact scale of the dollar amount may be a bit faulty, my memory of the scale and the idea of an enormous purchase isn't faulty in the slightest. That example, while extreme, is indicative of the thinking that tends to go on when it comes to the planning for customer-facing (and other) technology. The technology drives the decisions rather than enables the outcomes. To be clear:

IT is the last part of the strategic equation, not the first or second or anything else.

That said, the options when it comes to customer-engagement technologies are multiple and can be overwhelming. Ultimately, the primary way to plan for the technology selection you are looking at is to review what outcomes you are looking for, what results you want those outcomes to have, and to find the best-suited technology to enable it. What "best-suited" means for the IT selection process is well beyond the scope of this book, but some of the high-level considerations are:

The outcomes needed—Some random examples: Are you interested in tracking the customer journey? Do you need to build customer journeys? Do you want to be able to operationalize your sales, your marketing, your customer service? Do you need to provide web self-service with an intelligent knowledgebase that is responsive to customer requests? What channels are your customers communicating on about you and with you? On how many of them are you interested in reciprocating the communications? How many are you just monitoring? What kind of marketing do you want to do? What kind of sales process do you have? What about your need for customer engagement analytics?

The technical considerations—Are you running other technology systems already? Are you starting fresh or replacing something else? Are you looking at a technology that allows you to scale as a business or doing something stopgap? For example, several years ago, a midsized niche insurance provider was looking for an interim sales force automation solution to replace their Excel spreadsheets and chose NetSuite as their interim solution. Two years later they underwent an SFA selection process and kept NetSuite because it was proven to be cost-effective for them. It started as an interim solution that then proved to scale well. If it hadn't, it would have been replaced by something else.

Iterative feedback—Once you put your IT in place to enable your strategy and programs, you need to make sure that the users of the technology are involved in the improvement of its use and the enablement of its capabilities. Also, you must be sure that there is a way to change on the fly because engaging customers is both a fluid and a fickle process, and what you need to operationalize it can change quickly. The ones who will know what changes are needed are the users of the technology or those employees who are engaging with the customers. In addition, since self-service tools might be part of the engagement effort, the customers themselves should have a mechanism to suggest how to improve the tools and their use to bring the communications between the company and the customer closer to a frictionless experience.

Okay, enough of me. I'm now bringing a big gun to give you some further guidance. That would be the esteemed thought leader, and one of my closest friends, Esteban Kolsky.

THOUGHT LEADER: ESTEBAN KOLSKY

Esteban is recognized in the worlds of CRM, customer service, analytics, IoT—in fact, all things customer-facing—as one of the sharpest and most acerbic, yet big-hearted, people in the industry. As Managing Principal of ThinkJar, he has been an adviser to dozens of large enterprises on the very thing that this chapter is about. So, he knows from what he speaks. Listen up to this man. He's brilliant, he cares, and he knows how to write.

Yours, EK.

Thanks, Paul.

Throughout this chapter, Paul has given you plenty to think about regarding why an ecosystem makes sense and how to plan and strategize the design and implementation of ecosystems. I'm hard pressed to come with more details that those provided, but I am keen to extend a little bit from what he said.

While it is true that you cannot, in good conscience, believe that your "stuff" is the only thing that matters to your customers, there are plenty of people who think that their product is the beginning-and-the-end of the customers' needs.

Trust me, it's not.

We create our own complex ecosystems—some of them purposefully, some of them ad hoc. If you own a home, you will build an ecosystem of required service providers (gas, electricity, water, sewer, garbage, etc.) and then add optional providers (cable, internet, security systems, etc.) to fulfill your needs, how you see your life being complete. Although you can argue that internet, security, and cable are either not optional or not needed at all, the point is that, in addition to the basics, you need some "extras" that complete your perspective of what is necessary in life.

And you won't find a single provider to fulfill all your needs. Sure, in some places you can get electricity and gas from the same place, or sewer and water, or garbage and electricity, etc. We still don't have the single provider for everything, and that is because it is very, very different to deliver gas to a house than to make sure your cable infrastructure is working and constantly updated to reflect the latest technology and channel changes.

And the same happens to enterprises: even though for a long time we thought that suites of products were the best idea for companies (and we can trace the trend to the 1990s and the rise of CRM solutions when it comes to customer strategies), the main reason to believe that back then was the lack of technical prowess. The technologies and architectures at the time required extensive point-to-point integration that monolithic, on-premises solutions were great at delivering. They were also very poor at delivering end-to-end experiences, and they would not even consider customer engagement a priority. Their focus was delivering internal value to the processes that the company implemented to deal with customers.

Fast forward to the 2000s, and we have a different setup.

The rise of online communities and social networks, the (as Paul wrote before) customer gaining control of the conversation, the advent of inbound models that require better and more timely information—all coupled together with faster, more abundant, and better data collection, management, processing, and storage—yields a need for better access to more accurate information in a faster manner.

And, this is where on-premises solutions falter—dramatically.

The construction of those software packages to be the alpha and the omega of customer knowledge (remember 360-degree view of the customer?) meant that more data had to flow through them than was available to on-premises solutions. How can you access, in near real-time, information stored in a database five continents away, process it, act on it, and start again thousands of times every minute? The costs and the complexities of making that happen with monolithic suites was prohibitive. Not to mention that the functionality customers were demanding was not present (nor easy to add on) in suites.

The mid-2000s saw the rise of best-of-breed solutions, add-ons to the suites that made the company more responsive to the demands of the customers but that still required point-to-point integrations that were cumbersome and expensive both to implement and to maintain.

Thankfully we had the explosion of interest in cloud technologies come in and be the driver for the next decade. Cloud (the real, open, three-tier model with platforms at the heart of it, not just applications being offered in hosted-mode via browsers) changed everything. By connecting data sources and execution logic to platforms, we found a way to quickly and easily mix data and processes from anywhere and everywhere—in near real-time—without concern to the security, the expandability, and the pervasiveness of those solutions.

Fast forward to the 2010s and you see organizations finally getting the idea that the world revolves around their customers' expectations, not corporate needs. The desire to deliver to a new, empowered customer who is demanding end-to-end experiences is finally met with a set of tools and technologies that can do it. The emergence of corporate platforms, sometimes powered by vendors but mostly as a piece of a new customer-engagement strategy, gives rise to empowering customers to achieve their needs and have their expectations met, not by managing and controlling experiences, but by providing them an all-encompassing infrastructure that lets them do what they want, when and how they want.

This delivery model is focused on outcomes, not on results. The outcome is not just a metric or even a single-sided value proposition (e.g., make more money by upselling) but, rather, as Paul explained, a focus in the value chain: ensure that all parts of the experience co-create value both for the organization and the customer. If this happens, if the value chain is created and maintained, over time it becomes engagement: an outcome of well-delivered, end-to-end experiences with co-created value.

And that brings us back to the $64,000 question: how do you leverage ecosystems to build engagement?

Simple answer: generate engagement by making sure that every interaction between customer and organization co-creates value to both at every step of the way. To do that you need to always have: a) the most accurate information, b) simple and secure access to relevant applications, and c) fast processing and timely delivery. And for that you need a platform—or, rather, a collection of platforms—between your organization and your partners and providers, working together. That's called an ecosystem.

You need ecosystems to deliver on engagement; it cannot be done any other way. At least not economically and practically.

Back to you, Paul.

* * * * *

Thanks, bud.

THOUGHT LEADER: KARL WABST

I need to tell you about Karl Wabst because he is unique in this book. His experience spans far wider and yet more deeply than any other person I've ever known. Karl has led some of the most advanced and interesting technology projects. He has consulted with some of the largest firms in the world, ranging from IBM to DirecTV to a multiplicity of others. He has impacted a significant number of key initiatives in the world of CRM, cybersecurity, and senior levels of administration at multiple institutions.

But it's the rest of it that makes Karl so well suited to be talking to you about organizational strategy. Karl Wabst is one of the best problem solvers I know. He has taken on some of the most difficult problems in the tech world and come up with elegant solutions—even if it meant getting his employer angry. So, I'm going be quiet and let him tell you what and how he thinks of engagement, strategy, and business transformation.

The floor is yours, Karl.

* * * * *

Transformation is a radical shift, not a simple transition, of your strategy, structure, systems, processes, and/or technology. Since it is a radical shift, it requires leadership, not just management. Next, it requires a shift in your company's culture. Read "culture" here as a direct reference to your people's mindset, attitudes, and behaviors. Third, it won't be successful unless you can sustain all of that over time.

At a time when many reactionary pundits believe that strategy is dead, I contend that you need exactly that level of commitment to rally your troops, whether what you are facing is something as benign as overcoming siloed department bottlenecks or as deadly as a tornado or terrorist attack. Strategy is more than a plan and a budget. A strategy is a set of choices that starts with a declaration of your dreams. Begin by focusing on people (consumers, employees, and shareholders) wants, needs, and desires—not money.

Many companies begin with, for example, an aspiration to increase customer purchases and experience with their goods and services. That is not enough. Stop here for a moment. If you cannot state your aspiration as S.M.A.R.T. goals, do not continue. S.M.A.R.T. stands for Specific, Measurable, Assignable, Realistic, and Time-based. To be successful, the minimum required is to define the target time-frame and customer segment, communicate your value proposition, deploy an appropriate organizational design to institutionalize a set of critical capabilities, and agree upon a well-known measure and a percentage of improvement.

Strategy is the means to organize and publicly proclaim a unified structure, purpose vision, values, and mission. Use strategy to drive engagement with employees and to convince them of their role in engaging customers and their responsibility for enhancing customer experience.

Now, we take another step together. Trust me, this is an important piece. Since we are talking about customer engagement, the most important thing we are trying to accomplish is to have a specific, measurable, and attainable (positive) influence on "the ongoing interactions between company and customer, offered by the company, chosen by the customer."

The need for business transformation and its relationship with digital transformation and customer engagement did not spring to life one fine day. No, it evolved as is true of most volatile, complex situations. During periods of great conflict, it is normal for people to band together for survival. It is natural for people to loosen ties with external authorities and join with like-minded people to ask, "What is in it for me?"

Several other major changes are influencing businesses' relationships with customers. I have seen each of these have profound effects. Constantly evolving communications technology is an obvious example. Communications has changed, that is undeniable. What we have gained or lost is open for debate. The challenge for organizations is in figuring out and satisfying consumers' conflicting expectations of customization and privacy.

Technology precipitated a revolution in each individual's ability to communicate independently of brands. The company and its voice have to, often begrudgingly, share power. The influence of commercially available, consumer-adopted communications technology had a profound impact on a wide swath of organizations, including the military, religious institutions, not-for-profit organizations, and public corporations.

The influence is not all positive. While communications technology made people more independent, some contend that it has isolated us from each other. As we communicate using machines, we may be losing our abilities to come together and communicate face-to-face. I contend we are evolving. Paradoxically, we come together alone, from behind glowing screens.

When existing companies cannot meet the increased customer expectations Paul speaks of throughout this book, customers exercise their freedom to go else-where. Today's customers have their own designs, blueprints, knowledge, and even manufacturing capabilities. In this environment, managers and their desire to main-tain the status quo become less important. People inside and outside are looking for leaders. What is the difference between managers and leaders?

Think about an Army. During times of peace, these large organizations still main-tain large infrastructures. Many systems must be coordinated to maintain our ability to be prepared for conflict. Meals still have to be cooked. Mail delivered. Uniforms issued. Orders processed. This is a task for highly skilled managers.

Yet, when conflict does arise, our soldiers, sailors, and aviators do not seek out managers. They seek leaders whom they are willing to follow into battle. Leaders take people into places they have never been and motivate them to put a larger ideal ahead of their own lives.

To be a leader, you must engage your employees and customers to create a shared future, despite facing uncertainty and ambiguity. Where does this leave you? Lead, follow, or get ready to watch your competitors take your customers away.

To close, I want to give you some ideas about how to transform your organiza-tion for the future. I also want to point you to tools that you can adopt as you start your own journey. Transformation is always difficult. It is supposed to be! In this conflicted ecosystem, the task becomes Herculean. It is a time for leadership, not command and control. Employers who demand that employees or consumers jump, are likely to be challenged with "Why?" rather than the stereotypical, "How high, sir?"

TAKEAWAYS

Corporate, Team, and Business Unit Strategy

- Reinforce customers' belief that you are a partner in their dreams, not just another competitor for their wallet, and build their trust in you around per-sonalized interactions.

- Build a structure with rigor and creativity to combat vague and fuzzy con-cepts swirling around relentlessly volatile and complex markets.

- Recognize the need for new strategy to win in your market over the next 5 to 10+ years.

- Aspire to be a trusted brand and source for interactions, purchases of goods, services, tools, and experiences.

- Conquer challenges: communications revolution, competitor initiatives, technological innovation, globalization, and restructuring.

- Frame strategic options: corporate aspirations, your chosen playing field, how to win on that field, the critical capabilities, and management systems that will be required

    Tool Tip: Read *Playing to Win: How Strategy Really Works* by A.G. Lafley and Roger L. Martin. Supplement that with the collected works of Clayton Christensen.

Start with People

- Learn your chosen customers' point of view. Observe. Listen.

- Actively engage the minds, hearts, and hands of shareholders, boards, executives, staff, and consumers.

- Develop leadership. Management remains important, but leaders are your future.

- Investigate ethnography. Improve insights. Bring the voice of customers inside. By the way, employees are customers, too.

- Elicit desires, dreams, and concerns.

- Map to corporate objectives.

    Tool Tip: Read John Kotter's books on leadership and change. Start with *Leading Change* and then read *Accelerate*.

⁙ ⁙ ⁙ ⁙ ⁙

Thanks, Karl. Valuable and inspiring.

Strategy is driven by the knowledge of what you need, what your customers want, and what you can provide them given your constraints and the value that you each get because of the programmatic efforts you made. But your customers are not static entities. They are on the move, and, as sentient beings, feel things about you and not related to you that impact how they decide to transact and interact with you. That's why the core to developing any strategy is to understand the customer journey that your customers and prospects are on—in a B2C and a B2B environment. So, onward to Chapter 6, me hearties.

CHAPTER 6

Mapping the Journey

"Mapping the customer's journey" might be the most overused and misused phrase in the world of corporate strategy. It typically started from a fantasy about what would be a seamless, perfect buyer's journey in the seller's dreams and worked its way into misperceptions of how to design it, track it, analyze it, and then make the wrong decisions about it. I don't want to be mean about this, but getting the customer journey straight is going to take some repositioning of the thinking around it. Luckily, the repositioned thinking is already out there, so we don't have to start from scratch.

WHAT IS A CUSTOMER JOURNEY?

There are more definitions of the customer journey than I can count, but, thankfully, most of them are similar. Ultimately, this is the way I see it:

A customer journey is the overall set of dynamic customer interactions based on a series of decisions that an individual customer makes coupled with events that an individual customer is involved with related to a specific brand in any medium, from the path to a purchase to a customer-service interaction.

The journey can be impacted by a customer's long-time experience with the brand, by the results of their immediate interactions with it, or by events and emotional states completely unrelated to the brand.

Is this an adequate definition? It may be a little awkward, but, for the most part, I think it does the trick.

If you look at what most businesses define as a "typical" customer journey, the interactions are stuffed into five or six boxes. Here are a few examples:

- Awareness → Research → Evaluate → Decision → Buy (or Not) → Post Purchase

- Awareness → Consideration → Purchase → Retention → Advocacy
- Pre-engagement → Commercial → Consultation → Initiation → Coordination → Completion
- Awareness → Consideration → Acquisition → Service → Loyalty
- Thinking → Exploring → Understanding → Getting Assurance → Decision/Purchase

Noticeably, the end points tend to be different. That's because some are more aspirational than actual, e.g., advocacy or loyalty. Those are outcomes devoutly to be wished but they are not journey-map concepts. The journey map is how the customer engages in the *buying* process; it's not reflective of the commitment the customer has to the company at whatever level. Aside from this problematic approach to a journey map, dozens of others that are close to these listed above have slightly different emphases based on, perhaps, the department they are associated with, i.e., a service journey, a marketing journey, a seller's idea of a journey, or an industry-specific idea of a journey. The journey for a buyer in manufacturing will be markedly different than that for a buyer in health services.

Then there are the distinctions between B2B and B2C journeys. Selling to individuals is different than selling to businesses. Mostly. Even saying that, though, at the end of every B is still a C, which is a soundbite way of saying journeys are based on what actual individual human beings are doing to intersect with a company.

The first journey you see in the list above is the one that you are likely to see the most often. This is the "buyer's journey" or the "B2B journey." But the B2C journey follows a similar path.

This idea of the journey is, however, problematic. There is a presumption that the five or six steps you see here are how customers journey along a well-defined path. I call these journeys the seller's "I-wish-this-was-the-customer's-journey" customer journey because the hoped-for sequential path proposed is hardly ever the one that customers actually follow. While the steps themselves are how most of us come to decide about a purchase, we usually don't do it in the orderly way that sellers wished we did.

Customer journeys aren't neat. Yet the sequential steps proposed above have value, at least the ones that reflect a real journey do. They can serve as a benchmark for the customer journey. They can be used as a baseline so that, when using a tool like Salesforce's Journey Builder to build a customer engagement process map and workflow, you have a starting point and a perfect "I-wish" journey. They are ideal versions of what you would like to happen and, thus, using Journey Builder or a similar tool, how you would like to respond. But, realistically, the customer journey typically looks nothing like what you've built, except in principal. Real customer journeys are very sloppy and not only work "out of order" but veer off the ideal path at significant levels. How do you deal with that—especially at scale?

The first step involves looking at the purchasing process itself.

THE PURCHASING PROCESS

Most businesses face the problem that the customer requires a lot more personal attention than in the past. Those customers have a lot of choices for the same products and services your company provides at roughly the same prices thanks to ecommerce and relatively inexpensive shipping services (among other things, of course). Plus, due to the information available to them, those customers are a lot savvier than they used to be when it comes to knowing what you offer, how competitive you really are, and where they may get something better. In fact, the most conservative research, a report done by Consumer Executive Board (CEB) of 1,900 corporate decision makers in 2015, found that, minimally, buyers are 57 percent of the way through the buying process before they contact a potential vendor. Other research has indicated that it's between 70 percent and 85 percent. By 2017, 80 percent seemed to be a universally accepted number. Regardless of whose data you believe, buyers are well into the decision-making process before they talk to a vendor. In the B2B world, the amount of time spent on the journey year-over-year increases. From 2013 to 2014, per the B2B Landscape report by DemandGen, 58 percent of respondents said that more time was spent on the journey than in the past. From 2015 to 2016, 54 percent said that the length of the time spent on the B2B buying process increased again.

The reasons given for why the amount of time continues to increase include:

- Spend more time researching the products—80 percent
- Use more sources to research and evaluate—73 percent
- More reliance on peer recommendations—62 percent
- More detailed ROI analysis before making a final purchase decision—61 percent

    (Source: "The 2016 B2B Buyer's Survey Report," DemandGen)

Ironically, this longer evaluation period shows why customer-journey mapping creates a real opportunity. A lot of sellers view these numbers with alarm, fearful that the potential customer taking so long to talk to them has already made up their mind about the purchase. One I spoke with in 2016 said it well, at least in the latter part of the statement: "We can't be proactive with these people. They own the effort." The customer has assumed control of the process.

That's because a significant amount of the information they need is now available online, from the basic products and services collateral to the corporate financials to conversations about the specific products and services that they are interested in. The 2017 B2B Buyers Landscape survey found that relevant content was mission-critical to buying decisions and, thus, potential buyers spent the time they needed ferreting it out. Here are just a few indicators.

- 75 percent said it was very important that the site presented relevant content that spoke directly to their company

- 66 percent said it was very important that the website spoke directly to the needs of their industry, and the solution provider showed expertise in their area

- 93 percent of respondents valued vendors that "demonstrated experience with/knowledge of our industry"

The implications of the above are enormous. The more appropriate content you can provide to a prospect or customer, the greater the likelihood they will purchase from you. The more you know about that customer or prospect and their actual journey, the more appropriate content you can provide them—and, with current technology, make it available in real time, often automatically.

But each step, not just the journey as a whole, has significance and challenges. Shall we take an abbreviated look?

Awareness—While the idea is self-evident, the customer-to-be needs to find out about what you offer, and dealing with that isn't as easy as it used to be. I'll talk more about it in the marketing chapter, but, for now, be satisfied with the idea that this is the stage at which you get the attention of the future customer. Getting that attention means that you are trying to yell "yoo-hoo" with three thousand other messages per day from competitors doing the same thing. You are trying to create a signal in the midst of noise. How to do that, later.

Research—Once interest has been captured at any level, typically a buyer is going to start working on whether the products or services or experiences you provide fit the criteria they have for what they need. What's interesting are the channels and the touchpoints that are the go-tos for researchers.

Here's the breakdown per the same DemandGen buyer's survey report at the earliest stage of research and at the latest stage of research (in parentheses), to the point that evaluation begins.

- The web—46 percent (13 percent)
- The vendor website—18 percent (18 percent)
- Peer recommendations—17 percent (17 percent)
- Industry analysts—9 percent (16 percent)
- Others—10 percent (36 percent)

Evaluate—This is where the first heavy lifting toward making a decision goes on. The list of choices has been narrowed, the comparisons are being looked at, and the plusses and minuses are being decided on. Interestingly, but not necessarily obviously, trust enters the picture here. The research the buyer has done and the data the buyer has gathered to begin serious evaluation are dependent on the sources of that data being trusted sources. The Edelman Group, in the "Edelman Trust Barometer," found that, when it came to searches, millennials trusted online search first (72 percent) and traditional media second (64 percent) as their trusted sources of information. In Feb. 2017, Trust Radius released a report called "The B2B Buying Disconnect" in which they identified that the top four most trustworthy information sources for evaluation were free trials (roughly 3.7 on a scale of 4.0), then peer recommendations, product demos, and conversations with analysts (thank goodness—I still have a job!). In other words, I do it myself or I ask my most trusted sources, i.e., my friends or family, and the experts. The vendors themselves didn't rank too highly in the trust configuration. Various permutations of vendor offerings were the bottom four choices.

Decision (Buy/Not Buy)—This is obvious on its face. The decision to either purchase the products or services or to forget about it occurs here. In traditional journey mapping, this is the result of the others above. Is that always the case? Is the sale made (or not) based on the other facets of the benchmark journey? Well, to some extent yes, to some extent no. While certainly we'd like to think that the research and evaluation process provided the fodder for the decision, the decision to buy or not involves many social and psychological factors. At the most trivial level, a bad day at work could destroy or delay a buying decision. Additionally, influence now plays a role in B2C—brand influencers are a good example—and in B2B—for example, the trusted adviser who has the ear of the buyer at the company. These peers are often secondary decision makers, meaning they provide the opinion that makes or breaks the deal via a public or private forum.

Post-Purchase—This is basically customer service, content, and upsell/cross-selling. No more needs to be said.

The Benefits of Knowing

If they are so unpredictable and inconsistent from the standpoint of the business, why bother with mapping and then tracking the customer journey? Because the data shows that knowing the paths your customers follow makes your ability to optimize your response to that customer a lot more intelligent than if you didn't. Despite the buzz phrase, "mapping the customer journey," keep in mind that what it really means is understanding their behavior with your brand—how they engage with it, where they engage with it, what they expect of that engagement at any given point. And, overall, it means how effectively that expectation was met or exceeded, or failed to be met, and, most importantly and very often overlooked, how important was the result of that expectation to the customer—which answers in many cases, why they engage with it and what would be best for you to do about it.

At the end of this chapter I'll discuss technologies to build, map, and track the journey. How to map the journey and what you should know to do that, we'll address right here.

A Typical, Sloppy B2C Journey: Building a PC

One of the most enjoyable distractions I ever undertook was building my own gaming PC. I'm an avid gamer, but you already know that. I had only bought pre-built PCs in the past, and I thought it would be satisfying to my inner geek to build my own. In 2015, that's just what I did. But in 2017, I decided I wanted to build another one; and that is where this story of my "typical-of-most-of-you-out-there-too" customer journey comes in. I'll abbreviate it in the interests of time and space.

To build a PC, you need several basic components.

- Case
- CPU
- Motherboard
- DRAM
- One or two graphics cards
- Power supply

- Cooling system

- Storage drives (SSDs are currently in fashion)

- Display

- All the peripherals, e.g., keyboard, speakers, mouse, etc.

The buying process is complex and requires compatibility among the parts so they can interact and work well together. You are likely to buy from multiple product providers to get what you need, where often the main difference between the products is how well they test, e.g., how much heat does a graphics card from MSI generate versus how much from EVGA?

The buyer's journey is complicated because not only are you most likely buying from different product producers but also from different retailers, like Amazon, Newegg, and Microcenter. The former two are online while the latter is a physical store, and the experiences and interactions are quite different. What I buy at one could have an impact on what I buy from another of the retailers. The display from ASUS that I acquire via Microcenter, let's say, has an effect on my purchase of a graphics card (GPU) from MSI on Amazon. The process that I undertook and the effort and thinking that went into each piece as related to the whole journey makes it incredibly difficult to understand the journey—unless you look at it holistically and from the customer's point of view. You could look at each product provider and retailer's part and not fully understand my behavior unless you understood what I was doing with the other pieces purchased at the various retailers.

Plus, the steps I took to purchase weren't a smooth 1-2-3-4-5 case of "pick your journey from my list above." For example, when I was deciding on the GPU, I was researching the GTX 1080 card and assessing how I was thinking of using it given the displays I was evaluating from ASUS, LG, and Samsung. Then, the newest of the GPUs, Nvidia's GTX 1080 TI, was announced (and selling out fast); and I just jumped straight through from Research to Buy. There was no evaluation stage. That said, I had researched several dozen PC cases and decided to buy one from Lian Li, when I suddenly reversed course and bought one from Phanteks—which I had to return because it didn't handle the motherboard I had chosen. The rest of the process was equally complex, and where I got the components from were typically either Microcenter or Amazon, with one of the manufacturers being the outlier for one or another of the parts. There wasn't a single 1-2-3-4-5 moment in this whole process. For the case it was probably 1-2-4-4-9 (just missed buying) -1-2-5-6-2-5. In the case of the GPU it was 1-2-3-4-9-1-5. In some instances, I bought, then returned, and started over again—the case being a prime example. How can this by any stretch of the imagination be seen as tidy?

That is, in fact, what I mean by "sloppy." And that is typical of how you and I and most consumers travel on the customer journey. But therein lies a conundrum. It is *imperative* that a business understands the individual journeys of their customers because the benefit of doing so is great and the cost of not understanding it and being accordingly responsive, given the expectations of the customer for that highly personalized response, is even greater.

MAPPING THE JOURNEY

Mapping the customer journey not only impacts your relationship to the actual customer but also is likely to provide you with the kinds of insights that you need for bringing your processes and procedures into alignment with a customer-engaged perspective. We'll look at those aspects in Chapters 7–9, but our first step is mapping the journey.

The Fallacy of Composition

A journey map, if it is complete, covers both the web/online customer trip and the physical travels of that same customer. For example, Ikea's journey map covers the in-store experience; e.g., the showroom, warehouse, restaurant, and marketplace; the out-of-store experience, e.g., catalog, delivery, cookbook, pop-up stores; and the online website, e.g., kitchen planner, Facebook presence, etc. It also shows the relationships within the category and among the categories and each category's components. Sometimes that's easier said than done; but, if the physical is part of the engagement experience, then it needs to be accounted for in the customer journey. Most touchpoint journey maps miss something.

The typical customer journey map being put forth takes the following things into account (these examples are taken from a coffee-shop customer journey).

1. The overall customer's purpose for interacting with you, e.g., customer in a coffee shop who drinks coffee while working

2. The specific touchpoint where the customer interacts with the company—channel, location, etc., e.g., the customer wouldn't just be coming to a store and location as the touchpoint but would walk in through the door of a store at a specific location

3. What the company makes happen at that touchpoint, e.g., it could be a baseline experience/interaction that has specifics: wafting of coffee

aromas, a person who greets you with a hello, a view of a couch and chairs you can sit on and/tables you can sit at, or a sign with specials of the day, or the lighting is set at a specific level, among many other things

4. What the customer expects of the interaction at that touchpoint, e.g., the customer will go in and encounter a decently lit, comfortable, nice-smelling place

5. What happened to the customer at that touchpoint, e.g., the customer notices the layout is very narrow, the lighting is kind of dim, it's a bit chilly, but the chairs/couches look comfy, and it smells really good

6. Did it fail to meet, meet, or exceed the customer's expectations? At an individual level, it may have failed to meet expectations regarding the layout, lighting, and temperature; met expectations with chairs and couches; and exceeded expectations with the aromas wafting through. All in all, it barely met expectations but still did so if you took things on balance

Ah, but that's where the missing element in these assessments comes in. None of us as individuals treat everything entirely equally. We weigh the importance to us of things based on our existing self-interests through a complex series of behaviors and emotions and history far beyond the scope of this book and of my limited intelligence to convey. Thus, how important is failing to meet, or meeting and exceeding expectations, in particular circumstances at particular touchpoints at particular times to that specific individual? That would be element #7 of the map above.

For example, if it were a very cold winter day, then the chilly temperature inside the coffee shop that day might have greater importance than the smell of the coffee or the dim lighting or the couches/chairs, and it would seriously impact whether the shop met expectations overall at that touchpoint. In the summer, by contrast, the chilliness might be almost pleasant, and it would perhaps be meeting expectations—meaning the customer bias toward a bit of air conditioning might make the chilliness more tolerable and less important to deciding whether they liked their experience or not. Or, at another level, it might be that the dim lighting was not what they expected; but, all in all, they didn't care that much about it one way or the other. "So, yeah, the lighting was dim, and that's too bad, but so what, really? I like the coffee there." That means that while the lighting didn't meet expectations, the customer didn't have a lot of emotional investment in it.

So, the frequently missing part of customer-journey mapping which can't be overlooked is how much weight the customer gives to the outcome and the expectations concerning it.

The other problem that is inherent in journey mapping is that, while you might be able to find out what it is that the customer feels didn't meet expectations and start getting some insights into how to improve the service that you are providing, a whole other set of things that you have to be aware of are impacting the customer that have nothing to do with your brand. The obvious way to understand that is simple. Each person your brand interacts with has a life outside your brand, and what happens in that life impacts the day-to-day interactions that the customer has with your brand.

THE PERSONAL VALUE CHAIN (PVC)

Your life is not simple. I know you know that, but I'm not talking about your anxieties and your ennui or the love of your life you lost or that game where you dropped a sure touchdown in the end zone that you just should have had. I'm talking about all the organizations and individuals that impact your life each day and how the interactions with any one or a group of those institutions or people impact all the other ones that you interact with. This is your personal value chain.

We are all social beings whether we like it or not. We are impacting and impacted by others. Even the most isolated monastic is impacted by others. Ultimately, if they eat food, they must, one way or the other, participate in the commerce of the world in a way that they cross paths with people—some sporadically, some regularly. The most socially isolated person the world, whoever that may be, nonetheless has a personal value chain. (All I know is, that individual is *not* reading this book.)

What defines a personal value chain, though, isn't *all* the interactions with *all* the institutions and *all* the people you meet. It is defined by those that are consistent in your life that have some meaning in it. That personal value chain is comprised of elements like

- Family
- Friends
- Businesses
- Agencies
- Networks (e.g., transportation networks)

So, for me, there are some obvious ones, like my wife, Yvonne, or my brother Bob and his family, or Amazon as a business, or friends like Brent Leary, Esteban Kolsky, and Denis Pombriant, all contributors to this book with whom I have strong personal and professional relationships. But it goes a lot further.

There is Sal Azzarkani, a taxi driver who is both a friend and someone I have a professional relationship to, or my dentist, Dr. Nadder Hassan, with whom I have a similar set of relationships. Suffice it to say all these people and institutions that I've mentioned have a real impact, not just on my life in general but on my actions at any time. My personal value chain impacts my relationship to your business (if I have one of course), and that is something that you as a business should concern yourself with.

But before we look at the impact of the personal value chain on the customer journey, let me personalize it. The story of Sal Azzarkani will tell you enough to see how real the PVC can be.

The Sal Azzarkani Story

Sal Azzarkani drives for Manassas Taxi, which is now a division of Checker Cab. His history is rich and interesting. He is Jordanian by birth, has a wife, three sons, and a daughter who is early in her college life. He is a former decorated U.S. Army interpreter who was stationed in Iraq. His job was eliminated as the war in Iraq began to wind down.

Sal's relationship to me is both as a taxi driver and friend of the family. My wife and I know his kids, his wife, his mom. We have had meals together. There is also a business relationship that at times can seem murky, but most of the time is clearly delineated. He takes us where we have to go.

Why is he part of my personal value chain—the circle of people and institutions that impact my life and how I function that indirectly can impact what I buy and my mood when I'm buying it?

Because of his outlook when it comes to customers and engagement. He is fundamentally a good person who translates his goodness into proof that he values his own customers.

Sal's business is driven by loyal customers, including about 10–15 who use him regardless of anyone else if he is available, or, alternatively, they use drivers he sends and recommends. The reason is that he goes above and beyond when it comes to customer service. For example, he is the only driver that an autistic adult will trust, and he makes sure that each afternoon, no matter what, he is there to pick up that young gentlemen. He helps his elderly customers with things like signing their lease, finding a sturdy walker for them to purchase so that they are not unsteady on their feet, and making sure that the drunk customer gets *into* his or her house/apartment not just to it. In one case, one of his regulars was too drunk to go home, so Sal took this person to his house until they sobered up, and then drove the customer home. Amazing, but it's not just his great customer service—it's him.

That customer service level creates advocates, and it is why he is a firm part of my PVC. Not only is he a great person but he provides a service to me that I need regardless, and he is the trusted source for that service.

He is one representative of my personal value chain, but I'm sure that each of you have that story to tell in some form and with some highly personal business relationship or multiples of it. What is important to a business is to realize that the members of any given PVC impact the lives of the person whose chain it is and influence their decisions—either directly because they are a trusted source or indirectly in the emotional impact that person or institution has on interactions with the company due to things outside of the control of the company.

Personal Value Chains as They Impact the Customer Journey

By now you realize, from reading the earlier chapters of this book, and because of your own life, that our self-interestedness as individuals is indisputable. Right?

But, even though human beings are self-interested because they want to be happy individually, they are not fortresses of solitude. The environment around them and their relationships among friends, neighbors, family, and even those they run across maybe once, but purposefully, the way they trust, who they trust, and the norms established by the world they live in, all impact their happiness. That impact can occur with a single interaction or longer term and over time.

What do I mean? Let's roll with some more Amazon as an example. Imagine the following scenario. You are online at the Amazon site during a day that can be classified as non-eventful. You decide to order something and, for whatever reason, there is a lag time of about eleven seconds before the buy button even starts to virtually depress. But it has been a non-eventful day, so you wait, and the button depresses, and you are done. That's the first scenario.

In the second scenario, you're on Amazon but after a very bad fight with your significant other. You decide to buy something, you press the buy button, eleven seconds . . . oh, wait, you are already so irritated that eleven seconds in your annoyed brain is eleven days and, out of frustration that is primarily due to the residual anger from the fight with your spouse, you abandon the cart—and the order doesn't happen.

What does Amazon know? Only that you abandoned the cart. In those speeches where I would use this example, I often got the question, "How would Amazon find out the reason for the abandonment?" The actual answer to that question is . . . they won't ever find out. But the solution exists even without the data: fix the eleven-second lag. Deal with the problem at the source, and you won't need to find out why.

What this shows is how customer interactions with companies are continuously impacted by factors well outside the immediate interactions or the brand itself. The journey that the customer is taking with you at any given time is complex because of factors that you will not have control of or potentially even knowledge about.

So, how do you at least control the part of the customer journey that you *can* control? The first step is mapping the journey so you understand who the customer is and what they are doing relative to your brand. Then look at how to do that with technology at scale. But, first, the process and the content.

"TRADITIONAL" JOURNEY MAPPING

The customer journey is becoming a marketing staple, with Forrester Research in a 2016 report stating that 63 percent of marketers are using journey mapping to understand their customers better. The problem with that statistic, while it is great to see that so many marketers are understanding the importance of customer journey mapping, is that to truly understand customers and their intersection with the company at all the touchpoints, digital and physical—which is now being combined in the absolutely adorable "digical"— it can't just be a marketing exercise. It needs to be a corporate initiative that includes engagement with the customer and insights into customer behavior to improve marketing, sales, and customer service processes and interactions that drive an actual journey, not just a marketing initiative.

NITTY GRITTY: HOW DO YOU MAP AN INDIVIDUAL CUSTOMER JOURNEY?

When we scale to millions of customer journeys, it's pretty apparent that technology starts playing a major role. But to even understand how to scale and how to use the technology that I will discuss in due time, it is important to understand how to map customer journeys on a much smaller scale because it provides the core of the content that you will need when you want to do it at scale with the technology.

The Inputs

When I say inputs, I don't necessarily mean the customer's activities at all the touchpoints where they happen to interact with your company. I mean the kinds of things that you will need to implement to get information about the customer journey. Some of those include:

- Questionnaire with in-depth questions for each individual customer you interview

- Broad online questionnaire to send out to larger groups of individual customers

- Customer Advisory Board input

- Use of customer analytics, including sentiment analysis, to pick up discussions and conversations

But there is a cardinal principal that must be followed if you are to do this right, regardless of which inputs you choose to take advantage of.

> *You are coming into this with no preconceived notions of what the customers' journeys are and no idea of what results you are looking for beyond an accurate depiction of the journey both individually and at scale.*

No preconceived notions. None.

That is crucial. One of the biggest problems to overcome for companies that start down this path is that they already have an idea of what they *think* the customer journey is. That can be, at the least, distracting, and, at the most, deadly. For example, at David's Bridal many years ago when we did the journey mapping, the company held a presupposition that, when a customer came through the door at a David's Bridal store, they were expecting a boutique-level experience. The way that David's Bridal at that time had it set up was that a greeter would meet the customer as they walked in and "register" them to meet with a "consultant." There were two problems with this. First, David's Bridal was not a boutique nor was there a boutique-level experience to be had. It lived for high-sales volume. Second, registration wasn't a particularly memorable thing. As the journey mapping was being done, the David's Bridal leadership expected that people would indicate that they remembered registration and that it was a classy, boutique-y move. In fact, the results showed that hardly anyone remembered registering. Rather, their first impression through the door was, "Wow, there are a huge number of wedding dresses on the racks in this store!" This was nothing like what the leadership had presumed. That's what I'm talking about.

This is not as easy as it sounds. There is a fine line between evoking an emotionally honest and informative response and manipulating the customer into giving you the answer that you want.

Ultimately, your job as someone responsible to understand the customer journey is to evoke the emotional state, not manipulate it. To do that, you give the customer the control over how they want to interact with you within the environment that you can provide and get their responses to how successfully you've done that.

Customer Journey Mapping: The Individual Customer

To be clear, what I am describing here would be almost impossible at the scale of millions or even thousands of customers but is excellent for small samplings. Technologies for dealing with journey tracking at scale exist, and I'll talk about them later. This is mapping designed to get a detailed look at a small sample.

Once you've approached it with a mind clear of preconceptions, you can begin to create the questionnaire that the interviewers will use, decide who the interviewers will be, teach the interviewers how to do the interviews, and then decide how you are going to choose the customers that you will interview and how you are going to compensate your customers for the significant amount of time they will spend in the interview.

CREATING THE QUESTIONS

Obviously, I can't create questions for you. However, regardless of specific questions, the questions must be designed to describe the customer's experience at the point of interaction but not lead the customer to a conclusion. For example, you should ask, "How would you describe the mood/personality of the person who greeted you?" rather than, "Was the person who greeted you happy?" The questions should trigger the customer's memories, not guide them.

Each set should be specific to an area of interest along the journey. Here is a set of questions that are designed for identifying the experience around product selection with a sales associate, aka consultant.

- What did you think of the consultant you worked with? How would you describe their personality/mood?

- Did your consultant listen to your requests and show you (products) that were similar to your requests?

- Was your consultant knowledgeable about the product? The store policies?

- Did your consultant spend adequate time helping you?

- Can you describe your experience shopping? Who picked out the products that you looked at? You? Your consultant?

- Were you shown different styles? Similar products? Accessories associated with your chosen products?

- How did you feel while trying out your products?

- Did you visit the store more than once before deciding about the products? If yes, how many times?

Keep in mind, this was just one (slightly anonymized) question segment. There were roughly 12 segments like this that covered just the brick-and-mortar experience. Plus, there were several others that covered other points of communication/interaction, e.g., the web, emails, text, contact center, etc.

CHOOSING THE INTERVIEWERS/DOING THE INTERVIEW

Once again, I can't tell you specifically who you should choose as interviewers, but they should be prepared to spend several hours interviewing each customer in depth. Typically, they should be astute, observant people. Why? Sometimes the answer that the customer is giving you on how they feel about something isn't truthful, and the interviewer has to be able to "veer" a little to get the truth. For example, one interviewer at a retailer that I dealt with was told by the customer that the poor interaction they had wasn't important to her, but, while she was saying it, she was crying. So clearly it was more important than she was letting on. The interviewer had to go a little off script to find out what the real story was without being all that leading about it. It's hard to do, but a skilled interviewer can make the decisions and find the path.

I also highly recommend that the interviewers are chosen in part from senior management because of their general lack of interaction with customers, especially in the B2C world. Giving them some direct interaction like the interview helps them gain empathy for the customer (which we will cover in Chapter 9).

Customer journey mapping is not a simple matter—it's as complex as the humans involved in it. As I mentioned earlier, with each customer you are looking for

- What happened with the interaction?

- What was the experience like?

- Did it meet, fail to meet, or exceed expectations at that point?

- How important was that meeting, failing to meet, or exceeding expectations to that customer at that time?

You must evoke the results without manipulating the direction of the conversation to something you, as the company's representative, expected.

The other question I've gotten frequently is the size of the sample when it comes to the in-depth interviews. I've worked with groups as small as 20 and as large as 150. Ultimately, the size of sample depends on what you are comfortable with.

CHOOSING THE CUSTOMERS, COMPENSATING THEIR TIME

The key to journey mapping is that the point of view is the customer's, not yours. To understand the POV, you should know exactly what customers you are interviewing. What segments do they represent? Are they your highest-value customers? Your most upset customers? Your first-time buyers? Are they customers from New Jersey, California, Canada, the UK (post-Brexit of course)? Are they a specific financial demographic? Age demographic? Are they lapsed customers? Are they digital customers who failed to purchase even though they had items in the shopping cart?

Another way to look at the customer is a persona-based approach. Personas are archetypes. They represent a specific kind of customer with a specific profile who, in the B2B world, often does a specific job. In the B2B environment, the customer might be a CMO or a Vice President of Sales. A B2C persona might be a customer who likes buying high-ticket items from you, someone with the income to support that buy but who tends to take a long time. Ultimately, the profiles of the customers whose journeys you are mapping meet the description of an archetype. They are "personas like me" or "mes like the persona." Defining personas provides a lot of value, especially since the results and the stories associated with those personas help provide insight into customer behaviors and assist with successful engagement. But, for now, let's focus on their value as one way to approach a journey map.

Once you define which customers you are targeting and specifically name the customers who meet those criteria, and you get their agreement to participate in the interrogation . . . err . . . interview, you must show them that you appreciate their time. They are giving you a lot of their time. They are also customers who are looking to feel valued. Even though they aren't transacting with you in the moment, they are engaged with you by their willingness to participate and improve your company with the feedback and data they provide so that you can interpret it along with all the other signals used to flesh out the details of the journey.

Compensation is in order. It could be as simple as a thank you and a significant discount or a free product from your catalog, or it could be a monetary sum or a certificate for a free dinner. It's up to you to make that determination. But, please remember, they are always and still your customer, and they are going above and beyond, so they need to know that the effort they have expended is meaningful to you.

JOURNEY MAPS

If you are building a complete journey map from the responses that your customers give both individually and as a group, keep these tenets in mind.

- This is a visual effort, not a bunch of lists. You are creating visualizations of the journey. They can be as simple as lines and dots and checkboxes or as complex as drawings of human beings combined with charts combined with colors representing emotional states. But the journey must be visualized. All descriptive material is supporting the visualization with anecdotal evidence or mapped-to analytics data.

- You should show specific individual responses as well as an aggregate map with examples of responses to show what the aggregated results are per touchpoint

- The map should incorporate the interactions, the expectations at the points of interaction, the success or failure at meeting or exceeding those expectations, and the emotional states of the customers at those points. It should show the gaps, either good or bad, between the expectation and result, as well as the opportunities that arise to either correct a problem, maintain a success, or expand upon a success.

- The point of view should be the customer's, not the company's POV.

- Include the results of other formats, e.g., customer advisory boards; broader, less complex surveys; and interviews with employees are welcome additions to the mapping exercise and supportive of the results.

When scale and real-time start coming into play, engagement analytics are highly recommended.

Speaking of Scale and Real-Time Interaction (RTI)

Because we truly do live in a digital age, knowing what your customers are doing is more than a useful exercise. But even more important than understanding the customer's view of the dancefloor that they dance with you on is your ability to track their activities, their interactions, their transactions, and their behaviors in real time. Are they salsa dancers? Hip-hop? Broadway? Crunk? Remember, their expectation, due to the communications revolution of the past decade plus, is that you will be responsive to them in a personalized way, if not in real time then very quickly. That's fine if you're a small company with a small customer base, one that you almost know by name and even may have had over for dinner. But the question *du jour* is how do you track your customers' journeys when that customer base reaches thousands and even millions of people who are online every day, transacting and interacting, all of whom are expecting that personalized, quick response. Even if they are not expecting it, your business still benefits by providing it to them. This is where and when journey-tracking technology rears its beautiful head.

I'll be taking a good look with you at the engagement technology landscape in Chapters 13 and 14, naming the names of the companies that you might be interested in. But not here. Here, I'm just going to outline what customer journey tracking technology can do optimally in its current state. I'll use a story to describe it.

21st Century Customer Journey Tracking: Thunderhead Meets Marston's

Thunderhead is a tech company that provides the ONE (capitals theirs) Engagement Hub—a customer journey tracking technology that you'll hear more about in the technology section of this book. In 2016, they began working with UK-based Marston's, who are the world's largest brewer of cask ale. Marston's felt that they had gotten away from thinking social when it came to their customers and, in fact, had let customer information just disappear as it was created—not capturing it, not analyzing it, not using it. That made the customer's engagement with Marston's somewhat bland—which I can attest is not what their ale is. Thunderhead, using the ONE Engagement Hub, tracked the web and email interactions of Marston's customers as they followed their respective individual paths with the company. First, they matched 20,000 of the customers who were interacting in multiple ways via multiple channels to existing customer records. Using a rather unique tag management system, they tracked the interactions and captured them into adaptive profiles of thousands more anonymous customers who were traveling to and through Marston's. They captured info for both the identified customers and the anonymous customers, such as: Which beers did they prefer? Who did they go to a pub with? What pubs did they go to? What they did buy at those pubs? What were their favorite menu items?

If attaching engagement data to a system of record were all, I'd say nice but "meh" for the most part. But they took it further. Using the technology, they could interact digitally and in real time to use the insights they gained to make personalized offers to both the identified customers and the anonymous ones based on the information they had gathered. If the customer had browsed for some specialty beer on the Marston's website, given what they knew of the customer and the interaction, the customer saw, in real time, personalized offers, messages, and features that were meaningful to them. If they were browsing a children's menu on a specific pub's webpage, then they knew that the browsing customer was likely to have children and to go to that particular pub. Then the customer saw relevant info like the children's facilities at the particular pub, specials on the menus, etc. Nothing generic.

Using the journey tracking technology, they monitored brand conversations and, thus, identified how a customer felt about the brand, a beer, an employee, or a pub.

By tracking the times of the interactions, Marston's could then piece together the customer's journey from website to Facebook to email to the actual pub, for example, as it really happened, not as it was imagined by staff.

The response rate to their communications went up by 6X. But the journey tracking didn't stop with that. Based on the response to, say, an email, they could learn more about the preferences of that customer. If they liked getting an email about pie, checked the prices, and ordered it at a Marston's, they would receive menu suggestions about pie from the wait staff next time they came into a pub.

Keep in mind that the 6X uplift in response, matching the interactions of 20,000 customers to their customer records, the personalization of the responses, and the increase in the bond that the customer had with Marston's, were all effected within a few months in a trial. Thunderhead estimated that, over the course of a year, they could match up 200,000 customers of Marston's pubs, hotels, restaurants, etc.

If you read between the lines of this story, its outcomes and results, you can see clearly why technology is necessary when scale matters. When you are dealing with tens of thousands or more customers, they exhibit trends via their behavior that will indicate problems to be solved and improvements to be made either overall—to effect a more seamless journey—or at specific touchpoints—to fix a broken communications mechanism or improve what is already getting a good result. Also necessary is the ability to drill down to the individual customer's journey in real time and interact with them at the touchpoint with the kinds of personalized interactions they are likely looking for. The more you know about them, the better you can do that.

The strategy for engagement coupled with the deep knowledge of the customer inherent in the customer journey form the largest part of what must be done to begin to design the engagement programs. But one more thing must be addressed before that happens. It is, doubtless, the most boring part of the customer engagement game plan: the operationalization of the customer-facing departments of your business. Which is why Chapter 7 covers what is probably the most familiar territory in the book.

CHAPTER 7

Mapping the Operational Requirements

This is probably the most important part of your corporate engagement strategy—a plan to operationalize it—and it may be the most yawn-inducing. The reason it's yawn-inducing is that there is a decent chance that you've not only heard it before but done it before—perhaps with your CRM system. It doesn't differ too markedly from other plans to operationalize a business. But there are a few differences that I will be pointing out, particularly in what to build around. It is important because it's what you do to systematize your engagement strategy so that the efforts and results are repeatable when they need to be, and flexible when they need to be, and those same results are measurable against the expectations you have in ways that are valuable to you and your colleagues. Plus, it helps keep your business running.

This chapter is going to run a bit differently than the others. At the end of most of each of the other chapters, there has been a discussion by an outside expert or two about its subject matter. In this case, we are going to start with the outside expert, Bruce Culbert, because what he will give you might be the best overview of an operations plan I've seen in a short space. I'll elaborate on some of the significant elements from there. Several of them are addressed in this chapter, others in different chapters. I'm assuming that you're okay with all that.

THOUGHT LEADER: BRUCE CULBERT

Bruce Culbert is a legend and a best-kept secret. He is an important player in the history of CRM, as well as a business leader who knows how to execute a game plan and operationalize a business. He has a long history of successes, including being the creator of e-business at IBM, the EVP and General Manager of both supply chain and CRM at KPMG Consulting/BearingPoint in its heyday, and the head of professional services at Salesforce. Now, he is the Chief Service Officer and a partner at The Pedowitz Group, a smaller venue than his previous ventures but a frequently award-winning marketing technology consultancy—so the unbroken string continues. Two other things about Bruce. He is an incredibly good human being with a heart as big as a planet, and he knows his . . . stuff.

I'll leave it to him to tell you how to build your operating plan. Your mic, Bruce.

● ● ● ● ●

HOW TO CREATE A CUSTOMER ENGAGEMENT OPERATING PLAN: SIX PROVEN STEPS

What is the role of a company's operating plan? Quite simply, it is the brains behind the business, i.e., the blueprint upon which the business runs. The goal of the operating plan is to interpret, implement, and incorporate the customer strategies and engagement goals into a set of actions driven by people, processes, and technologies to achieve a set of measurable business results, including revenue generation. The plan should support the company's broader objectives in sales, service, and support. Today's successful operating plan demands integrated visibility and support of the customer's engagement lifecycle throughout the entire company.

When building an operating plan, consider this proven, six-pronged framework.

- Strategy

- Customer orientation—customer journey

- People

- Process

- Technology—including data

- Results—what outcomes are we trying to achieve and how can we measure them?

Each area should be rationalized in a cost/benefits statement or business case.

We will discuss each of these six items here, in greater or lesser detail as some are covered in other chapters in this book. Based on these insights, I will provide additional considerations for optimally operationalizing your customer-engagement strategy.

Strategy

The business and customer strategies defined in Chapter 5 will determine a good portion of a company's engagement plans. Based on a company's specific industry (retail, manufacturing, distribution, financial services, software, etc.), certain norms and expectations must be met. One must also factor in a set of repeatable, predictable interactions a customer goes through during the lifecycle of their relationship with a company (aka, the customer journey, as discussed in Chapter 6). The company must engage customers to the level expected or higher. The costs for e-commerce, customer support, and other forms of engagement need to be baked into the base operating and financial plan of the company as a cost of doing business.

Many leading companies today are using "customer experience" as their key differentiator. They are creating experiences that offer utility, control, transparency, emotional connection, and value through a series of differentiated interactions and engagements that meet the unique and individual needs of that customer. Companies such as Zappos and REI are passionate about knowing what their customers want and consistently exceeding those expectations, while simultaneously bringing measurable value back to the business. Investments in capability for the customer and company need to be viewed as an ongoing effort. For each advancement in strategy there should be a corresponding cost-and-benefits analysis keeping the company focused on what can be accomplished in a realistic time frame to drive the highest value for the customer and the company.

Customer Orientation: Customer Journey

No strategy or operating plan would be complete if it did not directly tie into the impact on customers. All operational planning should fully articulate the impact and ownership of customer results. Sometimes that is with end-user customers directly, other times this may be another department or function within or outside of the company. The customer journey that is discussed in detail in Chapter 6 lays out a way to look at the types of interactions, influences, consumable experiences, and engagements a typical customer might go through to consider and purchase an item or service. In our firm's operating plan, we want to have the details of who owns the key customer processes and results and what technologies and systems are required to support achieving our stated goals.

People

Customer outcomes are highly dependent on all the people in the company and particularly in the customer-facing parts of the business in marketing, sales, and support. Talent acquisition and development are paramount to building a winning team. Operating executives and managers need to have specific plans. Each department and business unit needs to answer these questions:

- What specific roles are necessary to support the customer-engagement model for the business?
- What total headcount over time do I need and how much is it projected to cost?

- What skills and experience are required for these roles?
- What is the current level of the team in terms of competence to need and capacity?
- How do we recruit, hire, onboard, train, grow, and retain the talent required to meet our objectives?
- How will the people be organized, incentivized, and measured?

Process

Even in the smallest business, many different processes require management and support. They seem to grow over time as the next opportunity and or problem requires another process or procedure. When it comes to key customer processes, we always want to first establish ownership. What business function and who is responsible for the effective outcome of a given process? Consider content syndication, which is an import engagement process to drive awareness before and during the research and consideration phases of the buyer journey. In my company, several people inside and outside our company are involved in content creation and syndication, but one person is responsible, our Director of Revenue Marketing, Amanda Shelly. She has the responsibility and resources required to run this engagement process and own the results.

Second, we want to clearly articulate the goals of the process. In this case, the goals are to boost web traffic, produce new business leads, and raise the company profile through thought leadership content. With an owner and goals, all key processes can be aligned to desired business outcomes.

A healthy exercise to do when a new process is required or an existing one modified is to ensure there are no unintended consequences. Look upstream and downstream at the inputs and outputs of the process to understand, coordinate, and communicate the impact. Good process engineering is always necessary with a key customer's process. At least once a year, it is healthy to review all processes with their owners to measure results and decide if they are worth keeping. I call this the "stop doing" list. What many companies find is that they are doing a lot of things that don't deliver the business results originally thought or are no longer needed and valued based on changes in customer needs and/or the business goals. This annual review and list are effective ways to simplifying the business while keeping operating costs in check.

Technology

Among other things, this book is a reference guide for some of the many different technologies and solutions that can be deployed to support a company's customer engagement strategies. When putting the operating plan together, we must identify the technologies that will support our key customer processes as identified and defined in step 4. As with each process, we must establish clear ownership of each technology or system. With the proliferation of SaaS solutions throughout a company, there is bound to be redundancy. All technology spending should be rationalized around fit to customer needs and around a common customer data model. Identify areas of redundancy to eliminate cost and support.

With thousands of sales, marketing, and support solutions on the market, there is no "one" solution to support all an organization's customer engagement requirements. It is more realistic and useful to take a higher-level view of a technology "engagement architecture" that optimally supports the customer engagement processes and the overall customer experience.

This architecture would consist of many SaaS solutions that work together supporting the processes and information (think customer data and data model) the business requires. This is why it so important to understand which engagement models and key customer processes we are supporting first. Then you select technologies and systems that maximize your capability and performance in those areas and can be supported and sustained in an affordable service model over time.

Results

Following my logic for creating the operating plan, it's clear we are walking through a set of cascading and interconnected business requirements. Naturally we need to understand, document, and establish ownership for all expected results of our customer engagement processes. It can be an individual, a department, or a division, or it can be shared by the whole company. The point is, we want to be transparent to all constituents (including customers) about what results we are looking for and who is responsible for delivering these results. There are literally hundreds if not thousands of potential measures of customer success, from "likes" to repeat business and everything in between. The list of what to measure will differ by each business, but each operating plan should seek to answer these common questions:

- What do we want/need to measure?

- How do we measure it?

- What is the one source of truth (aka, data integrity)? How do we maintain data accuracy over time? (Note: This is why data models and integrated technology architectures are so important. It is virtually impossible to get consistent and accurate reporting with a jumbled bunch of point solutions.)

- What are our target goals and desired results?

- Who is responsible for the achieving these results?

- Who and how is analysis and remediation done on the results and how often?

For all businesses, the results section of our operating plan is to establish clear goals, accountability, visibility, and ownership, with feedback, remediation, and action plans as appropriate.

By incorporating these elements into your operating plan, you create a strategy that delights customers with each engagement. Put your customers at the heart of your plan, and they will reward you by becoming customer advocates who will help your company soar.

. . . . . .

Thank you, Bruce. On point. Now it's my turn.

OPERATIONALIZING THE BUSINESS OF ENGAGEMENT

I've already covered significant elements of the operational plan—strategy (Chapter 5) and knowing the customer via the customer journey (Chapter 6). Bruce now has covered the operations outline for you. But, as Bruce makes very clear, several other considerations come into play. Ultimately, the idea isn't just to design and execute an engagement strategy that is an isolated part of your business. For this to work, unless you are an outlier who has a plan that can work for you—and there are some—you are going to have to transform your business model and change the culture of your organization. As you grow (which is the point, isn't it?), you'll have to provide the architecture and the framework for addressing customers as you scale without losing the means to personalize interactions with your individual customers. This "personalization at scale" operationally means building repeatable processes associated with business rules conjoined with the ability to measure the productivity and efficiency of the business. Technologically, it means automation of those processes and a business-rules engine that can drive their direction. It is also mission-critical for engagement that your customer-facing departments in particular—sales, marketing, customer service—are all effective and efficient. But that also goes for the back office, e.g., financial, human resources, supply chain. All these departments, indeed, your entire company, should be driven by an understanding that every process and every procedure that they use or implement is either impacting the customer or is impacted by the customer. Why this is the case will be thoroughly discussed in Chapter 9 when we start looking at the difference between a customer-centric and a customer-engaged culture. But for now, take it on faith.

What I'm going to concentrate on here is the effectiveness/efficiency of the customer-facing departments—the processes—and the ability to deal with customers at scale via repeatable processes and automation. Though I will address technology and systems here somewhat, they are examined in much more detail in Chapters 13 and 14. Here we focus on technology as an enabler of systems only.

THINKING ABOUT OPERATIONS

Thinking about business operations is not a lot different than thinking about how you are going to transform your company culture to "customer-engaged," the subject of Chapter 9. The idea, as Bruce certainly reinforces, is to think about the day-to-day business operations you need to run to accomplish something in a holistic sense—in this case, making sure that the customer's experience over time is substantially good enough to want to continue to engage with the company. In the past, biz ops as some call it, were focused around siloed efficiencies—even if it was the customer-facing departments that were being made more efficient. For example, the company would look to the sales department to see how to manage the opportunities that they had, to measure and track the pipeline, and to account for compensation and revenue. Marketing had to create, launch, track, and measure campaigns to drive leads. Customer service had to make sure that routine requests such as getting a Return Merchandise Authorization (RMA) number was easily handled, as well as having highly developed procedures for escalation of issues from low-level support staff at the call center to either technically proficient representatives or management-team troubleshooters to deal with issues. Individually, all of these were legitimate considerations when operationalizing the business. For example, how did you manage the compensation plan when a sales representative hit some sort of milestone? What was the follow-up to a customer who had gone several steps into a marketing campaign, e.g., they had clicked on something, downloaded something, etc. In customer service, you had to make decisions as to when you would address an issue by kicking it upstairs to a management-team troubleshooter as opposed to that level-two tech specialist. The key was to routinize these efforts so that the mystery and uncertainties were removed and the results were pretty much what were expected, even when human beings weren't part of the process. As much as this seems to be smart—it is siloed. Each department is handling its own business and its own approaches to the institutionalization of the business rules, processes, and protocols of its own group—and that doesn't necessarily mirror what the customer needs or what the employees need to do with the customer that is interacting with them. What about leads from a marketing campaign? What happens to them? Are there criteria to qualify them for a sales handoff? Given that marketing and sales alignment are more and more prevalent (see Chapters 10 and 11), how do you build processes that traverse both departments? Callidus Cloud, a $250 million vendor in the customer-facing space, promotes an end-to-end technology that covers a range of processes that they call lead-to-money, which involves marketing and sales as an integrated whole. Bpm'online, a significant player in the process-centered technology world, offers a fully integrated suite of sales, marketing, and customer-service processes and technology that break down silos and replace them with cross-functional capability. To translate: they all work together. The breakdown of silos and the organization of operations around a customer-focused set of outcomes is how a company that aims at successfully engaging its customers needs to be run. McKinsey suggests that business operations be organized around sets of high-value, high-touch customer journeys. For example, I bought a BMW in 2014 that had a number of optional packages. As a result, the car had to be specially fitted with the options, limiting the manufacturing facility to specific locales in Germany and none here in the United States. Thus, the car had to be built overseas and shipped by ocean-going container. I had to find a lender (either BMW or a bank that BMW recommended) that could help me with a favorable interest rate on the car loan. I had to work through a sales person at a dealer to buy the car. I had to take delivery of the car when I was informed that it had arrived at the dealership. I was able, to a limited extent, to track some of the overseas journey of the car online, though the experience could have been considerably better.

So, what does this mean internally? My journey involved the sales department, the customer service department, IT, the supply chain and logistics and inventory management back office, and the credit and accounting departments—among others. That meant that for me, as a customer, all those units had to work together seamlessly enough for me to not know that they all were working at all beyond what I had to do and what I received in return for doing it. It meant that they needed to have integrated processes. For example, the BMW manufacturer needed to be able to tell the shipping company that the car was ready for the trip, and then the shipping company had to keep BMW apprised of the car's movement as it headed to the U.S., and BMW had to let me know (via the web) where the car was according to what the shipping company told BMW. I had to buy the car in the first place and be approved for credit with payment terms, which then triggered the work order that started the ball rolling on the creation of the customized car.

That's just one example of one journey that, if BMW was thinking around customer engagement, would have been part of their operating model. With an operational model built around customer journeys, the approach they took to the effort with me was reproducible for thousands and maybe millions of other customers who would undergo a similar if not identical journey even if the customized car they bought was radically different—different model, different colors, different options chosen than mine. But the process and the procedures associated with it—approvals for the loan, the building of the car, approvals on the dock for the shipment, the actual crossing of the Atlantic—all are repeatable, reproducible and, thus, efficient.

But building business operations in this fashion can be difficult. First, in most cases, some kind of operational infrastructure is already in place. To think in terms of journeys and outcomes, requires, if not a complete rip and replace, at least a significant reorganization of the processes, with some dropped, some modified, and some added. Doing it this way, however, can be successful. Once again, McKinsey cites a major European bank that announced a multiyear plan to revamp its operating model to improve customer satisfaction and reduce the bank's costs by 35 percent overall. But the bank didn't revamp everything based on all the journeys that their customers could possibly engage in. Instead, they targeted what they found to be the ten most important journeys, "including the mortgage process, onboarding of new business and personal customers, and retirement planning. Eighteen months in, operating costs are lower, the number of online customers is up nearly 20 percent, and the number using its mobile app has risen more than 50 percent." Additionally, they also cited a telco that reduced its product portfolio by 80 percent and then streamlined its systems and technology. "After rationalizing its offerings, eliminating some process steps, and using readily available tools to automate others, it managed to cut its sign-up time for new customers by two-thirds."

I like McKinsey's approach here, so I'm going to share a little more of their thinking because it aligns so well with mine. This segment is from "Transitioning to the next-generation operating model starts with classifying and mapping key journeys" (the title really is that long), written in March 2017 by a cohort of McKinsey's finest.

Instead of working on separate initiatives inside organizational units, companies have to think holistically about how their operations can contribute to delivering a distinctive customer experience. The best way to do this is to focus on customer journeys and the internal processes that support them. These naturally cut across organizational siloes—for example, you need marketing, operations, credit, and IT to support a customer opening a bank account. Journeys—both customer-facing and end-to-end internal processes—are therefore the preferred organizing principle.

Transitioning to the next-generation operating model starts with classifying and mapping key journeys. At a bank, for example, customer-facing journeys can typically be divided into seven categories: signing up for a new account; setting up the account and getting it running; adding a new product or account; using the account; receiving and managing state- ments; making changes to accounts; and resolving problems. Journeys can vary by product/service line and customer segment. In our experience, tar- geting about 15–20 top journeys can unlock the most value in the shortest possible time."

If you do this successfully, you've taken care of most of what is necessary for a successful customer engagement-focused operations plan. Why would I say that this covers most but not all of what you need? Because if you are focusing on high-value customer journeys without level-setting, you are going to try to operationalize the wrong thing. You will try to make customer delight your institutional norm—and that's not what you want to do. You want to institu- tionalize things in a good enough way to keep the customer coming back for more. In other words, operations do what the customer needs and not more than that. That means making sure that the things that are routine for that cus- tomer stay that way. Delight is a different beast that I will address later.

Keeping the Ordinary, Ordinary: Processes

If you look at the literature, it pretty much says the same thing over and over: the clear majority of customer service interactions—between 90 percent and 98 percent depending on who you read—are nothing more than queries.

What that means is that customers are looking to get answers to questions most of the time, not bitching at a customer-service rep or their supervisor. These are enquiries on the order of, "How do I return this item," or "What's your address?" The benefit is that these are easy-to-answer queries. The danger is that, if you mess them up, let's just say the wrath of a customer scorned when doing a job that is akin to a no-brainer is unimaginable. Who messes up, "What's your address?"

Most of this can be automated via business processes. In fact, companies like bpm'online and Pegasystems specialize in this kind of automation, and almost every CRM-related company that carries core customer-service appli- cations can handle it at scale. Where it gets tricky is to be consistent with not just the response but the response time in the channels that the customer is using to look for an answer. What I mean is that if I communicate with you about getting an RMA number for a return via email, the web, Twitter, Facebook, or a phone call, I would expect that I would get an RMA number and that the response time will be as good as the best response time on any one channel. If your fastest average response time is one hour on Twitter, then I expect an hour response time via email. And if I choose to call in needing an RMA and ask that you email it to me, you do just that. Don't give me any grief—intended or unintended.

As a case in point, Amazon has a textbook approach to returns. You go to their site. You find your order. You hit a button that says return order. You say why in a few words. An RMA label for UPS appears, which can be printed on the spot, emailed to you, or emailed to someone else to print for you. Once printed, you attach it to the box that contains your item. Even though Amazon says that your money will be refunded in 8–10 business days, they refund it as soon as they are notified by UPS that you have dropped the package off. They provide multiple options to get the RMA, frame the expectations, and then exceed them automatically by trusting the customer to return the item. Additionally, of course, they have your credit card and the charge will remain until they are sure the item is returned. The experience is, for the most part, flawless and omnichannel. This is exactly what I mean by "keeping the ordinary, ordinary." The things that are simple and not complaints are also expected to not be messed up. Amazon doesn't mess them up and is smart enough to set expectations so that they can exceed them if they want to. Everyone is happy, even if Amazon only meets the customer's expectations. What makes this so powerful is that Amazon does this via process automation, not human interaction.

That is keeping the ordinary, ordinary. And that is enough useful information about it, I trust, to keep you reading this chapter, stress-free. Just enough.

PROCESSES: THE ACCOUNTABLE AND REPEATABLE HEART OF BUSINESS OPERATIONS

Okay, I presume you've bought into the idea that the bulk of the interactions that customers have with businesses are mundane. They are asking a question, buying something, reading something, finding something. But they aren't effusive. They are doing something that is pretty much a repetitive task—meaning they've done it many times before, both with the brand of the moment and any online or even offline interaction with any company. What is your address? Where do I go to get the price of this thing I'm going to buy? Who do I call to find out how to buy this thing online? How does the online buying process work? I want information on (fill in the blank). The answers need to be right.

That's great for businesses because it requires repeatable processes. But woe to the business that gets this wrong. Esteban Kolsky, who you heard from in Chapter 5, did some customer-service research back in 2015, which found that, when routine things go wrong, customers get very frustrated. For example, 84 percent of the respondents to his survey said that they get frustrated when a customer-service agent doesn't have the information they need. The problem that the business has is that only 1 in 26 of those frustrated customers let them know. The rest decide to either tell everyone else or just leave. In fact, the percentage of those silently upset people who churn is 91 percent. Ninety-one percent!

The numbers continue to be dismaying. Sixty-six percent leave due to poor service—which includes not being able to do something simple. Eighty-five percent said that it was preventable. Fifty-six percent just want a right answer.

How do they get their answers? Seventy-eight percent would be happy to get it from self-service. That many people saying "self-service" screams for effective processes so that they get the right answers without human beings mixed in to potentially bollox it up.

But repeatable automated processes still require a definition explaining what they are, how they impact things, and how they are impacted by things. Let's do that.

WHAT PROCESS REALLY IS

I'm operating from a baseline assumption that affects everything I will be saying about business processes and operational details, especially around customer engagement.

There isn't a business process in the world that isn't either impacting customers or impacted by customers.

That flies in the face of things that Six Sigma and other exercises that were popular in the 90s and the early oughts taught. They were (and are) designed to strip inefficiencies out of siloed processes so that they worked more effectively. Find the bottleneck, break the bottleneck, and introduce efficiencies into the process so that it works optimally. There is nothing wrong with that idea as long as it isn't seen in isolation. Processes impact how other processes work, and introduce issues even as the inefficiencies are removed.

For example, many years ago, a company that was on the lower end of midsized introduced a new accounting process that all-in-all saved them an estimated $40,000 a year—which, at that size, is a huge amount of money. It worked fine until they decided to start selling things online. The process, due to the way that it was set up, forced the customers who were trying to register and buy online to enter some of the same data twice. The customers forced to do this found it to be a nuisance in enough numbers that it came to the attention of the company. They tried to alter the process so that this wouldn't happen, but they found they couldn't do it without throwing it out altogether— thus eliminating the savings they had gained due to this particular process. But they risked losing customers if they didn't do something about the process. So, they bit the bullet and eliminated it. They were subsequently able to design a new process that saved them less money but, more importantly, saved them their customers.

This just illustrates the point, somewhat dramatically perhaps, that business processes are always impacting and are impacted by the customers of the company they serve.

But they are necessary for business operations and for routinely interfacing with customers.

If you are looking to create and implement a modern business process, you want to implement a workflow, with associated rules, that is designed to improve customer-facing activities—even if it is a back-end business process. For example, a business process that improves supply chain efficiency can impact how happy a customer is with you. If you have a set of processes that are designed to take your order, validate it, process it, and then send the order for preparation and shipping, you have to take into account at which warehouses the ordered product is stocked, how close that warehouse is to the person who paid for the order, how much time it will take to go from the warehouse to the shipping company, what type of delivery option was chosen (e.g., standard, second-day air, overnight), whether or not it needs a signature, if it needs a signature is there an override in case they aren't home to accept delivery, etc. But, all-in-all, most of what I outlined doesn't need a human other than to put the product in the box and get it ready for shipping—even for that a human might not be necessary—and to drive the vehicle that is delivering it. And, if Amazon and Google get their way, even the latter will be done by drone or driverless car in the not-too-distant future. That said, all the above has to be accounted for. To keep the customer happy, the promise that the company made to deliver it two days after the order went in has to be met. With the proper business rules and the right workflow—and the appropriate technology—this can be done even when it is scaled to millions of customers and hundreds of thousands of possible outcomes.

The question is, of course, how?

Well, traditionally, the tricky part of business process management (BPM), especially business process development, has been the need to have strong IT people with coding experience designing the processes, identifying the rules, and custom-coding the integrations and even the user interfaces. But changing conditions have dictated changing technology and new tools. The focus has gone from IT as a driver to IT as an enabler of outcomes. This changed who made (and makes) the decisions about the uses of information technology from the actual IT guys to the line-of-business leaders who are looking to achieve certain results that IT can help them with. The need to respond to customers in real time, and in a personalized way, has changed how companies have to think about their automated processes and their responsiveness. Now, results with customers need to be effectuated in nearly real time if not actual real time. That means that tweaks have to be made and then implemented almost on the spot.

This has transformed both the tools that are required for business process management and development and the holder/user of those tools. Speed-to-results and ease-of-use have become paramount. What used to take weeks of a developer's time has to be done in hours of a line-of-business user's day.

This led to the evolution of what Forrester Research and Gartner Group call low-code BPM tools. Forrester's definition of low-code, when it comes to process, is

> *Target applications that require coordination and collaboration across different employee and customer roles. To this end, process platforms provide a mix of process automation, case management, and social interaction features that can be configured to manage structured and unstructured business processes.*

In other words, while there is room for customization by developers, for the most part, the tools allow users to configure the processes they need to support large scale (or smaller scale if they so desire) customer interactions (at least in the context of customer engagement-related processes). Ultimately, these processes are creating specific work actions that are defined by the actions taken by the customers or those involved in the workflow. One example could be a sales person who needs permission from a marketing manager for changes to corporate collateral. Another example would be what collateral to send or what other action to take depending on how a customer receiving an email related to a marketing campaign responds to that email. If they open it and download something, in four days follow up with another email with an escalation of some kind. If they open it and don't download something, send a different email after two days, asking if they saw it. If they still don't respond, remove them from the list. If they respond by downloading the document, send them an offer within three days. If they are customers who want a company address, have a set of process steps that are designed to give them that address in the format (i.e., via the communications medium that they requested it in) without, of course, any human intervention needed.

What makes low-code business processes incredibly useful is that process-creation is easy to navigate with friendly user interfaces, and there is no need to use code.

When it comes to this idea, I'm not preaching to a small audience on the street—more like the choir, in fact. The Association for Information and Image Management (AIIM) did some research in 2016 which found that 55 percent of the companies they surveyed felt that BPM was either significant or imperative for their business. So, one can surmise, a small majority of companies get that automating processes via workflow and business rules can transform how they deal with their customers.

Mapping a Process

Before we move on, let's get all micro for a moment. To understand how all this works, it pays to see what a process looks like. Many companies have processes in place that number in the hundreds or maybe even in the thousands. I remember a long time ago and far, far away in Pennsylvania, York HVAC, now part of Johnson Controls, did a CRM project that involved Siebel Field Service replacing their existing, handmade, cobbled-together field service applications. The first thing they did to prepare for that project was to review their 250+ business processes—every last one—and they either added new ones, threw out old ones, or, in some cases, modified existing ones. But each process was brought under scrutiny with an idea toward how it would impact their field technicians' ability to service their customers. It was a revelation. I don't remember the exact numbers, but what I do remember is that the process "turnover" was significant. That meant more than a trivial amount of the existing processes were thrown out and more-likely-than-not replaced with brand-new processes that were more integrated with each other than the previous set had been. It's not that all of the ones they threw out were bad, but they were no longer useful given the new perspective: how those processes would routinely serve the field technicians in service of their customers.

What they (or anyone) looked at when examining each process was the following:

- Who owned it?

- What kinds of approvals were necessary to trigger it to take action?

- How was it measured (e.g., if it is a process re: a marketing campaign, how many people opened the email sent in response to the first action?)

- What was the interface like? Was it easy to navigate to and via the touchpoints and to set the actions that the process drove into motion?

- What goal was attached to creating an ideal version of the process? Perhaps competitive differentiation? Or the process contributed to a highly successful interaction with a customer, thus contributing to long-term customer experience.

- If specific technology was to be used, was the process available out-of-the-box, and was it appropriate to the company that wanted to use it?

- Finally, could the process be used without being imposed? That stems from a very simple but often ignored idea. You can't insert a process into something that ultimately causes the goals driving the processes to be altered. The process itself has to be organically useful to the achievement of the objective, especially when it comes to customer engagement. For example, one of the processes that York implemented had to do with the easy ability of the field technicians to insert best-practices kinds of tips on fixing HVAC equipment into the Siebel Field Service database without a lot of permissions needed. Because this was both an easy process and very useful to the field technicians, it generated 1,200 tips in the space of its first two weeks. It was a process that had been included to make note-taking easier (more or less) and its value was organic. Its effectiveness was due to the easy-going nature of the permissions and the ease-of-use of the user interface. It generated value beyond its expected value.

I have obviously focused heavily on processes because their importance in engagement-focused companies, due to their scalability and their efficiency, is greater than ordinary.

But processes aren't all that has a magnified value. And that leads us to the final topic of this chapter—the use of systems to support operations. I'm not going to dwell on it a lot here because I spend 60-plus pages on the technology in Chapters 13 and 14, but it is worth talking about in the context of operations and, especially, customer relationship management (CRM) as the operational core for customer engagement.

Technology: CRM as the Operational Core of Engagement

For those of you reading this who don't know about CRM, it stands for customer relationship management. My most recent definition of CRM follows.

> *Customer Relationship Management is a technology and system that sustains sales, marketing, and customer service activities. It is designed to capture and interpret customer data, both structured and unstructured, and to sustain the management of the business side of customer-related operations. CRM technology automates processes and workflows and helps organize and interpret data to support a company in engaging its customers more effectively.*

It is the operational heart of the customer-facing departments at any business. If you are looking at the system overall—and the technologies associated with it—all of it is designed to promote outcomes that lead to results, be they sales, marketing, or customer service.

Technology enables the systems that are needed to carry out both standard and customer-interfacing operations. Despite a lot of naysayers, CRM has grown to a nearly $40 billion industry in recent years. It has gone from "nice-to-have" to "need-to-have" in the span of a couple of decades. The reason is simple. Business operations such as managing leads, sales opportunities, sales pipeline, marketing campaigns, and customer-service case management all have to be handled and their success or failure measured and the proper protocols respecting those operations supported. In fact, the technology offerings are organized around systems to enable precisely those routine things—routine, but mission critical.

For example, leading CRM technology provider Salesforce has a product portfolio organized around their platform. They have their portfolio organized by "clouds," which is a fashionable way of talking about specifically grouped applications that are being delivered via the cloud. In Salesforce's case, they have Sales Cloud, Marketing Cloud, and Service Cloud as the core pillars, and several others, among them Analytics Cloud and Community Cloud, and vertically specific clouds such as Financial Services Cloud, Philanthropy Cloud, Health Services Cloud, all built on a single platform called the Customer Success Platform.

The Sales Cloud provides the functionality that you would expect of a Sales Force Automation (SFA) application.

- Account management
- Pipeline management
- Contact management
- Opportunity management
- Demand generation (e.g., lead management, which overlaps marketing)
- Scheduling and task management
- Business process and workflow engines

But those are the basics. Because of transformative business environments, vendors like Salesforce are building in entirely new capabilities. An entire market around additive value is growing rapidly. Some of the new additions being provided by multiple technology vendors include:

Sales onboarding—bringing news sales people into the fold with training and content related to the sales program and the sales processes of a given company.

Best-next-action—a prescriptive offering that tells the sales people what is the most likely next best action when it comes to a particular opportunity they are working on. These are based on the historical data available to the company about opportunities similar to the one being worked on.

Sales intelligence—which is exactly what it sounds like—getting external data on the companies and people, influences and events that can impact the opportunities that the sales team are involved with or the markets that the companies involved are in.

Customer engagement analytics—what are customers doing on their journeys that you need to know at the level of groups, segments, clusters, and individually.

The more forward-thinking companies, like Salesforce, are developing products and services that align themselves with the new organizational requirements of businesses as they adjust to that 21st century customer's demands and needs. For example, Salesforce has the misnamed but very good Salesforce Engage, which has nothing to do with customer engagement but has everything to do with the alignment of sales and marketing departments that is becoming increasingly prevalent. The workflows and processes are geared to, for example, getting permission of marketing managers for sales people to change the corporate collateral to suit their localized requirements.

This gives you a taste of what systems the technology enables, but one of the key requirements for successful business operations—especially that in service of the customer—is that you choose the right software and services to enable those systems.

There are a few cardinal rules for that worth going over to close out this chapter.

SELECTING AND IMPLEMENTING TECHNOLOGY

The first rule of software selection is to select the software and services you are going to use as the last thing you do immediately prior to executing your revamped business operations. Trust me. I've done a lot of this in my life.

General Rules for Software Vendor Selection

Have a well-formulated framework, strategy, program, and set of business requirements for each aspect of your game plan before you even think of software selection—The last thing you do is make your choice of software—not the first. Know what you want from it before you ever even consider which software you want. The reality is, the software is dumb, even with artificial intelligence. It will do what you tell it to do or want it to do, if it is built to be able to do that. If not, you don't want it. What it won't do is anything for you that *you* need to do. It just enables tasks, finds out information, and identifies strengths and weaknesses. But the heavy lifting is yours. This makes it lighter. It's the forklift, not the operator. So, once again, last, not first or in the middle.

Make sure you know what your business requirements are—You can't adjust to the software. It has to be capable of adjusting to your needs. In that York HVAC example, above, when they did their selection, one of their criteria was how much of what we want it to do is out-of-the-box and needs little customization—which, back then, was time consuming and expensive. That aspect is less important now than it was then, but it's still important to be clear on the limitations and the strengths of the possible software you are going to select.

Vendor selection—Remember you aren't just selecting technology systems, you are selecting a business partner who is going to have a lot to say about how your business operations are functioning. Sure, you have to know what the products available to you are, the services you need, whether it meets the functionality requirements you have, the kinds of issues that the software/services have had, how happy the customers are, and what the analysts think about it. But this is also a partner company who, if you are having trouble, you should be able to count on. That means you need to know if they are financially stable, if they are a good cultural fit for you, and whether they have a good track record of working with their customers when there are problems. Due diligence these days is easier than ever, with the availability of public information; conversations on the brand via the web; analyst organizations like Gartner, Forrester, and IDC; boutique market research firms, like Ray Wang's Constellation Research; independent analysts, many of whom you've heard from (or will hear from) in this book, like Esteban Kolsky, Denis Pombriant, Brent Leary, and me; and user-based review organizations like G2 Crowd. All in all, you get a well-rounded look. Combine that with some independent reference checks—find the customers and do the checking yourself rather than depend on the potential vendor's customer references. Talk to them, too, though. With some legwork, you have enough information in the public domain to make a pretty well-informed choice that isn't dependent on what the vendor candidate tells you.

I want to bookend the chapter with a short piece on how to design operations from the standpoint of customer engagement. Our author is Brian Curran.

THOUGHT LEADER: BRIAN CURRAN

Brian Curran, Oracle's Vice President of Customer Experience Strategy and Design, has been doing human-centered design for 30 years, which, if you look at him, makes you think he's been doing it since he was born. He's worked for and with multiple Fortune 100 Brands in senior executive roles ranging across operations, customer care, sales, marketing, and ecommerce in several different industries, ranging from automotive to high tech. This guy is impressive—he travels across the world helping customers figure out how they are going to transform their businesses—not just digitally but from the human side. He is a whole-brained man. Listen closely to what he has to say on designing operations for engagement. You won't regret it.

◦ ◦ ◦ ◦ ◦

To me, designing engagements is a combination of art and science. Understanding the human psychology of engagements and the attitudinal nature of needs, expectations, and experiences in the desirable portion of human-centered design must be balanced with the feasible and viable portions to ensure execution and, ultimately, results. To achieve this balance, one must marry the two in a process that translates great ideas into executable activities. These are the building blocks of a disruptive business model and the requirement of innovation, which should always be ideas that are executed.

The goal here is to transition from divergent ideation to a converged set of operational requirements in a way that honors the art and yet moves towards the science.

In the art portion, I have defined the moment where I want to engage in a different way and have determined the unmet need(s) at a useful, usable, and meaningful level. This is the foundation of my desired state: the needs of the customer; the desired outcome associated with meeting those needs at an attitudinal, behavioral, and financial basis; and an understanding of the issues or opportunities associated with meeting those needs.

I can proceed now to designing an interaction at that moment that takes into consideration empathetic factors such as context and expectations, along with engagement factors such as the appropriate use of channels, content, people, and other things that the customer will come into direct contact with during this interaction.

But how do I go from that diverged set of customer-centric ideas to a converged set of feasible and viable requirements that can eventually lead to execution? To do this, I must now start to take those loosely coupled sets of enablers and descriptions in my story board and start to map those out in a concise way. I need to think about these requirements as a list of activities that must be performed, the resources necessary to perform the activities, and any partners or others in an ecosystem needed to perform these activities. I will also need to take into consideration that there will more than likely be data that is collected and analyzed, decisions made and utilized during these activities, and I must account for that in my design. In addition to these requirements, I will also need to think about building an accountability model, so I will need to determine how I will measure the execution of this activity and the outcome associated with executing it.

I start at the top, with the activities directly engaging with the customer, such as, "Provide customer with multiple pictures of assembled chair." Now, I ask the question of resources, necessary only to provide that picture in the moment. Are there systems, human, physical, or other resources involved in that delivery? During this process, I am also determining the level of change necessary to perform this activity and whose responsibility it is to execute this activity. By defining this activity and associated resources, I have determined if this is self-service, assisted-service, or a hybrid.

But the activity list is not over. I now need to determine the activities it takes to support the direct engagement activity. Many people call this the back-stage activities it takes to drive the on-stage activity for the customer. These activities include questions like, "Where does the picture come from?" or "Who takes the picture?" or "How do you decide which picture to display?" Now I am starting to put the business rules and processes together as a set of activities and resources necessary to execute. I will eventually use Business Process Mapping (BPM), but this exercise helps drive a more cross-functional workgroup and starts the process of busting silos that get in the way of delivering to customer's needs.

Once I have all my activities mapped down many layers and have determined everything it takes across the company to deliver this moment, I can start to look at the data requirements and flow associated with each of these activities. I like to use string with stop and start points at each activity, and a description of what is happening to the data. For instance, "How do you decide which picture to display?" may have a data requirement to know which item was selected by the customer. But it may also need to know the customer's previous behaviors and previous purchase history to make it more personalized. We will need to show where we needed to get the data, how it was analyzed, how a decision was made, and, ultimately, how the data was used to interact in a personal way. This could be just data movement between the listed activities or it may require the team to list another activity that is just about data, such as how machine learning or NLP was used as a resource to, "Make decision to show previous purchase pictures with prospective purchase."

Finally, take each of these activities and determine how you are going to measure the execution of that activity to provide accountability, but also to connect all the activities to an outcome that all can share. This is about cross-functional teams understanding their role in delivering customer-centric and financial measurements attached to their operational measurements.

· · · · ·

Thanks, Brian.

A lot more that could be covered in this chapter, but I think an overall operations game plan and the discussion of processes and systems should do it for Chapter 7. As I said, a lot of this will be covered in subsequent chapters. This is merely the taste of one of the smaller entrees in an eight-course meal. Now to one of the mains: building a customer engagement program. Ready? Time to chow down.

CHAPTER 8

Beyond CRM: Programs for Successful Engagement

W hat makes customer-engagement programs different than, say, CRM programs, is that they are focused on provoking and reinforcing customer behavior that benefits both the company and the customer if the company is truly customer-engaged. The success or failure of those programs is based on the customer achieving some sort of comfort with and trust in the company, whether the programs are advocacy/loyalty-based programs, or efforts to provide systems of engagement to simultaneously facilitate a frictionless user experience and capture data about that customer's behavior. So, not only the content, but the design of the user interfaces, the user's ability to navigate through the programs without friction, and the narrative built around the program are components of successful customer-engagement program design. Our guru in this chapter, Brian Solis, is perhaps *the* expert in the design of the user/customer experience and the "look and feel" of engagement programs. You'll hear all about that later from both me and Brian, but mostly from him as he's far smarter than I am on this.

How do you create the programs once your strategy is clear, you've already operationalized the business, and you know who your customers are? Funny, you always seem to ask me the right questions in a truly timely way. Thank you.

BEFORE YOU DESIGN, YOU RESEARCH

Obviously, I'm assuming you've read the first seven chapters and have at least thought the things in those chapters through before you start building and executing programs. With that presumption, it is worth mapping what you have and what you need. I have to assume that you've attempted to do so systematically, or maybe not so much, and that you have some programs in place already. (I'm making no judgments whatever on how well or poorly you've done to date with your engagement strategy and programs.) But doing some research on where you stand is a great starting point for developing your customer-engagement programs.

Look at your current programs—customer feedback, systems of engagement (e.g., gamification), loyalty programs, communities, and personalized content—if you have anyone of them, that is. Then look at your more traditional efforts around your contact center, your approach to marketing, and your sales methodologies. What's worked? What hasn't? What has worked but is not likely to work in the context of your new strategy? In other words, make a ruthless and serious examination of the good, the bad, and the potential that your existing programs provide.

Get a substantial amount of customer feedback via the journey mapping described in Chapter 6, but also via engagement surveys that are designed to provide both broad and in-depth data that you can analyze. Monitor and capture data from social-media activity. Keep in mind with the feedback that it's not just how good or bad you are doing; it's more about what customers feel about you, how are they behaving with you, and what they want and expect from you.

Based on your analysis, decide which programs you should eliminate, which you can keep as they are, which you can keep but need to modify, and what you need that you don't have.

DESIGNING AND MANAGING CUSTOMER ENGAGEMENT PROGRAMS

Let's take a closer look at what goes into a successful customer-engagement program.

Tenets of the Program

The broadest, most universal objective for a customer-engagement program is that it is designed to make the customers' overall experience and particular interactions good enough to encourage them feel like they want to continue engaging with your business. To them, your brand is a "company like me," if the programs succeed as planned.

The ideal results come in four parts:

- The ongoing engagements are *good enough* to make the customer want to continue the engagement. Note that I did not say "delightful enough."

- The customers' expectations were and are met and *occasionally* exceeded.

- A flexible approach, processes/best practices, and ongoing cultural/ organizational support become institutionalized around your engagement programs. It's not enough for the company to activate the programs. The employees need to want to participate in their success and are supported for doing so. This must be an engrained part of the culture, and the processes and best practices of the company have to contribute to providing what is necessary to keep the customer engaged.

- The customer feels good about their involvement with you, no matter what form it takes. This isn't about multi-channel or omnichannel or channel-less engagement, or even about devices—it's about the interactions of human beings when they are customers and how they feel about those interactions in the moment and over time. Thumbs-up or better is an expected result if things are done well.

To achieve these kinds of results with your customers, you have to provide them with several things they need to be able to foster these interactions. First, and probably still foremost, they need access to the basic products and services that the company provides them and that made them interested in the company in the first place. Second, they need access to the kinds of differentiated consumable experiences that not only are available at a premium cost, more often than not, but define the brand, as we discussed in the American Girl example in Chapter 3. Finally, and arguably more important than ever, the tools that give those customers control over how they interact with the brand are now part of what is necessary. There is no program built around engagement that can ignore the tools provided to the customers, so interface and navigation become of mission-critical importance in the program design. We no longer live in a world where just products and services suffice to keep the customers happy with your brand.

Even though I suppose I could I drag this chapter out and talk to you about twenty-five elements of program design, I won't. When it comes down to it, there are three overarching parts that we should consider in the creation of customer-engagement programs. Who and what-sized audience are we trying to appeal to (the scope)? What is the content of the program (type and details)? And how does the program look and feel (user design and navigation, aka, UI/UX, format of the content, etc.)?

Scope: Program Objectives

This is all-encompassing. Not only are you determining what kind of program you want but also the size and focus of the audience you are aiming at and the results you are looking to achieve. The ultimate objective is to foster customer engagement for a selected sample of people, whether it's hundreds of thousands or a small, highly specific group. This can extend beyond consumers in the B2C world but can involve something of a much smaller size and a higher order of engagement.

For example, perhaps the most advanced form of engagement is co-creation, where the customer and the company produce a result by working together. The customer gets involved as a participant in the life of the organization in which they have some emotional investment.

Scope: Small—Objective: Big

CASE STUDY: NORRA DJURGÅRDSTADEN

One great example of this on a modest scale is not a customer-engagement program but a constituent-engagement program run by the district of (I hope I get this right) Norra Djurgårdstaden in central Stockholm, Sweden. They have been in the midst of serious urban redevelopment, incorporating a plan for long-term sustainability into the redesign and transformation of their district. The plan was to build 12,000 homes and 35,000 work areas to meet the needs of substantial population growth. But rather than undergo a "simple" transformation project, the Swedish Building Service (Svensk Byggtjänst) and city officials partnered with Paradox Games (one of my favorite PC games companies) to use a game developed by Colossal Order, *Cities: Skylines*. The idea was to not only to use the game to create environments and simulate outcomes, but, as the project director Staffan Lorentz said in an article in the August 2016 issue of *PC Gamer*, "Norra Djurgårdstaden is seeking new ways of engaging people that are not normally involved in the discussions of the future of our city, and how to plan for its desired direction. Games can be an entry port for a new group having a real say and having new ways of looking at things."

The program was set up as three weekend-long workshops with the Swedish Building Service, Stockholm city officials, developers from both game companies, and the citizens. The idea was to brainstorm and then actually create simulated neighborhood areas via *Cities: Skylines*. For example, they wanted to test a scenario with an environmentally sound neighborhood that would reduce fossil fuel consumption. That one was built in the game and tested well. The citizen input here was both on the idea and how well it worked, so they had direct input on whether they wanted it to be prioritized. Once the areas were sketched out in-game and as a physical model, the city planners went to that area live, then went back to the workshops and built multiple digital iterations of it. To expand the scope of the game itself to cover some more sophisticated models, they flew in a "modder"—a person who can use the tools provided by the game to modify it, often enriching and expanding its capabilities—who took in information and then built out modifications to the game to make it even more useful.

This is an engagement program that had a short life as far as the project it was involved in but a much longer one as a prototype for future efforts for citizen engagement. This isn't gamification. This is literally immersion from the citizenry to the benefit of the city. In addition to the engagement of the citizenry in the improvements made in their district, they've created a reproducible template that can be utilized in any district in the city and involves the co-creation of a newly renovated living, breathing neighborhood.

The difference between engagement and experience is well expressed in a local's comment from the same *PC Gamer* article:

> *"Engaging citizens is part of the future," says Norra Djurgårdstaden local Ann Edberg. "It's fantastic to be able to participate in the creation of a new part of Stockholm during its development process, rather than just experience it once it's done."*

But this was a relatively small project. What about when your customer base is millions of customers and the level of engagement is generally high but your objective is to increase the engagement level? That can be daunting. While the Svensk Byggtjänst project involved dozens of people from the staff and the citizen base, it had a more-than-modest goal, which was to get the citizens involved in the transformation of a district. When you are dealing with millions of customers, though, and each of them has an array of specific outcomes they are looking for from you, how do you develop that kind of program?

Time to tell you the story of Dialog Axiata.

Scope: Very Large—Objective: Very Big

CASE STUDY: DIALOG AXIATA GROUP

Dialog Axiata Group is the largest of the six telcos in Sri Lanka. It has 7.9 million customers that they take the time to get to know and to service, and, once they've done that, to elicit feedback from so they can see how well-engaged they are and how good the customer's experience is, both over time and during their engagement journey.

The results of their good works are such that Brand Finance calls them the top-valued brand in all of Sri Lanka. They've won six GSMA Mobile World

Awards, and they have been voted by Sri Lankan consumers as the Telecom Service Provider of the Year for five successive years and Internet Service Provider of the Year at the SLIM-Nielsen People's Choice Awards. Dialog has topped Sri Lanka's Corporate Accountability rankings for the past six years in succession. To top it off with a slice of investor heaven, their bonds are AAA rated.

PROGRAM PREPARATION

Dialog Axiata's engagement programs and customer experience initiatives have been wildly successful. Aside from being a very well-managed company, they have always operated from what I call a truly customer-engaged (beyond customer-centric) standpoint and are involved on a day-to-day basis and in real time with their customers. Their overarching strategy and subsequent programs were part of their mission, Chief Customer Officer Sandra De Zoysa told me as far back as 2011:

> *This has more to do with bonding and relationships for the long term. It's not just a phone. It's not just revenue to us. Wherever you go, there is Dialog in your life making it easy for you. It's all about how well Dialog fits into Sri Lankans' lifestyles.* **This is service from the heart.**

It has never wavered.

Her statement was reflected in their vision statement in their annual report in 2015:

> *To be the undisputed leader in the provision of multi-sensory connectivity resulting always in the empowerment and enrichment of Sri Lankan lives and enterprises.*

It is also reflected in their values—their culture—with the very first value being "service from the heart."

They had the vision, the culture to support the vision, and the framework to build the programs. They didn't treat this as empty rhetoric as a lot of companies do, where "vision" becomes marketing pablum. Service from the heart was also the soul of the company.

They understood that if they were going to keep their customers—both individual consumers and institutions—fully engaged they had to be integrally tied to the lives of their customers. The simplest premise that they built on was the most obvious one to all of us: a phone was no longer an instrument just for making calls but a device that served their customer's lives. But they also had a telco business to run—and a highly regulated business, at that. So, they took "service from the heart" as the foundation of their business objectives, and not just altruism. To build "service from the heart," what is it you should do? Here are the objectives they came up with:

- Manage customer experience from the "service-delivery end."

- Manage the customer lifecycle end to end.

- Get granular information about individual customers.

- Map customer engagement daily to understand the experiences that the customer was having across their lifecycle and at each interaction point—physical or digital.

- From all the data gathered and analyzed, promote an individually tailored portfolio of personalized programs and offers aimed at each customer or at least each customer group.

To accomplish these objectives, they undertook a series of internal initiatives to build out the processes and the measurements, as well as the internal and external institutions, that were needed to execute the service programs that they were building. They ranged from the process-focused Escalation Management to the creative- and behaviorally-focused User Experience Design to the feedback mechanisms like the Voice of the Customer forums to the ecosystems with Five Star Partners, plus about ten more.

Based on these objectives and their segmented customer data and their knowledge of the needs of both the groups and individual customers, they built multiple programs to satisfy consumer needs and monetize their business services and to continue to make sure that the engagement was good enough for the customer to want to continue the relationship.

THE PROGRAMS

The bulk of the programs that they initiated took the mobile lifestyle of their customers into account. That meant, for the most part, creating value-added services related to the mobile devices. What made these offerings so engaging was that they were tied both to the general desire on the part of their (and the rest of the world's) customers for personalized programs, as well as to the day-to-day lives of Sri Lankan citizens. These programs weren't glamorous, but they were incredibly smart business.

In 2014–2015, they added more than 20 new services and multiple product offerings. Per the 2015 annual report, these services were designed to "suit the needs of various customer segments in order to drive usage."

What makes them so good at what they do is that they are acutely aware of the need of personalized services for each of their customers, yet they are also aware of their own limitations in providing them. An example of a creative program that satisfies both sides of the equation was what they called "MyPlan." Their description of the reason for it in their 2015 annual report read, "individual preferences are different and flexibility is needed to create their own post-paid plan with combinations of Dialog to Dialog minutes, Dialog to Non-Dialog minutes, Dialog to Dialog SMS, Dialog to Non-Dialog SMS and Data."

What they did was to allow each customer to choose from a market basket of services and programs and pre-pay with the promise of no price hikes and flexible use of the services, meaning if you don't use one, you can use another. Dialog Axiata claimed this program drove a 144 percent year-over-year increase in their active user base.

On the one hand, this program reflected the need of individual customers to customize what they used and how they used it. On the other hand, it was a way to monetize the customer's personalized usage and, at the same time, satisfy the customer's need to feel as if they had control over how they operated with Dialog Axiata.

Other services were driven by specific lifestyle/cultural needs. For example, Dialog Axiom found that many pregnant women on their network had questions about pregnancy that were not big or urgent enough for a doctor's appointment. In response, they created a short-coded service (one that you paid for by having the service cost put on your phone bill and accessed via a text-messaged short alphanumeric code, e.g., 4321) that gave the pregnant women access to a qualified medical practitioner who could answer their questions without an appointment. This was a small but important service that gave the users peace of mind and was convenient—a surefire winner. On the larger scale, they had a related service that would set up medical appointments with qualified medical personnel for their telco customers.

Additionally, they designed and created devices. Suraksha is a mobile safety device that was designed for parents and kids. Unlike an unrestricted phone, this phone limited incoming and outgoing calls to four specified individuals that the parents chose. The device also had an SOS button for emergencies and active GPS location tracking. While I have no data, it was very popular according to Dialog Axiata.

While these are examples of services that were aligned with the engagement needs of their customers, they also had broader programs for customers that went beyond usage; they were designed to provide personalized services while gathering data that would provide Dialog Axiata with enough insights to suss out other specific services.

DIALOG AXIATA: CUSTOMER OWNERSHIP PROGRAM

Dialog Axiata understood that the services they provided, while tangible, were impacted by time, context, and the intangible emotions and behaviors of their customers—which could kill the value of the services as quickly as it arose. They also understood that customer experience was a long-term, long-tail concept. It evolved and changed, customer by customer, over time; and it could impact how poorly engaged or well engaged that customer was at any given moment. They took care of both of those concerns by developing a customer-ownership program.

Staff was assigned to continually monitor customer accounts in the background and measure customer experience every day, at scale. Based on the high volume of data they were able to gather, and the insights they gleaned from that data, they were able to tweak their interactions with individual customers on the microlevel—ranging from direct contact to website interactions—and, in the larger scheme, provide new and topically appropriate short-code monetized services in addition to the above-mentioned medical services, such as e-channeling, movie booking, concierge services for higher value customers and food delivery. The service would be opened and the phone account charged.

Dialog Axiata is nearly paradigmatic when it comes to how to think overall about designing and implementing customer-engagement programs that have shorter-term tactical transactional benefits. But this is also true for the longer-term "service from the heart" initiative, which made the company an inculcated and indispensable part of the life of Sri Lankan citizens.

LESSONS FROM DIALOG AXIATA

What are a few of the universal lessons?

- The customer's experience may take place over time, but it is always moving/changing and the programs you develop should account for that fluidity.

- The culture of the company must support "bonding" with the customers. It is never a soulless, purely process-driven or revenue-first-and-only effort. The effort to engage customers should be one that is living and breathing in the culture of the company. That means not only should the customers be engaged, but the employees should be engaged as well, and not only in the execution of the programs but in the evolution of them.

- Don't look at monetizing "experiences" as a copout or a bad thing. It's part of how to benefit from providing customers with a great experience over time and to keep them buying your goods. It helps you meet the criteria of successful engagement—both the company and the customer receive value from the transactions and interactions.

- The programs you design should codify what customers need, and, selectively, what the customer desires. Above all, though, the programs have to be organic to the relationships the customer already has and geared toward what you would like them to be.

Program Design—Not Always Exceeding but Always Meeting Expectations

The last item on Dialog Axiata's list above exposes an elephant in the engagement-program room—in fact, a mastodon—and that is whether or not we should design programs to exceed customer expectations, i.e., to delight the customers? The common response to this is, "Of course, we should always delight the customer." There are multiple examples of business after business saying that their core cultural value is "delighting our customers all the time," several of whom are companies I know well and who know me well and thus remain unnamed in the interests of preserving our friendship.

My answer to "should you" is unequivocally no.

Why would I say that? I think we established in Chapter 3 that customers have a set of basic utilitarian expectations when it comes to the acquisition of a product or a service. The program should do what it is supposed to do, i.e., carry out its expected basic function(s).

But what's on the other side of basic? Continuous customer delight. In theory, a great idea. In practice, a horrible one. The whole idea of customer delight is that the customer's expectations are exceeded by a company's action at a moment—*and that the customer doesn't expect it to happen again.* The latter is *the* key component here. The minute that the customers are expecting over-the-top service all the time is the minute that the bar is raised, your costs start to skyrocket, and, of course, what was exceeding becomes meeting expectations.

Even the Ritz Carlton, the epitome of superb customer service, delights deliberately only on occasion; or in ways that are so small that there's no financial onus. At every Ritz Carlton I have ever stayed in, I get a handwritten note at some point with a name signed to it from a member of the hotel staff telling me about their availability to answer a question or to take care of a request. The Ritz Carlton both sets my expectations by continuously doing that and manages them by continuing to do it in the manner they do—with little cost to them. The mini-delightful part that makes them stand out is the personal handwritten note from a staff member. It is a differentiator that adds very little cost to their efforts and makes an ordinary expectation seem a bit better. But, at the same time, I now expect to get it while I stay there. There's no escaping excellent repeat behavior becoming an expectation. You can manage expectations by preceding them with a framework for your customer-to-be on what to expect, but the actions you take with them over time drive what they will expect of you.

A couple of years ago, my wife and I went to New York to see *Hamilton*, and we stayed at the Ritz Carlton on Central Park South. They asked us at the front desk when we were checking in why we were visiting, and, of course, we told them. When we got back from the theater to the hotel, a bag was hanging on our door with a handwritten note in it that said, "I hope that Hamilton was everything you expected it to be." With it was the 2-CD *Hamilton* soundtrack. Wow. Delight, and just . . . wow.

Do I expect something like that every time I go to that Ritz Carlton? No, of course not. Do I expect something handwritten every time? I do because I've gotten it every time. Will I be upset if I don't get it? Not much because in some other way I'll have been made aware of the quality of the staff services, or my question will have been answered promptly and completely. I'll be a bit sorry, but the negative impact on my experience of not getting a handwritten note is far less than the positive one each time I do get it. That said, I would be very upset if my question remained unanswered. Remember also Chapter 3's "Margins of Utility."

What this means is that a company needs to make sure their programs incorporate what is good enough to keep the customer engaged, but not delighted all the time. The customer gets what they expect to get, and it works. Their basic needs are fulfilled in a way that makes the customer feel substantially satisfied and desirous of continuing the relationship.

In the July–August 2010 issue, the *Harvard Business Review* published what is now an iconic article in the annals of all-things-customer-related called "Stop Trying to Delight Your Customers," written by Matthew Dixon, Karen Freeman and Nicholas Toman. In that seminal piece, they cited the findings on the relationship of customer service to loyalty from a study done by the Customer Contact Council of more than 75,000 people who either had phone contact with contact-center agents or used customer self-service channels. They also conducted hundreds of interviews themselves. The findings boiled down to this, and I quote:

> . . .*delighting customers doesn't build loyalty; reducing their effort—the work they must do to get their problem solved—does. Second, acting*

deliberately on this insight can help improve customer service, reduce cus-
tomer service costs, and decrease customer churn.

Once again, you have proof that your primary focus should be on keeping the ordinary, ordinary. If customers need answers to their queries and they are asking those questions via email, text, phone, Facebook, Twitter, or web self-service, make sure that you have the answers to those questions available in all channels, or at least the means to answer the question in those channels. That's good enough. Imagine messing something routine up. You don't want to go there. That means that you take care of it by making sure that the first engagement programs you create are based on making sure that the interactions are frictionless and seamless and accomplish all the baseline things that need to be accomplished to keep the customer satisfactorily engaged. Occasionally, and I do mean, once in a while, calculatedly delight your customers with something personalized to them. Do all that, and you will keep them as your customers.

THE LOOK OF LOVE IS IN YOUR EYES—AND IN THE EYES OF YOUR CUSTOMER

Up to now, I've primarily been focusing on program content, scope, and audience, but as long as I am of sound mind and body (both questionable), I can't ignore one other key element of design—and that is the look and feel, appeal to the senses, appeal the emotions, appeal to the intellect, and the ease, speed, and seamlessness of navigation and use. The acronym for all this is UI/UX, which stands for "user interface/user experience." The "user" in this case means the customer. While I'm not going to spend a lot of time on the actual design elements and how to do them, which are well beyond any talents and knowledge I have, I am going to focus on what kinds of things need to be considered. I don't pretend to know everything about everything. Well, sometimes I do . . .

Pardon Me, Is That Laptop a Real Louis Vuitton: Style Matters

As far back as 2005, Harris Interactive did a study jointly commissioned by Toray Ultrasuede and Intel called "The Intel/Ultrasuede Laptop Style Study" (duh). As bad as the decisions were on what to do post-study, the study itself provided some very interesting insights. Here are a few:

- 73 percent of U.S. adult computer users want to buy technology products that reflect their personal style.

- 76 percent of those computer users who admit to glancing at someone else's laptop PC are checking out its style or design.

- 40 percent of U.S. adult computer users find their laptop to be generic, boring, dull, sterile, or lackluster.

What this shows and, as we will see, continues to show, is that people care about style (i.e., look-and-feel) when it comes to technology and pretty much everything else. How often have you seen a mobile device and thought, "I *want* that," without even knowing how to use it. The mere look of it and, perhaps, how it felt in your hand were enough to trigger desire and interest. You know those perfume or eau de toilette tear-out pages in magazines that have a bit of some contemporary scent for either men or women? Have you ever bought one of the advertised brands strictly based on what you sniffed in the magazine? Oh. Okay, then. Well, I have.

Think of the battle of the mobile devices now. We think about not only the look-and feel of the device itself but the accessories the device has supporting it, like the cases and the bling associated with it. We've come a long way from the purely utilitarian crushed keyboard look of the original Blackberry to the celebrity bling mobile Vertu, where you can get any one of dozens of models up to the Signature edition Clous De Paris Red Gold, which includes polished 18k red gold, black leather, polished ceramic pillow, a ruby Vertu key, and polished black sapphire face and keys for a mere $46,600 U.S. And it functions like a phone too—though it wasn't terribly well received for its mobile qualities, which, among other things, led to Vertu's demise in 2017.

This wasn't just an early-ought trend. In 2014, Nielsen did the "Connected Life Survey" with a section on wearables where they found that, of the nearly 4,000 consumers who responded, 62 percent said they wished wearables came in forms besides wrist bands and watches, and 53 percent wanted wearable devices that look more like jewelry—meaning look and feel mattered when it came to how they thought of technology. Finally, for the cherry on top, things have gotten to the point where, at present, we are seeing the fusion of fashion and technology as a harbinger of things to come.

In 2014, eBay did a survey on the interests of consumers in wearable technology, not just smart watches but clothes, too. A full 80 percent of respondents saw the coming trend—tech will seamlessly integrate with fashion in the near future—while 72 percent were open to wearing clothing that tracked their health, the earliest adopters of what is now called "smart clothing."

Okay, that's the physical fashion "hardware"—highly styled technology and technology embedded in fashion. But that principal carries over to engagement programs, too, because the look and feel of the systems of engagement that are used as the interfaces to the programs matters a great deal. It is so big a deal that the $5 billion enterprise software provider Infor hired more than a hundred creatives to work on their interfaces and user engagement design. What makes this internal group—an actual organized internal practice called Hook & Loop—unique is that the hundred-plus staff is almost all *not* tech-world hires. For example, they hired the chief creative designer for Michael Kors and, to warm the hearts of movie fans all over the world, the guy who did the special effects for the first few Transformers movies—the good ones. Their logic was impeccable—they can teach tech but they can't teach creativity. The results were and still are the most beautiful user interfaces of any technology vendor's offerings. What makes Hook & Loop so intriguing is that they are a competitive practice but also strictly an internal design agency for use of the company and its customers. They also designed Infor's remarkable and contemporary lower-Manhattan office. Design has become a staple of many technology companies and the consultancies like Accenture (Interactive), as well as a focus of almost every company that has any concerns with customer engagement and how a customer feels.

But the bar is high. Think of it this way. When YouTube first began, the novelty of the medium was such that anything that was uploaded was the subject of interest and everyone watched it. As YouTube became a commodity and homemade videos became a normal and easily available format for communications, production values began to matter. No longer will you (or anyone else) accept the grainy, close-to-unviewable videos that we were all willing to go with when YouTube began. Quality mattered because we were all raised with TV and the movies, and our expectations are in the vicinity of that kind of viewability. The bar is high for all communications media when it comes to the senses.

When it comes to customer interfaces, they are expected to be simple in conception and intuitive in navigation on the one hand, and visually appealing on the other.

ELEMENTS OF CUSTOMER-ENGAGED USER-INTERFACE DESIGN

At a high level then, how should the design look and feel? What will make it appealing to customers, making them want to use it again and again or be involved interactively in the programs of interest to them?

Frictionless interactions and navigation—Navigation through the program via the interface should be easy. If your customers need to find something, figuring out how to get there should not require digging through screen after screen. When they need to click a "contact us" button on a website, they shouldn't have to wonder how to find it. It should be where the customer expects it to be. Several years ago, a client of mine who shall remain nameless didn't have a contact-us button on their website because they didn't really have a contact center to deal with traffic, though they did have a skeletal customer-service staff who could have fielded calls if the customers could have figured out how to make them. Thus, with no outlets for the customer to vent or get easy problems solved, this company had a social media firestorm every time someone took their complaints to the "people like them" on Twitter or on customer-service-focused websites or into customer-service-focused communities. Not smart.

Convenience—This one is rarely talked about in program design but it is an important part of the thinking that should go on. Customers don't just want things that are easy to navigate; they want things that are convenient. That means, in effect, if they stretch their arms, they will bump into the program. You are well served if you can engage the customer where he or she is, not making them have to get to you. This isn't always necessary or even, at times, useful. But often, it is a real opportunity to foster engagement. Something as simple as planning to make a move from adding delivery to what has been strictly carry out yields significant opportunity. Denny Marie Post, CEO of Red Robin Gourmet Burgers and Brews, talked about this in a February 23, 2017, Loyalty 360 article entitled "Red Robin Sees Delivery as Potential to Heightened Customer Engagement, Customer Experience."

> *Convenience is being redefined . . . State of demand, among our target for carry-out at the unplanned dinner occasion, where we have traditionally done very well, has doubled in five years. The same guest who often went out for a movie or shopping is now frequently choosing to stay at home to binge-watch Netflix and shop online. They still don't want to cook all the time, so the option to carry out the foods they love most or to have those same foods delivered is taking on new importance.*

Personalized content—Even though not every customer, especially the more recent ones, is necessarily looking for personalized information—after all, they are still learning what your company provides—the more loyal or long term or interested the customer, the more likely they are to want personalized program content. But you may not know all the details about every individual. So, you use your customer advocates to build case studies, tell stories, and operate as extensions of your marketing department with content from them. Laura Ramos, a Forrester Research analyst and thought leader, found that when you are building the kind of advocacy content that you think may appeal to your customers and prospects, there are four types of content that work. They are:

Content that validates—case studies, references, social media sharing

Content that educates—customer communities and user forums

Content that rewards dedication—MVP programs, referrals, speaking engagements for customer advocates

Content that inspires—customer advisory boards, co-creation, and other forms of collaboration

This doesn't just consist of written content or videos. It includes the activities and efforts that the programs create for the customers and the rewards they receive in return.

Systems of engagement, fun to engage—Systems that are designed to foster communication and interaction between the company and its customers are sort of obvious requirements when it comes to developing programs. If customers can't interact with you, what kind of programs are you designing? I mean, really? But what should be considered while designing the programs are (a) how the customers want to communicate with you, and (b) what the business feels is in its best interests to provide to the customers for that communication. "There's an app for that" doesn't apply when you are discussing co-creation on the scale of, say, General Electric or IBM and their business partners and customers. However, the idea that customers will interact with you if they enjoy the interaction is spot on. That opens the door to thinking of things like gamification or the creation of customer communities to foster relationships between customers and between customers and management. But the systems for the interactions, the engagement systems, should be interesting in themselves. For example, creating an informal back channel for communication with your management team for the best customers—and making designated members of the management team easy to reach via Skype, Facebook, Twitter, or WeChat—should provide engaging and relaxed communications to break down barriers and make the interactions fun, engaging—and special. That's where systems of engagement coupled with programs that make specific customers feel valued in ways that are meaningful to them are a win-win for everyone concerned.

Visually, auditorily, emotionally appealing, consistent across communications media, but not necessarily identical—We know this. The idea that something is cool is sensate. We also know that feeling good is exactly that—a feeling. We know that beauty, when it comes to what we are interacting with, isn't skin deep, and it makes a difference. When you see a site where the landing page is crowded with images, the text appears in a small, hard-to-read font, and typos and misspellings are everywhere—your response is simple: *ugh!* But when you see stunning visuals that are highlighted by just enough text to help convey the meaning, and the text is presented in a font that is large enough, colorful enough, and, doggone it, sharp enough, then you not only become engaged with the meaning of the visuals and the text, but you *feel* good because it *looks* good. The images are eye-catching but not distracting, the headlines are clear, the blocks of text as big as needed. But there is another consideration. Something that looks good on your PC doesn't necessarily look so great on a phone with a 4.7″ or even a 5.5″ screen. And what you do to moderate the look and feel for that mobile device with the small screen isn't necessarily the same as what you do for a tablet with a 10″ screen. While the look and feel (logo, colors, etc.) must be consistent, the presentation can't be identical when it comes to the form factor. The content needs to be consistent, too, but not identical. How you present it in an email is going to be different than how you present it via a website or a video. A phrase that is meaningful when it comes to your customer viewing it on a website may look stilted and become the exact opposite of engaging if it is sent in an email—even though it's the exact same phrase.

Find out what works and test, test, test—Recognize that your customers' activities, moods, and behaviors are going to be "fluid" over the life of their journey with you. Their interests and passions will change, and their relationship to your company will change as surely as time itself continues to march on. Plus, some of your customers will churn, some will continue to be inert, some will be best left alone, some will be enormously responsive to you—all at any given time. That means what you design today as a program for engagement might be great for a while but, over time, become, let us say, not so great. Thus, you should spend the time needed to measure the results of the customer's activities, track their journeys, query their thinking, find out their likes and dislikes, and then do it again and again, and design and redesign accordingly.

THOUGHT LEADER: BRIAN SOLIS

Enough of me. It's time to listen to the real guru in this chapter. Brian Solis is someone I know as a thought leader at an exalted level—a true game changer.

He is the person who introduced "social" to public relations, changing the nature of the industry forever. He is one of the most listened-to voices of our era when it comes to engaging customers and designing experience. He is a master of this science because he understands its art. He is the author of several books, most recently, his bestselling *X: The Experience When Business Meets Design*, a seminal work on business and the value of creative design. But, best and most of all, he is a dear, dear friend. He has a lot to tell you on the subject of program design and customer behavior. I'll leave this in his hands.

Take it away, my great friend.

*   *   *   *   *

THE FUTURE OF CUSTOMER ENGAGEMENT STARTS WITH AN UPGRADE IN HUMAN PERSPECTIVE

While CRM, historically, has always had the foundation for engagement—its three-pillar approach with sales, marketing, and customer service—all things customer-facing, while still appropriate, are not sufficient to compete in a digital economy. Customers are changing faster than most CRM systems can evolve. More so, how executives see and perceive customers and how they invest in customer experience (CX) efforts are also not keeping up with the times. Though CRM's three-pillar approach is a necessary foundation of any core engagement program, connected customers are learning to expect more personalized and real-time engagement that mimics their favorite apps and mobile services. Customer experience and the perspective necessary to see how customers are changing need an upgrade from the front-line to the back office all the way to the C-suite. And that starts with the one thing often missing from CX strategy . . . empathy.

Connected customers see and experience the world differently than many executives assume or presume. Executives simply do not live digital lifestyles similar to their increasingly sophisticated, always-on customers. Instead, they are immersed day-in and day-out in managing businesses toward delivering shareholder and stakeholder value. Of course, driving for business objectives is critical. The challenge is that, without exploring new investments in innovation and digital transformation, organizations are doubling down and over-tapping existing resources. But there's only so much momentum and treasure left for every business before facing the need to change or augment efforts in the pursuit of new sources of wealth.

Empathy is a human antenna that helps executives hone in on what people really do, feel, want, and value to inspire meaningful innovation and digital transformation. An awakening of this kind is crucial to see where initiatives are misdirected, completely missing, or currently failing.

But what is empathy and how does it relate to designing the customer's experience to engage them in ways where they *feel* something worth experiencing again and again?

Empathy is the ability to understand and share the feelings of another. Often, when CX strategies are formulated, they do so without consideration of how customers actually feel and what they think in existing touchpoints. Furthermore, they do not appraise the experiences desirable customers have with their favorite startups, online and mobile services, and real-world experiences of companies outside of their industry. Customer experience, for all intents and purposes, largely seeks to improve the customer journey "as it is" versus exploring innovative options of "what's possible" based on what people prefer, expect, and adore.

People Have Experiences Whether You Design for Them or Not

It's been said that customers do not want products, they want experiences. Connected consumers are saying they want more than transactional engagements, clever gimmicks, or outright marketing. And customers are expressing their discontent by taking action. 89 percent of customers say they have switched brands because of poor customer experiences. But for those companies that invest in experiences, customers are more than ready to stand by you. In fact, a staggering 86 percent of customers have said that they are willing to pay up to 25 percent more for a superior experience.

Let me ask you this. What is the experience you want people to have and share? Does the answer align with your brand promise? Does either align with the experiences people are sharing about you right now? In my research, I've found that more often than not, businesses are indeed investing in improving customer experiences. But they are not explicitly designing intentional experiences, in each moment of truth, and then driving the level of change and investments necessary to deliver them consistently throughout the customer journey and lifecycle. Instead, they are looking at ways to improve experiences that people have at transactional levels.

- Let's expedite the time for someone to talk to a representative.
- Let's retrain representatives to be more helpful.
- Let's get a fully loaded app to serve DIY customers.
- Let's make our web site responsive for mobile users.
- Let's improve our return policies.
- Let's invest in the latest media in creative ways to reach people where their attention is focused.
- Let's find out what's happening with AI, chatbots, and messaging apps to engage people their way!

While these are important steps forward, they aren't examples of true experience design. They are acts to improve slivers of experiences. This is still important. But, fixing what's broken and/or removing friction in the customer journey are just the beginning. That's iteration in customer experience, where customers do the same thing but better. This is also a time for innovation where you can introduce new things that create new value. Experience design is an opportunity to both iterate and innovate to set the foundation, to write the book, for what people should think, feel, and do, as well as how these human elements assemble the desired brand essence and experience.

Customers don't see departments or transactions independently. Each engagement, each moment, individually and then collectively, forms the universal experience people feel and remember. When you look at each moment of truth, every department, whether it's sales, web, channel, social, email, even customer support, contributes to or takes away from the experience you set out to deliver. Yet knowing this, each function operates independently and often competitively, creating a disjointed customer experience thus. This takes away from the brand experience and, over time, opens the door for customers to find alternatives that better align with their expectations, behaviors, and values.

Customer Experience Takes Digital Transformation

Leading analysts around the world agree that customer experience is the new battleground for businesses to differentiate and compete. Delightful, frictionless, and memorable customer experiences contribute to the bottom line of any business, yield increased customer satisfaction, loyalty, advocacy, and customer lifetime value. One of the biggest CX trends in industries around the world is digital transformation, which represents the investment in upgraded technologies, processes, and infrastructure to compete for a new generation of connected customers. This sets the stage for a more agile organization, one that is more capable of introducing and supporting new services and processes, better and at scale. But technology and agility are just the beginning.

In my research over the years, I find that, while businesses are ready to take on the challenge of digital transformation and customer experience, it is done through a lens of legacy rather than with an updated vision of what's possible. Yet, what your customers *experience* is shaped as a whole, and thus requires thoughtful design to engage customers, in whole and in each part, to first deliver against expectations and eventually exceed them.

Meet Your New Customer Segment—Generation C (Connected)

Even though you think you're already customer-centric, you may not be. I believe you believe you are. But customer-centricity is measured in action and inaction. Many companies, I've learned, are customer-centric in principle but not in practice. The truth is that, most of the time decisions are made in favor of shareholder or stakeholder value over what's in the best interest of customers.

Several years ago, I published a series of reports and books introducing what I called the "Dynamic Customer Journey," which was meant to outline in detail how connected customers traveled through the customer journey. It redrew the traditional funnel and highlighted the emergence of new touch points ranging from social to mobile to video to peer-to-peer reviews. More so, it introduced "Generation C," a growing influential customer segment that shared similar behaviors, interests, and aspirations unlike previously documented demographics. The "C" represents connectedness, and everything about how, where, and why they make decisions is highly evolved and evolving. This is a critical distinction in consumerism in that those who live active digital lifestyles shared similarities in customer journeys across all age groups. Rather than just looking at millennials vs. boomers or Gen Xers vs. centennials, Generation C is inclusive of multiple demographics and warrants a digital (and mobile) first approach to CX and the design of products, services, and all experiences.

By studying traditional customers and Generation C, CX strategists can uncover new insights and inspiration to build relevance and market share in this and the next economy.

Shifting Perspective to Rethink Product and Service Design

One thing I find consistently in my research is that customer experience is often led by technology initiatives as part of overall modernization efforts. But customer experience is in the eye of the beholder. It is not anything you can solve for from a technology-first roadmap. As strange as this sounds, customers are human and it is their experiences that should be front-and-center of any CX strategy. Believe it or not, customers aren't at the center of customer-centric investments.

Executive decision-makers are not representatives of or champions for evolving customer segments. They don't think or behave like modern customers. They operate through a complex organizational culture and report to shareholders and stakeholders, which makes it difficult to see customers (as people) clearly and genuinely. Yet, executives often think they are their customer and make decisions accordingly. This sets the stage for what I refer to as an experience divide where executive mindsets and investments and customer preferences and aspirations are increasingly growing apart.

I want to get you thinking about this with a little test.

Imagine a crowd along a railing at a parade or attending a concert or some other attention-worthy event. Now picture the crowd modestly close up and only that crowd. Among the crowd is a mix of middle-aged people, boomers, and younger people. What do you *see* when you think of the different age groups convening on a momentous event? Depending on who you ask, you get different answers. But, what do *you* see?

Most of the time, we see scores of people with their phones up, capturing the moment rather than *being in* the moment.

How do you react to that observation?

Are you one of the people with their phones raised enthusiastically? Are you living digital and physical moments hoping to share what you are witnessing with friends and followers on your favorite networks and apps?

Or, do you see those attempting to be in the moment but distracted by all of the phones around them.

These days there are always those with their phones and those without. Although, every day, those without phones are becoming a relic of the past.

When certain genres of people focus on those with phones, they tend not to appreciate their behavior but, instead, question it.

"In my day, I would *be* in the moment. Why do people bother showing up if they can't look up!?"

For everyone else, it's simply second nature. It's how they live life. It's how they experience (and share) everything.

When you stop and think about it, there's an "us vs. them" reaction to the evolving differences between what was and what is normal. And, if you notice, any time someone starts a sentence with "in my day," they should be automatically disqualified from designing engagement or experience solutions for emerging generations of connected customers.

Let's take a step back to think about this.

Many customer journeys, systems, processes, and policies are designed for customers without smart phones. They're simply "the customers we've known for a long time." Any time you design new CX strategies, customer touch points, apps, or mobile services, or consider new technologies, this group is holding you back from the future of business. All they inspire is business-as-usual with some new tech bolted on to it.

All too often, this is the center of reference for many strategists today (and the board that governs all new investments). As such, it's easy to see always-on consumers and the technology that they use as fringe, the latest in hot trends, or something that is different from you and the world you know so it must not be critical. This leads to a few different types of experience design approaches, including:

- Iterate on existing services to deliver the same old thing but maybe better.

- Capitalize on a tech trend to try to "be hip" and emphasize tech over value or usability.

- Repackage existing products and incentivize them with new gimmicks.

- Create physical and online experiences with the latest tech without understanding how to blend tech and experience in culturally relevant ways that captivate connected customers.

Either way, you may miss what's really going on.

Some see people on their phones prioritizing tech over the moment. Others see that they are not only in the moment, but they're able to straddle digital and physical worlds to share the moment with others in real time, thus making the moment bigger than just to those present. Everyone in this picture is in the moment. The question is, can you design experiences that cater to traditional customers and the evolving expectations of your connected customers?

Hint: you can, and you can't.

But understanding what you know and don't know is exactly how you win. The future of digital transformation and innovative customer experiences can only go so far as the products, services, processes, systems, operations, et al. are designed to support. This is why customer experience, design, innovation, and leadership must work in lockstep to fuse the connection between usefulness, user experience, value, and enchantment. Change gains momentum with a new mindset that sees customers, markets, and opportunities through a lens of possibility and invention, not legacy perspectives.

Innovation Takes Design for Connected Generations

It is how customers, for all their differences and similarities, feel about your business and its ethos as tied to their objectives, values, and how they correlate to other great/ negative experiences they have in other facets of their life. That means, in addition to building an agile infrastructure, organizations must also consider the relationship customers have with technology and how that changes their standards for service, engagement, and experience. More so, executives and technologists must also understand people, what they value, what they expect, what makes them happy, and why. Otherwise, new technology is, at best, novelty and, at worst, an inconvenience. The same plays out with products and services and also every touch point from the first mile to the last mile.

Let's start with a direct but layered question, "What value does your business offer connected customers today versus the value you can deliver if you took a new look at the state of the world today?"

What your business means to shareholders and stakeholders may well, in fact, be different to Generation C. To them, a magazine is an iPad that doesn't work. To you, analog-first decision-making is natural because that's how you learned throughout your life. But Generation C, for example, use mobile devices as their first or only "PC" and live on services such as Uber, Lyft, Postmates, Airbnb, TaskRabbit, Filld, et al. Their standards for engagement, utility, and value are different than yours, and designing for what matters to them without genuine empathy is imprudent.

The standard for traditional customers might mean call centers, online chat, email service, PC-based and mobile-ready websites, having a physical location to conduct manual transactions, etc. On the other side of the equation, Generation C might manage money with different intents and goals. How they engage with information or transactions emulates the user interfaces and experiences of their favorite networking and messaging apps, such as Tinder, Instagram, Kik, Snapchat, and the like.

I know, you're thinking, "What do those services have to do with my business?" At a cursory level, the answer is "not much." But when it comes to user experience, the answer shifts to "everything."

The design cues inherent in each of these apps cater to a connected mindset, making interaction frictionless if not invisible and hyper-transactional. And, these apps seamlessly bridge offline and online interaction.

Then there's the emerging trend of "no UI is the next UI," setting the state for voice commands, AI, and a new foray of engagement opportunities that further shift customer standards and expectations. The point is, these apps become your competitors and also sources of inspiration to innovate.

Be Human. Humanity Is the Killer App of Digital Transformation

You can't see the new customer if you're in denial of their market impact and influence. This isn't a trend. People aren't going back to the way things were, which conveniently aligns with how executives see the world and the processes that support legacy standards for customer engagement.

In my research, I found that only 54 percent of companies undergoing digital transformation have completely mapped out the customer journey. Of that number, only 20 percent have mapped out the customer's mobile journey.

There's no way to get ahead of customer evolution if you have no idea what it is. It's also impossible to deliver meaningful and shareable experiences if you have zero empathy for the digital customer.

If you have aspects of the three pillars of CRM that meet or exceed customer expectations but fail or under-deliver in others, the customer experience can never be 100 percent. This is because technology cannot feel or empathize with customers—not even with artificial intelligence. The problem is that companies do not take a human-centered perspective. CRM is still rooted in technology-first paradigms that by design do not deliver or foster authentic, emotional, and integrated experiences. To design human-centered customer experiences takes intention and a combination of informational and emotional architecture. This facilitates how customer engagement is cultivated through technology and empathy to deliver experiences that people feel and value.

This means that we need to rethink the very definition of CX. Technology-first approaches miss the human element. When you consider customer experience from the vantage point of what customers experience and what experiences they love and those that they can do without, by default it evokes empathy. Next-generation customer experiences cannot be defined by technology, processes, systems, and other operational components without first seeing the customer journey through a human lens. As such, we need an upgraded definition of CX . . .

Customer experience is the sum of all engagements a customer has with your company, in each moment of truth, in each touchpoint, throughout the customer journey and the customer lifecycle. It's not any one thing that you do well; it's everything.

While we're at it, we need a new appreciation and understanding of what the word "experience" even means. It is not an NPS score. It is not CSAT or CLV. It is also not time-to-resolution. Experience is an emotion. Experience is something you feel, something you sense and interpret, and it's measured by how you react. You either feel that an experience is delightful and worth remembering and sharing or it's not, and it's either forgettable or memorable and shareable for reasons that are not beneficial to the brand. For companies that care, the best experiences become memories, and memories become the foundation for customer loyalty and advocacy.

Innovation in CX is all the work you do to conform to expectations and aspirations of people as they evolve instead of making them conform to your legacy perspectives, assumptions, processes, and metrics of success.

To win in customer experience, to win the hearts and minds of Generation C and all customers alike, start by taking some steps toward the digital transformation of your perspective and beliefs.

- Accept you are not your customer.

- Establish a game plan that begins with the insights that matter to customers and the outcomes that matter to your business, otherwise nothing else matters.

- Study your physical, digital, and mobile customer journey and assess where there is friction, where you're excelling, and where you're absent.

- Study the customer journeys, user experiences, and value propositions of companies outside of your industry that are effectively engaging Generation C.

- Assess their preferences, expectations, behaviors, and values.

- Identify new ways to add value to the customer's experience.

- Educate all stakeholders and shareholders on the state of the evolving market and do so in ways that the C-suite understands.

- Define an experiential standard for which all those working on CX and the technology to support it can work collaboratively and in alignment.

- Implement new metrics that track experience design against real-world customer experiences.

- Learn and improve.

. . . . .

Now that was just the right combination of art and science. Brian, thank you.

I think that Brian provided clarity about the design we should consider, and now we're well underway when it comes to customer engagement. Agreed? If you do, then it's time to start thinking about the biggest question of all—how do we build a culture to sustain all of . . . this (picture a wide sweep of the hand). Check it out in Chapter 9.

CHAPTER 9

A "Company Like Me": Customer-Centric Is Not Enough

P rograms, strategies, definitions, best practices, stories about doing something right, techniques and tips . . . all the topics of the prior chapters are great. No doubt about it. However, if your company doesn't have the culture to support all of that in a sustainable way—and *then* some—then it is all for naught, and you may existentially despair. It would be your right.

The culture you need to support a customer-engaged—and note I did not say customer-centric—company is within your grasp, though it will take some work to understand the defining characteristics. That's what I'm going to do in this chapter: show you the characteristics of a customer-engaged culture. How to implement the organizational change is another person's book, not mine.

A "COMPANY LIKE ME": THE CHARACTERISTICS OF A CUSTOMER-ENGAGED CULTURE

If any terms are being tossed around somewhat loosely in this era of the customer, they are "transparency" and "authenticity." And, for that matter, "era of the customer." Now, if you go to the various business resources where terms like this get defined, here's what you find—or at least these are the definitions that I like best:

Transparency (from BusinessDictionary.com)—"[L]ack of hidden agendas or conditions, accompanied by the availability of full information required for collaboration, cooperation, and collective decision making."

Authenticity (from *Fast Company*)—"It's about being consistent in word and deed, having the same fundamental character in different roles, and being comfortable with your past."

The problem with both at this juncture is that, despite these nicely formulated definitions, they are more buzzwords than, pause for the irony, authentic expressions of what companies are doing to gain the trust of their customers. Transparency and authenticity, while entirely laudable, are conditions that, on the face of it, are difficult to achieve. This is especially true of transparency since, to some extent, regulation requires some corporate opacity.

I'm going to take things in another direction. While transparency and authenticity are certainly important, I think that to build the kind of company that can demonstrate successful customer engagement requires a culture that would foster a relationship between the company and its customers characterized by believable honesty and empathy. That's what customers are looking for anyway. You're a customer. You know that you require a relationship that makes you comfortable with the company. Optimally, if you care enough, you'd feel that the company is trustworthy and that it "understands" something about you. They don't exaggerate, they don't lie, they don't hide things. They are believably honest. They know enough about you to want to provide you with what you need as a customer to derive value from the company.

I call what you want a "company like me." I'll explain, but you'll have to bear with me.

Establishing Who and How

How do you go about reaching this nirvana, this exalted state of a "company like me?" First, understand who the customer and your employees trust. Also, *how* they trust.

Back in 2000, Edelman, the Public Relations company par excellence, released the first Edelman Trust Barometer. The report was created to become the go-to as the annual report of record for who and how people trusted. The broad framework was simple—ask people who were their most trusted sources. In the seventeen years it has existed, the Barometer has become the most trusted source for who is your most trusted source. The socioeconomic value of the report is its ability to see how robust or how weak is the trust in mainstream institutions. For example, the 2017 report found that two-thirds of the countries surveyed are now "distrusters," which means "under 50 percent trust in the mainstream institutions of business, government, media, and NGOs to do what is right."

In the earliest incarnations, back in the 2000–2004 era, the Edelman Trust Barometer, in a clear fit of irony, identified industry analysts and financial advisers as trusted sources. But in 2004, a new category of trusted humans emerged—23 percent said "a person like me" was one of their foremost trusted sources.

Who Exactly Is a "Person Like Me"?

Let me reassure you, there is no one exactly like you (or me) on this planet. But, that said, a "person like me" is someone who you *feel* has similar interests to you—perhaps similar or identical hobbies or favorite sports teams or business interests or language or food or beverages. Think about it this way. You often use review sites of some kind, correct? Raise your hand if you don't. That's what I thought. When you are looking at a review for the best steak in Chicago, you are on Yelp, scanning the ratings/rankings of the restaurants in question. First, you look at how many stars the restaurant has and probably, though not absolutely, eliminate the one- and maybe the two-star restaurants. But then, with the three-, four-, and five-star restaurants you are reading reviews that say things like "the ribeye was aged Wagyu beef but the service was slow." Or "the service was exquisite and the tenderloin a very good cut and cooked close to my specifications." Let's say you see about 20 reviews that are in line with what you are looking for. Your filters start working: I care a lot about the service, even more than the quality of beef. Another person cares more about the beef and the convenience of the location, or the parking lot, or the price, and so on. In other words, you choose based on the set of criteria that matter to you. The net effect is that you choose the restaurant that makes most sense to you.

But do you know what you just did? Without thinking twice about it, you trusted the reviewers. In other words, people like you—and yet all you may know about that one reviewer is that his email handle is rabiddog@gmail.com. And another reviewer, well, they love steak, but that was the point, wasn't it? But because you felt that he or she had similar interests to you, and even though you never met them, you feel as if they are comparable to you—and, thus, you trust them automatically. You know I'm right.

That's a "person like me." In 2004, 23 percent saw them as a most trusted source. By 2006 that categorical person like me was considered a credible public spokesperson, which means that, for the first time, we were seeing the rise of influencers—especially brand influencers. By 2016, the number of people who felt that a person like me was a trusted source was 82 percent and by 2017, that same peer was identified as a very or extremely credible spokesperson by 60 percent, tied for first place with academic or technical experts. That means that peer trust has become the most powerful source of belief.

What Exactly Is a "Company Like Me," Then?

What does that mean for a company? It means that the customer, to be engaged in a way that is meaningful with the company, must trust the company to the point that they feel the company consists of peers and those peers are found in all areas of the company that touch the customer—sales, marketing, and customer service, in particular. The company must show itself to be trustworthy, empathetic, believable, and respectful. None of these attitudes and behaviors is easy to measure because they are often intangible in any way beyond a feeling, but your business can make concrete efforts and establish concrete programs and deliver a supportive culture to make this work the way it should.

Why don't we examine each of these four traits—trustworthiness, empathy, believability, and respect—and then look at how to build a culture that gives employees and customers the kind of support that leads to, not just a customer-centric organization, but a customer-engaged one.

A "COMPANY LIKE ME": TRUSTWORTHY

The communications revolution that I discussed in Chapter 1, with all the things it led to, also did one other thing that was perhaps the most important of all—it led to a change in who and how we trust. If you believe, as I hope you see I obviously do, that the most important thing that your company can do for its customers is to establish a trusted relationship, then this is a momentous change. Being capable of building that trust with the customer should be an integral part of your business culture.

What exactly do we mean by trust in a business or a brand? Let's define it without using the term "brand promise," please. I'm sick of it.

Does it mean that trust is based on successful and frictionless transactions?—Meaning the customer trusts that, when they buy from you, they will get the products or services they paid for, the quality of products or services they expect, and the transaction is protected from theft and frictionless in the interchange? For example, and it is the best example, Amazon not only makes the purchasing process and the delivery process easy for its customers, but they make the return process as simple and easy and without rancor or approbation as the purchasing process, thus guaranteeing the trust of their customers in the purchase and the associated processes. Additionally, they have a merchant vetting process for all third-party merchants and take responsibility themselves for those merchants. This removes the fear that the customer might have of being stuck with a shoddy product without recourse.

Does it mean trust in the interactions between company and customer?—Meaning promises made are kept? This isn't necessarily someone telling a customer, "I promise that I will. . . ." It's FedEx and UPS delivering packages averaging a 99 percent on-time success rate. It is *not* GE Appliances saying that you will have the parts you need in three-to-five days and failing to deliver any parts at all ever—twice. (Sadly, a true story.)

Does it mean trust in the truth of what is said?—Meaning the company is being honest with the customer about whatever the subject, whether good or bad? For example, we all saw the United Airlines PR fiasco due to not only stupidly—even though they were legally removing a paying customer from an airplane—but also due to the callous way they handled it on day one without honestly acknowledging what had happened. The United CEO's *mea culpa* 24 hours after his first response was 24 hours too late. "Honesty is the best policy," goes the old saying. It's an old saying because it still holds after all this time. Truth in business means trust in business. Let's make *that* an old saying.

Does it mean the company is acting as a trusted adviser to the customer?—Meaning the company is showing that they have a self-interested but agnostic way of thinking about their customers (whether individuals or institutions) and are willing to help them think through their strategies, practices, and approaches without the primary focus being the products or services the company sells. For example, Salesforce, one of the world's largest and certainly fastest-growing business software companies, has a program called Ignite that consists of staff members whose only job is to work with Salesforce customers to innovate with and for the customer's company. Salesforce software and services have literally nothing to do with the innovation. They are there to brainstorm and develop programs for digital transformation (among other things) for their customers. Their objective is to be the trusted adviser of their customers' companies, not just the purveyor of products.

All the above are the right answers and good starts to achieving that trust. But there is another facet to this. Your business needs to be able to trust its employees in how they deal with customers. That means that there needs to be formal organizational support for the empowerment of those employees. In Chapter 2, we saw the example of the Philadelphia Flyers, who empowered each employee to work with customers to resolve issues and answer questions no matter what it took to do so. But also, if you remember, the employees were rewarded for outstanding performance when it came to the results of their efforts with the fans at the arena and elsewhere. This is a hint of what it takes to start putting the building blocks of an exceptional culture in place. Build trust with the customers, trust the employees by empowering them to deal with the customers in the name of the company, and then make sure that the employees are rewarded for successfully adding to the building blocks of that trust with the customers by compensating the employees and thus supporting their efforts with concrete rewards. Institutionalization of trust is a core principle of a customer-engaged culture.

But, of course, this isn't enough.

A "COMPANY LIKE ME": EMPATHETIC

You might think that empathy is a stupid idea for a company; or you might think that, while it's lovely in principle, an empathetic company does no good for shareholder value or revenue or any of the left-brained metrics that companies live and die with.

You would be dead wrong.

Before we get into what an empathetic corporate culture means, let's look at some numbers from The Empathy Business (yes, that's real), a UK-based organization who are focused on measuring "actionable empathy" at businesses. Their definition of empathy in business is more than suitable.

We define corporate empathy, not compassion or sympathy, as the emotional impact a company has on its people—staff and customers—and society—the next generation.

What makes The Empathy Business very interesting is that it measures empathy—takes something that has often been mistaken as just "feel the customer's pain" and left at that—and instead expands the definition and fleshes out what makes a company empathetic. The things that they investigate and score are, by category:

- Ethics
- Leadership
- Existing culture
- Brand perception
- Public messaging on social media
- Employee perceptions of the company
- Diversity and inclusion initiatives
- Environmental concerns and sustainability efforts

The Empathy Index has its detractors, including those who feel that you can't quantitatively measure empathy and others who question the methodology. I have concerns, but my concerns are more the latter than the former. What I don't see even implied, which I always include in determining whether a company is empathetic, is corporate philanthropy. To me, at least, that is a surprising gap.

Questions about the methodology notwithstanding, they are doing interesting work in quantifying empathy and showing the impact that empathy has on business and financial results at companies.

What they have found is that the top ten scorers on their Empathy Index (more on that in a second) increased their market capitalizations more than twice as much as the bottom ten, and they generated 50 percent more earnings per employee from 2015 to 2016. That in itself isn't so interesting because it could be a matter of better-run companies doing far better than poorly run companies. But well-run companies include empathy as part of their game plan.

Before I get to showing you what you need to do to make your company more empathetic, I want to make something clear, since I'm sure that several of you are appalled at the idea that empathy would be a business attribute as opposed to just simply a personal attribute from the heart. When it comes to customer engagement, it is both. Remember what Dialog Axiata CCO, Sandra De Zoysa said in Chapter 8:

> *This has more to do with bonding and relationships for the long term. It's not just a phone. It's not just revenue to us. Wherever you go, there is Dialog in your life making it easy for you. It's all about how well Dialog fits into Sri Lankans' lifestyles. This is service from the heart."*

This is business empathy at its best—having a deep knowledge of the customers' wants, desires, pain, and needs—and then building the organizational culture to support that, with the overarching reminder that this is a business and the purpose of it is to sell things. In the case of Dialog Axiata, they are selling services that are meaningful to their customers and spending the time to get to know them in ways that others don't. Their attitude is one that says, "We may be a business, but we are also Sri Lankans, and we want to be a part of your life—if you will let us."

Contrast this to a change made by Ryanair toward a more customer-centric approach, which was motivated by their underperformance in 2013—a year that carried two profit warnings. To deal with this, they instituted the "Always Getting Better" program in late 2013, which included:

- A more easily navigable website—for example, to book a flight went from 17 to 5 clicks

- 24-hour grace period to make booking changes, rather than charging for the changes as soon as the flight is booked
- Cut in baggage fees
- Free second cabin bag
- Allocated seating
- Allowing the use of portable electronic devices, pretty much at the level that all airlines currently do (a "table stakes" upgrade in policy)

All of this is, without a doubt, customer-centric; but it doesn't go to the heart of customer-engaged. And, though the Empathy Index might anecdotally think otherwise, it is not empathetic. Contrast the truly empathetic Sandra De Zoysa statement above with what Ryanair CEO Michael O'Leary said after the implementation of Always Getting Better: "If I'd only known being nice to customers was going to work so well, I'd have started many years ago."

Ugh. That is simply cold. It also shows the contrast in thinking between a company that is trying to be more customer-centric for business reasons only, and a truly customer-engaged company. It also violates a fundamental principal of an empathetic company.

An empathetic company needs to be made up of empathetic people from the top down.

Customer-centrism, while still a good thing, can be a corporate thrust for tactical reasons, as with Ryanair. Customer-engaged culture has to be embedded in the DNA—it's strategic—part of the company's lifeblood, regardless of initiatives at any given time. Customer-centrism does some good for customers, but the business motivation for doing it is "what goes around comes around," getting something out of it. Customer-engaged companies are driven by mutual value exchange at the molecular level and at all times, even when the exchange is "imbalanced," i.e., when the customers benefit more.

So, what do you do to make your business truly empathetic on its way to becoming a customer-engaged company?

Listen to the customers, and the detractors—Customers who are buying from you often have something to say about you. Those who really don't like you, have a reason that they really don't like you. Find out what the customers are thinking and *hear* it. Even if it is painful. Many years ago, one of my retail clients was forming a customer advisory board and the first person they reached out to recruit was one of their most active detractors. She became the first advisory board member and, within a short while, a firm advocate for the company. Because they paid attention. Taking feedback good and bad is important, but equally important is doing something with it and reporting back to those who gave it telling them what you did with it. The report-back aspect is most often disregarded and thus the feedback providers have no idea if they are giving you anything of value, nor do they have any idea that they are valued.

Ethics, diversity, sustainability, corporate philanthropy are all active C-level and board responsibilities—Salesforce has a Corporate Equality Officer, Tony Prophet, who's entire job is to see that ethics, diversity, and sustainability are all part of the corporate portfolio and the corporate culture, regardless of their direct relationship to sales. Salesforce handles corporate philanthropy via their Salesforce Foundation, which had given out somewhere around $600,000,000 in grants by the end of 2016.

It starts from the top—The CEO on down to the officers and staff must be able to reflect and transmit that empathy. This should not only be publicly obvious but reflected in the actions of the company's leading individuals. In 2015, my wife and I had to cancel a cruise that we were about to embark on from Rio de Janeiro on Oceania Cruises due to a death in the family. We had insurance, so we were covered on getting the money returned for this rather expensive vacation. In all our interactions with the company, not only did we barely hear, "Sorry for your loss," which would have been tolerable, but there was an enormous and disturbing emphasis on, "We don't owe you any money because your cancellation was last minute," despite the fact we weren't even asking for anything. This was compounded by a direct mail letter from their customer-experience director (I'm not kidding) in response to my wife writing to the President of the company, who said, pretty much in sum, "Sorry for your loss, but we want to make it clear we are not liable." That is close to verbatim. We have never taken that cruise line again, and after several emails and letters asking them to stop sending their sales literature—which they have completely ignored—we now just rip them up and recycle them. All because of the lack of empathy. Or, in this case, even sympathy.

Transparency and accountability as policy, not buzzwords—Customers want to know who you are as a company and how you conduct your business. If you are an empathetic company, you want to let them know, good or bad. Sandvik AB, the European mining and construction tools and machinery manufacturer has a publicly available Code of Conduct that is the foundation of its operations and governance. It is a combination of pledges and procedures that makes them publicly accountable. Along with that, they include themselves in the Financial Times Stock Exchange FTS-E4Good Index, which is listed as a sustainability index but covers far more than that. The FTSE4Good Index requires public disclosure of information, including your success and failure in three primary pillars that include (but are only a small portion of 300 items):

- **Environmental:** Biodiversity, Climate Change, Pollution and Resources, Supply Chain Environment, Water Use
- **Social:** Customer Responsibility, Health and Safety, Human Rights and Community, Labor Standards, Supply Chain Social
- **Governance:** Anti-Corruption, Corporate Governance, Risk Management, Tax Transparency

Their willingness to be transparent and accountable, and their success in achieving their goals related to all the above, have gotten them included in the RobecoSAM Sustainability Yearbook for eight consecutive years, a highly prestigious yearbook that awards companies who have overachieved in sustainability categories. The results are a profitable $10.5 billion company that is trusted worldwide.

Creating an empathetic culture is not easy, but it is eminently doable as the several examples here show. Keep in mind that it is another facet of a customer-engaged culture, but not the only one. We need to look at a couple of others.

A "COMPANY LIKE ME": BELIEVABLE, PERSONABLE

Interestingly, this is different than trustworthy and if anything is closest to authentic. The idea is not that you believe what the company says, but that you believe that the company has real people with warmth and personality and, thus, is a good company. It is believable to you as a customer because you can see elements of yourself as a "regular person" in the leadership or staff of the company in question. This means there must be a willingness to expose not just the human side of the company in whatever medium it is in at any given time, but also that the real people who make up the company get to speak in their own voices. For example, using Twitter or Facebook judiciously to allow empowered and/or assigned employees to communicate in their real voices is far more powerful than pushing a sales or marketing message via those same social media. But it requires exposure via more than social media. The Golden State Warriors, the marquee team of the National Basketball Association, are also the world's most popular and recognized basketball team. One of the reasons for that, beyond their winning ways, is their willingness to allow their stars, such as Steph Curry, to show their human side. Steph Curry's family is very involved in his basketball life. His daughter Riley is in multiple videos, as are his wife and his dad and mom. Riley, in fact, went viral when she was front-and-center in a press conference that Steph Curry gave in 2015 after the Warriors won the championship. She crawled all over the table with the mics and made comments that a 2-year-old wise beyond her years would make. It humanized the Warriors and made them believable.

A "COMPANY LIKE ME": RESPECTFUL

Finally, to become a customer-engaged company, you should show that you are respectful of the customers you have, the companies you compete with in the markets you are in, the employees you hired, and the world in general. While there are a lot of facets to this, I'm going to briefly focus on those aspects of respect directed to customer engagement.

The most important sign of respect for your customer—and the one that must be culturally encouraged—is the respect for a customers' information privacy. I'm not going to get into a deep discussion on what should remain private and what should be fair game when it comes to both storage and use of that information. That is a discussion for another time and another place—over a whiskey perhaps? You know how to reach me.

That said, the best way to start is with a policy that respects the customer's choices of privacy.

Ultimately, if you are talking about building a culture that fosters engagement with a customer, the company should respect the notion of customer choice. The customer has provided you with information. If freely acquired, that information is available for potential use. It could be used for learning more about the preferences of the customer, a relatively benign purpose. It could be used, as Facebook and Google do, to provide personalized ads—a little less benign. It could be used for running the kind of analytics that suggest what the best next action is to take with the individual customer—even less benign. But, whatever it is, the customer needs to willingly provide it and let you use it for agreed-upon purposes.

A significant number of companies either bury the use in terms and conditions that most customers sign when they use a website for something or get something in return for providing the information. The more diabolical approach is to support opting out—meaning that you have a policy that says we are going to use it unless you tell us not to—which is disingenuous at best. Even though opt-in—meaning the customer intentionally gives the company permission to use the information—is less advantageous to the company, it reflects respect for the customer. Think of it this way. How many of you have had auto-renewal of something that you ordered for a year, didn't really pay enough attention to the terms of service to know that it was turned on unless you turned it off, and found out too late when you were irrevocably charged for something you no longer had an interest in? Raise your hand. (Paul raises his a few times.) That's opt-out. Opt-in means the customer has control over how they want to continue to interact and, as we see, sometimes transact with you. When the company policy supports opt-in, it is a sign of respect for the customer and their needs—even though disadvantageous in an immediate sense for the company in question.

Laws like the European Union's mandatory General Data Protection Regulation (GDPR) require a company request opt-in as well as be accountable for the uses that they put the data to. The premise of GDPR is that the customer owns his or her data and has the right to its control. That means anyone who operates a business that is one way or the other in the EU, meaning headquartered or doing business with an HQed EU business regardless of location is required to adhere to the GDPR under still penalty for violation. The GDPR has had impact well beyond its borders, and we are in the midst of a transformation that will enforcement the customer's control of his/her own data if it isn't freely given. So, now that this is the present, the wisest possible approach a business can take is to show the respect, regulated or not, by not using the customer's data without their permission.

Now, wait! Before you move on to the next chapter, there's more! I want you to meet Silvana Buljan.

THOUGHT LEADER: SILVANA BULJAN

At first, when I was thinking about what I wanted to include in this chapter, I thought, incorrectly of course, that I would discuss organizational change and leadership and how to think about the framework for the culture that you are going to need to reach your engagement goals. Then I realized, "Greenberg, you're nuts. You aren't that smart." But I knew who was. That, my friends, would be Silvana Buljan. I've known Silvana more than fifteen years, and I've seen her company, Buljan and Associates, become one of the most significant and influential businesses in Europe. Her *raison d'etre* is not just driving change but providing the methods, means, programs, strategies, and frameworks for permanent transformation to a customer-focused culture at companies large and small. Silvana is also a recognized thought leader in the world of organizational change and customer culture. Somehow, with all those accolades, she still manages to be one of the nicest people I've ever known.

I figured that I'll let her talk to the considerations of leadership and organizational change because she's so much smarter on that topic than I am. One note before I hand it over to her, though: what she is calling customer-centric here is what I call customer-engaged. Just to be clear.

Here's the mic, Silvana.

Attitude is a little thing that makes a big difference.
—Churchill

Engaging customers has to do with a series of things, as has been exposed in previous chapters of this book. One of them is a "customer-centric" corporate culture, or, to ask the million-dollar question, "How can we achieve the goal that the whole organization (meaning each and every employee) is focused on truly engaging with customers rather than fulfilling rules and procedures?"

To answer this question, we need to look at some distinctions, and I have chosen those most convincing to me in terms of simplicity and clarity.

CULTURE

> ...the way of life, especially the general customs and beliefs, of a particular group of people at a particular time.

As they relate to organizations, we can translate "general customs and beliefs" into tangible aspects like vision, mission statement, corporate values, and organizational structure. Nowadays, there's no company in the world not publicly communicating these. And we have aspects of organizations that we cannot describe, which are also called "basic assumptions" (see Schein's *Organizational Culture: A Dynamic Model*) or "how things work here." Basic assumptions are the actual reality for employees and for customers interacting with the company as an organization. They are the key aspect to focus on when you want to describe a company's corporate culture. That's why I like to distinguish basic assumptions as the "make or break" criteria for a true customer-centric culture.

Going back to our definition, "a particular group of people" is the sum of all persons representing an organization or a brand in the context of corporate culture. "At a particular time" is, however, the second-most important distinction we want to focus on for a defining a customer-centric culture and its impact on customer engagement.

Here a concrete example: if we take a look at the leading-edge companies with a true customer-centric culture, we find names like Nordstrom's, Chipotle, Amazon, Marriott, Virgin, and Apple—just to mention some of them. All of them have something in common in their basic assumptions: *serving customers is a privilege; this is what we are here for.* Period.

Their priority is to exceed customers' expectations in each and every interaction, and to attract, develop, and empower customer-centric talent to ensure an excellent customer experience over time. Everything works around customer needs, expectations, and requirements, not around corporate policies designed by legal departments. And this is exactly how we start fostering customer engagement: people serving and interacting with people. (Even in automated interactions we have people behind the scenes who have first designed the processes and the language of interaction.)

Another thing these companies all have in common that implicitly relates to time is their leadership style with customer-centric founders and leaders.

Organizations and families have a similar psychological pattern: we do what we observe in our parents and superiors. We can have the best strategic plan for customer engagement, a great digital identity that promises great things to customers, and so on. If our leaders neither believe nor actively practice a customer-centric approach for managing their businesses, customer-centricity just won't work. This currently relates to about 80% of companies across the globe. The top 20% is not only characterized by "believing practitioners," but by consistency and discipline in making the customer-centric culture stick. This is especially true because they know that leadership style is bound to time if it's not specifically structured in a binding leadership model to be lived by all employees with team-leading functions.

How do they do it? Here are some examples, and an approach to answering our pending million-dollar question.

First, we need to have a look at the personality of customer-centric leaders, which can be described as follows:

- A natural and commonsense understanding of the importance of customers. If we have no customers, we have nobody to send invoices to.

- Emphasis on the purpose of their business and what it stands for. No customer-centric leader stands for making profits or becoming the richest person in the world when starting his/her entrepreneurial adventure. There has to have been a "game-changing" purpose to found the business in the first place.

- Respect and consideration of every person without thinking in hierarchies

- Openness for receiving feedback and bad news (both from customers and employees)

- Seeing the glass always half full and never half empty

- Questioning everything to impulse-breaking existing rules

- Resistance to fear

Personality is driven by values that are received in the first phase of "socialization" (up to 12 years), and it is very difficult to change someone's personality as an adult. This means we must look for a "cultural fit" for leaders with the customer-centric corporate culture. If there's a misfit, it directly converts into an obstacle for leading a customer-centric organization. As simply as that.

Apart from personality, a customer-centric leader has a set of competencies. Good news: this is something we can learn and develop in others. So, let's have a look at them. A customer-centric leader:

- "Impulses" the vision of the customer as the priority for business in every employee, all the time

- Involves and empowers employees to fulfill the brand promise for customers

- Ensures resources for employees to give the best customer experience (training, complaint budget, etc.)

- Motivates others to work for and not against customers

- Transforms the emotions of others in a positive way

- Contributes to give the best customer experience by having regular direct contact with customers and employees

- Eliminates procedures that are of no value, neither for customers nor employees (within the legal and tax framework)

When these competencies are applied by all employees with team-leading functions, the most difficult part for ensuring a customer-centric culture that drives customer engagement has been fulfilled. The rest is, figuratively speaking, "peanuts."

ENGAGEMENT

Engagement in the context of business means creating a continuous interest in what we are and what we do as an organization. There must be a connection between the organization and its stakeholders—customers, employees, partners, etc. The prerequisite for connection is being in touch, which means being in a relationship characterized by interactions and conversations. There is no customer engagement if there's no regular interaction or conversation, even if it takes place only once in a year (or less). It's not about annoying frequency; it's about providing authentic value in interactions and conversations. Many companies truly fail in this because they battle for "mindshare" rather than "emotional share."

Let me give you an example. I am absolutely engaged with one single airline, and I'm a frequent traveler with several airlines. This airline never sends me offers to fly with them, but they do send me interesting newsletters and valuable information three days before taking a booked flight. Twenty-four hours before the flight, they make it easy for me to check in just by making two clicks in an email they send me. There is no rocket science behind it; they respect my choice of not wanting to receive any promotional interactions, and they stick to it. The in-flight experience with them is exceptional, as are all the interactions across my personal customer journey. And they never have disappointed me, never have failed in all the flights I enjoyed with them. I feel totally engaged with this company. They are not the cheapest in the market. And you know what? Their CEO has a clear vision of the purpose of his business: to take customers safely from A to B because they have trusted their lives into the hands of the airline. Wow! This is exactly why their culture is different and motivates employees to give customers the best experience: they are focused on taking customers safely to their destination, not on generating more profits for their company.

To put this all in a nutshell: your customer-engagement efforts might bring positive results in the short term because you have a punctual product or service that customers are willing to buy, but if you do not invest in ensuring a true customer-centric corporate culture, there's no recurrent business and sustainability that you can achieve by doing things right from the beginning.

Culture eats strategy for breakfast.

Peter Drucker said that. How right he is.

* * * * *

Thank you, Silvana. That's why she's the expert.

A "company like me" is the ideal that those of us focused on customer engagement strive for when building our businesses. As I've implied, there are differences between what has been traditionally a customer-centric company and a customer-engaged company. A customer-centric company is certainly something to aspire to and accomplish. It focuses its efforts on supporting the customer-facing departments of the company to make sure that the customers and prospects in the orbit of the company have what they need to make the relationship valuable to each. Optimally, its target goal would be loyal and at-least satisfied customers. The customer-engaged company—with a culture that encourages empathy, trust, respect, and believability—aims for advocates and settles for loyal customers. (The differences between satisfaction, loyalty, and advocacy—and in the business results based on them—will be the subject of Chapter 15.) A "company like me" is a company that the customer wants to help succeed, and is happy about its success. It's not a purely utilitarian transactional relationship. To be clear, there is nothing wrong with a customer-centric company. But we need to aspire higher.

Now, it's time to start looking at the customer-facing departments—marketing, sales, and customer service—to see how they individually and together foster customer engagement. Are you ready?

SECTION FOUR

The Details: Specific

. . . and drill down to the specific. Here I cover thinking about the specifics of customer-facing disciplines—sales, marketing, customer service—now that you've mastered the rest.

CHAPTER 10

Marketing: Beyond the First Line of Engagement

I think now that we're old friends and have figured out the foundation for customer engagement, and the culture to sustain that foundation, we should start examining the kind of impact a customer-engaged culture might have on the old, stalwart, customer-facing departments, those foundations of CRM: sales, marketing, and customer service.

If you were ordering this in proper form—meaning the likely point in the customer journey that a single customer would first engage with the company—it would be something like this: they are found via the marketing department, sold to via the sales department (duh), and maintained in a relationship until they are sold to anew and beyond by the customer-service department.

Would that it were so simple. Sigh. Marketing, sales, and customer service in combination with business back-office activities like inventory management, logistics, human resources (I refuse to call it the incredibly cold "human capital management"), and financial tasks and systems are all increasingly integrated. Are the silos gone? No, but the awareness that they are silos and detrimental to the health of the business if treated that way is greater than it has been at any time. The actual integration and alignments are in progress in many more businesses than they were just a few short years ago. For example, the alignment of sales and marketing is now *de rigueur* for many enterprises. Additionally, as I covered in Chapter 7, none of the processes that are associated with these departments are seen as agnostic any longer. They either impact the customer or are impacted by the customer. Nonetheless, so this book doesn't get out of hand, the order for the next three chapters is based on the order of the three pillars and when customers engage with each. In Chapter 11, on sales, though,

I will address the alignment of sales and marketing because of its importance to engagement. The lines are starting to blur in so many ways. As are my eyes.

But, regardless, we begin with marketing.

Several years ago, when I began examining how marketing has changed, and the set of challenges that created, I limited my look to what I thought was its transformed purpose. I saw marketing as the first line of engagement—the effort to capture the attention of the customer. That was vital, without any doubt. The first connection that the prospective customer had with the company, either in B2C or B2B transactions, was typically a result of the marketer's efforts. In a mildly smug way, I thought I nailed it when it came to marketing's relationship to customer engagement.

So much for being smug. I was nowhere near right. I was far too limited in my thinking. What became apparent, not long after my first hypothesis, was that contemporary marketing is not just the front line of engagement but continues throughout the customer lifecycle. If marketers were able to get the customer's attention at the beginning with the well-thought-out distribution of content, with the personalized attention that named-accounts needed, with the ability to make sure that the content addressed the specific personalized needs of the prospect, with the provision of content in the post-sales life of that customer to help them understand the company better and answer their questions, and, most importantly, with the creation and articulation of the corporate narrative and all other stories associated with it, then marketing's role was considerably more expansive—and important—than it had been at any time in history.

So where does it all start? Your attention, please.

THE FIRST LINE: SHOPPERS, MAY I HAVE YOUR ATTENTION PLEASE?

All of us are besieged with messages every day of the week. They can be physical (e.g., direct mail pieces, billboards, flyers, or, even more likely, digital messages available to us through everything from movies and TV to social channels such as Twitter and Facebook. They can come to us via email, banner ads on a website, Google ads, or ad placement inside a video game. But, one way or the other, they are advertising for a product, service, or possibly even a consumable experience that is designed to do one thing initially: get our attention.

But the sheer availability of the consumer channels, digital channels, and physical entities for those ads mean that we are getting bombarded by them to the tune, depending on who you believe, of several hundred to 20,000 per day.

The standard for years has been a Yankelovich study that was done in 2004, which stated we are bombarded by 3,000 brand impressions a day. Regardless of who's number you believe, every study, bar none, says that you are being blasted with so many messages per day that your mind, to protect itself, zones out all but a few that catch your attention—whether it be brief awareness or a protracted look. If you don't think that's true, or that the data is inaccurate, just take a moment and think about your own experience. In a day, how many messages do you either remember seeing or are you peripherally aware of? I doubt you can give me a number, but you probably "feel" the number is "a lot." When you get your direct mail at home, a lot less these days if you're like most people, you still don't really want to look at it; a significant amount of it gets chucked unopened. The pieces you open are bills, legal notices—(You get them too, right? No? Uh, oh.)—and perhaps a handful per week of direct mail items that may be interesting enough to look at. Being bombarded by messages is not only your experience and mine, but the experience of millions of people across the globe who are either getting burnt out by this amorphous, undifferentiated noise or zoning out to protect themselves.

This is not only the message recipient's dilemma but the marketer's dilemma in a digital era. In the past, they would simple competing for the interest of the potential customers against their competitors. Nestle's chocolate syrup competed with Hershey's chocolate syrup who competed with Yoo-hoo chocolate syrup. While this is certainly still among marketer's concerns, it is not the fundamental first task that they deal with anymore. Now, contemporary marketing professionals are competing for the attention of the consumer or business buyer against, not just competitors, but every single message that each of us gets in a day. The fundamental first task of a marketer is, "How do I capture the attention of a person long enough to see if they can be made into a viable prospect—and eventually become a lead?"

What makes this even more difficult than it would have been even if this problem existed in days long, long ago is, as I think we have established, customers have expectations of personalized responses, messages, and interactions. They will not respond as well to more generic "let's throw it out there and see what happens" kinds of marketing. I know that I fit the demographic of seniors (65+) who love the Yankees (I do) but don't live in NYC (I don't) and are Jewish (I am). But I'm also Paul Greenberg, and, given that it's a fairly common name, there may be 200 Paul Greenbergs who fit the identical demographic. As a customer, though, I don't care about the 199 others who fit that demographic. I care about me, and I expect you to know enough about me as an individual to pique my interest.

Yet, you are competing to get my attention in the midst of an unprecedented volume and velocity and density of information being thrown at me,
the customer, which doesn't change my expectations of you one bit. Even
though I am part of your target audience, I am hearing noise that might not be
specifically related to anything I am interested in all day and, thus, have a hard
time focusing on any one message specifically.

Dr. Walker Smith, the Yankelovich chief, did a good job of stating the problem and identifying the outline of the solution (broadly) in 2015, when he said:

> *Advertising clutter is the single biggest problem with marketing. Not just
> today, but as long as advertising has been around. People are annoyed by
> ads that show up in unfamiliar places, but become used to them over time.
> So marketers respond by finding even more unfamiliar places. It's cumula-
> tive and it's getting worse. Yet, consumers can process no more information
> today than they could before, and perhaps even less. Multi-tasking is just
> a fancy word for paying little attention to many more things at once. If we
> really want to do good marketing, then we have to get out of the clutter
> business and stay solidly in the communication business. It's tempting to
> try and address our challenges by adding more weight to our media buys,
> but this only raises the cost of doing advertising, and it never goes down in
> this arms race. We wind up in a place where it costs ever more to get the
> same old—and sometimes declining—response. Clutter is a fundamental
> problem for us.*

The issue of attention has garnered so much . . . attention . . . that an economic concept (I hesitate to elevate it to an economic school or theory) has
been circulating for several years identified as the "attention economy."

The attention economy's centerpiece is that attention is currency because
we have only so much of it to give and that we are subject to a lot of opportunities to give it, so we should be compensated for it. One idiotic extreme
school suggested that we substitute attention compensation for actual currency—like U.S. dollars—though I am hard pressed to figure out how to buy
food with attention. Aside from that absurdity, the concept is not terribly far
off. To capture attention, you should give the customer something they want. It
doesn't have to be monetary or even a physical "thing"—it could be emotional.
For example, one way that Adobe Digital Marketing captures attention is via
national TV commercials that are just simply funny. One of their most effective attention grabbers was a national TV commercial of a baby who is hitting
a buy button over and over via iPad on an encyclopedia website. This leads to
the fictional "Encyclopedia Atlantica" believing that they are back in business

again in a big way, and it sets a chain of events in motion—demand for more trees to produce the paper, more trucks to transport the encyclopedias, and, because of this, the lumber futures market goes crazy—all, of course, done because the baby keeps hitting the iPad buy button on their page. It's really funny. You should see it. Here is the URL (youtube.com/watch?v=N1ltwg2n-TK432T). What it does is capture your attention, and you are "paid" by the fact that it's funny and memorable and you want to talk about it.

More directly, many games available on tablets, typically those you can play for free but have in-app purchases, give away free "stuff" that benefits you in the game (e.g., gold, currency, points) if you voluntarily watch a video advertising something—often another mobile game. That's a perfect example of attention as currency.

But, keep in mind, the distraction of attention isn't limited to the mind-numbing multiplicity of messages. We are distracted by apps, we are distracted by texts, we are distracted by notifications from our mobile devices, and to make a metaphysical point, we are distracted by the way we conduct our lives in general. So, really paying attention to something truly is an increasingly scarce commodity. Getting your attention is marketing's fundamental first-level problem.

THE SECOND LINE: HOW LONG CAN YOU KEEP IT GOING?

Once you have captured the attention of the customer or prospect, there is no guarantee you will keep the attention of that person. As a marketer, your next job is to nurture them once you have them until the time you can get them placed in the sales pipeline. Historically, at that point, the marketer left the loop and sales took it from there. Not so much anymore. It's taking the full value chain of a company to be able to compete to close deals for many of the reasons stated throughout the book—foremost being the demands and the intelligence of the digital customer. Now the marketer is responsible for not only identifying and qualifying a lead, but providing content for that prospect once the lead is part of the sales pipeline. This continued effort by the marketer throughout the customer's lifecycle and the sales cycle is forcing companies to rethink the relationship between sales and marketing and to rethink the way they market. In Chapter 11, we'll address the alignment between sales and marketing. I had to put it in either this chapter or that one, and, not entirely arbitrarily, I chose to put it in the chapter on sales. In what remains, here, though, I'm going to rocket through what I think is now marketing's most important charter—telling stories, the kinds of marketing that are now more germane than ever, and what this means for the role of the CMO and the marketer.

MARKETING'S TRANSFORMATION

If you are focused on engagement, the customer journey becomes your paramount way of identifying, understanding, and reaching customers. While there is the initial engagement mentioned above—providing a signal that appeals to individual customers to separate yourselves from the noise—marketing is so much more than that. Marketers are required to understand the customer from the time they begin the journey to the engagement they have with the company early on to the point that the customer becomes fully engaged or even disengaged. It means that, in effect, a marketer's job is to provide personalized attention to each of the potentially millions of customers in the commonwealth of self-interest that makes up the 21st century customer's "institution of record and engagement." In the past, pushing sharp and demographically targeted messages via campaigns, and then understanding and tweaking the results, was the primary duty of the marketer. The Chief Marketing Officer (CMO) owned the strategy and execution of that marketing plan.

But things changed dramatically when customers were not only able to demand more and leverage their control of the conversations about the brand, but were also able to research vendors online, learn about the real-world experience others had with those brands, and get information that in the past was available to the brand only. The world had come a long way from when, to get information, you clipped a coupon in a magazine and sent it in or had to wait for the company you were interested in to tell you about themselves. Now, with peer reviews and opinions available online, our insatiable appetite to find and consume information, and tools that make it a nearly, though not totally, frictionless process, marketing has been transformed to something much bigger, more expansive, more immediate, and more important than at any time in its history.

What does this mean for marketing itself? There are so many approaches to marketing that are available as either reasonable extensions of traditional marketing, complete faux panaceas, or actual marketing methodologies and practical techniques that meet the requirements for modern marketers to succeed. How do you choose?

I'm suggesting two forms of marketing that I think are more than panaceas, more than fads, and are significant, practical ways of addressing the real-time needs of a digital customer. This is by no means anywhere near a total marketing strategy, as cutting-edge as these two marketing practices are. This is a representative sampler of two of the most interesting and applicable marketing practices that are also gaining mainstream acceptance. They are paradigm approaches for fostering engagement.

Two Practices: (1) Account-Based Marketing (ABM)

Account Based Marketing (ABM) is the product of an age of individualization and personalization. Its rapid adoption is arguably the most significant trend in marketing per se, at least in the last two or three years. My great friend, Laura Kratchnova, CEO of ScratchMM, did some research on ABM's adoption and found that, as of this year, 37 percent of the companies that she surveyed had adopted ABM already, and another 33 percent were either launching or considering it. SiriusDecisions, in their 2016 report, "State of Account Based Marketing," found that marketing departments were targeting between 11 percent and 30 percent of their total budgets to ABM. This is up from a high of 19 percent the year before.

ABM's appeal lies in its effectiveness in B2B efforts. Rather than mass marketing, it relies on focusing time, effort, and insight into designing approaches and campaigns personalized to named accounts.

To be fair, it's not a shiny, new concept. The forerunner of ABM was the work done by the incredible Don Peppers and Martha Rogers in 1993, when they pioneered a complete customer-centered one-to-one marketing worldview and methodology in their seminal work, "The One-to-One Future." Over the last couple of decades, similar approaches to marketing, including Targeted Account Marketing, have been dabbled with. But what didn't exist until now is the demand from the customer that drives the adoption. The customers in the last several decades weren't as brand savvy or content-consuming as the contemporary customer is, nor did they have the information available to them or the social leverage they have now. ABM adoption grew from customer pressure, not sales pressure.

ABM typically works this way:

1. Identify the accounts via the data that you have and the markets that you are in or want to be in.

2. Align the sales and marketing teams (remember, Chapter 11) so that they agree on definitions, objectives, rules of engagement, process flow, and accountability.

3. Map the accounts. Who are the decision makers? Who are the influencers? What are the challenges that the named accounts each have?

4. Create specific personalized content for each account. Make it relevant and note that potentially it could be in real time.

5. Identify the channels that you will use to communicate with the named accounts.

6. Launch marketing campaigns in conjunction with sales.

7. Evaluate the results—often using analytics to help get some insight. Learn from successes and failures.

8. Rinse and repeat.

As straightforward is it sounds, ABM has significant challenges, with the biggest one being what is probably obvious: how do you deliver a personalized engagement for each of your named accounts?

That said, if you master ABM, you can get some impressive results. In the ScratchMM study, they used an anonymous case study—presumably their client—a hundred-employee B2B software company that sells "virtual desktop management software to mid-market and enterprise." The results were impressive:

- Average deal size went up from $18,000 to more than $50,000, a 178 percent increase.

- Average sales development rep (SDR)—inbound sales—generated 200 percent more pipeline, to $900,000 per month (up from $300,000 per month).

- Opportunity conversion went from 18 percent to 22 percent.

On the larger stage, ITSMA, the organization that claims to have pioneered ABM in 2004, found that 85 percent of the marketers they've surveyed feel that ABM gives them the greatest return of any marketing discipline.

Two Practices: (2) Content Marketing

The Content Marketing Institute's (yes, it has its own institute) definition of content marketing is very good. It is as follows:

> *Content marketing is a strategic marketing approach focused on creating and distributing valuable, relevant, and consistent content to attract and retain a clearly defined audience—and, ultimately, to drive profitable customer action.*

Content marketing is based on providing, not necessarily pushing, (e.g., self-service) the appropriate content to a specific audience, which could be a segment or an individual, in the way that the audience wants to receive it. It can be exceptionally valuable when it is focused around providing active opportunities with relevant content to whatever stage of the process they may be in. In the well-regarded "B2B Buyers Landscape Report" from DemandGen, two things stood out. First, 90 percent of the respondents said that the provision of relevant content was the fourth most prevalent reason that B2B buyers chose the winning vendor. Equally as important, it showed the single most important thing that a buyer-to-be is looking for on a vendor website is relevant content—69 percent. There is a resemblance in the B2C world to the latter, since the individual customer is looking to see if the content they need to make buying decisions is available on the vendor's site. The one dilemma that content marketers have is to be able to handle the individual needs of the customers who are looking for the relevant content, which can be a real-time need. The corollary issue is that, while they can provide the documents, video, podcasts, etc., that the customer might need, what kind of return for the vendor can be projected? Technologies that are coming onto the market now can handle highly personalized content such as Pitney Bowe's EngageOne personalized video solution (pitneybowes.com/us/customer-engagement-marketing/personalized-media/engageone-video-personalized-video.html) and measure the return on investment of content creation, distribution, and consumption, Captora's Advanced Personalization tool being a prime example of one that works (captora.com/advanced-personalization/).

Clearly, content marketing overlaps to some extent with ABM. Both are concerned with getting relevant, timely content to customers. But, when you need to do it at scale, it can be daunting. Plus, while you may be dealing with millions of customers simultaneously, each of them is demanding something slightly different.

American Express is always dealing at scale. Over the past several years, in my analyst guise, I've met with their varying representatives when they are typically the customers of a tech company. They are among the masters at providing personalized content. Two examples:

(1) In 2015, I met with an Amex representative who oversaw optimizing a customer's experience on their consumer card websites. She explained that they were constantly using Adobe A/B testing tools to optimize the content provided to each customer that crossed their websites' paths. Based on the customer's journey, which they were monitoring and continuously testing, the content that would appear to each customer on the site landing page would constantly change. If the customer was looking for a card, and they were also spending a lot of time on an American Express travel site, then the order of the content that appeared on the landing page was different than if a person had been looking over consumer goods of some kind. This was done with continuous testing and ongoing optimization and real-time change in the look and order of the content provided.

(2) American Express partnered with the Global Business Travel Association to do a market-research report on the satisfaction of business

travelers. If this were the 20th century, the report would have been done and it would be made available to whoever American Express wanted it made available to. But in the world of massive information consumption, that wasn't sufficient. Instead, of just treating the research as an isolated one-off report, they created a content hub that had the original research, further new research, a blog, infographics, presentations—either original videos or videos of events and listicles. (No, they are not like popsicles. They are "the top ten . . . blah, blah, blah." You know. Those little lists we all love to see, argue about, debate endlessly as to why our top ten is better than that top ten, and then claim that they are bogus. Those listicles.) This was a thought leadership effort, pure and simple. The objective was to educate B2B companies' suppliers on how to handle expense management and what technologies and tools were available to do that. The results were outstanding. They had a reach of 100 million publications and a 100 percent higher engagement rate on LinkedIn than their benchmark. They are a go-to when it comes to knowledge about expense management, thus increasing both mindshare as a go-to and their role as a "trusted adviser" to businesses on expense management—increasing faith in the company and thus in their products.

Many other kinds of marketing have emerged (e.g., influencer marketing, relationship marketing, and data-driven marketing, which is not the same as data marketing). The traditional marketing approaches, like product marketing, and basics, like campaign management, are never going to decline. But the demands on marketers are white-hot now and only going to increase in intensity since they are almost required to operate in real time to meet customers' greedy needs. Luckily, the marketing technology exists to handle scale and speed. But even more importantly, marketers recognize that things have to change—and change quickly—to meet market needs head on.

The Chief Marketing Officer (CMO) is becoming a different beast.

THE NEW CMO

The CMO at a customer-engaged company holds a pivotal role. The responsibilities of this executive go well beyond the traditional marketing-strategy role. They are now responsible for a significant part of all customer-facing activities—directly in the case of some, and as the key "liaison" in the case of others. For example, the alignment of sales and marketing, which I'll address at the end of the chapter, is a perfect example of "liaison."

The results of this reconfiguration of the CMO's role are that the CMO now has more responsibilities than he or she had traditionally and is also under a great deal of pressure to succeed quickly—and, not so parenthetically, take some responsibility for the revenue of the company.

In many cases, the additional responsibility is more along the lines of technology budget management and technology selection. This is not a small responsibility. The industry has gone from less than 150 identified marketing technology solutions in 2011 to 6,829 (!) marketing technology solutions identified in the now iconic Marketing Technology Landscape SuperGraphic released every year by Martech thought leader Scott Brinker. What makes this so important is that if, minimally, you are planning on scaling and analyzing results, this technology is necessary, so the choices you make need to be wise. If you are going to interact in real time with the selected customers who's journey you are tracking, then choosing the right MarTech is the same as choosing the right CRM system (which would incorporate MarTech), or the right ecommerce system to track sales and transactions, among many other things.

But many of the largest enterprise are taking the CMO's changed role even further. Some are extending the role (Citi Group put all its consumer businesses under a single CMO); some are merging roles (Mars integrated the CMO and Chief Customer Officer into a single role as CMO); and some are getting rid of the CMO (J. Crew, which has been a troubled brand as of late, eliminated the position and put it under the COO). Coca Cola got rid of the title CMO and gave an expanded portfolio to a person with the title of Corporate Growth Officer, which includes marketing. This neo-CMO is at the leading edge of a pivotal change in the marketing world.

Marketing is still marketing—meaning it's the way strangers and now customers are engaged, both individually and en masse. It is broad and encompassing, but the basics never change. CMOs run campaigns, which are efforts to impact someone or some group over time with your message and, more importantly, make them aware of your story. What makes this role increasingly important is that, for the business to succeed, nothing is more important, and, let me repeat, *nothing is more important,* than a story—a corporate narrative—and marketing is not only the story's craftsperson but the chief storyteller.

THE OVERARCHING REQUIREMENT: STORYTELLING

No matter what the mission and vision, the messages, the campaigns that a marketer is responsible for, they have one overarching requirement: they are responsible for creating and telling the corporate narrative and the other stories associated with that narrative, be they human and lifestyle-related or departmental or persona-based. This is the fundamental task of an organization that is trying to impact a market or engage its customers.

I could talk all day about the marketing funnel (which I will not do since this is a book about customer engagement, not marketing tradition) and about click throughs, ad spend, and A/B testing; but marketing's primary focus should be to create a picture that reflects the personality, the story, of a company. The purpose of marketing is also the same as successful customer engagement—it supports the creation of an ongoing bond of trust between the customer and the company. To do that, the customer has to trust the company's processes, their products and services, the experiences, and interactions that they have with the company, the people they meet from the company, the promises the company makes, and, actually encompassing all of this, the story that the company tells. They also should be able to not just trust that the story is what it is, but that they can see themselves as part of that story.

What makes Marc Benioff, CEO of Salesforce, both the ideal visionary and arguably the best C-level marketing person at any company, is not just that he can present a vision of what the company wants to be, but that he can get people to buy into that vision, including his customers, prospects and employees, and he takes the actions necessary to establish the truth of that story.

Our marketing guru, Alan Berkson, will talk to you about the elements of the corporate narrative, but I want to speak to why storytelling is important in the first place.

Human beings have been telling stories to each other for more than 20,000 years. What makes stories so wonderful is that they evoke an emotional (and corresponding physiological) reaction in the people telling them and hearing them—one that can lead to the person hearing them gaining an insight or making an association that allows them to understand what it is that you are trying to tell them. Sometimes it's a verbal thing; other times its best expressed visually. For example, several years ago, a senior executive I know was reviewing another software company's technology at my request. I told him, prior to his meeting with the them, that they would be unable to explain what the technology does, so he would have to tell them, "I don't have a clue what you're talking about, just show me." That is exactly what happened and exactly what he did and the result was he nailed their purpose by "seeing" their story. The result was a strategic partnership with the company my executive friend represented—and it has resulted in significant revenue for both companies.

What makes a business story viable is the ability of the customer or viewer/reader to connect to it in a personal way. The story can be in print, digital, or actual; it can be video, audio, or any other medium that works. Some of the most emotionally engaging stories are videos. But, no matter what medium, there are certain characteristics that govern its success at engaging customers.

CHARACTERISTICS OF A BUSINESS STORY

It is emotional—The story evokes something in the person hearing or seeing it that makes them feel good in some way, perhaps via humor or a cute animal or even something that has a great outcome, or a passion, that they share.

It is believable—The customer can relate to it in some way. The story should be told in the voice of the company or the people telling it. That way, the story is authentic. Customers will feel that it is a tale that adds value to *their* life—not life in general.

Its purpose, lessons, and outcomes are satisfying—Unless there is a deliberate reason to be counterintuitive, it has an ending that is what the person hearing, reading, or seeing it expects it to have and still manages to reflect the sentiment and the message that the company wants it to.

It is consistent—The look, the feel, the emotional DNA of the story is corroborated by what the company says and does in its everyday life. If the company makes a big deal of its corporate social responsibility, it needs to show that it contributes to worthy causes in a regular manner, watches its carbon footprint, works to have a sustainable business, promotes equal pay to all, and/or other things that are so culturally embedded the story isn't seen as a marketing message but instead reflects who that company is.

It is actionable—That means not only can the audience identify with the story being told, but the story moves them to action beyond merely identifying with it.

For example, Ideo, perhaps the world's preeminent creative experience design agency, tells the story of their work with the Chicago Fire, a Major League Soccer (MLS) team that needed to fill seats in a town of passionate fans who were committed to the Cubs, White Sox, Bears, Bulls, and Blackhawks. (I hope you know what sports they represent. Really? Okay, in order, baseball, baseball, football, basketball, and hockey.) The Chicago Fire had been working with generic messages such as "Chicago on Fire," which appealed to no one by trying to appeal to everyone. Ideo built a storyboard that was based on a specific group of highly passionate fans who attended all Fire games and never sat for one second during the games, cheering on their favorites. At first, once they had the apparently reluctant buy-in of the Fire, they extracted the qualities of these passionate fans. They

Are authentic—transparent and open

Are gritty—unpolished (something like the satiric version on Saturday Night Live of "Da Bears" fans)

Have pride—proud of Chicago. Having lived there for 22 years, I can attest to the real pride that the residents of the city took in being a Chicagoan.

Are globally curious—interested in the sport, the players, the city they lived in, etc.

Have an indie attitude—with a chip on their shoulder, in a nice way.

Are irreverent—funny, sense of humor, playful

This led to a much more personalized kind of approach, including slogans like "Don't Stop Living in the Red," "Where's Your Soul At?" etc., and funky merchandise with pictures of amped-up players. In other words, the story of the Fire became not a generic "fired up" one, but one of passion and commitment and grit. In one year, attendance rose 21 percent due to the story that the Fire told—one that reflected the qualities of those passionate fans. As I call it, the Chicago Fire went from another MLS team to become "a company like me" that fans could identify with.

In fact, storytelling is not just an art but also a science that has been distilled down to a sequential series of steps that have been around since Aristotle. It's called Freytag's Pyramid, a colorful name for a story's dramatic structure. It pretty much boils down to the following sequence:

1. **Exposition**—The introduction of the story: setting, characters, back stories, plot lines, etc.

2. **Complication**—Rising actions that lead to the key elements of the plot. These are the parts of the story that carry throughout. This is the most important part.

3. **Climax**—A turning point for the main character(s). If things were good, they go bad; if they were bad, they go good (so to speak).

4. **Reversal**—The moments/actions that lead to where everything but the final resolution is done.

5. **Denouement**—Final conflicts are resolved in a cathartic release, or maybe something less than that, but release nonetheless.

You might be cringing right now with the formality of the structure, but that storytelling arc is the one that most novels, movies, TV shows, and commercials with a story (e.g., Super Bowl commercials with the Clydesdale horses and puppies) use if they are successful. For example, Adobe used the humor with that baby hitting the buy (encyclopedia) button to great success. Break it down using Freytag's Pyramid:

1. **Exposition**—*Encyclopedia Atlantica*, a failing print encyclopedia company, starts getting an unaccountably large number of orders.

2. **Complication**—The CEO of the company issues instructions to buy more paper, which drives the wood market, which drives the futures market.

3. **Climax**—The production of the encyclopedia requires more trucks to deliver them to the customers, but . . . oops!

4. **Reversal**—It turns out it's a baby hitting an *Encyclopedia Atlantica* "buy" button repeatedly on their website, but of course they had no idea it was this.

5. **Denouement**—Buy Adobe Digital Marketing so you can find out who is actually buying. That's how you solve this. Release.

Am I advocating for the use of Freytag's Pyramid in your marketing efforts? No, but it is a helpful structure that can provide you with a framework for how you can go about constructing the videos you do, the collateral you produce, and the commercials you write. But even simple stories can work.

Case Studies, Data, Use Cases: Furthering the Narrative

As you probably noticed, I'm a conversational writer. I like to tell stories and corroborate my suppositions by providing data to back it up. Additionally, though I haven't done much of this here, I am a fan of identifying the use cases (more on this in Chapter 11) that support an approach to doing something. But if you put all of these things into a bigger picture—the use of case studies, use cases, and data—all of them support one thing: furthering a narrative. Ultimately, everything we do in business, from marketing to sales to customer service to any other form of communication or conversation that goes on between a company and a customer, is a means to develop, sustain, support, and further a story that each party in the conversation is comfortable with, allowing them to continue the interaction. As a customer, that means I would trust the company to show me via the case studies I receive, the use cases I read about, and the data provided, that they understand my needs as the representative of a business or as an individual interested in their products and services. But when I say "my," I literally mean my individual needs, not just the company I represent nor the demographic I am a part of. Mine. I will respond to signals that indicate that you are giving me something I value—such as a real-life example of how well something was done using this product, via a case study or an individual testimonial. Or maybe you'll show me a way that I can use what you provide in a way I hadn't thought of before. By telling me the stories I need to hear to help me decide what I need to do, you are showing me that you value me.

For example, an iconic product marketing video done in 2011 by Corning Glass called "Corning: A Day Made of Glass" (youtube.com/watch?v=6C-f7IL_eZ38&t=25s) has had more than 26 million views. What makes this so special is that it tells a story that anyone watching can relate to. It is the story of a family, from the time that they wake up in the morning and do their daily work and routines, to the time they go home in the evening and eventually go to sleep, showing how they use glass of varying kinds throughout the day. The genius of this video is that not a word spoken the entire time. The only sign of "advertising" is that each kind of glass used is identified with its name and a tag line (e.g., "Photovoltaic Glass: High Efficiency, Optically Versatile, Durable"), which flashes onscreen for a few seconds as photovoltaic glass is used to show the wakeup time on a glass wall panel and provide menus to carry out other actions. This goes on for five plus minutes set in a near future that we didn't have in 2011 and now have parts of but is still aspirational.

Again, not a word spoken. Yet it reaches each of us because we can see that the life depicted, while not ours or anyone's outside a lab or Epcot Center's right now, is a life that we can have in a few years—with the implication, of course, that Corning will provide it.

Okay, I'm done with what I need to say about marketing. To make it clear that storytelling is more than just messaging, though, I've brought in one of the world's leading story craftsmen—Alan Berkson.

THOUGHT LEADER: ALAN BERKSON

I've known Alan for years. I met him at the Pivot Conference several years ago. I realized I was speaking to not only a warm, good human being, but a master story creator. At the time, he was a partner in a business that designed corporate narratives primarily for enterprises. His methodology blew me away. Since then, he has gone on to work for CRM technology vendor Freshdesk as their Global Director of Community Outreach.

I had him write a guest post on the corporate narrative for my ZDNet blog "Social CRM: The Conversation," which I have been writing for around a decade. It became the most popular guest post in the blog's history.

So, we're lucky to have him with us today, aren't we? You know we are.

What's the story, Alan?

. . . . .

The old world of broadcast advertising is gone. We now skip through commercials on DVRs and online videos, or suffer through them, grudgingly. We have moved from a world where storytelling was the domain of elite practitioners to a world where *every individual is a storyteller.*

A brand's corporate narrative is no longer just the stories they tell about themselves. The days of brand campaigns and interrupt-driven messaging have been replaced by a pervasive communications environment with a sea of voices. Consumers are no longer, well, just consumers. They are creators and participators who now have the power to add to a brand's corporate narrative, with voices as loud and powerful as any other.

Digital and social media have given power to consumers to be part of the conversation, often bypassing brands completely in their "buyer's journey." From a Yelp review, to a tweet, to a YouTube fan video, consumers have been empowered to express themselves and have an impact on how others see a brand.

TRANSPARENCY, WHETHER YOU LIKE IT OR NOT

Corporate narrative, today, is more than just the stories we tell as companies, as marketers, or as advertisers. To be successful, you must distill what is both unique and universal about your products or services into a *brand essence,* a framework that goes beyond simple mission and vision statements. This essence must pass muster by *all* your brand stakeholders. Your employees, customers, partners, investors—all parties who have a vested interest in your brand—need a clear understanding of not only your vision, ethos, and founding principles, but also the messages and aspirational drivers behind each specific brand. It behooves everyone to see that this essence is accurately reflected, both in your products and in the actions your company takes. If your *company* is communicating messages that are different from what your *brand* is communicating, you will generate cognitive dissonance both within the company and within your consumer base. The result can be confusion, indifference, or even active antagonism.

How do you navigate this new messaging landscape?

Digital and traditional distribution platforms can be leveraged in concert to build relationships with mass audiences and grow a brand. In the age of pervasive communications, the most important driver of brand awareness across multiple media platforms is **story**.

Story, and the sharing of story, is now the most powerful activator of consumer behavior.

ELEMENTS OF CORPORATE NARRATIVE

Corporate narrative is not just for the marketing department. It requires buy-in from all divisions of your organization, with your company message infused in everything from product development to customer service. A deep and engaging narrative must be developed that connects your employees to your message because their actions will convey the message you want your customers to receive.

Corporate narrative is about listening. You need to put in place the right tools and processes to hear and understand the consumer. Through listening you can innovate mechanisms to help weave the consumer into your narrative, and validate and celebrate participation in your brand. Listening with care and authenticity also supports the placement of rapid-response frameworks to identify opportunities and quickly react to events that impact your brand.

Corporate narrative is not about playing solo, but more like conducting the orchestra. The digital landscape is complex and each channel has unique traits and features. It is critical to understand the distinctions between media platforms, so that the message can be modified and customized to leverage the medium and maximize engagement.

If the old corporative narrative was *read-only*, the new corporate narrative is decidedly *read-write*. We are moving from a messaging economy based on time (the classic advertising model) to one based on attention. To get your message through the cacophony of voices and distractions consumers face daily, you need to fortify your brand with the following elements of a strong corporate narrative:

Focus on your brand essence—What is unique and universal about your product? How does it appeal to the customer's personal aspirations? What message does it have to give to the world? The pace and tempo of digital media requires brands to empower all stakeholders for swift and improvisational response. The most successful brands will be the ones whose team members best understand the core of their brand and then best communicate it. It also provides a framework for your stakeholders to maintain a dialog around the brand, even under adverse conditions.

Build a culture of listening—In a world of broadcasters, if all you do is broadcast, you are setting yourself up for failure. Listen, acknowledge, validate, and celebrate participation by *all* your stakeholders, including your customers and potential customers. This is how you earn attention and break through the noise. It's also how you inoculate your brand against potentially toxic events or news. That's when you need an army of advocates by your side.

Lead the narrative—You may not be the only voice in your corporate or brand narrative, but you are still an important one. Find ways to add your voice in concert with others, and conduct your narrative across multiple channels, platforms, and touch points. The result will be an immersive, orchestral wave of storytelling, some of which will be yours, but most of which will be your happy customers.'

. . . . .

Thanks, Alan.

So, marketing is storytelling, content and signal separated from noise. The CMO has to be alert to translating all that into actions for the marketing team and the company in order to impact the markets that the company plays in. But even marketing is there to drive demand and thus opportunity and thus sales—and it is only part of the customer-engagement story. How important is it that it plays nice with sales? What does that mean for demand-generation in a digital age? How much interest do the sales and marketing departments have in working with each other? Why can't we all just get along? Let's find out if they (and we) can.

CHAPTER II

Sales Gets Personal

J ust to be clear, this isn't a chapter on the sales process or how to generate leads or anything like that. How sales people sell, not the process that defines sales, is undergoing change. I'm going to show you what that change is and how sales departments are impacted by customer-engagement strategies, programs, and transformed customer demands.

Sales people may be the most besieged "species" on the planet. Their job puts them under immediate pressures. They have to sell regardless of changing economic climate, public perception, or need for their particular products or services. They are under pressure to not just meet quotas, but meet them by hard-and-fast deadlines. According to CSO Insights, in 2014, only 58 percent of them made their quotas, giving them what probably feels like a tenuous hold on their employment. In fact, according to the Sales Readiness Group, also in 2014, the average lifespan of a salesperson on the job was less than 2 years, and for a sales manager it was 19 months. Because their compensation is tied to performance more than most other jobs, and their job tenure is so short, they are continually concerned about their ability to take care of their families over the long term. Thus, they are paranoid about their jobs, not just because they are held accountable, but because failure is met often with extreme measures—no, not *that* extreme, for Pete's sakes. But they often are let go. One tech company in the early part of the 2000s was notorious (it could have been urban legend, but, knowing the reputation of the company, I doubt it) for firing the bottom 10 percent of performers every quarter, regardless of reason—even if surgery was what kept one out of action for the quarter. Whether true or not, this story getting any credence at all shows that it was considered possible and, thus, shows what kind of pressures salespeople are under.

These stresses created early-adoption problems for Sales Force Automation (SFA) systems, which were supposed to help salespeople do their job. A pressured salesperson felt the need to always be out there selling; doing the tasks that weren't "selling" (e.g., entering data into systems related to the opportunities that they had open, accounts they were working and managing) seemed to be, at best, a distraction. More ominously, it was perceived as a threat because the use of SFA required salespeople to expose their pipeline information to their managers, making them even more paranoid, since many salespeople thought (and many still do think) that their leverage with the company was their "personal" network of clients. Thus, they protected that network from their managers and other salespeople as if it were the crown jewels and their managers and the other sales reps were jewel thieves. SFA systems exposed that network, taking away the protection, and thus made salespeople even more paranoid and resistant to adoption.

But the times they are a-changin'. Now SFA systems are standard operating procedure at the bulk of enterprises, with just south of 70 percent adoption depending on whose studies you believe. They are part of how a salesperson runs their day, and, because they are now cloud-based systems and have strong mobile footprints, the time-suck they were in the past is a lot less the case since the data can be entered on the go. So, that part of the job is less stressful.

In fact, the adoption rates and acceptance of the "need to have" status of sales force automation is at an all-time high. In late 2017, Cite Research, commissioned by SugarCRM, did a study of 400 sales executives, which found that a "CRM system" (by which, I presume, they mean, as do most people, a sales force automation system) is the most used and most valuable tool for the sales team. Seventy percent of respondents said their sales teams used CRM systems—that's more than any other technology tool. The most telling number, though, was that 92 percent said the CRM system is extremely or somewhat valuable to increasing the effectiveness of their sales teams. That is a staggering increase over the last decade.

But the sales team requires a lot more of a village than it did in the past to close a deal. This is partially because, as we examined in Chapter 10, it takes so much more to just get and then hold the attention of a prospect than it did in the past, and partially because the demands of a customer-to-be or existing customer are so much greater and more variegated than before. All of this makes it harder for the salesperson to go it alone any more. On the one hand, this means greater internal cooperation with other customer-facing departments like marketing is necessary. On the other hand, collaboration helps meet that much more complex set of customer demands. Collaboration requires that others have access to the pipelines of individual salespeople. Ultimately, while there is almost always a lead salesperson responsible for, if not initiating engagement, then at least maintaining engagement and interaction and turning an opportunity into a sale and a transaction, the collaboration between the sales department and the marketing department—and internal collaboration among the sales professionals—tends to lead to better results than the go-it-alone approach of the past.

HERE'S HOW . . . THOROUGHLY MODERN SALES

Unlike in the past, when they operated almost at cross purposes—at least one would think that they did if you talked to sales and marketing people then—it is now very hard to separate sales and marketing efforts from one another. It's not that they are getting indistinct from each other—each has its own raison d'etre—but the need to align them in a 21st century business environment is not only important but becoming paramount.

In the past, they had different objectives, different outlooks. Sales focused on the short term, with marketing looking at the longer term. They operated at different cadences—slow for marketing, fast for sales. But that led to them often being at odds with each other, and that led to distrust between the two departments. They were a dysfunctional couple who were required to work together and were often unable to do so.

Was that universally the result? No. Was it commonly the result? Yes.

A lot of that outcome rested on the distrust of marketing. I couldn't really say what I'm about to in the previous chapter since that was the marketing chapter, and I couldn't very well diss them in their own chapter, could I? But we're in the sales chapter now, so I can speak more freely about what sales departments and CEOs really think about marketing. CEOs have had a hard time trusting marketing. The Fournaise Group did a study in 2012, which found that 80 percent of the CEOs who responded didn't trust marketing due to what they saw as marketing's disconnection from financial reality. That severe disrespect is oddly corroborated by 76 percent of the marketers who responded to a Forrester Research study in 2013, who felt that, if they could track ROI, they would gain greater respect. Of course, that's what *they* think, not what the CEOs think. So. . .

Wait. We are here to talk about sales, not to diss marketing. How do we establish a sales team that understands that their likelihood of closing a business deal is greater if you have higher degrees of customer engagement? What is it they have to think about and do to make that happen?

For this to happen, the salesperson must accept that it is now a buyer's world, which is just sales-speak for the fact that we now live in a world in which the customer controls the conversation. Barry Trailer, who is one of the foremost sales thought leaders in the world (and who you will hear from at the end of this chapter), set forth the state of the relationship between buyer and seller in 2013 when he said:

> *It's well known that buyers have taken on a greater role in educating themselves about possible solutions to their various needs; they have in turn relied less on a rep's product knowledge and have instead increased their demand for reps understanding the buyers' industry, their organization, and their business challenges.*

This is a significant reorganization of the relationship. In the past, buyers relied on the sellers for information about whatever it was they were interested in buying, and customer references were often the needed "third-party" validation. Of course, those references were handpicked by the seller more often than not. Now, as we saw with the data on how buyers do research and who they trust back in Chapter 6, the shoe is on the other foot. The buyer controls the journey. And they can find a review of the shoe, regardless of what foot it's on.

However, if handled well, this is a huge opportunity for the sales person. If it's true that the bulk of the research is done by the time the buyer contacts the seller, which means that the seller has been identified by that potential buyer as a legitimate candidate for the purchase and, thus, the potential buyer is almost qualifying themselves as a legitimate lead. But if you are looking to be the deal winner, as a salesperson, you need to engage the prospect—and that takes a different kind of sales person in this part of the 21st century.

What makes selling so much more difficult now is not just battling with other sales people at competitive companies, but, as discussed in Chapter 10, competition for attention. Plus, the buyers are far more savvy, whether buying for their business or buying for themselves, than they have ever been. Additionally, self-service via ecommerce and the web eliminates the direct interaction with the salesperson when an individual consumer is buying directly, and that works even in the B2B environment to some degree. Amazon Business, which is the B2B ecommerce arm of Amazon and has almost the same interfaces and user navigation as the consumer side, did more than a billion dollars' worth of business as of 2016, a year after it launched, and has grown to $10 billion as of 2018—eliminating the salesperson in a B2B sales environment.

Combine this with the increased demands of the customers, the ability of that customer to get the data and the opinions that he or she needs to make a decision, and it becomes imperative that the contemporary sales person change how he or she sells, as well as what they attempt to do and be. They must look at the entire lead-to-money opportunity in a different light and use the resources available to them to do just that.

A contemporary salesperson, in an era of customer engagement, cannot be just a product pusher any longer. Selling to the customer is no longer a matter of just having either the best product or the best sales patter, either. It is no longer a matter of having rich features and functions or even just a great price. It's a matter of having knowledge and understanding, and building the relationships with individuals at the buyer's business who are going to be involved with you as a partner. Thinking about the customer or prospect now is thinking about the subject of a partnership, not the object of a sale.

In order to start meeting these requirements, a 21st century sales person needs to

- Be outcomes-based
- Accept that you are going to be a point of contact even post-sale
- Be a subject-matter expert
- Use contemporary technologies for insight
- Make sure that sales enablement is a functional piece of the sales department
- Be aligned with marketing

Thoroughly Modern: Outcomes-Based

When it boils down to it, the customer doesn't care about whether your product is a good product or has a plethora of uses for a lot of different kinds of companies. What he or she cares about is how does it help their company and, equally if not more importantly, how does it help them get the outcomes that they need to reach whatever their goals are. To illustrate the point, several years ago I was at a party with a very senior executive of a big company who made some of his company's larger buying decisions. I asked him about a software selection, since he seemed to be particularly savvy when it came to technology. I said, "If you were down to two choices, one which had a 100 percent benefit to the company and none to you and the other which was 80 percent beneficial to the company but had some benefit to you, which would you take?" His answer, with literally no hesitation was, "The second one." When I asked why, he said, "It has some benefit to me." This isn't terribly surprising. Like all other human beings, your customers or prospects need to see how the products and services you provide are going to help them achieve the outcomes that are relevant to them. To that end, one of the smartest efforts at product marketing I've ever seen was done in its earlier days by the sales optimization business software company Lattice Engines. Their customer testimonials weren't just about how the software benefited their customer companies, but instead were testimonials from individuals on how they got promoted because of their success with Lattice Engines. The sales approach means show the customer how it gets the outcomes that benefit the business *and* the individual buyer.

The value of outcomes-based selling goes to the heart of self-interest. I want to know what it is you can enable that gets me to these places I need to be so that I can achieve my goal and thereby benefit the company I work for. But it's not just the sales and/or marketing people selling enablement—it's also product design teams working to create a product that helps achieve the outcome. It's the approach that service design people call "value in use." The oldest cliché around it is that you aren't looking to purchase a screwdriver; you are looking to purchase something that can help you put together a cabinet. Think about it, though. If that is the case, the desired outcome might need one kind of screwdriver; but if you are tightening a computer motherboard screw, it might need an Allen wrench instead of a screwdriver. Each of them supports an outcome that has a different result and different approach—and the sales team and the product development teams should know what that projected outcome is supposed to be to create the appropriate products or provide the appropriate services that will solve the problem or enable the outcome, i.e., do the job.

Thoroughly Modern: Point of Contact

This isn't really a product of contemporary thinking of any kind. In the past, when a big business deal was sold, and something went south, the person who was called by the customer was the salesperson who sold the deal. One of the reasons, as pointed out in the book *Strategic Customer Service* by John A. Goodman (Amacom, 2009), is that the salesperson historically hands the customer his card and says, "Call me if you have a problem," which is not really the job of the salesperson. Either way, the customer perceives the salesperson to be the point of contact because that is the person the customer has been most engaged with. Think of it by analogy. If you have a delivery problem with something from Amazon, you don't query the carrier, you query Amazon, who you see as the primary stakeholder in this equation. Same with the salesperson—who, now, does have to be ready to be that point of contact.

But salespeople have to sell—that's their job—and that creates a conundrum: how do they service existing customers if there is no revenue involved?

Goodman suggested assigning specific customer service agents to specific sales people and their accounts—but that was 2009. Now, at least in the tech industry, there is a somewhat more elegant solution. It is called "customer success management."

The customer success manager's job is to work with the customer accounts to make sure that their use of technology works optimally for a company. If they have any issues, the CSM becomes a go-to person for dealing with the problem, and the CSM is compensated accordingly. Their KPIs are not revenue-related at all.

CSMs work closely with sales. For reasons that are unfathomable, the only place that customer success management exists systematically is the tech world, though there is a significant amount of movement as of this writing to broaden the appeal. This makes the sales person a lot more available to do what he or she does best—selling—and leaves the heavy lifting with the customer in the hands of the CSM.

This approach fosters engagement because the customer has a permanent point of contact, making the customer's communications chain simple and straightforward. The salesperson can still be available if need be but, ultimately, they are free to sell.

Thoroughly Modern: Subject Matter Expert

As if shifting how you sell and customers expecting salespeople to be available wasn't enough, the contemporary salesperson would do well to be a highly visible subject-matter expert.

What do I mean by that? If you look at the common thread in the point of contact and the subject-matter expert, it goes to the heart of what I've already discussed in other parts of this book: the customer needs to see the company and its representatives as trusted advisers. At the same time, one of the most important competitive differentiators for a salesperson is to be a subject-matter expert—someone that the customer can go to, not just to buy from, but to learn from, perhaps about an industry or a product or a trend or something that makes the salesperson, once again, a trusted adviser. Historically, there were salespeople and then there were subject-matter experts who were not necessarily sales people—likely were not, in fact. But now, the trend is toward the salesperson being the subject-matter expert.

I'm not saying that this has to be done one-to-one. Given the proliferation of smart devices, communications channels, and publication media, it is very possible for the salesperson SME to become a public resource, whose reputation extends beyond his/her immediate client base.

This isn't as big a leap as it may seem. For a salesperson to be good at what they do, they should be subject-matter experts already. If they are selling solar panels, they are likely experts in how the solar panel's efficiency benefits the customer, or how it works, or, perhaps, what the regulations are that govern the solar panels' use in commercial buildings, etc. Distilling this expertise to thought leadership, meaning the information is provided as a service rather than as a selling point, isn't a giant leap when it comes to practical activity. It's a matter of the salesperson understanding that he or she has a new part to play, and then playing it.

This has been going on since the advent of the communications revolution early in the 21st century. As far back as 2008, Caterpillar, the farm and industry equipment manufacturer, found that they were getting a high volume of inquiries on the use of electric-power generators. Thus, that year, they created a blog on electric power generation called "Power Perspectives" that has since morphed into a blog and an online community. The early blog was written by salespeople, among others, and was so successful that it generated a three-day symposium on generator set enclosures in 2011. To be honest, I still don't know what a generator set enclosure is, but it was apparently quite a three days, with 2,000 attendees who probably did know. The results were exceptional, with the creation of solid sales leads such as a European order for the rental of 740 dump trucks.

This aligns well to the data that has been showing up the last several years. According to IDC's "2011 Buyer Experience" survey, independent blogs and communities are most valued by IT buyers, followed by vendor blogs and communities.

But blogs are just one of the channels that the sales SME can address. Of course, Twitter and Facebook are avenues for communication. LinkedIn is an increasingly popular publishing platform for business. But, to participate in these channels, the wise salesperson should know the protocols of the channels they are communicating in. Seth Godin nailed it a few years back at an insurance sales conference I happened to be speaking at when he spoke via Skype on engaging your customers.

In the case of online communities and forums, participate as an expert and member rather than a sales pusher. Provide expertise to help solve problems. Converse with prospects or customers on relevant topics. Don't push a "pitch." Consider developing a regular podcast, an internet-based radio show, to provide some useful pontification on a subject of interest to your customers.

Luckily, for the contemporary sales person, their options to communicate expertise are substantial and often fun: they can tweet, post Facebook messages, blog, do LinkedIn posts, do podcasts, produce videos, and participate in the online communities and forums. The options for creativity are endless. The salesperson has to figure out how to direct their expertise and then target both the locations and the media that their target audiences favor—and be prepared for using multiple media since, as I hope I've established, we live in an omnichannel world.

A collateral benefit of salesperson-as-SME is that they can support marketing in advising them on which content would their prospect find helpful, depending on the stage of the opportunity.

Thoroughly Modern: The Use of Sales Intelligence

Salespeople now are lucky. They have a huge range of tools available that can provide them with the kinds of information they need to gain the insights that can make or break a deal. Sales intelligence technology, such as that provided by InsideView (real-time and near-real-time company, individual, or opportunity data and information), or Lattice Engines (measuring comparative behaviors and prescriptive analytics, including best next-action advice), PROs (predictive and prescriptive pricing analytics, among other things) or even Thunderhead (tracking the customer journey) abound everywhere. What they all ultimately do is provide data and more structured information, allowing the salesperson to make a more intelligent judgment on how they are going to proceed to the next level or even take the next step with a prospective customer. They are the foundation for insights.

The benefit of using tools for sales intelligence (for example) is unmistakable. Aberdeen Group, who spends a lot of time looking at best-in-class practices for organizations, found that when it came to sales intelligence the primary drivers for its use were:

- Improving lead quantity and quality to maximize selling time (61 percent)
- Improving the sales rep's knowledge of territory, accounts, and industries "for more educated, consultative conversations" (36 percent)
- Identifying high-value prospects through trigger events (27 percent)

  (Source: Sales Intelligence: "Best-in-Class Strategies Adopted by Salesforce Data.com Customers," Aberdeen Group, July 2013)

The kind of information they get from sales intelligence, which is scanning both structured (CRM) and unstructured (social) data, can range from specific information on companies (e.g., corporate management, financial data if publicly traded, and competitor information) to executive biographies, conversations about the company or conversations by employees of the company, and industry-related knowledge that can impact an opportunity or person involved in the opportunity. This benefit becomes particularly powerful when integrated into a CRM system of record down to the level of the account or the individual. Having this on a smart device via a mobile platform makes it even more valuable since it allows the identification and use of the knowledge in real or near real time.

The other thing that sales intelligence tools, such as those offered by Introhive, can do is surface relationships in a prospect company's corporate hierarchy that can impact a deal.

Thoroughly Modern: Sales Enablement

The value of technology and intelligence is obvious, I would think. But they are just parts of a larger sales-enablement initiative to support an internal departmental transformation to a cooperative sales culture.

CSO, the organization that our guru Barry Trailer helped found, defines sales enablement as:

> *A strategic, cross-functional discipline designed to increase sales results and productivity by providing integrated content, training, and coaching services for salespeople and frontline sales managers along the entire customer's journey, powered by technology.*

I am adopting this as my official definition (always with attribution of course). Sales enablement encourages cooperation among the sales people, sales managers, channel managers, business development people, sales engineers, subject-matter experts (if they are independent), and, of course, marketing and customer service personnel. The entire idea is to provide ongoing support to the individuals who need it, in combination with highly visible objectives, successes, and failures, along with well-aligned efforts to make sure that all those concerned are in the same book if not on the same page.

Content at all stages of sales experience is an important part of the sales-enablement lifecycle. If you are new and in the midst of the onboarding process, you need the standard paperwork; but you also need the basic collateral, the pitch decks, the rules of engagement, the case studies, the price lists, and then knowledge of the sales process that the company uses. More experienced sales people need materials that support their subject-matter expertise, updates to existing content, and newer price lists, new case studies, data, and collateral on new products and services, and refresher courses to enhance their sales skills.

There are a lot of supportive technologies for this. Callidus Cloud (an SAP company as of 2017), a sales performance automation vendor out of Dublin, California, has a strong sales onboarding technology that not only covers the blocking and tackling up to and including the background checks, but, more importantly, pays attention to the organization and provision of content, both chosen by the salesperson and suggested for the salesperson. Allego provides a video sales training technology driven by a rather incredible video compression algorithm that not only handles the training videos but the processes associated with them, as well as the testing if that is part of the process—all on mobile devices. The enablement technologies out there are substantial and mature enough to be more than a nice thought—or an unfulfilled promise.

The value of sales enablement goes to the heart of "more than a village" to be successful at sales. It really is an internal sales alignment that crosses over to other departments to work. If you look at the "CSO Insights 2016 Sales Enablement Optimization Study," and put together the optimally aligned sales-enabled organization, it would look like the following, which is largely compiled from the CSO Insights report.

- It would have a formal sales enablement charter that covers vision, services, road-map, and success metrics—only 15.3 percent of the organizations CSO Insights queried had that level of organization.

- The view would be holistic, covering people, processes, technology, knowledge, and skills.

- It would change what it needs to as it is needed rather than all at once.

- Ideally, the cross-functional collaboration would extend to sales, marketing, human resources, sales operations, sales management, product management, event management, customer service, training, legal, and the executive team. Looking at the numbers, the respondents said that they were happy (more than 50 percent good enough) with the collaboration with marketing, sales management, customer service, legal, executive team, and sales operations. The others needed help.

- It would align the sales process to the customer journey and, I trust, not the other way around. That means it would track the customer journey and adjust the sales process and workflow and efforts accordingly. More than 55 percent of the companies responding said that they were doing just that, with about half having a formal process for it and, more interestingly, the other half doing the alignment dynamically.

Journey-tracking technology, with a few rare exceptions like Thunderhead, is not as advanced as the thinking reflected here. However, CSO Insights found that there was a 15 percent increase in the deal win-rate when the customer journey and sales process was aligned. That's major.

- Leveraging the knowledge of the customer journey, a formal approach to social interactions, the tools needed to communicate with the customers on the journey would be in place. Those with formal processes saw the benefits as an increased number of leads (57 percent) and then "deeper relationships with clients" (56 percent).

- Content quality would be assessed with a process that, at the same time, was organized to get the content out the door in an effective and timely way. The content itself would be appropriate to where the customer is in the journey. Data on the value of that can be found in Chapter 6.

- Training would be continuous and valuable to the enhancement of the skills and experience of the individual salesperson.

While sales enablement covers cross-functional collaboration, I want to spend a lot more time on sales and marketing alignment than any other piece because it is becoming almost mandatory for successful sales performance. To keep the customers and prospects engaged requires a close collaboration, some of which was touched on in the last chapter on marketing. But I want to drill down because of its importance.

Thoroughly Modern: Sales/Marketing Alignment

The first big step to 21st century sales success (I hate that it sounds so "salesy" when I say that) is to focus on the outcomes that are produced by what you are selling. But a larger company effort is needed to make this work well, and that's the alignment of the sales and marketing organizations. The historic disconnects that drive the dissonance between sales and marketing need to end because the value chain—the seamless end-to-end functioning of the organization—needs to be in great working order to optimize your potential to close deals. Victory in deals comes not just from the great individual salesperson, but now involves the whole company. This especially means sales and marketing working together to accomplish the financial objectives of the company—and to make the engagement with the customer as seamless as possible. I'd say frictionless, but anything that involves price and possible negotiation of terms is never going to be frictionless even in a perfect world.

The Disconnects

The complaints and the disconnects that have haunted the dysfunction between sales and marketing are commonly known. Among them are the following.

- Marketing campaigns don't take advantage of sales insights since the teams don't really talk to each other. Nor does one allow access to the data of the other in the sales and marketing automation systems, even if they share a common system of record.

- Sales people are known to rewrite marketing collateral without informing marketing that they've changed the collateral and, at times, ruining a corporate campaign initiative or two.

- Conversely, marketing will write collateral without consulting with sales to find out what they actually need to do their job.

- Definitions are very different, especially the definition of a marketing-qualified lead (MQL) or sales-qualified lead (SQL). Also, when the lead handoffs from marketing to sales should occur is often left as ad hoc and murky.

- The two departments work at different speeds and cadences, with sales taking a short, fast route and marketing thinking long-tail and slow, except for highly specific campaigns.

- Both departments are, more often than not, measured completely differently. The different KPIs and compensation plans attached accordingly tend not to make it in the interest of one department to support another.

These are just the common complaints, but they are so pervasive that, on July 4, 2013, Heinz Marketing, a very well-regarded marketing agency, humorously released a "Declaration of Independence for Modern Marketers," the underlying purpose of which was to advocate an alignment between the two departments—though it was couched in a really clever way. Here is a small excerpt from a long document.

IN UNISON, July 4, 2013.

The unanimous Declaration of Modern Sales & Marketing Professionals the World Over

When in the Course of the latest fiscal year or quarter, it becomes necessary for sales & marketing departments to dissolve the political & organizational constraints which have both connected and kept them from one another, and to assume among the powers of the earth, the new, integrated and collaborative station to which the Laws of Nature and of Nature's God entitle them, a decent respect to the opinions of mankind requires that they should declare the causes which impel them to the separation from past practices and embrace of the new reality.

Such has been the patient sufferance of these Sales & Marketing professionals; and such is now the necessity which constrains them to alter their former Systems of Operations. The history of the historic, ineffective Sales & Marketing system is a history of repeated injuries and usurpations, all having in direct object the establishment of an absolute Tyranny over these teams and objectives. To prove this, let Facts be submitted to a candid world.

It goes on to list more disconnects than I have room to cover and calls for alignment of sales and marketing. If you are interested in reading the rest, you can find it at

heinzmarketing.com/2013/07/a-declaration-of-independence-rewrite-for-modern-marketers

Sales-and-marketing alignment is on the table not just to solve disconnects or to get the CEO to trust marketers or allow sales people to make changes to collateral without approbation. It's becoming an increasingly valuable way to begin the process of capturing mindshare and converting it to market share, i.e., to translate interactions to transactions.

The Costs

But it isn't just the disconnects between the departments and the loss of efficiency that matter. Lost sales productivity and wasted marketing budgets cost companies around $1 trillion per year according to B2B Lead in their white paper "101 B2B Marketing and Sales Tips." The same white paper points out that not only do salespeople ignore 50 percent of the marketing leads they receive, but they also waste 50 percent of their time on unproductive prospecting. It makes you think, "Well if they didn't ignore 50 percent of the marketing leads, maybe those unreliable prospecting efforts wouldn't go to waste at the level they do." Regardless of how much credence you put in the specific numbers, there is a clearly a significant cost when marketing and sales are dysfunctional.

Alignment

Why wasn't this obvious from the beginning you might ask? Or maybe you might not.

It was discussed in detail for the first time as recently as 2006 when marketing thought leader, Phillip Kotler wrote a piece in the *Harvard Business*

Review called "Ending the War Between Sales and Marketing," which posited alignment between the two for the first time. But it began to gain momentum when marketing pioneers Don Peppers and Martha Rogers (they keep showing up!) wrote in 2008 what became a seminal piece entitled "Sales and Marketing: The New Power Couple." That document not only spurred the sales/marketing alignment discussion but was the foundation for several companies leading the way to that new relationship between the two. The value of the alignment was corroborated in 2011 when The Aberdeen did research on the value of the impact of successful sales and marketing alignment with the rather strangely named "Sales and Marketing Alignment: The New Power Couple." Don't ask.

Okay, you're interested. Your sales teams are ready to roll, and the marketing folks have now bought in. How do you go about it? What steps do you take?

WHAT IS TO BE DONE: RULES OF, AHEM, ENGAGEMENT

What is nice about aligning the two departments and the plans for them is that, for the most part, the participants begin talk to each other and then agree on things. Here is a list of what you have to agree on and then plan for. Sales and marketing must jointly agree on messages, definitions, measurements, and objectives. That means agreeing on:

- Metrics such as win rates, lead acceptance, opportunities conversion
- Definitions such as what constitutes a marketing-qualified lead (MQL) and a sales-qualified lead (SQL)
- The process that determines when the handoff of leads from marketing to sales happens and how it is coordinated
- How the revenue is recognized and apportioned. This one is harder for marketing to swallow, but they become accountable for revenue. The key performance indicators for each department are created accordingly.
- The processes of content creation and distribution, so sales supports marketing's global responsibilities, and marketing supports sales' need to have specific collateral appropriate to their needs. This means a process needs to be created that allows for changes, with the approvals necessary for smooth operations.

WHAT IS TO BE DONE? EXTEND THE HEADLINE

Once the agreements, definitions, and processes are in place, then practices need to change, especially in relationship to how marketing and sales sees the customer. We start from the beginning of the customer lifecycle, when their attention is captured, and we move from there to the captive audience member who becomes a lead, then we see them transform into an opportunity in the pipeline, and, then, if the deal closes, they are handed off to the customer-success team—if you have one. Marketing travels this path by providing the qualified leads and the content that the sales person needs along the journey, and that's the key.

When sales and marketing alignment is successful, they are aligned one other way—along the path of the customer's journey. To discharge their responsibilities, they need to not only understand what the customer wants but why they want it. To make it translate to what I said earlier, they need to be aware of the outcomes that the customer is looking for to tailor their efforts toward showing them how they can achieve them with the use of the products, services, experiences, and tools that the business provides. Sales needs to make the case; marketing needs to create the content that supports it. Salespeople become subject-matter experts; marketing supplies what the sales people need to make their case. Both are following the customer's journey, not just touch-points here and there. That allows them to personalize the relationships they are developing via either thought leadership or direct interaction. The net effect is that sales knows the company they are courting and the people they need to know and the industry they are dealing with. They become relevant to the prospects. Christine Crandall, a thought leader in the space, said it well in a 2014 *Forbes* article:

> ...relevance is a table stake across the entire lifecycle of a seller-buyer relationship, not just when you are making the sale or answering a customer service question.

Results

What makes marketing and sales alignment so powerful is that the value of the effort is verifiable. In 2011, the Aberdeen Group's "The New Power Couple" paper on alignment identified the best practices of best-in-class companies and the value derived from those practices.

- 91 percent of marketers at best-in-class companies understood sales goals.
- 73 percent of salespeople understood marketing goals.
- They experienced a 67 percent better probability that marketing-qualified leads would close.

- Marketing-qualified leads made a 209 percent "stronger" contribution to revenue.

- One very striking data point: 40 percent of the sales pipeline forecast was generated by marketing.

- There was 31.6 percent year-over-year growth by best-in-class companies, where average companies had 22 percent and below-average laggards had 18.2 percent growth.

Aberdeen found significant benefit in aligning sales and marketing. Even with this data, there are always naysayers who are skeptical of value. One of the constant questions, aka repetitious litanies, that I hear in my conversations about how sales/marketing alignment aids is, "What about B2B? How does it work there?"

Let me put your concerns to rest. Both SiriusDecisions and MarketingProfs have been doing consistent research in business-performance success, including the success that can be attributed to sales and marketing alignment in a B2B environment. Here are the numbers, a story unto themselves.

- 24 percent faster three-year revenue growth (Source: SiriusDecisions)

- 27 percent faster three-year profit growth (Source: SiriusDecisions)

- 36 percent higher customer-retention rates (Source: MarketingProfs)

- 38 percent higher sales win rates (Source: MarketingProfs)

That, I hope, at least starts to put the story to bed. To pull the covers up and over, I'm going to end my part of this chapter with another story—a case study of a division of a company that was able start its life with sales and marketing aligned. This is a highly unusual state. Usually, venerable practices have to be thrown out, other practices modified, organization reporting structures changed, benchmarks and KPIs replaced, and sales and marketing people who have been doing things a different way for years, convinced—and it's an awkward, difficult, and usually incremental process that takes a while to put in place.

But the case of Telefonica/O2 starts with no baggage at all, and with sales and marketing alignment the game plan.

Telefonica/O2: Pure as the Driven . . . Revenue

Telefonica/O2 can be an innovative company, willing to invest in new ventures with new business models. You'll hear from them in the next chapter, too, but for now I'm going to tell you the tale of a Telefonica/O2 enterprise division.

In 2011, Telefonica/O2 formed an enterprise division to provide out of the box services and products to larger businesses and to large public-sector organizations. These services were not typical but, instead, experimental even though lower-risk due to their support via solid market research. For example, they developed a comprehensive offering to provide customer engagement services within the four walls of a retail store, with significant digital capabilities. The concept was to provide optimized offers on your mobile device depending on the journey you were taking in the store in real time.

Another example was to provide mobile connectivity services via 4G for nurses and social workers so they could respond with minimum friction to things that potentially required a real-time response. Not that sexy, but possibly lifesaving.

They recognized that to succeed with out-of-the-box products and services they would have to have a close working relationship between marketing and sales so that the tension between the two departments was reduced to almost zero and the response time to taking and completing initiatives was near real time—and that the organizational structure of the division could support this.

Keep in mind, they were starting from scratch. While the Telefonica/O2 brand was well known, its traditional mobile services revenue had been declining, along with the reputation of the brand. This new division was competing for mobile hegemony in the largest, most coveted, and most saturated market—the enterprise. But Telefonica/O2 decided to take some risks and build up a contemporary commercial division with a fresh from-the-ground-up approach.

They started by hiring 150 sales and 20 marketing staff who had to be able to work together to build the reputation of the division.

This was the raw meat. I mean that nicely. But they had to mold and shape the sales and marketing proposition. They started with the basics, their go-to-market proposition, which they called, wait for it, "Go-To-Market." This was a joint planning and strategy effort that set the foundations of their game plan.

The first phase was characterized by setting joint targets and then defining how they were going to coordinate the effort. They looked at what they defined as their available target pool—potentially about 4,000 organizations that met their criteria. They carved out several key vertical industries that they felt they could provide these services to, e.g., the mobile 4G services to nurses in the healthcare industry, and so on. From that total pool, they set an objective of 240 leads generated for the first year, converting 6 percent of the total to leads that were also distributed vertically.

Once they defined their markets, identified their target, and set the numbers, they created sales compensation packages tied to both lead conversion and, of course, deal closure.

But how did something become a lead? What was the point that the marketing team would hand off the lead to the sales team? Both teams jointly agreed on not just the handoff criteria but who would be accountable for what. Sales was made accountable for the speed with which leads were followed up, marketing was accountable for the number and quality of leads.

That was the first phase.

In the second phase, with the target markets established, the KPIs set, the compensation packages built, and the definitions and accountability agreed on, they put together dedicated groups around the multiple vertical solutions, among them health services, local government, and retail. That meant teams of sales and marketing people were specifically assigned to each vertical.

That was well and good, but then they did something that I should say was unique, somewhat risky, and kind of brilliant.

Rather than assigning budgets to each department, they allocated the total budget dollars along the following lines:

- 30 percent of the total to sales enablement/education (i.e., materials)

- 50 percent to content and communications

- 20 percent to data and systems

Think about this for a second. Marketing and sales held joint responsibility to see that the budget allocations were used according to outcomes needed. This wasn't marketing being accountable for the budget for content—both departments were responsible for the total budget as it was distributed.

What Telefonica/O2 built with this division was a sales and marketing pure play—no baggage to discard—with cooperation and joint planning in the interests of both and the company as a whole from the beginning. What kind of results can you get from something like this? Not only is this a real-life example, but an interesting sandbox to see how a pure sales/marketing alignment could and would work.

The results? The formal economic term for it is amazeballs.

At end of 2012—after one year of existence—they had exceeded that 240-lead quota by roughly 25 percent, with 304 leads delivered. Nice. But there is so much more than that. They had 50 customers with a contract value of over $300 million U.S. and a pipeline at 160 percent of target, which put them over $1 billion. That is an almost unbelievable success rate. Yet, there it is.

But it didn't stop in 2012. Telefonica/O2 continued to have a great deal of success. In 2015, they initiated the "Start Small" program to reach their targets around highly specific vertical accounts and step up their activity. But this, rather than strictly revenue-based, was a Start Small with one account; they expected significant growth around the use of ABM. Their 2016 numbers were off the charts—though, of course, on the books. Take a look:

- 325 percent of target business won
- 118:1 ROI (investment to closed deals)
- 313 percent of target pipeline goals
- 67 percent sales qualified lead conversion rate

This was based on 40 accounts, up from the one account of the year before.

By 2017 they decided to get even more ambitious. This success led to a bold 2017 growth target—34 percent.

They have been wildly successful—much of it due to the alignment of sales and marketing.

Ultimately, all these changes to how a salesperson has to approach his/her job are based on the need to personalize the interactions with the sales prospects—to heighten the engagement. How do you even think about this? I'm going to let our guru, Barry Trailer, tell you that.

THOUGHT LEADER: BARRY TRAILER

When I met Barry Trailer, he was inextricably tied to Jim Dickie at an organization the two of them ran called CSO Insights. I read all their research and was blown away, not just by the quality of the research, but the actual conclusions they drew on how sales was evolving, as well as how to reformulate the thinking around sales because of the evolution of the discipline and, even more so, because of the evolution of the buyer, who was more demanding than ever before.

After having read their stuff for several years, avidly, I had the opportunity and the good fortune to get to know Barry pretty well, and to not only appreciate his incredibly keen mind and his articulation of the insights around sales, but his sense of humor. The man was always smiling. What was mildly disingenuous about this is that, while he was smiling, he was one of the key influencers in transforming how sales was done forever—and he remains that way to this day. And he's still smiling.

So, Barry, time to let these readers know what you know—behind that smile. Take it away.

. . . . .

There are 5 reasons people won't buy from you: 1) no money; 2) no need; 3) no desire; 4) no urgency; and 5) no trust. This last reason likely has killed more deals than the other 4 combined. You've heard it before: a deal too good to be true probably is. The weakest close is, "Trust me." Trust, synonymous with credibility, is a thing either earned by you (e.g., past performance, reputation, etc.) or transferred to you (i.e., referrals). It can be difficult and take a long time to earn and, yet, can be lost in an instant.

What is this elusive lubricant to relationships and does it have a diminished role in today's high-speed and, increasingly, disconnected exchanges?

At a recent conference, a speaker talked about Amazon and their need for speed. The example, their pages were too slow when taking 500 microseconds (μs) to load—that's right, half a second was too long. They focused on reducing the time to load a page to 100μs! Web surfers get antsy at 3 seconds and are ready to explode if a page takes several seconds or longer.

With this as background, here's an experiment I've been doing the past few years. Shake hands with someone in the usual fashion: firm (not punishing) grip, solid eye contact, not rushed, not clinging, and introduce yourself. Now, introduce yourself again, only with a "cold/dead fish" grip. While the exercise appears the same to an observer, the person you're shaking hands with will almost universally have an adverse reaction, either stepping back, making a frown, and/or shaking their head while saying, "No way."

Two things to note. First, the reaction time is even less than 100μs—it's instantaneous. Second, the person did not think about their reaction—it was visceral.

Technology is evolving at an amazing, and accelerating, pace; but our DNA is fixed for, at least, a couple generations before and after us. Boomers and millennials—and every demographic sub-group between them—are essentially identical in this regard.

And it's not just a cocktail-party game. CSO Insights' research over a 10-year period shows higher levels of sales performance directly correlate to higher levels of relationship. And, in workshops over this same time, the first element reported to increase with higher levels of relationship is trust. Other things increasing include knowledge of the customer's business, industry/domain expertise, referrals, repeat business, etc. But, always, the first thing is trust.

The question then becomes, how do we give the experience of a trustworthy handshake when interactions are increasingly disconnected, high-speed, and remote? How to establish trust?

One clue has already been provided above: your reputation precedes you (and follows you). This is especially true in today's online search/social environment. Establishing, maintaining, and growing a reputation of being both knowledgeable and trustworthy can be facilitated via *social engagement* (not "social selling"). Demonstrating product/industry/application knowledge in blogs, online group discussions, and social postings is a good place to begin.

Soon, (this is being written in Summer '17) we may see sellers (B2B, B2C, B2B2C) being rated via Yelp or another online application, the way Uber drivers, restaurants, and other service providers are today. We may see the coming of a "seller's pledge" (including a badge on LinkedIn profiles) that I will not stalk you, spam you, or otherwise be an Internet Troll you do not welcome into your sphere.

Yes, things are rapidly changing in the world of sales, but trust will continue to be the bedrock upon which relationships are established and elevated. The modern seller will be out there with social outreach and connection as the earlier generations were "out there riding on a shoeshine and a smile."

Then what are the to-dos needed to increase trust?

Do Your Homework *Before* Class

- Ask rifle-shot questions based on your understanding of the client's business situation/challenges.

- *Listen* to the answers and reflect back your understanding in your own words (don't simply "parrot" what the buyer said).

- Present relevant insights/information; if they want more detail, buyers will ask for it.

Don't Play with "Live Ammo"

- Plan your call/presentation and rehearse in advance, if necessary.

- Anticipate likely and/or difficult questions and research your answers in advance.

- Practice/role play so that your delivery is comfortable and allows you to be yourself.

Cultivate and Ask for Referrals

- Being referred into a prospect always heightens your initial credibility. LinkedIn and other social platforms can be leveraged in this regard, and you should become a skilled and frequent user.

- Be sure to do your best in preparing and showing up, so as not to damage the credibility of the person that referred you.

- Thank the person that referred you and keep them updated on progress you're making (they'll tell you when they no longer want to hear about it).

That should help those of you who are ardent sales folks, I should think. As you may (or may not) know, CSOi has defined five levels of relationship, from Approved

Vendor (lowest level) up through Trusted Partner (highest level). Look at the list below and tell me that being trusted doesn't matter.

Percentage of reps making quota when perceived as:

- Trusted Partner—59.7 percent
- Strategic Contributor—57.3 percent
- Solutions Consultant—51.2 percent
- Preferred Supplier—57.7 percent
- Approved Vendor—46.7 percent

Not only does being a trusted partner feel really good, but the results have a tangible effect on your company and on you. That's about as good a win-win-win as you will ever see, don't you think?

* * * * *

Thank you, Barry. That truly helps.

We've looked at the advanced models for two of the traditional customer-facing pillars so far—sales and marketing—both becoming inextricably linked. But what about the newer models for customer service? How do we start approaching them?

CHAPTER 12

Customer Service: Ambassadors for the Brand

There is an almost ironic (though not in the Alanis Morissette sense of the word) contradiction in customer service's evolution. On the one hand, customer service is arguably the area that most directly impacts customer engagement. How a customer feels about a company is often the result of their experience with the customer-service department, whether that interaction is with a human representative, a bot, a judgmental algorithm, or self-service. Regardless of the mode of the service interaction, they all have one thing in common. They are queries seeking an answer. It might be a utilitarian query such as, "What's your address? I need to return this." Or it might be an emotionally charged plea, such as, "This thing is broken, and I can't get it to work, and I need your help now because I need it to work now." Or it might even be a demand fueled by rage such as, "You just bumped me from a flight, and I have a speaking engagement in six hours, and no other flight will get me there on time you . . . jerks! Fix this!"

On the other hand, for all its direct impact, there is an amorphous, ethereal cloudiness to what customer service has become. With the growth of self-service and the high-volume increase in customer interactions, customer service now seems to be a wrapper encompassing all customer-facing processes, which, in turn, seems to reduce the role of the department itself. For example, sales people are expected to handle customer issues as a point of contact; customer-service representatives are at times being given revenue objectives for upselling and cross-selling to customers; marketers are providing the content that customers using self-service need to quickly resolve an issue in a way that mitigates the need for a human interaction. So, who is the customer-service rep? The salesperson? The marketer? The customer? Or the *actual* customer service rep? No matter what the answer, one constant remains. When it comes to customer service, the anticipated outcome is an answer to a customer query, received via whatever medium, with some expectations wrapped around how they are going to receive that answer.

In other words, it's complicated.

Who is going to deliver the answer in any given service query remains to be sorted out, and—a big hint—the answer can be "all of the above." As of now, though, the customer-service rep (CSR) is still the prime point of contact.

Some of the responsibility for the expanded scope of customer service rests with the significant changes in the ways that customers have come to want to access it. At the departmental level, here are some examples of what has changed.

- The media that customers use to communicate their queries and effect their interactions

- How much choice the customers have in how much they choose to be involved with the companies that they engage with

- The customers' expectations of the quality and speed of responses by the companies to their queries

- The advanced state of the technologies that are available to, minimally, enable and, optimally, foster the new customer-service models

Even with this, what remains customer service's biggest change is that its footprint has expanded to Yeti-sized proportions. Thus, customer service has begun a transition from a constrained, managed, departmental initiative to a companywide employee initiative that is intertwined with the overall customer experience and the continuous company-customer engagement. The result? Customer service delivery models are changing.

A brief note before I continue: I'm not covering the contact center per se in this chapter. This is a chapter on customer service that has multiple delivery models, of which contact centers are one—along with web-based self-service, communities, and mobile chatbots. Since they are a traditional medium in transition, contact centers will be addressed another day; otherwise, the chapter would become endless. Call this an editorial decision if you need to call it something not obscene. I will, however, cover the transition of traditional customer service to the newer models. Contact centers play a role in this.

What's caused the change? In general, the communications revolution that I have repeatedly been discussing throughout the book has created the means and desire for different avenues of customer interaction.

But there is a bit of "the more things change the more they remain the same" involved too. Seriously. I'm not just saying that to use the cliché.

CHANNELING THE CUSTOMER

Back in 2007, Forrester Research in their quarterly NATRMCE&SB survey found that the preferred channel for customer service, even among millennials, or as they still were known back then, Gen Y, was the phone.

In their "2017 Customer Service Trends: Operations Become Smarter and More Strategic" report subtitled "Vision: The Contact Centers for Customer Service Playbook," written by one of their most influential and astute analysts, Kate Leggett, they found that the channel with the highest percentage of use in a twelve-month period was . . . the phone.

Ahh, you're thinking, so nothing has really changed. Well, as you can probably guess, I tricked you. While it's true that the phone remains number one, what's important is that the second-most-accessed channel is either the Help link or Frequently Asked Questions on a company website, aka self-service, which trails phone by a slim 3 percentage points. Self-service wasn't even a blip in 2007. As you can see below, with the complete chart from Kate Leggett's report, not only is self-service surging but there is one other notable thing—increased use of non-traditional channels such as service communities and virtual agents (chatbots). In the following list, the first five are self-service channels, while the last four are live-assist channels.

- Help or FAQs on a company's website—64 percent

- Voice self-service (either touchtone or speech recognition)—43 percent

- Online forum or community—39 percent

- Use of an online virtual agent from a website—37 percent

- Use of a virtual agent on a smartphone (e.g., Siri on an iPhone)—35 percent

- Conversation with a customer-service rep or agent via telephone—67 percent

- Response to an email sent to customer service—60 percent

- Instant message/online chat with a live person—46 percent

- Contact of a company using Twitter—32 percent

But how responsive have companies been to the queries—both in terms of percent of queries responded to and time to response? Not very. Eptica, a

UK-based customer-engagement suite provider, did a Multichannel Customer Experience Study (2016) that verified this rather sad conclusion. They found that only 38 percent of emailed questions were answered, 48 percent of Tweets asking questions were answered, and 44 percent of queries by Facebook were answered. Across all channels only 51 percent of the questions were answered satisfactorily.

Even worse was the amount of time taken to answer those queries. Email queries averaged 34 hours and 15 minutes per answer, with ranges from as little as 3 minutes to as much as 4 days. Queries submitted through Twitter had by far the best average response time, averaging 4 hours 14 minutes. Facebook more than doubled that to 8 hours and 37 minutes on average. Not surprisingly, web self-service was the best channel, with 66 percent of the questions answered successfully. It's easier to look up something on your own if the answer is available. But it also is less stressful to do it yourself when you feel that the other customer services avenues you have are dismal.

What Customers Want

Gladly, a young company that developed a product that consolidates customer-service data, especially support tickets regardless of the channel on which they were received, did a "Customer Service Expectations Survey" in mid-2017 that reflects what our digital-age customers are thinking, expecting, and demanding. This data paints a picture like no other.

- 91 percent want companies they do repeat business with to know who they are and their history.

- 68 percent agreed that: "I want to be greeted by name, not asked for a ticket number."

- 67 percent of customers say big companies they are regular customers of treat them like a ticket number rather than a unique customer.

- People use an average of 3 different channels to reach customer service.

- 82 percent of consumers want to use multiple methods to communicate with customer service.

- 71 percent say if they switch channels mid-conversation, they expect the company to know about previous interactions.

- 78 percent said that customer service was a factor in their decision to make a repeat purchase.

- 81 percent are more likely to purchase again if they had a positive customer-service experience.

What's also interesting about this survey is how evenly it's distributed across generations. For example—and this is a common theme—the 91 percent who want companies to know who they are break down across generations like this: 93 percent baby boomers; 92 percent Gen Xers; 87 percent millennials. This small differential is universal across the data, going to the point I've made more than once that this is not a matter of generations any longer but of connected customers.

What else we can learn from the data that holds water elsewhere is that customers are expecting high degrees of personalized interaction, and the place that they want to see it in its most obvious way is customer service. A "company like me" is responsible to know who you are and to then make you feel valued accordingly. A great or good customer-service experience can provide that value exchange.

Customers have one other important service-engagement expectation. For customers, consistency and continuity matter a great deal. Here's how the survey defined them (and I agree, though with a small caveat).

> For customers, consistency (that channels and agents didn't give conflicting advice) and continuity (that they don't have to repeat themselves should they switch channels or agents midway) came out as most important in a support interaction.

The caveat is in the definition of consistency. I would add that it's not only a matter of consistent advice but a consistent overall experience across channels. It's not only a matter of picking up on one channel where you left off on another. It also means that the customer can navigate the customer-service channels without having to relearn terminology or having to find the data from the other interactions on other channels, and interaction navigation should be seamless regardless of channel.

That said, it was *their* survey, so I'll run with their definition. The failure rate in being consistent and/or continuous is high. Here are the numbers.

- 25 percent of the customers polled reported experiencing continuity when they switched channels.
- 39 percent said that they experienced continuity sometimes.
- 36 percent experienced continuity almost never.
- 92 percent said they were frustrated with having to repeat themselves multiple times to multiple agents.

What can we discover from this telling survey?

First, we see that customers are not demanding the sun and the moon. They are demanding what you would expect a digital customer to demand—some idea that they are valued and customer service that is responsive to their needs as an individual customer, not a group. This was borne out by the following data.

> *When asked what the one thing was that customer service agents could do to make them feel like unique, valued customers, the top answer (48 percent) was surprisingly simple: that the customer service agent should have knowledge of their previous interactions with the company.*

Remember my earlier dictum about customers: the idea of value to a customer is feeling valued.

They are prepared to reward the company that makes them feel valued, not only with continued business but with peer advocacy. The numbers for that are brilliant, as my friends across the pond would say. Of the best customers, 95 percent say that good customer service impacts purchase decisions, while 93 percent say it influences the decision to recommend to friends and family. Big return on this.

But there is a gap. To close the gap between customers' desires and the actual company's performance in an era where, due to the impact of social channels, scale affects even those small companies with a small customer base, new customer-service models become paramount. While this book doesn't have the scope to handle all of them—just being honest here—I will cover two of the most viable in this chapter to give you a flavor of what you can do with customer service for higher levels of engagement with your customers. Both of these models accelerate that:

- Self-Service and Knowledge Management
- Service Communities

A third that goes beyond just customer service—the use of chatbots, artificial intelligence, and mobile devices—will be covered by Brent Leary and me in Chapter 14.

NEW CUSTOMER SERVICE MODELS

> *Internally, customer service is a component of customer experience. Customer experience includes having the lowest price, having the fastest delivery, having it reliable enough so you don't have to contact anyone. Then you save customer service for those truly unusual situations.*

> —JEFF BEZOS, CEO, AMAZON

One of the more interesting effects of the communications revolution was how well it pointed out what had become ineffective or insufficient. For example, because customers can go elsewhere to find the solutions to problems (e.g., a community, a user forum, YouTube, social media, a blog, etc.), they are less dependent on customer-service representatives at a contact center. What makes this good for the company at some level is that customer-service costs are reduced as they rely a bit less on human contact. What makes this a potential nightmare, however, is that the company has no quality control over the material that is out there nor the people—who may not be affiliated with the brand—providing the answer to the customer service question. Uh. Oh.

The problem that companies face, then, is how to be able to, on the one hand, provide the customer with the avenues they want for their service queries and, on the other, provide the quality control that is needed so that the queries don't turn into issues and the issues don't turn into firestorms. Which, to be blunt, means not just quality control, but control—which means keeping it behind the firewall.

As ominous as this sounds, it isn't. Ultimately, both ends of the equation can be satisfied. *And* the models, channels, and practices to do it are already available—as is the public track record for you to gauge its success.

In General

If you look at Forrester's numbers, you'll see something very interesting. Substantial percentages are attached to a wide number of customer-service channels. While it remains true that phone and, thus, contact centers are the most frequented, and that the largest growth channel is self-service, it's notable that the number of channels used that are over 30 percent is . . . all of them. The channel with the lowest level of use for customer service is Twitter, and it's used by 32 percent of the respondents. As I pointed out in our earlier chat on omnichannel, this means your business must be ready to handle or proactively participate in all the channels that the customers use to get their answers.

Realistically, if you are committed to doing what customer service is supposed to do—answer queries and solve problems—and you are willing to make sure that the ordinary day-to-day queries are answered in the most frictionless way possible, then you can provide the various communications media to your customers for their conversations and correspondence with you. Once again, the paramount foundation is keeping the ordinary, ordinary. That takes work, plans, programs, technology systems, and cultural alignment, but so does all of customer engagement—if that isn't abundantly clear yet.

Case management will always be needed, and, as most of us have experienced, call centers are increasingly becoming contact centers—omnichannel entities that are designed for communications through everything ranging from phones to text to social channels, with agents who are either specialists in each or prepared for all. That transition is ongoing and, even though the shape of the new contact center is still a bit uncertain, what we can say is that it will be available for customers at the end of the day, even if it is no longer what it was as the millennium arrived.

But digital customers aren't as worried about human contact being the way they get information. The internet has been good to them when it comes to that. So, we are seeing digital service models rise to the top of the charts, with self-service being one model that more and more companies are turning too as a major avenue.

Self-Service on the Rise

Perhaps the most important change in customer service in the last decade has been the rise of self-service as not only an acceptable alternative, but a desirable one. From a pure cost perspective, it's got an obvious benefit for the business. Each self-service interaction costs pennies, while a live service interaction via phone, e-mail, or webchat costs more than seven dollars for a B2C company and more than thirteen dollars for a B2B company—a *lot* more. (Source: "Kick-Ass Customer Service," *Harvard Business Review*, Jan-Feb 2017.) The value when it comes to cost efficiency is obvious.

But there is another side. Customers are not wedded to how they get their problem solved or query answered, but they are wedded to getting their problem solved and query answered and with as little friction as possible. If it is possible to get it solved without a human being, so be it. In fact, that's easier.

Self-service can be handled through a lot of different channels. Behind the firewall, it can take the form of help files, frequently asked questions (FAQ), and a query to a knowledgebase on a website. Outside the firewall, it can be a YouTube video, an answer in a Reddit subgroup, a discussion in a user group built around a product or service, or an article online. Of course, the difference between the choices of providing answers behind the firewall and outside are the differences between quality control and the possibility of an unsubstantiated or incorrect answer respectively.

Keep in mind, self-service isn't only accomplished using knowledgebases, FAQs, and help files. It's done by the customer taking an action via an app or a website without another human involved. As mentioned in Chapter 7, my ability to generate a return label from Amazon without a person issuing it and sending it to me or asking an agent to do it is a huge timesaver and trust builder.

Since self-service is a popular choice now, and a cost-effective one, it becomes a smart move for the company to get their customers to come behind the firewall. The best possible way to do that when involving customer service is to have more complete knowledgebases that are easy to search, even if the query is complex.

When it comes to managing that, there are a few things that are both no-brainers and absolute necessities.

- Information should be accessible 24/7, as should the means to take actions.

- The information that the customers have available to them must be available to the agent at the contact center (if there is one, of course), and the ability for the customer to deal with a human should more often than not be a routine option.

- Strong workflow and business rules must be in place so that additional information can be hidden from the customer and made available to the agents, if the customer-service department decides it should.

- Search tools should be able to craft highly personalized customer queries. The more they draw on customer records, the better for providing an answer. Analytics that provide customer information should, therefore, sit on the back end.

- The sources can be the help files and the FAQs but also can be videos, articles, and best-practices white papers. Sufficient information should be available to help a customer make an intelligent decision on what they want to do—what action they need to take, what information they need to know, what experience they will have.

- The idea of capturing and qualifying the answers to customer questions needs to be part of the practice and the culture of the organization, or else valuable information will be lost.

- The decision as to who provides that knowledge, the employees and/or the customers, once made, means that the tools for either or both groups have to be made freely available.

Self-service is trickier than it looks and comes with enormous challenges. These challenges are broad and encompassing. Here is a partial list to give you an idea of why this isn't just a matter of posting a knowledgebase with best practices and a few answers to a bunch of questions.

- An extraordinary range of customer problems, inquiries, and required actions must be dealt with. The questions can range from utilitarian (e.g., what's your address, who is the supervisor of customer-service tier-one support) to product-based (e.g., how do I fix this problem with your "thing") to pricing questions (e.g., how much will this cost if I want to do I this way?). It's almost impossible to anticipate all but the most common and obvious questions and provide their answers. But customer self-service may also involve being able to pay a bill, make a reservation, buy a book, or, more broadly, take any action that might have needed a human representative in the past. With apps on a mobile device, you don't need humans to sell you something any longer or to take your credit card. You do it all yourself while walking down the street.

- Many of the problems are discussed outside the firewall. When you receive it, the query might be the tail end of a much more "emphatic" discussion outside the firewall, so the urgency could be misread.

- Problems often need to be addressed in real time. Sometimes it's a matter of putting out a fire. How do you do that with self-service? You don't, really.

- Info needs to be captured via multiple channels. This is standard operating procedure, but, as we will see in Chapters 13 and 14, this is also a very doable process with the right tools in place.

- One of the biggest challenges is separating what is merely information without value from information that can be an asset. If you are capturing data from external sources, the answer given might not be the right answer, or it might not be a repeatable practice or process and is only valuable for a single query. How do you distinguish that?

- Legal accountability for information provided to customers—what you put in a self-service knowledgebase—is often legally binding. For example, if a query to a pharmaceutical company about what drugs are possibly able to help a specific medical condition causes a patient to react badly to a suggested drug, it can be the basis for a lawsuit.

- Distinctions must be made between what is employee-only or customer-available information. Some information should only be made available to the CSRs, some to the customers. What goes into the knowledgebases that should be publicly visible?

- Real-time metrics are needed. How do you measure the cost of a self-service interaction, the results of the interaction, the level of customer satisfaction it produces, etc?

Handling Self-Service

Self-service, with all its challenges, still manages to provide a high level of engagement for the customer. It meets the cardinal rule—the customer engages with the company the way that they want to. But that means the company needs to spend the time to make sure that the knowledge they provide is well organized, easily accessible, and can be personalized to the specific interests of the customer or customer group. As stupidly simple and obvious as this may sound, it also needs to be up to date. That means that all sources of that knowledge, be they formal databases, employee knowledge, or unstructured data such as conversations or videos, should be continually plumbed. The data has to be captured and put through whatever quality-control procedures are in place to certify the new information for its validity and value. Only then can it be placed into service. Yet this is constrained by the need for speed—it has to happen quickly.

Both ends sound daunting, don't they? First, you must be continually updating appropriate information, and then you need to be making it easily available to customers. This is especially demanding if you're a big company. But here is where technology plays a major role. To give you a sense of how technology can personalize self-service at scale, I'm going to tell you how GoPro, the hip live-action videocam company, uses Coveo, which was identified as the leader in the 2017 Gartner Group "Magic Quadrant for Insight Engines," to do just that. Plus, it's story time anyway.

From Daunting to Manageable: The Case of GoPro

I'm betting that, of the millions of you reading this book (hey, a fella can dream—or fantasize—can't he?), most have heard of GoPro. The videocam became a sensation for a considerable time and set the consumer standard for professional-grade (hence the name) amateur action videos of people surfing, skiing, and doing other feats of derring-do. GoPro also has a considerable community of advocates and, with around 300 total employees as of 2017, a much smaller staff than the size of its community. So, self-service for them became not just a good idea but a necessity before their customer base overwhelmed their staff's ability to meet service needs.

One of their problems was that data was scattered in disparate formats, distributed across multiple repositories such as customer records in Salesforce, best practices documents, and customer-created videos on YouTube. There was no way to aggregate them to a fixed, single system of record; but they could employ Coveo to do the aggregation in real time and near real time and make personalized query responses available through a self-service portal that not only put it all in one place, despite the number of databases involved, but allowed the customer easy access to the answer to their specific question by typing it in. They didn't have to get a formal answer to a formal question.

But GoPro took self-service even further. They already had a way to submit a case online. Coveo was used to proactively fill in information for the individual based on the customer record, thus completing the online form for the case in a much shorter time frame. The result was significant call deflection: twice as many potential cases went to self-service sources.

Finally, Coveo was used by the contact-center agents to access knowledgebases by entering highly specific queries to help them answer calls that needed on-the-spot answers, increasing first-contact resolution by a significant margin.

Who else is doing self-service well? I put the question to Esteban Kolsky, who I introduced you to in Chapter 5. In case you didn't know this because you've been marooned on Lian Yu (one for you *Arrow* fans), he is also one of the world's thought leaders in customer service. His answer is telling—a true indicator of how difficult comprehensive self-service is. When you read this, please realize that self-service is a model for customer-service delivery, but its functions are not just customer-service-department-related. It can be sales, marketing, etc. It continues to make the point that customer service today is broad and encompassing, not narrowly focused on case management. Here's Esteban's response.

> *Tough question, actually.*
>
> *Banking sites are still some of the best examples, due to their evolution and their trying new features (things like add-on products) and new and useful functions). Depositing checks without going to the branch is actually closing down branches and raising customer satisfaction.*
>
> *Amazon lets you do virtually everything you need via their website. But it's bad on user experience and navigation.*
>
> *Starbucks has some good things going for them. Their app manages rewards and loyalty very well—it has grown to represent more than one-third of all payments (via stored gift cards and loyalty cards)—and remote ordering before going to the store is awesome. The remote-ordering function, as good as it may be as an entry point for customer engagement, shows a weak area in end-to-end experiences for customers, however. In high-traffic stores, during peak hours, the baristas must choose whether to prepare remote orders or in-store orders—meaning one of the groups will have their feelings hurt (too long of a wait for their coffee); they cannot accommodate all orders in a timely manner.*

Virtually all major insurance companies (Progressive, Geico, the one from Allstate that's online only) have good apps to do most of it, including filing and tracking and even contesting a claim.

Some of the gaming apps let you do service without leaving the game— like within the effing thing.

Porsche lets you schedule service from the car when it's needed. And add reminders. It also gives you offers to special events as you drive around town.

Emirates Airlines lets you (in certain cities) schedule luggage pickup and delivery for your flight at check-in via their phone app.

Even the IRS has a self-service site to let you know your balance— which is 45% of phone inquiries. Imagine the savings and reduced wait times (on Monday am you could wait up to 3 hours to get to a person on the phone—or 10 days via us mail).

I don't think there's a web site per se. It's finding what customers are desperately asking for/want/need and offering that which makes a self-service function awesome.

If you still want a site—Amazon for completeness, I guess. Closest thing I've seen to being able to do it all.

Self-service, especially in the service of customer service (service[3]?) is a given in developing any game plan for engagement with your customers. The First Rule of Engagement Club is "provide the means to allow the customer to interact in the way they want to interact at the level they want to interact." Self-service as an option, borne out by the data, borne out by the success of those who have embraced it, and borne out by anecdotal evidence, now becomes a standard.

That leaves one more new service model up for discussion: support communities.

WHAT DO WE MEAN BY COMMUNITIES?

Communities, especially service communities, are not only increasingly a subject of interest in the business world but are coming online with mounting frequency. Technology companies like Lithium and Salesforce.com built the community platforms that are technologically necessary. The extant body of communities have had public success to the point that they are seen as a safe investment and, increasingly, as an important one. Their value is evident enough that The Community Roundtable, my go-to organization when it comes to all-things-community, reported in their "State of Community

Management 2017" that not only were community managers reporting budget increases versus budget cuts at 3:1, but 67 percent of them were identifying increases in measurable value year-over-year. Jeez. Those are serious numbers.

I'm sure you think that's as great as I do, right? Wait. You might want to know what a community is and how it applies to customer service, I would guess.

The definition of community that The Community Roundtable gives for all communities is simple: "A community is a group of people with shared values, behaviors, and artifacts." That seems reasonable enough and provides a basic foundation to run with. People who congregate in communities—at least the digital ones—tend to congregate to discuss and interact and share information about something in particular that drives their interest. Physical communities—actual neighborhoods—don't necessarily share values or behaviors, though they do share artifacts (e.g., a dwelling). So, please note that this definition is restricted to digital, as least as far as I, and, thus, this book and chapter are concerned.

Typically, communities tend to revolve around two types—communities of interest and communities of practice. A community of interest is a shared subject of interest—such as a BMW user group or a New York Yankees fan community. One community of interest you find frequently is a community of people who all have a specific medical condition or who are involved in a specific drug regimen.

A community of practice is a community of practitioners. One example of a highly successful community of practice is the SAP Community Network, which is a mature community (it has been around since 2003) of more than 3.5 million SAP practitioners, employees, students, and others related to the organization. It gets more than 2 million unique user views per month and has 430 subgroups devoted to subjects like HANA and ABAP development—which are meaningless acronyms unless you know something about SAP.

These are the prevalent "types" of communities. The definitions are so broad with "practice" and "interest" that they cover anything you could throw at them and meet the challenge.

Support communities are interest and practice combined, which makes them both a little unusual and very powerful. They have multiple configurations, though what they all have in common is that they serve a group of people who interact around a specific need set of needs or topic(s) of discussion.

They can be communities where any customers can go to get their questions answered by either/both qualified customer service representatives and/or qualified and authorized customers. An example of the latter is composed of the Microsoft MVP communities that flourish outside the firewall, where you can get tech answers from people whom Microsoft has certified not as customer service representatives but as their most qualified technical practitioners.

They can be communities where selected customers or categories of customers get support. For example, before it was made generally available in 2011, Cisco had their Service Support Community set up as a portal that would provide both self-service and interactive support for Cisco partners. Even when it was made available to all, the 12,000-strong community was targeted to users involved in Cisco service contract management and quoting or ordering activities.

They can be communities entirely driven by customers who play the role of customer service representatives. Giffgaff, the mobile virtual network operator (MVNO) in the UK, is a perfect example of this.

THE MODEL TRANSFORMED: GIFFGAFF

Several years ago, I was heading to London on a business trip, and I had an Apple iPhone that needed a nano SIM card, which, at the time, was a new requirement. I was a giffgaff user for the UK as my carrier there but had no nano SIM to be able to use the phone. I contacted a VP there that I knew about getting one. He referred me to a customer of theirs who was cutting the nano SIMs for them and would provide me one. I emailed the guy, who asked for my address and said he would get it to me in time for the trip to London three weeks hence. I asked him the cost—nothing. I offered to pay postage—nonsense. Two weeks later, I had the nanosim in hand—free of charge.

This is the model of customer support that giffgaff uses—the customers are the customer-service representatives.

Before I get too far ahead of myself, let me introduce giffgaff. Giffgaff is a mobile virtual network operator (MVNO), an organization that provides carrier-level services like phone calls, internet connectivity, and data services, but doesn't own the wireless network infrastructure that they use. They are the creation of Gav Thompson, the then Director of Innovation at O2, and are currently wholly owned by Telefonica/O2, whose wireless infrastructure they use for their services. The business model is based on the purchase of services in a 30-day package called a "goodybag" that are accessed via a free SIM card. They have been very successful in Britain due to the model they use, which is a combination of incredibly inexpensive carrier services for calls, text, and data in combination with services that are administered by and products that are co-created with their customers. Their very name, a Scottish term for "mutual giving," is exactly their business model.

They do the standard stuff, including soliciting opinions on social media and social networks like Facebook, etc. But their crown jewels are their communities, which operate at scale. To give you an idea of how extensive that scale is, here is the snapshot for December 24, 2018, of just their customer service community engagement. The numbers are the totals for the year to-date.

- Announcements: 120,671
- Help & Support: 8,297,293
- Service Updates: 6,683
- Welcome & Join: 350,695
- Giffgaff Gameplan: 35,597
- Contribute: 451,549
- General Discussion: 3,988,202
- Tips & Guides: 121,790
- Photography: 37,402
- Blog: 96,889

What makes this more than just a typical support community is that, not only are the giffgaff customers functioning as the CSRs, including a team of power users who are designated to handle more serious and difficult questions, but there are rewards for participation in the community—from the simplest level of being a member, which gets you discounts, to the more advanced levels of being an in-effect CSR, which gets you rewards and awards, especially if your answers get voted up as a top answer. This leads to even greater awards if you either are one of the power users or you provide ideas for services that eventually get used on the forums or via the giffgaff Labs. The reward tends to be free airtime, data services, and text services, or, at the smallest level, discounts for those same services. Giffgaff rewards its members with roughly $5 million per year in these free services—which can be used or given to charity. Additionally, they have "exclusive" closed invitation-only groups for both content creators and super recruiters—so there is an opportunity to be recognized by your peers as an "elite."

A typical question-and-answer goes something like this one submitted on June 2, 2017:

Sim won't activate
    Started by: morganchambers42
    On: 02/06/2017 | 17:30

Replies: 2
Message 1 of 3
0 Kudos
by: lynda1962
on: 02/06/2017 | 17:33
@morganchambers42, hi there, try using a different browser and empty cache then try again.
guide on how to activate your sim
http://community.giffgaff.com/t5/Getting-started/Activating-your-new-SIM/ta-p/3521635

You can see in this simple interaction a customer asking a question, a customer answering a question, a ranking engine (Kudos), a series of links to knowledgebases, and, finally, even though it isn't showing here, the possibility of escalation to an actual giffgaff employee if need be ("agent will help you").

What makes this incredible, with all this activity, is that the average response time is 90 seconds.

Sometimes the problem-solving gets far more "above and beyond." In one case, a community member had forgotten their passport and was at the airport. Another member drove to their house, picked up their passport, and took it to the airport in time for the traveler to board the plane.

The delivery model is also quite sophisticated. Remember that nano SIM I received above? Here's the story behind the story.

The nano SIM was introduced with the release of the iPhone 5. Since Apple, due to a bit of both arrogance and shrewdness on their part, doesn't really show their actual hand (i.e., the product) until the actual launch, giffgaff couldn't risk purchasing something that *might* work in advance; which meant, at launch, giffgaff was likely to not be prepared to support its community. The community itself stepped up and solved the problem, creating their own accurate nano SIMs from the slightly bigger giffgaff SIMs, then creating an ordering site and a distribution network, so that on launch day, they were ready to support . . . themselves. And me, of course.

This business model has been successful in keeping costs of consumer services down and also the cost of customer service, the actual work being done more typically by a CSR. Even though the data is a bit outdated at this point, back in 2011 Cap Gemini did a study on giffgaff that found if this customer service model was applied to the entirety of Telefonica/O2 it would save them 20 million pounds a year in customer service costs. I'm not saying that this was feasible; just reporting the facts, ma'am.

In 2017, according to then giffgaff Community Manager Gregg Baker, they found that for each answered question they save £8. Couple that savings with a response time per question of 90 seconds on the average and you have, not only savings, but a great customer experience—mutual value exchange.

The millions of minutes spent per year by multiple community members led giffgaff to CSAT scores of 98 percent and NPS scores of 60 in 2017, by far the UK telco industry's highest. The average NPS for the mobile industry is a miserable 22. (All the data is from the 2018 version of an annual telco customer satisfaction study done by Ofcom on the UK telecommunications industry.)

But it is service like this that tells you why I am a devoted fan of this company. It works for me, and it works for them. It is a paradigm of customer service, and you literally can't get better than that. It's a model that works for everyone concerned.

So, we've seen the transformation of customer service well beyond its traditional case solutions and query responses into a company-wide and community-wide initiative that fosters engagement. It not only required a transition from the old communications media and information exchange but also the creation of brand-new forms of media and information exchange via communities, self-service, and, as the future unfolds, possibly chatbots and mobile experiences. But we'll leave that for Chapter 14.

Now, we've reached that nearly constant spot in a chapter where you are likely sick of me spouting off, so I'm bringing in a fresh voice.

THOUGHT LEADER: BILL PATTERSON

This piece by Bill Patterson tells you something about Bill. He is a thought leader who can translate the biggest and most significant ideas into action—in other words, he's the best kind of thought leader. He's been there, done that, and created that too. I've known Bill for more than 14 years and watched him grow into one of the foremost leaders in the customer-facing world. At present, he is the EVP, Product Management and General Manager of Salesforce's Service Cloud, one of the big three of Salesforce's offerings—a position of huge responsibility, and one he is well-suited for by skills, temperament, and experience. I think of Bill as a truly warm person who is a true leader with real accomplishments to point to, and a great friend.

° ° ° ° °

Transforming *Customer Service* in an era driven by the engaged customer requires that organizations rethink the paradigm of service delivery away from an inbound response-function to a new process of delivering ongoing care and value to customers. To accomplish this, we must shift away from delivering service as an operational necessity and to an approach where service offers new ways of differentiating your products, services and experiences. Consider the following three paths of change: Going Digital, Getting Personal, and Giving Proactive Care to enhance your service-engagement proposition.

GOING DIGITAL

We are increasingly becoming creatures of digital habit. Most consumers today are tethered to a digital device of some shape or form. Organizations are responding by introducing new service channels, such as establishing new Customer Service teams to monitor Facebook for outcry on social media. With each new channel comes new customer expectations of response and resolution timing. And, yet, many businesses operate across channels in an independent manner, causing inconsistency and incomplete service experiences to occur. It is, therefore, paramount that organizations embrace more holistic support tools and processes that drive consistency across these high-scale interaction channels—as, otherwise, service will vary greatly depending on the point of origination in the support funnel.

GETTING PERSONAL

Following digitalization comes the expectation to deliver personalized customer service. Remember, in the case of a service interaction, your customer does not actually *want* to be contacting you; rather, they are in a place where they are *needing* to contact you because they largely weren't able to solve their issue themselves. Customers are looking for both help and resolution to *their* problems quickly, where optimizing for their time becomes the most precious commodity.

It is, therefore, critical that businesses aim to introduce new options for personalized care into their support functions to eliminate waste and to optimize the support funnel for the needs of specific customer issues. For instance, rather than employ static, pre-canned Interactive Voice Response (IVR) systems that prompt first by the entire list of product and problem combinations, shifting navigation to first identify the customer, followed by presenting issues experienced only by the products they own, can greatly save the time and effort made by customers. It is small shifts like these that can enhance the overall support experience. It is also where our final transformation pillar, Giving Proactive Care, shows even greater promise.

GIVE PROACTIVE CARE

Giving Proactive Care, is about *embedding* Customer Service into the products, applications, and experiences that your organization offers to customers. This final pillar of transformation also holds the greatest opportunity to drive differentiation for your organization, but it requires an advanced shift in the way in which service is defined and offered.

Take for example the automotive industry, where the automobile is no longer just a collection of an engine, drivetrain, and wheels, but now a device combined with thousands of sensors and services that track status and communicate the automobile's health with other devices and service providers. These sensors communicate into service centers and schedule appointments when automobiles encounter issues. The automobile becomes a fully transformed product that allows customers to take control of their ownership experience and greatly enhances the serviceability of this new premium product.

The future of customer service will continue to evolve based on the demands of customers and the willingness of businesses to cater to their needs. Businesses will need to innovate, and, as customers ourselves, this is a great thing.

* * * * *

Thank you, Mr. Patterson.

I hope that I've been successful getting you focused on engagement with the ideas and gurus I presented and with the stories I've told. If so, I'd love to be able to rest, but, in truth, I can't. I have to still take you down the path to enablement via technology systems, the outcomes that you might achieve if you are successfully engaged with those pesky customers, and how you can measure the financial impact directly and indirectly on your business. *Then* I can rest.

SECTION FIVE

Technology and Its Uses

W hy is technology the last thing that you plan, and why is it one of the most important things that you do? How do specific customer-engagement-focused technologies benefit your business? How do you use your insights to personalize at scale? I will take care of that for you. But I don't do laundry.

CHAPTER 13

Does This Mean We're Engaged?— Systems of Record Meet Systems of Engagement

As you may (or may not) have noticed, I've studiously avoided a significant discussion of technology until now, though, of course, I have mentioned it here and there. I have my reasons. I've dealt with technology for more than two decades—hell, the bulk of my current clients are major enterprise technology companies—but I have always known a couple of things about technology that seem to escape a lot of the practitioners who are just encountering it at their companies for the first time. First, they don't understand that technology isn't a panacea. It's primarily an enabler, though at times it can even be a driver. Second, the technology you use to accomplish whatever you are trying to accomplish is the last thing you select, after you've determined your strategy and programs, designed your business processes and workflows, created your business rules, and identified the specific needs and requirements you have for the technology—and not until then.

I'm starting the chapter this way for a reason. I want you to be entirely clear on this and on the fact the technologies I am speaking about in this section are not being designed for your specific needs. I don't have a clue what your needs are. I give examples of the types that are needed to enable and foster engagement at a company, not yours per se, although they might be right for you.

Each company's technology needs are specific and can't be accounted for in a book or a speech. The framework is what I hope that you get from this and the next chapter, the foundation for thinking about and planning for the technologies and data you need for execution of a customer-engagement strategy and program. Also, the examples of tech out there might be useful enough to provoke some investigation on your part because its already out there and plays an obvious role in successful customer engagement.

You may wonder why even use technology when we are talking about customer engagement? What does it have to do with anything? If engagement has to do with behaviors, and you can't enable how someone feels, why use technology to enable your engagement strategy?

If you are a growing company, the question is how can you *not* use technology—especially if you're dealing with a customer base made up of more than two individual customers? Ultimately, technology becomes an important component of your business planning, especially if you're serious about engaging with your customers.

You will find a lot of overlap and interchangeable material in this and the next chapter. I made some choices as to what would go where. This chapter is focused on the back end of the customer-engagement technology deployment—the data and the backend systems. Chapter 14 is focused on the front end—the products, the services, and the tools. Please, though, don't get on my case about what I put where. For example, I put artificial intelligence in Chapter 14—primarily due to the growing body of use cases that justify investments in AI. I could have put it here just as well.

Now that we are mind-melded, let's move on to taking a look at the key component of any technology strategy—the data.

THE DATA

One thing we can be sure of. We need to know more and more about our individual customers, not just what slot they fit in a demographic analysis.

No one is going to disagree with that. In fact, the lip service to this is so rife that chapped lips are becoming a serious medical problem in the business world. But immediately following the nodding of the head you will get when you make that statement, you often hear a permutation of this: "Well, this is the era of big data and therefore . . ." And from there, you'll hear some stats related to petabytes or zettabytes and some homily to the amount of data available, etc. If you hear that statement it means someone, and I won't mention names, isn't getting it.

Understand that it isn't the amount of big data that matters, it's the specific kinds of data that matter, as well as the insights you gain from it. In the past couple of decades, we have had prodigious amounts of industrial-strength transactional data and demographic information about individual customers. What makes this era unique and incredibly exciting is that we now have gobs (a scientific term for *huge*) amounts of behavioral data that, when applied in conjunction with the transactional and demographic data, provides us with a copious, detailed customer profile of an individual and how they are acting at any given time. When analytics programs do what they do, this data give us insights into those individual customers in real time and allows us to respond to them based on either present or anticipated behavior.

While it seems obvious to you and me that behavioral data is customer gold, it apparently isn't so obvious to most marketers. In 2015, eMarketer reported on a study done by Researchscape that identified the metrics that marketers used to devise their campaigns and their efforts toward individual customers. Surprisingly, even with all the declarations about getting to know customers, intimacy with the customer, putting the customers in control, and blah blah blah from the marketing world, the data they rely on for personalization efforts is the traditional demographic and transactional data. Among the types are email addresses (57 percent) and demographics (40 percent). The behavioral data, not so much, is focused on location-related data (18 percent), lifestyle data (15 percent), and psychographics (a miserable 8 percent).

Something is wrong with that picture. What is wrong is those marketers are behind the curve when it comes to understanding what customers want, who they are, and what they are doing. While they pay homage to being more engaged with their customers, which requires their knowledge of who, what, when, where, how, and even why their customers are doing what they are doing, they neither focus on the effort to find those things out nor do they actually gather the information that they need to make the appropriate judgment.

Luckily, a significant number of companies are making efforts to be engaged with their customers in a more immersive way, which means, of course, getting to "know" the individual customers and how they act and what they do and what they like. The lesson is the same, no matter where in this tome or anywhere else you look. When you are trying to personalize your relationship to your customers, of course you need the demographic and transactional data you always have needed, but having behavioral data is where you start to distinguish yourself. The challenges that come with the data, however, are significant.

The Challenges

The challenges that contemporary technology is designed to meet are, to put it politely, non-trivial. Think: scale, volume, velocity, variability, veracity, and making sure you ask the right questions. Now, let's commit to them to paper, or at least to digital paper.

Scale—Capital One (my bank): 45 million customers (I feel so insignificant); Amazon (my preferred shopping): 300 million customers (I feel important); Verizon Wireless (my mobile carrier): 146 million customers (I feel so misunderstood).

Let me explain. If you think of it in total, I'm three of 491 million customers. Yet, I don't care what the other 490,999,997 customers want of those three companies—nor do they care about what I want. What I want from each company is specific.

- Some explanation as to why I can't get specific information about my account at Capital One without having conniptions—I feel so insignificant.

- Why the product that Amazon shipped second-day air didn't arrive in time. In response, I get an explanation and a free month of Amazon Prime for my troubles—I feel important.

- Why I continue to get offers that are completely unrelated to me or my status with Verizon Wireless—I feel so misunderstood.

Each of them, even Amazon, could provide me with what I want with the right data about, not just my transactions, but my interactions and other behavior related to the company. However, the dilemma they face is how to do this for their entire customer base. Now, at the moment, I'm not discussing the engagement strategy, which might tell you that you don't have to do it for *all* of the other customers. I'm assuming that all customers are important and not that some are more important than others—even though they are. By assuming that, I'm also assuming, as the title of this book would want me to do, that each customer is self-interested. Consequently, it isn't easy providing what ultimately each customer wants, personalized interactions that scream: "HEY, WE KNOW YOU—AND WE CARE," or at least say that in lower case. But technology allows for the identification of relevant individual customer data, the capture of that data, the storage of that data, actions taken on that data, and the organization of the results of those actions into usable form (i.e., transitioning that data into information). When the employee using that data tries to glean some insights from the organized reporting of that data, the information becomes knowledge, and that leads to insights that can then be applied. The industry cliché—for all of you who love to use industry clichés to show how smart you are—is "actionable insight." You are *so* smart. Personally, I'm just snarky; not so smart.

Volume/velocity—There are so many articles and posts about the 4.4 zettabytes of data (2013), which are projected to grow to 180 zettabytes by 2025

(IDC's forecast), that, if we just cut them out, we'd probably reduce the total data to 2.2 zettabytes. While that's an interesting stat, what is more interesting and far more daunting is the velocity of the data being produced—the continual increase in the rate of the data produced, year over year. That, in combination with the total amount, is what has been called "big data."

Back in the days when people were concerned about what to do with all the data being created, people got so concerned with the amount they made it seem as if big data were the equivalent of overpopulation of the species (which, to be clear, I don't believe is an actual issue). Where were we going to put all this data? What were we going to do with it? Technology, it was said, couldn't handle the volume or the velocity.

Well, that was nonsense. As is almost always the case, technology was designed and developed to handle it. Now the germane question—a real one—is: how do we gain insight from that data? The phrase often used is, "big data, small insights." I'll talk more about that later.

Variability—The kinds and sources of data that have to be dealt with varies widely. It can be transactional data, other types of structured data, data from the social web, SMS, sentiment, communities, mobile devices, sensors, video data, audio data, geospatial data, data from apps usage. There are more sources and many more data types too, but this is enough to make the point. While, even to this day, many of the queries still target the structured data from internal systems, the need for individual customer information and the response time available to answer customer queries make the value of other data sources immense. The shortness of the window of opportunity to respond is also why having enough customer-journey data to anticipate the customers' behavior using predictive and, eventually, prescriptive analytics is an increasingly appealing option, particularly when the customer base is very large.

Veracity/clarity—The quality of the data, the right context for the information, is one of the major challenges you have to deal with. In the past, when most of the data you were concerned with was names, addresses, etc.—i.e., the structured transactional data that traditional CRM storehouses held—your concern was along the lines of was: "Brad Pitt, Bradley Pitt, Brad Pit, are they all the same person?" Then, as social media use became widespread, the concern was: "Brad Pitt the name and address in Los Angeles, is it the same as bradpitt on LinkedIn, as @bradpittoceans11 and @bradpittoceans12 on Twitter and facebook/bradpittaloneagain on

Facebook?" Tech companies like Gigya make identity verification a lucrative business. At last count in 2018, Gigya had 1.2 billion verified social IDs. Major business value. Pitney Bowes has the largest address verification database in the world. But it has gone well beyond just name and address ID verification and even beyond social ID verification with the expansion of available sources and data types that need to be verified, accurate, and ready to be analyzed. For example, now, clarity matters as much as veracity. You have to deal with misspelled text in tweets, or the context of the conversation on a social site, and the sentiment being expressed in context. For example, since Twitter is such a great source of examples, how would sentiment analysis interpret this tweet? "I find that @SouthwestAir (curse word with "ing") themselves with terrible policies and bad customer service is great. Love it." Aside from the grammatical head scratching that this sentence induces, how would an algorithm interpret this—terrible, bad, great, love it? Additionally, you must deal with industry-specific jargon, multiple languages, different meanings of the same thing in different cultures, abbreviations, visual data interpretation, and the geospatial side. You must deal with influencers and influence—how does the data you capture resonate with others, and who is actually putting that data out there? Clarity and veracity are a complex challenge that can, if improperly done or ignored, impact results so severely that you will make the wrong decisions or respond the wrong way to your individual customers and damage rather than improve the relationship. But the right way? The benefits can be significant, as we will see.

The right questions—One theme you will see always and threaded everywhere when it comes to data, analytics, artificial intelligence, and machine learning is that you should ask the right questions to get the right answers. You can ask the wrong questions and get the right answer to the wrong question, which is, for your actual purposes, the wrong answer. But it will seem right. For example, many years ago Sony was trying to figure out the best way to distribute inventory across the globe for moving specific products. They ran analytics based on what they thought was the right question and got the answer to that question. But, because it was the wrong question, it ultimately cost them millions of dollars since they couldn't deliver the product in a timely manner. Wrong question. Even machine learning is dumb: it needs to be pointed in the right direction to learn the right answers. Asking the right questions, knowing what you are seeking to find, is vital to the successful use of data for insight.

In other words, big data, small insights potentially lead to happy customers, and maybe, just maybe, loyal customers, if you can meet the challenges.

How you capture the data, how you store the data, how you report, analyze, and interpret the data and do so in a way that gives you and your customers what you want . . . well, that's what systems of record and systems of engagement are there for.

These aren't abstract challenges or challenges germane to just a small sampling of companies or industries. Institutions across the planet are hit with the same questions that need to be answered.

To put a final period on the point, I bring you Lauren Vargas, who is not only one of the leading thinkers in community engagement but also a master of the library—our version of a real-life librarian but super-powered. Though she's not a librarian by vocation and, in fact, is currently Head of Employee Digital Engagement and Collaboration at Fidelity Investments, she is a qualified expert with all the right degrees in library science. I invited her here to show you how even libraries are being affected by the challenges of data—and if repositories of knowledge are being impacted by large data movement, then pretty much everything is.

Lauren, tell 'em what the story is.

* * * * *

Over the past fifty years, hackers [or agents of change] of all backgrounds have built a world that scales to the complexity of a larger connected community—designed or enhanced by an increasing number of architects. The volume, velocity, and variety of data today are influencing change across "informational ecologies," originally defined by Thomas Davenport (1997) and the definition expanded by other knowledge-management researchers as "the system of people, practices, values, and technologies in a particular local environment" (Nardi and O'Day, 1999: 49). By changing from an inside-out perspective to an outside-in perspective, organizations have the power to change the relationship between the consumer and the organization and develop a collaborative relationship versus a one-sided experience.

Museums are just one example of an industry coming to terms with being a public servant instead of serving the public. Until the modern advancements in data collection and use, museum systems were primarily focused on the collections. Now, systems are being designed to bring together collections and visitor-specific data. With the knowledge of the power of "big data" and its rapid growth, museums can adapt or adopt communications personalized for unique cultural experiences.

This transformation is much needed. Since the first of the 21st century economic recessions began in 2001, consumers are spending less money on luxury items and museums are competing with other entertainment venues for every dollar. Settling for a bigger audience with general or mysterious value will not solve revenue issues for cultural institutions or any other industry; to meet their goals, these organizations need to understand the diverse needs and groups within the community.

Organizations are recognizing the need to go beyond single-variable learning and learn more about how the communities they serve think and act differently, while forging their own customer journeys versus those paths thrust upon them by organizations. If organizations developed a framework embracing the development of data collection and use strategy blending big and small datasets with an infrastructure designed for big data with systems integration and networked data sets, then small data (via visitor personalization opportunities and omnichannel experiences) have the potential to become more consistent and attainable. The goal: hone in on consumer experience by building and improving the supporting infrastructure. Today, every industry is gearing up for a period of advancement to view a holistic customer journey—one that actively engages the consumer both inside and outside the physical walls of the organization.

● ● ● ● ●

Thank you, ma'am.

So, then, the question is how do you do something with that data? Make it valuable enough to help you foster engagement? Systems of record, meet systems of engagement.

SYSTEMS OF . . . WHAT?

A few years ago, an executive of a major software technology firm made a rather overenthusiastic and just plain wrong statement: "Systems of record will be replaced by systems of engagement." That will never happen. They are mangos and strawberries. They each have a *raison d'etre*. They each can work independently, but they work better together—like strawberries and mangoes—each awesome unto themselves, but as a smoothie . . . yum. To start out, let's chat about what they are. Doing that will give you what you need to understand how technology can enable high degrees of personalization at scale and thus even higher levels of customer engagement.

I'm assuming you aren't a particularly geeky individual, so some of what I'm going to do is define terms. If you are familiar with the terminology, by all means, skip ahead.

DEFINITION: SYSTEM OF RECORD

When CRM began hitting its apex, it began to not only serve the needs of sales, marketing, and customer service departments in a functional way, but, even more importantly, took all the data that was gathered as a result of the interactions with single customers in those departments and aggregated it to a single customer record. Initially, it stored core CRM-related data such as what I bought, what I was upset enough about to call customer service on and the resolution of the problem, what marketing campaigns I responded to and when, etc. But as time went on, more and more frequently it became important to know which media I used to communicate, what videos I was looking at online, what I was saying about the specific brands in conversations with my peers, what reviews I was writing and responding to, what content I downloaded, and a multiplicity of other data. But this created a lot of problems because of the vastly different forms that the data were in and the different schemas that had to be reconciled to make the data reportable. For example, while the transactional data—what you bought—was structured for the traditional customer of record, the conversational data—the social media back and forth—was called "unstructured." That meant, realistically, the data was structured according to the norms of the medium that recorded the conversation, which varied by platform. But ultimately, even that unstructured data had to be captured and organized in combination with the traditionally structured transactional data to allow analytics engines, algorithms, and human beings to make some sense of the data so that it could be used for insights and, thus, have a meaningful purpose. A meaningful purpose meant applying those insights to something that would let the customer know, at least metaphorically, "Hey, we're listening to you, and we know you." Even if it was only an algorithmic frontend responding. Now, of course, the respondent is as likely to be an artificial-intelligence-driven chatbot. Or a person. Or not. Probably not an alien.

As it stands now, systems of record are mature, and they are structured to hold data they had never been able to in the past. Broadly, they don't only apply to the customer-facing side of a business but can encompass human-resources or accounting or inventory-management records. As we saw in Chapter 7, these are impacted by or are impacting customers but, nonetheless, the data isn't directly information about a customer. Yet, it can be part of a system of record.

Place that on your brain's back burner. It's important to know, but we are concerned with the customer record.

Before roughly 2010, a typical customer record consisted of the following:

- Account data
- Order data from brick-and-mortar stores, phone orders, ecommerce
- Billing information
- Credit information, including third parties like Dun & Bradstreet, Experian, etc.
- Customer-cost allocations data
- Interactions related to transactions data, including emails, phone conversations, online chats
- Service data, including tickets—open and closed, successful, and failed; service-request resolutions, contact-center interactions, queries, etc.
- Marketing data, including campaign responses, promotions offered, successful and unsuccessful results
- Segmentation data, including standard demographics, household information, geographical information

But with the advent of the high volume of available behavioral data and data from external media, and the need to personalize at scale, the data required for a successful ongoing engagement with individual customers changed and, thus, what was needed for the customer record did too.

Now, in addition to the above "traditional" data, the customer record needs:

- Unstructured individual customer conversations found via social-media monitoring and text analysis, which might include comments, discussions in threaded forums, blogposts, etc.
- Profile information gleaned from Facebook, LinkedIn, Twitter, and other social networks and communities
- Records of the content created by the individual influencer or customer
- Third-party information associated with an account, including competitive intelligence or contemporary news
- The nature of the customer's role as a decision-maker within a business (in a B2B transaction), the influence they wield, and how and whom they influence
- Perhaps most importantly, customer-journey data

Let's chat a bit more about customer-journey data because it requires a changed data architecture to make it useful for real-time evaluation and orchestration, and for the historical record, thus preparing it for analytics action. It is difficult because the journey data is best served with fava beans and a nice chianti, um, I mean, is best served when used real-time. Doing this in real time creates its own set of problems because the customer's journey is ongoing and can contain a significant number of channels and sources, such as websites, emails, and even IoT sensors. The other "problem" is that you have to be able to pinpoint the individual's footprints when there are thousands running this omnichannel marathon in very similar sneakers—and they are running at record speed without let up. High speed, high volume, pinpoint accuracy of an individual's data, is tied to capture of the data, storage of the data, action on the data, and a response to the insights and actions suggested by the analysis of the data. All in real time or nearly so. This suggests that traditional data architectures don't work all that well. But, before we even get to what data architecture works for the new world, there are two other things that we have to factor in—the system of engagement that the customer is communicating with (which is providing the new velocities and volumes of data) and the evolution of the systems of record. They aren't sitting still but are growing out rather than transmogrifying into something entirely new.

Then we'll talk about the new data architecture.

Progress Marches On: The Network of Record, the Ecosystem of Record, Customer Data Platforms

Even though that overenthusiastic senior executive called the demise of the system of record the wave of the future, it actually has been evolving. In the past couple of years, it has become clear that the system of record that CRM always defined—which held the transactional data—was too limited given the need to learn from the data that each customer generates since it is available for harvesting or at least is accessible in potentially dozens of channels. The system of record's scope had to change.

In 2016, insight engine vendor Coveo rather cleverly began calling what they utilized an "ecosystem of record"—which is, in a purely literary way, really clever. But, beyond its literary merits, it is a smart way to imagine an expanded system of record. The way to conceptualize this is to think of thousands of data sources, even millions. A pipe is sunk into each of these data sources. Each time a query is created, all the data sources are searched, and the pertinent information is carried by the pipe to a central clearinghouse, where it is aggregated, analyzed, and then made visible on a screen at the clearinghouse to the customer or whoever is asking the question. But the data is never moved from its original source. It is (in effect, not technically) copied from its original source and made readable and relevant. But the data itself stays at its source and remains dynamically available and is *not* stored in a customer record per se—though the query and its results may be.

This differs from the schema of the Network of Record, which has been put forward by B2B Intelligence Platform provider, Radius. If I had to characterize the Network of Record, it is a meta-system of record—a system of records of systems of record. It takes all the systems of record out there, and the data captured from engagement systems and the data sources, and aggregates them (and stores them) in the cloud as a humungous data store. It is a different and equally valid approach to what Coveo is doing.

Here's John Hurley, Marketing Director at Radius, with his take on the Network of Record, explaining it far better than I can.

> *The abundance of data is overshadowed by major shortcomings in the quality of that data. The C-suite depends on data to drive strategy and individual contributors rely on data to operationalize go-to-market activities, but intelligence predicated on inaccurate and stale data can be harmful to their success at scale. I fully understand the quandary business executives are in right now. Achieving critical mass with data and intelligence takes time—time they feel they don't have. But here's the alternative: They remain tethered to traditional datasets and continue to find themselves late to every sales and marketing opportunity. Or, worse yet, they miss them altogether due to bad data.*
>
> *A network-effect-driven model is used by very few, if any, business-to-business applications, but the most disruptive consumer platforms (Facebook, Amazon, Uber, AirBnB) use the methodology as the foundation for their defensible positions. It is defined by a product that improves with every new user that joins. The Network of Record combines hundreds of data sources with data aggregated and anonymized from more than 760 million records contributed from their customers' systems of record. It effectively connects hundreds of CRM systems together to create a single source of truth.*
>
> *This accurate data is passed on to their clients, who are able to connect with more of their prospects, improve sales and marketing efficiency, and access richer intelligence. A Network of Record, to paraphrase Forrester Research, combines sourced and customer-contributed data, which could potentially create the largest cloud-based B2B data source and house the most up-to-date business information without the need for manual verification or the inaccuracy of purely crowd-sourced methods, leading to very high match rates and accuracies that do not degrade over time as quickly as other approaches.*

These approaches—the network of record and the ecosystem of record—regardless of what you choose to call them, are the cutting edge of systems of record and are well suited for dealing with data's volume and velocity, and the future.

These meta-systems are one of the directions that we are seeing with systems of record. They are not moving to oblivion and replacement by systems of engagement but to greater "thickness" by their evolution to something more meta than they have been in the past.

But it's not the only approach.

Another approach that is almost directly counter to these meta-systems has been gaining credence for a few years—customer data platforms.

Unlike the network of record or the ecosystem of record, the customer data platform (CDP) is an aggregate sort of data that has been optimized for marketers only, meaning that it is data with a highly specific focus.

There are three attributes of a customer data platform according the CPD Institute Director and marketing technology thought leader David Raab.

It has to be controllable by the marketer—In other words, what the system will do and what data will be included is the choice of the marketer

The data has to be unified and persistent—Marketing-relevant customer data must be assembled from multiple sources and made available permanently in a single place.

The system needs to be accessible by other systems—Through the use of APIs or tools that can extract specific useful data for use in other systems or via query languages the data is available to use in, say, a standard CRM customer record, which might include the transactional data or the case-management data. This becomes increasingly valuable as marketing departments align more and more with sales.

In late 2018, David expanded the scope of CDP's definition to this:

A Customer Data Platform is packaged software that creates a persistent, unified customer database that is accessible to other systems.

What's notable about this is that it is no longer for the marketer only.

All of these are increasingly valuable extensions of system of record at both a meta level (network of record, ecosystem of record) and a micro level to macro level (CDP). All are invaluable to the accessibility of the data needed to foster engagement, so take heed to these advances.

I hope you see that systems of engagement aren't going to be replacing systems of record, ever, but they are equally as important as systems of record, and together they make magic. The immediately pressing question, however, is what are they?

DEFINITION: SYSTEM OF ENGAGEMENT

At the simplest level, these are systems that allow communication and interaction between the company and customer. Technically, gamification systems, feedback systems, real-time interaction management systems (RTIM), and interaction engines (e.g., Infor's Epiphany or the Salesforce Marketing Cloud Interaction Studio, which is actually about 85 percent of Thunderhead's journey orchestration technology embedded as a white labeled Salesforce product), mobile messaging systems (like Skype, WeChat, Facebook Messenger, WhatsApp), and community feeds all fall under the umbrella of systems of engagement.

Ray Wang, CEO and founder of Constellation Research, who you met in Chapter 1, as far back as 2011 in the October 20 issue of *Harvard Business Review*, identified nine common characteristics of systems of engagement. By and large, I have no arguments whatever and think they are foundational characteristics. That said, I eliminated one and added one (identified below) that I think needs to be added. All the commentary is mine, unless I otherwise say so.

Design for sense and response—The systems are optimized to listen and then respond, which means—once they identify the context, sentiment, and the relationship of the interaction/communication to others in the conversation—they can determine a "best next action" to respond to the resulting assessment.

Design for usability, friendliness, easy navigation—They are created with the idea that, regardless of platform or device, they are easy to navigate and interesting to use. Currently, there is no guarantee that the conversation started on one channel can be easily continued on another. (This characteristic was added by me.)

Address massive social scale—This one is obvious. The scope and velocity of the conversations can be handled.

Foster conversation—They are designed explicitly to allow a company and its customers and other constituents to interact. They also encourage collaboration between or among parties.

Utilize a multitude of media styles for user experience—Omnichannel is the term du jour when it comes to communications strategies for a reason. There are thousands of channels and media to communicate on or to use to interact. They can be video, Twitter, Facebook, text, etc. They also can be systems that support explicit approaches to interaction, not just the media itself, such as gamification or feedback systems or communities.

Deliver speed in real time—Real-time listening and real-time response, which I outlined above.

Reach to multi-channel networks—I'll quote Ray here: "Engagement systems touch corporate, personal, and machine-based networks. A Skype call or instant message reaches out to both the corporate directory and your own personal network."

Factor in new types of information management—The data structure of the different media is, well, different in each case and, thus, not necessarily interoperable. Using them in combination with the newer extended systems of record (and the traditional ones) requires a newer kind of data architecture.

Rely on smarter intelligence and flexible tools—(I added tools.) The engagement systems rely on business rules and workflows like any system that involves movement of information. It has to go somewhere to someone so something can be done with it. But these systems need to be more flexible because the data is dynamic and continuous and flowing at a larger scale than anything we've ever seen. Rather than immutable processes, rather than tools that only skilled technicians can use, the tools that are associated with the business rules and workflows need to provide the flexibility for us to change them—even at the user level—if and when needed.

Systems of engagement enable customer communications with their companies of choice, if the company is smart enough to provide them. Having such a system makes your business so much better because the customers have the avenues they need to engage.

That said, when the systems of record and engagement are working together. . .

SYSTEMS OF RECORD AND ENGAGEMENT INTERTWINED

What a mind you have! Not *that* way.

What makes the relationship between systems of record and engagement unique is their symbiosis. The systems of engagement not only effect communication between the company and the customer but provide data to the systems of record, which then parse that data and feed optimized, personalized knowledge back to the systems of engagement so that the customer can respond to a personalized offer or other prompt from an AI-driven chatbot that keeps the customer interested (or more) in continuing to interact with the company, even if a human being never was involved in the conversation. That then garners a response by the customer, which provides more data, which . . . you get the message, right? The system of engagement provides the activity and behavioral data captured and stored in the system of record for analysis and reporting.

Of course, this takes us right back to the data architecture. A traditional data architecture that supports a more rigid, or at least highly structured data set, and doesn't need to factor in real-time responsiveness, isn't realistic any more. It leaves too much time between query and response, so to speak. A new data architecture that can work—say it again, kids—at scale and at high speed, is now necessary.

THE NEW DATA ARCHITECTURE FOR THE NEW CUSTOMER

The easy reason to think that a new data architecture is important is that big data necessitates it. While true, it is considerably more than that. It is also driven by the need for real-time responsiveness. Traditional data architectures—though they can handle scale to some extent—are not built to handle scale in real-time.

To be entirely candid, I'm not technical enough to tell you what that data architecture needs beyond the very simplest of lay terms. I have a great friend, however, who is a true visionary data architect—Ray Gerber. Aside from his creative responsibilities as a thinker, he is the Chief Product Officer of Thunderhead, the customer journey orchestration technology company I spoke about in Chapter 6 and will be talking about again in Chapter 14. He lays it out here for you.

*   *   *   *   *

Most data architectures in use today are focused on the tracking of transactional data. These data structures were designed in the era where most customers were engaged in a single channel at a time and were satisfied with "delayed" responses, meaning they were willing to wait a while to get answers to issues and questions, and even to get delivery of purchased products.

These data structures were focused on providing insights at a moment of time, (e.g., your current bank balance).

The proliferation of smart devices and the subsequent changes in customer expectations has, however, changed the requirements for these data structures. Customers want a seamless and fluent experience, and they want things (answers, products, etc.) NOW.

To properly engage with this new type of customer, brands need to:

- Be everywhere the customer is, all the time

- Understand the interaction context (i.e., device type and geolocation)

- Track cross-channel behavior

- Understand how customers behave over time to better understand when customers are ready to act (i.e., make purchases, etc.)

The key aspects of a data architecture needed to support these requirements are:

- A single corporate-wide data repository

  - All customer decisions are made from a single source of data to ensure consistency in outcomes

  - The data architecture builds itself out as brands gather additional and new insights into customers

- Support for the ability to have a data structure that can vary by each individual customer, (i.e., customer A can have 20 attributes while customer B can have only 5 attributes)

- Support for each record being extended with new data attributes without the need to rebuild the whole database table

- Multi-key identities

  - Support for multiple ways to identify customers as they use different touchpoints to engage

- Tracking of customers across lifecycle stages

  - Ability to track all interactions from when the visitor first interacted with the brand or thought becoming a customer, through the advocacy and retention stages

  - A single corporate-wide vocabulary that will translate data coming from foreign data sources into the single set of attributes that is used by the whole organization

    - This element is built into the architecture so that the translation happens in real time

- Track change in customer attributes over time. (There are two key architecture requirements here)

  - Track change in individual customer attributes over time

- This is required to see how individual attributes change over time (i.e., how interest in a product has increased or decreased in the last two weeks)

- Track the relationship between changes in multiple attributes over time (i.e., interest in product A increased by x percentage in the last week, while interest in product B decreased over the same time)

- Track behavior change over time

  - Support is needed for full end-to-end visualization and understanding of the customer journey

  - The key concept is that of sequence regardless of channel/touchpoint. The data therefore needs to be continually "reordered" as new interaction data comes in.

The final architecture requirement and probably the most significant one is the need to consume new data and translate it into insights in real time (near real time is not good enough anymore).

* * * * *

Thanks, Ray.

These are the parts we now have: a data architecture that is aligned with the scale and speed of data and customer needs, systems to capture and store that data, and systems that not only provide the means for customers and companies to communicate but allow for the capture of the communications data, too. You might be thinking, "Who gives a ____?" Despite your possible lack of enthusiasm, there are lots of reasons to be excited. Because this means we have the underpinnings for what may be the most important reason to use technology in service of customer engagement—personalization at scale and in real time.

PERSONALIZATION AT SCALE: THE TECHNOLOGY

In an era where engagement is a key strategy and where customers expect you to provide them with what they need to do whatever it is they are doing with you, data and insight become incredibly important for providing a personalized experience. But more than just identifying the products, services, tools, and consumable experiences necessary for the customer to sculpt their own choice of engagement with the company, businesses are now in a position where they must anticipate customer behavior and then develop optimized offers or programs for those individual customers in real time or close to that. While algorithms never determine those insights, the data analyzed and presented in the right way provide the basis for the insights. How can these insights be used?

The difficulties inherent in the identification of an insight are increased by magnitudes when two other factors come into play. Scale (i.e., the size of your customer base) and speed (i.e., the expectation that the action suggested by the insight will be taken live rather than later) more often than not add complexity to a situation that was already complex. As the customers are on their thousands and even millions of journeys, how do you find out what they are doing, interpret what you know about their activities, decide how you are going to respond to them, build the response, and communicate that response—all while the customers are still on their various journeys. Equally importantly, how are you going to do this in a meaningful, individualized way for thousands, maybe even millions, of people?

This is the dilemma of personalization at scale. Yet, because I know you've memorized every word you've read so far, you don't have to go back to Chapter 4 to be reminded of the benefits. Regardless of the difficulty, it is what you have to do; and the technology is there to do it. Memorize that.

FROM DATA TO INFORMATION TO KNOWLEDGE TO INSIGHT

Data is useless. No, I'm not kidding. Data is useless . . . until it is used in context. Think of it this way. How often has someone told you something, and your response, if you weren't being nice, was, "So what? Why'd you tell me that?" Whoever told you that, of course, thought they were telling you something of importance. But you had no idea why they told you that, right? The person who told you the "thing" had context—in other words, they had a reason to tell you. But you had no context, and so didn't understand what (or why) you were being told.

What you received was information without context and, thus, no meaningful actions could be taken. That is data. It becomes information when you give it context. It becomes knowledge when you define what the information's value is to you and its purpose. It is insight when you figure out how to use it effectively.

Think of it this way.

DATA:

- 17.5 ounces white flour, plus extra for dusting
- 2 tsp. salt

- ¼ ounce fast-action yeast

- 3 tbsp. olive oil

- 10.5 fluid ounces water

INFORMATION:

This is a recipe for making bread.

KNOWLEDGE:

Here's how you make the bread.

INSIGHT:

Judging from the comments on those who ate the bread made with this recipe, this is a good-tasting bread that can be made even more healthy and taste equally good with multigrain flour instead of white flour, but it would need 1 tbsp. more olive oil.

Of course, what isn't easy is to figure out how to take what is data and make it useful knowledge and ultimately gain some actionable insights. The technologies are there to parse the data and then run the algorithms that provide you with what you need to see to gain the insights, as long as you are not overwhelmed by the amounts of data available to you. Scale can be frightening. But the approach to handling big data coming at you at high velocity is simple: take control of it. Follow these steps so that you can gain value from the data you have.

1. Don't treat it as big data.
2. You want something from it.
3. Decide what it is you're looking for.
4. Develop a hypothesis.
5. Decide on what specific information is going to be needed.
6. Plan accordingly.
7. Gather the information—which means find the data, organize it, and build the reports that provide it to you in the form you need.
8. Run the analytics on the data—the analytics can be descriptive, predictive, or prescriptive (more on that shortly).
9. Use the knowledge you have to produce the insights you need.
10. Apply those insights (e.g., make an optimized offer to a particular customer).

GOOD ANALYSIS MEANS NO THERAPY

Before we really get into analytics, I'm going to stop here and take a breath. I have to focus. No, not because I'm losing it, though I have been accused of that more than once, but because we're only going to be talking about customer-engagement-related analytics here, not analytics in general. I'm guessing you have a pretty good idea of what analytics are. If not, read the excellent Thomas Davenport article "Analytics 3.0" in the December 2013 issue of *Harvard Business Review* (hbr.org/2013/12/analytics-30). It's worth your time. Then finish reading this chapter, though it's pretty self-explanatory.

CAN ALGORITHMS SHOW YOUR LOVE . . . IF THAT'S WHAT YOU THINK IT IS?

Given the large number of data types and the sources and difficulty with providing clarity, how do we use analytics to find the optimal customer-engagement actions we have to take? What are we analyzing?

The science of customer engagement is the attempt to systematize how humans interact and then to create a methodology to make the efforts, processes, and results repeatable and reusable so they can be applied to any size of endeavor. Ultimately, to be able to make that happen, you need to recognize its greatest limitation. At best, the effort can reproduce the model of an *approximation* of how humans interact and, thus, give you the basis for insights on how to anticipate future human behavior, either *en masse* or at an individual level. But that predicted behavior is also, at best, a reasonable assumption, no more. Why is it only, effectively, a good guess? First, because, in real life, each human interacts with other humans and institutions in a different way than every other human. That means that, for example, I interact with you, differently than I interact with your brother, and he interacts with me differently than you do, and you interact with him differently than you interact with me, etc. This is true even if the interactions are for the same purpose. What? Yeah, I know your brother. Moving on. To add nuance, while an infinite number of interactions are possible, each human has a set of constraints that exist to limit how they can respond. They are constrained by their individual bandwidth, which, in much simpler terms, means no one human can respond to everyone they have the opportunity to interact with in a given time frame. So they have to decide who they are going to interact with and, given many considerations, of the infinite number of ways they can interact with someone or something, how they are going to interact. That means, if the interaction is with your business, the customer has a reason they chose to interact with your business and not someone else's. They have a context for how they chose to interact with you. So a single interaction out of context might end up with the wrong response from you because you didn't understand why they interacted that way.

Confused? Let's revisit an example from back in Chapter 6 but come at it differently this time.

Remember the example of a purchase attempt made on Amazon in a normal frame of mind contrasted with one made in an irritated state of mind due to a fight with a significant other? If you remember, the item in the cart was temporarily abandoned in the first scenario and permanently abandoned in the second. But in the two-hour window before the purchase, without any context, there was no difference in the actual action taken of leaving the item in the cart. The context (not irritated, and irritated) determined the final outcome, which was different in each case. The customer's behavior was dictated by their emotional state.

Now let's throw in a twist and add predictive analytics to the mix (along with social listening). Amazon would like to be able to anticipate the outcome of your actions based on past behavior, the behavior of people like you, etc. If the only data they have is your transactional data, then there isn't much they can really figure out because the propensity to purchase that book is based on things like books like that you bought versus books you've considered and abandoned, etc. But that can't account for your bad day or your emotional state. So, as I said, in Chapter 6, their only recourse is to fix the lag since they have no idea why you were so upset. (And that's something they should do even if they did know.)

But imagine if you were "vocal" about that bad state of mind on social media or you even more specifically tweeted "#Amazon lag time is driving me nuts—and so are all of you! #drivemecrazy #arrrggh." If they had that data and had incorporated it into the data they were looking at, it might suggest that the reason the cart was apparently abandoned wasn't just the lag time. It gives the data some potential context and, thus, it might provide a better indication of future behavior. Having said that, though, decisions do have to be made as to whether it is worth the effort to find that out or to just fix the lag.

As we established in Chapter 4, human beings are self-interested, so they are expecting a response that appeals to them as individuals, not as a group. Which means understanding individual and segmented behavior. Even though the customer demands individual attention, you still have to understand their common behaviors and their similar interests (they don't have to be identical), which allows you to effectively create responses that can appeal to a larger group at the level of the individual.

PREDICTIVE ANALYTICS AND THE BEST NEXT ANALYTICS: PRESCRIPTIVE

Applying analytics allows you to make the best interpretation of the data you have. If you are using predictive methodologies and algorithms, you can make a best guess—often correctly—as to how individual customers will behave in a specific situation (e.g., a marketing campaign). You can, using prescriptive analytics, decide what your best next action will be in, for example, a sales opportunity—use this presentation, make this the offer, or speak to this influencer of that decisionmaker. Companies like Lattice Engines do that for sales and marketing, Thunderhead do that for customer journeys, and Pegasystems do that for marketing, sales, and customer service. As an example, PROS, a technology company based in Houston, Texas, optimizes pricing to produce anything from a quote for industrial equipment to dynamic prices for airline seats. PROS uses advanced algorithms that work in real time to look at the demand, history, external conditions, airline industry comparisons, weather, and a whole variety of other factors that go into the price of your airline seat.

To provide optimal engagement, the analytics models have to take into account more than the transactional history. The model has to account for the known behaviors, preferences, and tastes of the customers. The models have to account for the demographic and geographic differences that are reflected in the individual behaviors.

To give you a bit more of the technological picture, I'm going to give you a few examples of the kinds of models that are used for engagement analytics.

The Model

I'm not a data scientist. I can't pretend to get into the math that goes into building these analytics models, but I can give you the types of models that are appropriate to developing queries around customer engagement. Let's look at three. One note: they are often used in tandem.

> **Clustering analysis**—Cluster analysis is an appropriately named model that is designed to take the survey samples and then surface groups that organically have similar affinities. In principal, it's a very simple model. Similarly answered surveys lead to the creation of a group populated by those who gave the similar answers. But it actually takes a lot of work to build the model, especially when the survey questions are focused around attitude or behavior. Criteria have to be established for what "similarity"

is. The results are not the same as segmentation by age, gender, location, or job status. The results of clustering lead to groups like those mentioned below in the Telenor case study—Sure Things, Persuadables, Lost Causes, and Sleeping Dogs. I'll leave it to you to read the case study to find out what they mean, but they are grouped by likely behaviors.

Propensity models—This is a commonly used model. You've probably heard it most frequently as "propensity to buy." All in all, it means that you are developing models to identify customers who are likely to do or not do something. It can be likely to churn, likely to respond to a particular offer, likely to do x if y, z, and ab are presented or occur. Typically, there is a score associated with the likelihood.

Collaborative filtering—The likely way you've seen the results of collaborative filtering are via recommendation engines. Along those lines, "because of your past transactions, your current web behavior, the purchasing and viewing behaviors of others who have similar tastes and preferences to you, we recommend this first, this second, and this third." In the newer, narrower sense, collaborative filtering is a method of making automatic predictions (filtering) about the interests of a user by collecting preferences or taste information from many users (collaborating). The underlying assumption of collaborative filtering is the same as the concept of a "person like me." Give the similar tastes and preferences of person A and person B, the likelihood of their similarity on other things is greater than would be the case with a random other person.

I'm not going to dwell on the models any further, but these are useful to show the constructs that drive the analytics.

Customer Engagement Metrics: A Sampling

The difficulty in writing this chapter is that to fully cover customer engagement data and analytics would require a book unto itself, but, due to space limitations, we can only scan the available concepts, models, sources, and metrics at a high level.

When it comes to the kinds of results you're looking for, it can vary because, as I hope by now you figured out, customer engagement covers every single customer-facing activity and organization at a company. So, there are marketing-engagement metrics, community metrics, sales metrics, customer-journey metrics, customer-service metrics, social-media metrics . . . the list is endless.

Here are a couple of somewhat more recent examples to highlight what I mean.

COMMUNITY ENGAGEMENT

- Visits converted to community new registrations (i.e., visits to the website that convert into registrations for the online community)
- Registered community logins to comments and responses (i.e., how active are the community members)

MARKETING ENGAGEMENT

- Clicks, conversions, shares
- Email opens
- Content ROI

SALES ENGAGEMENT

- Customer lifetime value
- Revenues per customer
- Overall revenue increases

These are simple metrics. They all reflect customer-engagement success (or failure). However, to drive this home, I'm going to give you a bit of a deeper dive into customer-journey analytics, what they measure, and how they are derived. This is based on Thunderhead, the customer journey orchestration platform advanced analytics model. So put on your suits and get ready to hit the water.

JOURNEYLITICS

To table-set, if we are looking at the full Thunderhead analytics package we find there are three types: profile analytics, journey analytics, and conversation analytics. I'm only concerned with journey analytics.

The same way CRM is the operational core for engagement, the customer journey is the center for knowledge of the customer's interactions and behaviors. When Thunderhead developed the analytics models for what they called "Journeylitics," they identified what they were looking for, the outcomes that the analytics needed to produce, and the metrics that would define those outcomes.

What They Were Looking For

Thunderhead understood that if they were going to develop a valuable analytics platform they needed to identify certain outcomes. The ones for journey analytics they found most compelling were:

Preferred cross-channel behavior—What sets of channels did customers at scale and individual customers prefer for their communication and interaction?

Number of touchpoint transitions needed to achieve goal—How many different types of places, digital or otherwise, did the customer have to go to before their task was completed?

Number of interactions needed to achieve goal—This one is self-explanatory.

Similarity of people that behaved in the most common manner—This goes to the heart of the analytic models for engagement above. This is clustering analysis.

Time delay to conversion—This means the touchpoints that were closest in time to the customer's conversion gets the greatest "credit" for that conversion.

Churn detection—Who is most likely to churn? (see below); who is least likely to churn?

Behavior post-employee engagement—How is the customer acting after interacting with an employee, either in the immediate environment or over time.

Following their identification of the set of desired outcomes they wanted to measure, the next steps for Journeylitics was to identify an aggregate set of analytics "types" that would provide the most useful picture of the customer's or customers' journey(s). The basket:

Best path—Based on various metrics (e.g., count, cost, duration), including path-based Adaptive Engagement Profile (AEP) clustering.

Attribution analysis—This measures the success or failure of campaigns as they occur during the customer journey.

Moments of Truth (MoT) analysis—A way of determining (anticipating) the key places and times where the company can impact the customer most effectively with a chosen action.

Root cause analysis—This is analysis that determines why something happened, not just what happened.

Path predictions—Which way will the customer or a group of customers be likely to go?

Path alteration recommendations—To optimize the value that the customer can provide, what path would you redirect the customer or group of customers on?

With the analytics frameworks in place and running, proprietary algorithms perform common path analysis based on presence of a target node that would be specific to the type of analysis. A "target node," for those of you as technically ignorant as I am, would be, in its simplest form on a sales journey, a "purchase node." The analytics would identify all the journeys that had to travel to that purchase node. If it were more complex—and the idea would be, for example, who called the contact center to get more detail around a product—the target node could be, for example, the intersection of the "Assisted Channel" (the call center) and the journey stage called "Knowledge" (information about the product). All journeys that showed a visit to the Assisted Channel and had a conversation about a product, i.e., a product-knowledge discussion, would be surfaced via the algorithms.

If for some reason there are no available target nodes, Thunderhead's engine fires up the DBScan algorithm, which does path clustering (see cluster analysis above) to find the organic available groupings and how they behave along a specific path or paths that are uncovered by the clustering.

The next step is the application of AEP clustering that then takes these identified clusters and looks at the affinities between how people behave across their journeys and their profile status.

Once that is done, and the data is captured in real time, the data can be analyzed to find out things like:

Most common path—What touchpoints, activity types, and sequences are preferred by most customers?

Cheapest path—What is the cheapest path (based on cost per channel) preferred?

Shortest path—What is the shortest path that customers take from start to end point?

Least-effort path—What paths for what customers, all in all, use the fewest steps, take the shortest time, and have the least transitions?

The reason I've spent the time doing, not really a deep dive, but more a walk in the deeper end of the pool here is that it gives you a non-technical idea of not only how analytics for engagement work but also how to think about the outcomes you need to associate with it.

I'm going to start bringing it home now with a case study about Telenor, a Norwegian telco; but before I do, since churn and telcos cohabit, I'm going to discuss churn because it is a widespread example of how and why customers disengage.

CHURN, BABY, CHURN

I'm sure that if you have ever had anything to with anything related to business whatsoever, you've had an issue with churn. The churn I'm talking about is not the process of making butter, though that's got a far better result than the one I mean. The churn I'm nattering on about is a loss of customers—those customers who voluntarily leave companies each and every year, often faster than the gain in customers. One industry that has staggering problems with churn and has had for a *long* time is telecommunications. The annual telco churn rate is so bad, anywhere from 10 percent to 67 percent according to the 2017 numbers of the Database Marketing Institute, that the telcos measure their precipitous fall in monthly average rates to soften the PR blow but also to micromanage and to be able to intervene to reduce the loss in a timelier way.

I'm sure you'll realize, if you think about it, you've got to take some responsibility for the telecommunications industry's misery yourself—unless you've only had one carrier your whole life. You've probably moved seats somewhere in the Verizon/AT&T/T-Mobile/Other Smaller Carrier merry-go-round at some point. Plus, your tolerance for problems that carriers cause is probably considerably lower for your wireless carrier than it is for other types of companies you use for services, isn't it? So, some trigger caused you to disengage from a carrier at some point.

Keep in mind there are serious customer-engagement costs to the carriers each time you leave, and, even though you leave, the bad taste in your mouth doesn't. The process of disengagement costs that company 13 percent of the normally expected revenue, share-of-wallet, etc., as you are leaving and, when you go, it costs 100 percent, of course.

If the solution to the problem was simply reducing customer loss, there would no real need for predictive analytics. But it's more complex than that. The complexity comes in two places: the reasons for the churn and the kind of customer you are dealing with as you target potential churn.

The types of churn vary a great deal. First, the intent to churn can be active (they are planning to leave because they are so fed up with the carrier already), passive (a trigger causes them to leave even though they didn't plan it), or involuntary (they are moving to a city that has no coverage by their current carrier).

The reasons for the churn vary as greatly. For example:

Fed up with carrier—This is the bulk of churners. One strange statistic: according to the Database Marketing Institute, 17 to 20 million subscribers sign up with a new provider every year. Sounds okay so far, doesn't it? Well, 75 percent of those new subscribers are people who left another carrier. So, the bulk of new subscribers are customers who couldn't be retained by someone else. I mean . . . what?

Promotional churn—The subscriber leaves due to a promotional offer from another carrier.

Contagious churn—A brand influencer starts to trash a telco, or any company really, and, as a result of that dissing, others leave the company. But, keep in mind, in this particular case, the inclination to leave really needs to have been there already. If they were happy and not in a cult, the say-so of a brand influencer isn't necessarily going to be enough to get customers to depart.

Churn is also impacted a great deal by inertia, and it is dangerous if misinterpreted. The cost of change is often higher than the perceived value of moving, and that leads to inertia. But it doesn't stay that way. That's part of the complexity of churn. How do you know that the reason that the customers aren't leaving isn't just the cost is currently too great and at some point, due to a trigger or just a better deal, the costs are no longer an obstacle. At that point, watch out. *Or* be smart, figure out why the customer is staying, and decide on a course of action to keep them—which means, in some cases, transforming the inertia to loyalty or at least some minimal standard of happiness with the company.

How can you use analytics to interpret your customers, provide the basis for insights, and then decide on a course of action for those customers based on the insights? For that, ladies and gents, I'm going take you on a trip to Norway. Metaphorically, of course. I can't afford to actually take you. That would be way too expensive.

TELENOR MEETS PREDICTIVE ANALYTICS

Telenor is a Norwegian telco that primarily services all of Scandinavia or the Nordics, depending on your level of political correctness. They have 177 million mobile subscribers (2017) throughout Europe and Asia, with total revenues of $13 billion by the end of 2017. They have an immense market share in Norway—well over 50 percent. They touch on all the right things for a responsible company: gender equality, sustainability, inclusion, innovation efforts, artificial intelligence research, etc. They are making efforts to stop cyber-bullying. They are constantly building their infrastructure, with 5G initiatives to expand their speed and bandwidth. Yet, they have had significant churn over the years. But because they are a smart, progressive company, they realized that they had to start using tools with their data to reduce that churn. Any reduction in churn—even a single percentage point—is worth millions of dollars to a telco. But the efforts to reduce churn—especially the traditional efforts that telcos made, which were usually aimed at an undifferentiated customer base—could be costly. How to manage this?

Their biggest problem was low-cost acquisition programs by competitors. Their defections were significant because they were, at least at the time, unable to offer similar programs. Also, they were blind to which customers were prone to suggestion when offers like this were made by their competitors.

Telenor realized that they had to begin aggressive, proactive marketing campaigns that were designed to retain those customers. But to do that effectively, at a reasonable cost, meant they had to know how to target the customers rather than throw an undifferentiated campaign at a conglomerate mass of customer blobs.

To figure out how to differentiate their customers and anticipate the possibility of churn in various customer groups, they used an approach to analytics called uplift modeling. Uplift modeling predicts not just the likelihood of the performance of an action but can also anticipate a change in the likelihood of performing that action. By understanding the context of the customers' actions, the time and timing of those actions, and the impact of others on the actions and of the actions on others, it can measure not just the propensity to churn of an individual but the actual impact of an action on that individual (for instance, as we mentioned earlier, the impact on a particular person or a brand influencer blasting Telenor for some reason).

Once they decided on uplift modeling, they had to decide on the data that, for this specific project, was meaningful. In this case, they primarily used internal transactional data from billing systems, customer service, and sales. Social, not so much. They had nothing inherently against social data, but the internal data served the purpose, was more efficiently organized, and was more cost-effective.

They hunted for a number of variables within that data to help them distinguish the customer "groups" that they were trying to type. In part, those variables included the size of the plan the customer had, the call volume, the additional products beyond basic services, and the propensity to either attrite or, conversely, to respond positively to an offer, based on historic data.

They weren't working blindly from the data, hoping to suss out insights without any real idea of what they wanted. They had a game plan. There were four distinct customer "types" that they felt were important to identify:

Sure Things—Customers who are loyal and committed. They will stay and, thus, no time has to be spent persuading them to stay.

Persuadables—They could leave but are amenable to suggestion. They can be persuaded to stay with offers

Lost Causes—It doesn't matter what Telenor would do, they will leave. Same as the Sure Things, no point in spending any time on them.

Sleeping Dogs—This may be the trickiest group. They are fine because they are inert and not thinking about taking any actions other than paying their bill each month. But, if you send them an offer, it might awaken their brain cells to the point that they decide to leave. Again, a really tricky group to interpret.

The idea was that once you were able to identify which customers fit into what groups, you could develop a plan for each group. The most obvious approaches were: for Sure Things and Lost Causes, do nothing at all. For Sleeping Dogs, it was a bit tricky; but if Telenor did anything, it would be low-key and relentlessly positive. They chose, however, to do nothing with the Sleeping Dogs. They, ahem, let them lie. Persuadables were clearly the focal point, and the time, money, and labor were put into this group.

The results were excellent. Those who used traditional modeling and analytics got, typically, a 5 percent reduction in churn. But using uplift modeling, predictive analytics, and, then, based on the results, targeting only the Persuadables—who turned out to be 60 percent of the potential churners—Telenor got a 6.8 percent attrition reduction (a 36 percent better result), at a 40 percent cost reduction, saving them millions of dollars, or, if you prefer the local currency, tens of millions of Norwegian Kroner. Analytics done right lead to insight, which lead to churn reduction, which means continued engagement with customers who might well have disengaged.

I'm pretty tired, now, and I've done all the talking. So, I'm going to turn the conversation over to two of our gurus. They have so much more to tell you about the technology out there and how it's being used. So much.

First up, David Myron

THOUGHT LEADER: DAVID MYRON

David Myron has been one of the most consistent voices in the CRM world. I've known him more than 10 years. Until recently, he has been the editorial director of *CRM Magazine.* Now he is the editor-in-chief of *ProSales* magazine.

But what he always is, aside from a man with a big heart, is an astute observer of the outside world and a highly knowledgeable CRM practitioner and thought leader.

I grabbed David at the tail end of his sojourn at *CRM Magazine* to write this piece because it is an area that has to be addressed—systems of record vs. systems of engagement. He, as the wordsmith he is, addresses it so well.

Take a listen to David.

*   *   *   *   *

Customer relationship management has taken on many different definitions over the years, but one aspect of CRM that many can agree on is that, when used well, the CRM database is the customer record for organizations. It's where you can find valuable customer demographic and behavioral information that has been captured by the company over the course of its relationship with customers. Having access to this information is incredibly valuable to marketing, sales, and customer-service professionals as it enables them to provide more personalized interactions. But as people conduct more of their interactions and transactions over digital channels, and especially as many of these interactions become automated, new opportunities for pairing systems of record with systems of engagement will emerge.

Systems of engagement are the systems that customers use to interact with a product and/or company. Whether it's a website, a kiosk, an agent-facing customer-support application, a speech-enabled interactive voice-response system, or a smart watch, systems of engagement are digitally connected devices or systems that interface with employees, partners, prospects, and customers.

Some of these systems already connect to CRM systems. For example, an agent-facing customer support application can connect to a CRM system to pull up a customer's account so the agent can view the activity in the account. For other emerging systems of engagement (think mobile, social, and the Internet of Things) that aren't yet connecting to CRM systems, the opportunities are endless.

What happens when an organization forces employees to use a system of record without focusing on how that experience affects their engagement? It runs the risk of creating task-oriented processes. Salespeople have long viewed entering customer data into their CRM system as a burdensome task that distracts them from the thing they want to do most—sell. Naturally, this breeds resentment toward the

CRM system and often derails CRM adoption. If a company does nothing to address this, and it doesn't mind creating task-oriented processes for employees, that attitude toward CRM often trickles down to its customers.

For those who have called into a contact center and have been forced to repeat their account number or other personal information to different agents on the same call, they know what it feels like to become victims of a task-oriented mindset. This happens when an organization focuses too much on the task and not enough on the customer experience. As a result, customers feel as though they're being processed through the system and not valued, which naturally degrades the customer experience.

This is what prompted the "outside-in" or "customer first" mentality in the CRM industry, which encourages organizations to think about customers' needs before the company's needs. Before a process or technology upgrade, executives must ask the following question: "Will this change negatively affect the customer experience? If the answer is "yes," it's time to rethink the plan.

Systems of engagement, however, tend to put the customer first. These systems aim to help customers not only accomplish their tasks, but do so as quickly as customers need and as thoroughly as they want. For example, organizations that build speech-enabled IVRs to automate customer service calls often hire human-factors analysts who study how people interact with machines. If these analysts find there's a bottleneck in the system, they'll troubleshoot it and make recommendations for improvement. It's not unlike the way a customer strategist might create a customer-journey map to evaluate customer-engagement bottlenecks.

When organizations pair their systems of engagement with their system of record, they're not only connecting valuable customer information with customer-facing systems, they're forced to think about CRM in a new way—from a task-oriented mentality to customer-experience mentality that puts the customers' needs first.

Think about what this might mean as organizations embrace the Internet of Things. Because digitally connected devices can record customer usage patterns, products can capture that information to facilitate transactions. Already, customers who own an LG Smart Manager refrigerator can access the fridge's inventory through an iOS or Android app, so owners can keep track of what they need to buy. It can also monitor its contents and automatically add food to a user's online shopping account when supplies are running low.

Connected products can help manufacturers to engage with their customers, suppliers, partners, and distributors like never before. Once-ordinary objects can become smart, context-aware, and connected, further bridging the gap between physical and digital realms.

For manufacturers to enable their systems of record to connect with systems of engagement, they should consider the technology drivers of the IoT—cloud, mobile, and social media. They should also look for functionality, such as email integration, which can drive user adoption. Finally, manufacturers should seek a CRM solution designed for their industry and integrated with major business solutions such as ERP, business intelligence, and marketing automation applications to help them operate more efficiently and deliver an exceptional customer experience.

· · · · ·

Thank you, David. Next up is Dr. Michael Wu.

THOUGHT LEADER: DR. MICHAEL WU

What can I tell you about Michael Wu? He is a leading voice and visionary when it comes to the science of technology. He has designed systems, created algorithms, cloned alien entities—okay, maybe not the last one. And while doing all this work first as the Chief Scientist at community platform tech company, Lithium, and now as the Chief AI Scientist for PROS, he has managed to travel the world as a thought leader in areas as diverse as gamification, influence, big data, and so many others that I can't even begin to share them all. But, if you meet him, and you should, he is so humble that you'd have no idea that he is as accomplished as he is. He won't tell you. So, I will. He is *very* accomplished, which is why I have him here to talk to you about customer engagement, data, and AI.

Michael, take it away with that big heart of yours.

· · · · ·

Today most enterprises are drowning in data but starving for insights. Although the big data industry provided the infrastructure for capturing, storing, processing, and retrieving huge volumes of data economically, most companies are not realizing the full potential of their big data assets. There is a big data gap between what the industry provides and what businesses really need, which are the information and insights derived from the big data. Information and insights are what help businesses make better decisions, engage their customers more effectively, and drive more profitability.

Due to the natural correlation within any data set, the amount of information that can be extracted from big data is actually quite small; and the insights that can be gleaned, even smaller. Despite its scarcity, you might not need a lot of insights to win in the market. Just as a single grain of rice can tip the balance, a single bit of insight can mean the difference between winning and losing.

The story of Bronwyn Cook illustrates this point. Bronwyn has been a 20-year customer of an Australian mobile provider who is reaching the renewal point of her contract. After some shopping around, she tweeted her current provider to inquire if they have any multi-device plans, which are offered by a competitor. To her surprise, the competitor's agent responded first, even though she didn't use their twitter handle in her original tweet. But what's more surprising was the tweet itself, which says

@broncook76 Sounds like your Living On A Prayer Bronwyn, if you get off the Lost Highway I'd be happy to have a chat! Have A Nice Day – Sav

After several back-and-forth tweets and chats with both her current provider and the competitor, the competing provider eventually converted her. Obviously, the competing provider has the plan she needs, the customer experience (CX) with their agent was excellent, and the application process painless. But it all started because Sav, the competitor's agent, had a critical piece of insight—Bronwyn is a Bon Jovi fan. Sav's initial reply referenced three Bon Jovi songs that Bronwyn immediately recognized (i.e., Living On A Prayer, Lost Highway, and Have A Nice Day). This piece of insight is only a few bytes of text on Bronwyn's twitter profile, hiding among several hundred million others (i.e., big data). But it was used well, so Sav was able to engage Bronwyn effectively and eventually drive profitability for his company.

The moral of this story is that big data is undoubtedly important; but, in its raw form, it's too big to be actionable. It needs to be distilled, filtered, and reduced down to information and insights that are actionable to be useful. Currently, data scientists are responsible for this data-reduction process. They use analytics to distill possibly zettabytes of big data down to a few bytes, and sometimes to a single bit (i.e., 1/8 of a byte), so humans can decide which course of actions to take.

Because insights are, by definition, new information that isn't known beforehand, having access to insights will usually change people's decisions. This will alter the subsequent actions and potentially the outcome. In the context of engagement, insight about the customers (or consumers in general) will change how we engage them. The engagement will become more relevant and more personal. This could lead to a different outcome, though it's not guaranteed.

In our example with Bronwyn Cooke, Sav would probably have engaged her very differently if it hadn't been for the insight that she's a Bon Jovi fan. But because Sav discovered this insight, he was able to engage her at a much more personal level that get her attention immediately. Although this ultimately converted Bronwyn, we can't prove that she wouldn't have been converted otherwise because it's counterfactual. Even if it is the case that she would've been converted anyway, and this insight did not produce immediate value in this particular engagement, it could still be valuable in future engagements.

One of the most important consequences of engagement is the development of a stronger customer relationship, which manifests in customer loyalty. Customer insights provide a deeper understanding of customers and open the door to a whole new level of personalized engagement. This will increase the efficacy of the engagement, which builds loyalty and drives profitability.

The inception of artificial intelligence (AI) is an inevitable evolution of big data, analytics, and automation. Traditional business analytics have limited accuracy due to constraints imposed by the data, the model, and sheer computing power. Thus, regardless of what the analytics suggest, humans always have the final decision. Today's big data and distributed computing infrastructure changed this. Machine learning can train models to produce results that closely match that of human experts. By leveraging training data from multiple human experts, modern analytics can even produce results that are better than any individual. This makes human decisions seem redundant.

It's only a matter of time before we endow machines with the power to make decisions, cutting humans out of the loop. This automation of decisions and subsequent actions is the birth of AI. For example, traditional analytics may show us performance data and forecasts that suggest certain transactions to optimize our portfolio value, but it's up to us to decide whether we want to to make those trades or not. Today, AI-powered robo-advisors can make the decision and execute those trades on our behalf. One of the simplest prescriptive analytics is a GPS, which prescribes an optimal route to our destination; but we can always decide when and where we want to follow the route. In the near future, AI-powered self-driving vehicles can simply automate those decisions and just take us to our destination.

The rise of AI also has a significant implications for customer engagement. Innovative enterprises are already using chatbots to engage customers at various touch-points along the customer's journey. Although human engagements are more personal, they are inconsistent and error-prone. This is because humans fatigue over time, and they are easily influenced by their moods and the environment. It would be very difficult for Sav to come up with an equally creative response to every customer he engages, even if the same level of insights are available. Moreover, a different agent is likely to provide a completely different CX. Business processes are often required to minimize these human inconsistencies and mitigate the impact of careless human errors.

As with any machine automation, AI can provide consistency and compliance to the engagement without sacrificing scale and speed. Keep in mind that consistency of customer experience doesn't mean the exact same experience every time with every customer. Rather, it means the same level of politeness, verbosity, patience, humor, etc., which can all be tuned and standardized in an AI. It also means the engage agent (or bot) will have the same level of technical expertise and personalization, which can also be normalized by having access to the same knowledge bases and CRM data.

Access to big data beyond the enterprise, however, and the capacity to distill them into actionable insights, can provide the next level of personalization to engagement, as in the case with Bronwyn Cook. This was very difficult to operationalize at high speed and large scale while maintaining a consistent CX across the entire customer base until AI came along. At that point, how much personalization we want is merely a function of how much data we are comfortable sharing. Customers can essentially specify the desired level of personalization in their brand engagement. If we want, perhaps someday we can all get an equally creative response as Bronwyn Cook from brands we engage.

* * * * *

Michael was great, wasn't he? As always.

Luckily, by both David and Michael speaking for awhile, it gave me the time to catch my breath, take a nap, and get refreshed. I'm going to need it because Chapter 14 is the "other" chapter on technology and the front end to this backend. The scope is seriously big. So turn the page and take a breath.

CHAPTER 14

Enabling It All: Products, Services, Tools

I kind of came into the discussion about technology backwards by starting it in Chapter 13 with what goes on and what you need to do when you have the data for personalization. But there is *so* much more going on—before you get data, while you have it, and after it gets analyzed—than you can imagine. So, rather than leave it to your imagination, I'm going to describe the front end—the applications, the services, and the tools—that are used by the company and provided by the company to the customers to foster more effective customer engagement. To get there, though, I need to spend a little time delineating some things so that there is no confusion if you ever are in the market for customer-engagement-related technology. By design, this and the previous chapter are the longest in the book, so I can cover engagement technology with some clarity, which isn't easy when it is in a protoplasmic state. But I try, oh, how I try.

THE CUSTOMER ENGAGEMENT TECHNOLOGY "MARKET"

As of this writing, there is no customer engagement technology "market." Much as I'd like to think otherwise, the customer engagement technology landscape is far too immature at this juncture to be called anything resembling a market. It is more a protoplasmic entity that is still trying to figure out what it wants to be when it grows up. That isn't to say that there isn't an evolving customer engagement technology basket of products, services, and tools available for your business pleasure. Because customer engagement, as we established early on, is a top-of-mind C-level initiative, the tech companies are building new products, or tweaking their existing products, changing their messaging and rebranding to meet the functional needs and to trip the emotional wires around customer engagement. For example, Marketo, who, in 2018, were acquired by Adobe, changed its messaging from "revenue performance management," which was their idea of marketing automation, to "engagement marketing," a rather dramatic re-messaging. Gamification as a separate technology category has gone away and is now "engagement." Microsoft has changed its Dynamics CRM product name to Intelligent Customer Engagement, which is now part of Dynamics 365. The enterprise feedback management (EFM) category is now called an engagement platform. I can keep going, but I won't.

Ultimately, the problem for those companies in the market for selection of a customer engagement enabling application, solution, or platform, is that what vendors call customer-engagement technologies aren't necessarily even remotely similar, though they each may legitimately be part of a customer-engagement technology matrix, or ecosystem. It simply means there are a lot of variables that go into an end-to-end customer engagement technology matrix.

For example, go to the website of Capterra, an organization that provides comparative assessments of varying types of software for selection. Type in "customer engagement" and look at the options. Here are some examples.

Lithium—A "customer engagement platform," which I personally call a community platform and that Lithium thinks is a digital-experience platform. Whoever you believe, they fall within the spectrum of customer-engagement technology.

Five9—A customer-service-focused platform

Yotpo—An online-review-generation application (ugh)

WalkMe—Engagement through "enterprise-grade guidance." A highly sophisticated contextual help platform

VeriShow—Their own description: "VeriShow's sales technology provides everything a salesperson needs to connect, present and close with prospects online."

Capterra, as of the end of 2018, has all in all 103 total categories tagged as "customer engagement software," and a mindboggling 14,958 products with each very different than the other. Which is the problem. Yet, it isn't that these companies are being deceptive—or at least, not most of them. They do foster customer engagement. The question you should concern yourself with is how valuable or important is the technology to your specific engagement strategy? Don't worry what it's called; find out what it does for you, not just what it does in general.

All that said, there is an identifiable customer-engagement technology eco-system that, if you could fully embrace it, would allow you to enable a truly end-to-end capability. But the one *big* caveat: there is no way in hell that you will be able to do *all* of what would be a complete ecosystem, and there is no way that a single vendor can provide you with the full spectrum. No way.

It's still important to see what the total ecosystem looks like so that you can make some sense of the software and services you want to use to enable your strategy.

So, what I'm going to do here is construct the ecosystem and deconstruct the parts as best I can. One more, and final, caveat: this is a work in progress, so changes are likely over time. If you are interested in the status of this, find me at paul-greenberg3@the56group.com, and I'll give you a status update on the matrix.

THE CUSTOMER ENGAGEMENT TECHNOLOGY MATRIX

There are 29 technology categories (not Capterra's loosely defined 103) that I can reasonably identify as customer-engagement related. While I'm not going to take you through the 29 (though they are available in detail on my site, the56group.com), I am going to focus on what we Yankees fans, during other, happier times, called "The Core Four." For Yankees fans, that was Derek Jeter, Jorge Posada, Mariano Rivera, and Andy Pettite. Arguably there was a High Five (my name and my name only)—which should have included Bernie Williams. But that's an argument for another day.

The customer engagement Core Four includes:

- CRM, which is the operational core for customer-facing departments, including a strong business-process engine (as outlined in Chapter 7), workflow-development tool, and, of course, sales, marketing, and customer service—its standard pillars.

- Mobile platforms because mobile devices are now the centerpieces of how we communicate and how we consume information in both our work and home lives. This includes not only the device platforms but things like mobile messaging platforms and mobile versions of enterprise applications.

- Customer journey technologies to build the benchmark journeys, track your customers in real time, and respond accordingly. This is a core technology because its outcomes align with what your customers are demanding at this point.

- Analytics to support the personalized responses in real time (as discussed in Chapter 13).

- Arguably, though not covered here, there is a High Five for this matrix too—ecommerce, the transactional core of a larger customer-engagement ecosystem.

Since I've spent a fair amount of time on both CRM and analytics already, I'm going to approach them somewhat differently than I will the other two. Mobile and Customer Journey Orchestration will get the full treatment. When it comes to analytics, I'm going to refer you back to Chapter 13. When it comes to CRM, I'm going to ask you to read what we have going on here. Not what is CRM, which I've already explained, but how to deploy it and how to think about the deployment when you've made your decision. To do so, I've invited Philips Global via their Global CRM Head, Marta Federici, to not only present a case study that is textbook when it comes to implementing CRM, but to let us have the benefit of hearing Marta speak to us on the thinking that goes into it a little later in this chapter. That's how we'll welcome this core customer-facing operations system into our discussion.

CRM

If you want a lot of detail on CRM, please feel free to purchase my book *CRM at the Speed of Light, 4th Edition,* which provides 650 pages of detail on *just* CRM. Otherwise, I'd like to start by taking you on a trip to the Netherlands that ultimately spans the globe.

Deploying the Core Technology: Philips Global CRM Transformation

Philips' application of core customer-engagement technologies was paradigmatic for its actual successful implementation, the context it was done in, and the results it had. At 10,000 feet, it was a business transformation project. By the time the parachute reached 2,000 feet, it was obviously designed to achieve more successful customer engagement in both a B2C and a B2B environment—and the metrics show just that.

What I'm going to do, with Marta's support, will be give you a sense of how it's done properly, and the results that can be expected when it is. But, as I said earlier, a cautionary note first.

Do not attempt this same way at your company. This is Philips-specific. But how they went about it is a universal lesson in approaching a project of this magnitude. While the advice may be obvious, remember the above-referenced Indonesian pharmaceutical company. Maybe it's not so obvious after all.

THE STORY BEGINS. . .

Philips is a Dutch company with a rich, long history. It has survived wars, cataclysm, and the global depression of the 30s, and it still thrives after 125-plus years. This is in a world where 88 percent of all Fortune 500 companies on the list in 1955 were gone by 2016. One of the secrets of Philips's survival is that it understands the world that it lives in, and, at the same time, makes adjustments to that world without holding on to its corporate legacy, but not disregarding it either. By understanding that world, by being attuned to changes, Philips gains a truly agile approach to business, making changes and transforming its model as the need arises—a lesson that those 88 percent never learned. For example, for the last several years, Philips has been the largest securer of patents in Europe. They not only respect their past and live in the present, but they plan for the future.

To that end, in late 2013, Philips began what they called the Digital @Scale Transformation Program. The game plan was what the title implied: the digital transformation of Philips and the empowerment of its 4,000 digital and marketing employees across the globe. Their problem was that Philips's scope is immense. They were active in 17 markets in more than 60 countries and in multiple businesses that scaled both B2B (e.g., health systems) and B2C (e.g., personal health). They had to find a common way to deploy and operate to achieve some efficiencies and for simply more effective operations and engagement with the customers. They built the initiative around six key digital capabilities: search, analytics, campaign (which was what Phillips termed CRM), content, digital sales, and social media.

CRM was the most significant part of this transformation program. As I've stated numerous times, CRM is the operational core for any customer-engagement program or, for that matter, digital-transformation program. But it also might be the most difficult to deploy due to what Marta said were the "heavy technology, data, and operations components," especially since you are deploying it globally in 60 countries and across both B2B and B2C units.

But it worked—although it took time. To give you an idea of the timeframe, it took two years overall, with the B2B component taking more than a full year to deploy to all markets/businesses.

They used some of the most mature CRM technologies. For their B2C initiative, they implemented Eloqua, now the Oracle Marketing Cloud because it is a stable, mature platform with significant room and tools for customization, which was important because Philips had never deployed a marketing automation technology—and they were doing it at scale and had to integrate it with other systems. For example, they tied it directly to their B2C Master database, a Teradata product.

That was the easy part.

B2B was more technically complex because of the advanced campaign management required, and the integration to other systems. They used Eloqua B2B and did a bidirectional integration with Salesforce, which handled demand generation, lead management, and opportunity management—all baked into the Salesforce Sales Cloud.

The reason that this large implementation worked as well as it did was because the technology selection came at the end of a longer process that involved designing and building business cases; identifying the processes, roles, and workflows that Philips needed to use to deploy their strategy and programs successfully; creating the data models; the IT plan; the reporting and KPIs and benchmarks that would define the standards for the success of the deployment; and the campaign strategies and blueprints for them that were needed upon launch—and then creating the training materials. All of this was either done prior to or during the selection process for the technology and prior to its implementation. Every department across the entire global organization cooperated in the efforts. Each department at the company had multiple inputs that shaped the design, functionality, and implementation of the technology. They provided these inputs prior to the effort and feedback during the effort so that the result would be successful when the systems and new ways of working were finally implemented. The departments had to sign off before Marta's team would move forward on the design, creation, and production of specific configurations or features.

Once the plans were signed off on, each department had a face-to-face, market-by-market deployment that was supported by the larger company-wide Market to Order (M2O) organization and by department-by-department change management initiatives. At the end of the day, each department, as well as the company, not only got it right but also was able to "talk to" other departments. Silos around CRM were eliminated, but, simultaneously, departments could use their specific instances of the system to their own advantage without impinging on other departments.

By early 2017, both the B2B and B2C deployments were done. It was an initiative of immense scale that, from the start of planning to the full deployment in both instances took two years, a remarkable time from door-to-door.

DID IT WORK?

Yes, it did. On the B2C side, Philips, in 2016, with the successful implementation of the core operational marketing systems, saw outcomes like this: more than 80 percent increase in engagement from 2015 to 2016; increased emails sent by 170 percent over the same time.

To be clear, when Philips says "engagement," they are talking about people who browse on their website, open or click into an email, register a product, create an account, or interact in any way with any Philips-owned channel—a significant range of activities and interactions on media involved in a customer's possible journey. That's what makes the more than 80 percent number a big deal.

But they didn't stop with B2C. They did equally as well on B2B. They were able to actually operationalize marketing by:

- Centralizing their customer data

- Integrating their marketing automation efforts via Eloqua/Oracle Marketing Cloud with Salesforce's Sales Cloud

- Identifying a framework for demand generation, especially lead management. They not only agreed on the criteria but built the handoffs into the technology's capabilities

- Applying "business rules to make customer data collection progressive and easier, fully in line with more restrictive laws all over the Globe"

- Onboarding over 95 percent of the sales and marketing staff to teach them the new technology and the new ways of working

Their B2B results reflected the successful enablement of sales and marketing operations. After only nine months of the implementation in the UK and Irish markets, they doubled the sales opportunity pipeline and increased marketing qualified leads by a multiple of 6x.

What makes this interesting is that it wasn't just a CRM deployment, but, as I stated earlier in the chapter, it was a strategic technology initiative that, since its initial success, was rolled out to the entirety of Royal Philips and has been extended to marketing related "re-engagement" campaigns. They started with the core customer-engagement-related operational side of marketing and, when it worked, they made it wider and deeper throughout the company. That's what happens when you do things the right way.

THOUGHT LEADER: MARTA FEDERICI

Before I go further, I want to introduce you to the person who led this effort, Marta Federici, Philips's Global Head of B2C&B2B CRM and Loyalty. I asked her for her perspective on this because she is one of the most accomplished practitioners that I've ever run across. I'm going to have her spend some time with you to tell you how she went about it. The reason I'm dwelling on the core technology implementation is that it is rarely done as well as she and her team did it; and what she has to say, in combination with the case study above, is truly instructive when it comes how to think about, and then go about implementing, the systems necessary to keep customers engaged and the businesses running smoothly while that occurs.

Marta?

* * * * *

We are living in the *Age of the Customer.* Companies are investing vast amounts of energy at every level to adapt to their customers' perspective. We are listening to them intently, attempting to understanding and anticipate their needs, and building "one on one" experiences tailored to more fully encompass and connect all our products and businesses.

There is little doubt that in everyday corporate life, transforming and enhancing CRM/1:1 customer engagement becomes a long-lasting, challenging exercise that flows through building and then embracing new capabilities. I think, and my experience bears this out, that the changes are much more than changes: they are a revolution!

Roughly four years ago, my team and I began a global B2C & B2B digital CRM transformation for Royal Philips. Though difficult to achieve and time-consuming to implement, it nonetheless was thoroughly engaging and perhaps the most interesting and rewarding project I have managed in my career. While shaping and re-shaping all the various "outputs" based on new needs, new and unexpected directions, additional requirements, and even organizational changes, I learned so much along the way without losing focus on what should have been brought to life.

It all started with a strong management commitment and willingness to transform Philips into a forward-thinking digital company. With this aim in mind, we set enhanced foundations around 6 key digital capabilities through the global adoption of a single way of working. CRM (aka Digital Campaign B2C&B2B) was one of the core capabilities and the one with the highest impact on customer engagement and revenue-generation opportunity.

Designing and building a B2C & B2B CRM/Digital Campaign from the ground up turned out to be quite complex. This was not only because of each capability's component nature, but also because every single part needed to connect with other parts and work together perfectly. A certain amount of harmony is required when processes (IT tooling, databases, data models), together with roles within the organization (KPI's, reporting and CRM operations) are all crucial pieces of your puzzle and need to be properly configured to support all your customer-engagement ambitions.

To accomplish this transformation, you must be genuinely open to change and to really embrace the challenge! This has been a long journey and continues to present new challenges, but it has also provided opportunities for learning invaluable lessons, lessons that *you* could use in pursuing similar paths of change. Here is an outline.

Breaking through the silo—The best way to face the challenge and manage the complexity is to meaningfully engage with all functions in the organization. You must interact with all the stakeholders from the beginning, welcoming input and feedback at every step—daily, weekly, and monthly. The goal is to invest everyone in a horizontal priority to fully embed this cross-functional mindset. This leads to truly collaborative efforts and constructive results. With greater ambition, and keeping an eye on the bigger picture, we have to overtake the standard business-operating procedure, especially in large organizations. It is a truly eye-opening exercise, enabling full understanding of the multi-faceted journey you need to make to succeed.

Co-create: engage key stakeholders from day one—A globally led business transformation often comes directly on top of all of the day-to-day workload, where everyone needs to juggle short- and mid-term results. That's why marketing and business service's buy-in is crucial for success, keeping their focus and motivation high. The first step to take is to build in collaboration, involving key marketing and business representatives in a joint effort. What is needed is to translate and transfer business needs and marketing's first-hand customers' point of view into the new, big picture you are envisioning on a global scale. One of the biggest challenges in large organizations is, indeed, to learn how to adapt to the single-consumer perspective: we are so many; he or she is just one.

Don't be afraid to improvise—Be clear: focus on the defined goal, the objectives, the methodology used, the content that needs to be prepared. While doing this, never underestimate the importance of listening. Being too rigid, resisting suggestions or insights, or rejecting slight modifications because they don't fit the method are all missed opportunities that, in the end, could have greatly enriched the outcome. Keep an open mind for something that might have a positive impact on your business, as much as on the freshness of your plan.

It's a huge mindset change, for everybody—It's about sharing the same new business principles and values across markets, business units, and functions. It's a given that skepticism and reluctance to change will be your worst enemies along the way. But, believe it or not, nobody will be the same from start to finish, nobody will keep thinking the same way, as everybody will change and transform. It's just a matter of time.

When you can, leverage relationship marketing rules—Make your transformation meaningful and relevant, impactful and fun for your internal audience. Stay focused and be engaging, at all times and in any way, from a webcast to a training session, from an executive steering committee to a weekly operational meeting. Your story needs to inspire. Sharing lessons learned or accomplishments from markets (i.e., Philips geographic locations and businesses; both B2B and B2C business units) is a game-changer as it boosts confidence and eagerness to win. Always keep in mind: the more stakeholder engagement you have, the better your result.

Simplify and speed up adoption of new ways of working—Make the transition easier, so it will happen faster. A good idea is to co-build (piloting and optimizing first) CRM campaigns together with some markets. In this way, the multi-step engagement journey, including audiences, creative assets, KPI's, reporting, and even broadcasting strategy, will become the new ready-to-use blueprint for all the others. It's all about leading and teaching the way by showcasing good and effective examples.

In 2016, at Philips, we achieved an increase in customer engagement of 80% on B2C and 50% on B2B, with a strong growing trend for the future.

Transformation never stops.

We change and grow every day, as professionals and as individuals, both inside and outside the companies where we work. The need for change is not solely a business priority or just a clever program, it's a way of being, a necessary attitude we need to improve ourselves and grow. Our goal is to keep listening, learning, creating, and innovating every day by sharing and spreading the same perspective for a common goal. If we succeed at this, the speed of the transformation will be driven by the level of engagement we create among our internal stakeholders and then by our customers.

* * * * *

Thank you, Marta.

So, that's the way that you might want to frame your thinking on CRM. You've seen the approach, the methodology, the thought processes and the technology-systems implementation and results. CRM as a required piece of your business effort is unavoidable.

Interestingly, the other unavoidable piece is mobile—something which, a decade ago, was more than a novelty but less than ubiquitous and not mission-critical yet. It is, perhaps, now the most important piece of your planning and implementation. How do you deploy your products, services, experiences, tools, and communications on a device that someone is carrying in their pocket?

THE IMPORTANCE OF BEING MOBILE

If you look around you, the one thing that you always see is someone on a mobile device. Sometimes, in San Francisco, it's the only thing you'd see . . . if you weren't looking at your own device. It could be a phone or a tablet or even a laptop. But the smaller the better. The mobile devices that we use now—iPhone, Samsung Galaxy, etc.—are the repositories, not just for the apps that we use in our daily lives, but for information-gathering, conversations via multiple channels, playing games, buying stuff, and taking millions of different kinds of actions based on the apps, platforms, and devices that any one person or group may be using at any given moment. It all seems so normal. We are engaged routinely with our devices. Make no mistake, it is the mobile device that we use to engage with others, and we are also engaged with the device—and that is normal. It's not even the new normal. It's just how we live now. Using your mobile device is no less ordinary than using a door to go in and out of things. In fact, in March 2017, Flurry, an analytics firm with a funny name, found in their research on mobile usage that U.S. consumers spend an average of 5 hours a day on their mobile devices—more than 20 percent of their entire day, and, assuming we have about 16 waking hours if we are smart about sleeping, 32 percent of our waking hours. Holy cow! Put that in the context of the fact that 95 percent of U.S. adults own a cell phone and 77 percent of those own a smartphone of some kind. That's a lot of hours.

What we do in those five hours makes this even more interesting. First, how Flurry measures what we are doing is telling. They start by looking at time spent on mobile apps versus on a mobile browser. The results aren't even close—92 percent on apps, 8 percent on browsers. The usage breakdown:

1. Facebook—19 percent

2. Music, media, entertainment—15 percent

3. Messaging—12 percent

4. Gaming—11 percent

5. Utilities—9 percent

6. Productivity—9 percent

7. Browser—8 percent

8. Other—8 percent

9. Lifestyle/shopping—5 percent

10. YouTube—3 percent

11. News/weather—3 percent

12. Sports—2 percent

13. Snapchat—2 percent

That adds up to 106 percent, and I don't know why that is, but the distribution is a great indicator of how much we rely on our mobile devices day to day.

But it took a while and a lot of work to get to this state. Here's a bit of history slathered with insight about how to think of mobile regarding engagement, then and now, from Srikrishnan Ganesan, Director of Chat Products at CRM vendor Freshworks.

By 2013–14, it was clear to brands that mobile was taking away the time and mind space of their target customers, and they needed more than a presence on mobile. Their "Version 1" was to take the website and shrink it into a mobile screen. (Forrester rightly gave this approach the name "Shrink and Squeeze.") Most of them were websites disguised as apps and usually built "multi-platform" to minimize development and maintenance efforts. Obviously, there was no compelling reason for customers to use these apps, and the inference often drawn was, "Mobile isn't big for us." But brands also saw new mobile start-ups disrupting them. So, they thought, "It's about getting users to download the app and engagement tactics to get them to use the app more often." Version 2 was about these three changes: marketing to get it in more hands, push notifications to send offers (to stay top of mind), and a better-looking native app. On the marketing front, the app download driver was discounts to buy on mobile—push someone already buying from you to use your app to do the same. Then re-engage them through push notifications. Their metrics then told them they had no luck with increasing stickiness. Most of the apps were deleted after the discount was claimed. Only then came the dawning moment. Version 3—which is where most companies are today. Version 3 for brands has been about realizing that their mobile app isn't for everyone. It is for specific-use cases. Quite often it is only for the brand's loyalists. The story changed from, "I can spend more to acquire users on mobile because there's more loyalty for apps," to, "Only my loyal customers will use my app." The folks who transact with us often. The folks who have a much higher lifetime value (LTV). As part of this move to Version 3, we've had a bunch of wonderful apps focused on helping people achieve tasks on the go or perform repetitive tasks with ease. But this still is typically restricted to the "core" features.

So how do you think about things the right way for mobile? Of course, the cliché of empathizing with your customer and understanding what they want to do on the move is necessary. There's also the aspect of thinking mobile-first, designing mobile-first, or even mobile-only with assumptions around cameras, location, timing. But a first-principles way to think of this is: if you need a commitment from the customer (e.g., download and subsequent retention of the app on their phone), what value are you adding to them in return, and over what period? "Is this app important enough to have on my phone?" is how a customer thinks. Segment your customer into your VIP customers, frequent users, brand loyalists, occasional users, etc., and figure out what the value could be for each of them in different contexts. Focus on only those where you can deliver real value. Don't force the app on the rest, and provide the rest a superior experience on whichever platform you expect them to use to engage you—mobile web perhaps? When they turn into loyalists or frequent users or whatever segment benefits most from the app, they will move to the app. Also, if the app is indeed for the loyalists or VIPs, let every aspect of customer experience (CX) reflect the fact that it is for them—not just the app's core discovery or transaction features. It matters how you do engagement, how you do customer support, and how the app feels in every aspect. A brand can unlock more ways of delivering value to the customer with a holistic approach of thinking through CX. That's more likely to make it attractive for people to consider becoming "frequent users" or "loyalists" and moving over.

That's good history and good advice. We are always dealing with customers whose relationship to a company can be differentiated by their transactions and, thus, measured, if you are a savvy enough bunch, by their customer lifetime value (CLV), an indicator of what the household of the customer will be worth to your company over some determined timeframe with the company. But to maintain that engagement so that the lifetime value is realized means that the convenience of the action and the eye-pleasing interfaces, which allow for frictionless ease of use and navigation on the device are a necessary part of the planning for customer engagement strategies and programs.

Keep in mind, as much as I can talk to the data showing the pervasiveness of mobile device usage and wide distribution of services that are associated with it, the real value is in the personalized interactions the devices allow businesses to have with their customers. The level of engagement with the device itself escalates the intensity of the involvement.

You don't think that people are all that connected to their devices? Think of this. Have you ever left your iPhone somewhere and you weren't exactly sure where? How did you feel? Panicked? Freaked out that you didn't have your syringe, errrr, iPhone? Nearly desperate to get it back? That's what I mean. We have reached the point that 10 percent of the population uses only a smartphone for all their actual phone calls, no landlines at home at all—a smartphone dependency. This is most prevalent, as you would expect, with digital-native millennials, where roughly 18 percent of them are only using their smartphones. No more tethering.

As much as I'd like to rave enthusiastically about using mobile devices, this is a business book about customer engagement, which requires me to focus on the area of mobile I think carries the most business promise for the near future—mobile messaging.

MOBILE MESSAGING

I will confess that I don't think of myself as a messaging expert. But due to an Oracle speaking engagement in 2017, I had to research messaging. Prior to that, I thought that messaging focused primarily on communications with, of course, text messaging (SMS) being a frequently used means for interactions between two and sometimes more parties. I was far too limited in my thinking. After extensive reading and conversations with experts, I came to the realization that mobile messaging is not just a communications medium but, primarily, a service-delivery platform. I found that the ability to engage customers via mobile devices and to monetize that engagement was magnified exponentially by the evolution of mobile messaging platforms—and they represented one of the greatest opportunities for mobile engagement and the monetization of that engagement that we've seen in a while.

MESSAGING "APPS" USAGE DRIVES US ... CRAZY

There is no doubt about the ubiquity of mobile devices, but that penetration also applies to the usage of messaging apps on those mobile devices.

Here's some fodder for your left brain on mobile messaging penetration. In October 2018, according to Statista's ongoing research:

- WhatsApp (owned by Facebook) had 1.5 billion active users

- Facebook Messenger had 1.3 billion active users

- WeChat (China) had 1.06 billion active users

- QQ Mobile (China) had 803 million active users

Then it drops precipitously to Skype and Snapchat with around 300 million active users each—which isn't a small number but only seems so relatively. The irony is that Skype is already so pervasive it's a verb, but it's "only" got 300 million users despite its history and the current ownership by Microsoft, in large part because it has yet to be used seriously as a platform. It could be much, much more.

But the knowledge that the data provides isn't as simple as the obvious numbers suggest. Despite the global blanketing of mobile use, the reasons that people use their devices and the things that they use them for are highly personalized, driven by age, culture, bandwidth availability, country of origin, lifestyle, financial status, and technology savvy, among other things. For example, in the U.S., Facebook Messenger is the #1 app used for communication; but WhatsApp has significantly more global appeal, especially in emerging markets.

Both Messenger and WhatsApp combined have close to 3 billion users, not accounting for a likely significant number of people who use both. When Facebook acquired WhatsApp in 2013, it provided an alternate text-messaging service with the ability to send photos as well as text, and, because it was an app, it wasn't subject to SMS text-messaging fees from wireless carriers. Since the acquisition, it has expanded to include location-based services, audio and video calling, and the ability to send documents.

Facebook Messenger, in an appeal to its U.S. market, has been experimenting with adding services such as the ability call an Uber or to send money from within Messenger. That's not as strange as it sounds. Think of it this way. If you get a plea for money on Facebook, generally, meaning somewhere in your public conversation, the odds are strong that you will think it's a scam. If you get a request for funds inside of Messenger, the odds are at least better that you will consider sending money because you trust the message from the sender asking you for it. The level of trust is different because of the nature of the intimacy of the medium.

Until recently, QQ Mobile had more users than WeChat in China, but it is a legacy app. WeChat (more on them shortly) leads the way in Asia, with the largest number of active Asian users. But also leads the world in how to ambitiously go beyond the idea of an app-as-such to an app as a service, which fosters engagement much more deeply.

The level of engagement with these devices and apps is astonishing. WeChat users are accessing the app an average of ten times a day. Couple that with the use by U.S. consumers of messaging apps of all kinds at the rate of 23 minutes per day, according to market intelligence firm SimilarWeb, and you start to see the pattern. Then, just do some anecdotal research. Take a normal day out of your life and see how many people are sending at least one text per day, if not more. To do that, though, you're going to have to stop texting.

That shows a rather intense level of engagement, but, all in all, for your business, other than perhaps customer support, and maybe a small amount of marketing, mobile messaging doesn't seem to hold that much hope of transactional heaven, does it? Or does it?

It does if you stop thinking of mobile messaging apps and start looking at mobile messaging platforms. That way the ability to carry out a two-way communication turns into a one- or two-way interaction and even a transaction.

But that also means the technology that you are using for your mobile activity should be a platform, not just an app.

MOBILE MESSAGING PLATFORMS

There are dozens of mobile messaging platforms, but the dominant ones are WeChat, Facebook Messenger, Slack, and WhatsApp. Ultimately, what identifies each of them as a platform is the ability, through the API tools, to build applications and services via the platform that also are distributed and consumed through the platform.

The use of these platforms allows for the monetization of services via the platform. One of the simplest forms is what I mentioned in Chapter 8 that Dialog Axiata was doing: short code services that involve texting a number sequence via SMS and, in return, it activates a service that you respond to via text. A small charge associated with your carrier account shows up on your bill next month. The price, of course, depends on the service activated.

The next level of this is represented by Facebook's flirtation with hailing an Uber, sending money via its payment system, and a handful of other services. For Facebook, these are experimental and promising, but early stage. Ultimately, though, all the other platforms pale in comparison to WeChat as a platform.

Part of the power of WeChat is the dependence of the Chinese mobile population on its availability. Ninety-five percent of WeChat (known as Weixin in China) users are on WeChat every day and, as mentioned above, 61 percent are there at least 10 times a day. In fact, Tencent, the Chinese telco that owns WeChat, said that WeChat is responsible for 35 percent of all Chinese mobile activity. This isn't only significant because of the scale of the opportunity for WeChat, but because it allows them to develop the platform and the services associated with it at scale from the beginning.

The game plan has been the ability to use WeChat to purchase services and goods directly through the various apps. Because it's a platform, it is device-agnostic, meaning it can function without concern for any one mobile operating system—working on Apple's iOS as well as on Android. Plug in the app, enter the portal, and do what you do in a day with WeChat regardless of the device that you are doing it on.

But, like Dialog Axiata, WeChat is a business. Thus, the backbone service for their platform is WeChat Pay, a digital wallet built to handle transactions of all kinds via any mobile device with any third-party provider. Each WeChat user has a WeChat Pay account attached to a credit or debit card. Additionally, it's possible to receive money from other WeChat users. In fact, for the 2014 Chinese New Year, WeChat took advantage of an old Chinese tradition for exchanging money envelopes among friends and family during the holidays. They introduced virtual red envelopes, which allowed you to send money directly to contacts or groups created in WeChat. The money sent to the groups is distributed equally or randomly (nicknamed "lucky money"). After broad publicity, this feature drove adoption of WeChat Pay to the point that there are now 600 million active users of the system. In 2016, during the holiday period, 3.2 billion envelopes were sent! Whoa.

One thing to note here is how culturally attuned this was, taking a long-standing Chinese tradition and digitizing it to make it appealing to a contemporary audience. You couldn't replicate it in, say, the United States in the same way because the history isn't there.

The foundation of the WeChat platform is what they call mini-programs. So, for example, you can buy groceries at a physical grocery store and then scan a QR code on your device and pay for the groceries—somewhat similar in concept, though not design, to Apple Pay. You can book a hotel room and reserve a train seat and pay for them via WeChat. You can receive a virtual red envelope and use what you received as pocket money. You can buy food at restaurants or have it delivered. What makes it more advanced than any other mobile platform is that there are thousands of services available to the WeChat user.

That, in combination with the ability to do what you normally do on devices—buy and play games, communicate with friends, read reviews, track messages, etc.—constitutes an encompassing ecosystem that lets you run a significant portion of your daily life on the go without ever leaving WeChat. Additionally, they have an Enterprise WeChat that not only allows secure collaboration and communication within the office but has a built-in feature that allows employees to keep track of their annual leave days, reimbursable expenses, and the means to interactively request time off or to clock in.

Obviously, if you are one of the users of a mobile platform, the likelihood of sticky engagement is great. The question has never been the ability of the platform, application, or device to engage—it's already how we live—but how to monetize that engagement. Mobile messaging is one of the answers that ring true.

This isn't lost on anyone. I'm assuming that, to some extent, I'm preaching to the choir. Some data from Forrester Research in their 2017 Mobile and Technology Priorities for Marketers survey was telling. By FAR, the number-one priority for 2017 was the use of third-party mobile messaging platforms. Twenty-five percent said they were already fully operational and 15 percent said they were piloting it and 30 percent said they were planning to start using it in 2017. The numbers tell the story.

HOW TO TRACK A CUSTOMER OR TWO . . . MILLION

Chapter 6 was focused entirely on how to think about a customer journey, what it was, and how to map it. It's not an easy process, no matter how small the customer base is. But it gets terribly difficult when you are tasked to track, analyze, and respond to millions of customer journeys. To be able to orchestrate the journey, technology here is not just a good idea but necessary. Since this technology is one of the pillars of engagement, I'm going to take you through a user-friendly technology journey using what is my favorite customer-journey orchestration technology, the Thunderhead ONE Engagement Hub.

The Landscape's Beauty: Thunderhead

I start this with a disclaimer. Thunderhead is a client of mine. As a rule, however, I am agnostic when it comes to which companies win the competitive technology wars. For example, Microsoft, Salesforce, SAP, and Oracle are all fiery competitors, yet they are or have been each and all my clients. I don't pick and choose sides. I want the industry to succeed. Regardless of my connection to the company, Thunderhead's journey orchestration technology will show you how journey orchestration works, which is something you honestly need to know.

The Journey Through the Journey: Trek Through Tech

Thunderhead's ONE Engagement is unique in its own category because it can track and personalize conversations with anonymous customers as they travel their various paths to get done whatever it is they are trying to do. To do this, The ONE Engagement Hub (called ONE from hereon) is operated horizontally, i.e., as a layer across many channels and data sources. For example, ONE may be in play while a single customer or millions of customers are traveling on Facebook, Twitter, the web, email, or in a physical store that has a digital point of sale system, which may be using Microsoft Intelligent Customer Engagement for customer service and Salesforce Marketing Cloud for marketing. ONE can follow the customer as they traverse the mobile world via their iPhone and iOS or via their Samsung Galaxy S10 via Android. It simply doesn't matter. All the data they need will be gathered, analyzed, and spit out either as an analysis of the journey and its strengths and weaknesses, as millions make the pilgrimage, or as an optimized personalized conversation with a customer whose name they may or may not know.

To make this system work, ONE is integrated with potentially many other systems, be they CRM operational systems or data sources. It integrates with (as I write this) Salesforce, Microsoft, SAP, and Sitecore, among several others when it comes to CRM or engagement-related systems. The same with data sources. But, as I hope is already apparent, this is a constantly changing landscape, and new products, services, and data sources are always coming online and catching fire, making flexibility a necessary capability. So, to that end, ONE provides data adapters that can link to RESTful services, the architecture du jour, to grab data from and send data to any systems that subscribe to REST—which is pretty much all of them.

LISTEN...

The technology, once deployed, starts with what Thunderhead calls Touchpoint Listening. This is where they become aware of the channels being traversed by the customers they are trying to listen to. For example, if we are talking about web activity, they use a JavaScript-based tag, called the ONE tag. This consists of (mostly metaphorically), the attachment of a tracking device—a piece of JavaScript that uses first-party cookies to track a customer's journey by creating a tag that becomes the customer's temporary ID as they wander the pathway. That means, even without a name, the customer is identified by his or her (or its if it's a cat) tag so that they can be tracked, recorded, analyzed, and responded to while they are on the path.

If it's mobile, iOS- and Android-specific software development kits (SDKs) allow you to build listening support.

If it's email, a tracking pixel is dropped into each individual email, which allows you to see things like, "They opened the email," "They clicked on the link," etc.

The agent-based contact centers and traditional customer-service representatives aren't ignored either, the integrations with the customer-service applications residing within the CRM product of choice.

Otherwise, for anything more "bespoke," SDKs in multiple languages are available with the APIs needed to do the integration to the touchpoints.

LEARN...

Once you've listened and thus have the data you need to start thinking about how to respond to this winsome traveler, you have the technology available to apply what Thunderhead calls "Journeylitics," which is their version of journey analytics. I discussed them in great detail in Chapter 13, so I won't repeat all that here. I'd suggest that you go back and take a look at what I said earlier if you don't remember. These engagement analytics provide you with both a visual and in-depth way to identify the faithfulness of the thousands on the journey to the path that you optimally hope they would choose. If there are deviations, these analytics give you the means to find out what the deviation is, why it happened, and how to correct the path—clear the rocks, the fallen tree, the floods, whatever. If it's down to the individual, it gives you the knowledge you need to figure out how to best converse (i.e., interact) with this individual to optimize both their experience with you that day or to promote a sale of something to them that triggers their desire to buy.

What makes this particularly interesting is the use of the Adaptive Engagement Profile (AEP), the unique customer identification profile that ONE provides. Essentially, as a customer takes a journey, it creates a profile in real time, so, as it learns about the customer's behavior, likes, and dislikes, brand affinity, interest in specific areas, etc., it places that information in a customer record that is either already there, with associated transactional history, and other data that may have been gathered from other systems, or it creates one for the anonymous traveler using the JavaScript tag I mentioned earlier. It is learning as it goes and harvesting constantly. This information is part of what Journeylitics uses to decide how to respond to the customer.

The ONE Journeylitics are particularly visual and designed to let you actually see the paths rather than have to use your mind's eye and mathematician's degree to identify the holes and gaps—and what went right, too, by the way.

OPTIMIZE AND ENGAGE

Once you've tracked the journey and analyzed the data, the next level is touchpoint optimization—the response to the customer at the place they are traversing. That can take a variety of forms based on the channel that the customer is communicating in. For example, if it is a web-based journey, the customer will see content optimized to what they are doing at the time and their history with your brand. This can be either desktop or mobile, too. ONE uses content overlays. If it is a customer-service action at a contact center, the system will send a suggestion to an agent about the "next best conversation." In other words, it is particularized to the individual customer and is a possibility based on the successes with it in similar situations in the past.

To do that, ONE includes a decision-making framework that basically does what is called conversation arbitration. Keep in mind, the word "conversation" in ONE parlance really means all forms of bi-directional interaction, not just actual talking or social-media dialogue. Arbitration means choosing the best conversation from all the possible ones based on what the system knows about the customer as of the time it is deciding. It does that in context too—meaning part of the decision-making is based on the context of the already-existing interactions. If it is a customer-service call that goes on for three hours, the system, combined with other factors, can infer that it was a bad-news call and, therefore, wouldn't offer upsell or cross-sell as a choice of conversation.

The journey I just took you on is how customer journey orchestration technology enables customer engagement. But this is by no means the end of it all.

MOVING ON TO THE CUTTING EDGE: BOTS, AR, AND WHO KNOWS WHAT?

Technology, especially technology in service of engagement, never sleeps. In fact, the people who develop software never sleep either, and that's a big health issue at this point. But not to worry: we have bots coming that will develop the software, and bots don't have to sleep. Right?

Before we get to our man of the next several pages ("man of the hour" doesn't work inside a book) who will take over the discussion of the near future in tech, I want to make something of a statement re: artificial intelligence and bots.

As the chief scientist at Salesforce once said in a discussion with analysts on the future: "AI doesn't want anything." What he meant was that, yes, artificial intelligence learns, but it has to be directed to the subject it's going to learn about. It doesn't make those kinds of decisions. The algorithms still need human beings to tell the AI where it should start learning. That means we aren't at Skynet, and there are more benefits than anything to fear with artificial intelligence, machine learning, and bots.

On to our next section and next guest. I decided to let our guru, Brent Leary, actually tell you about the near future in technology and how it will get applied in service of customer engagement. You down with that, Brent?

THOUGHT LEADER: BRENT LEARY

Before we get to this, let me tell you about Brent. He is the managing principal of CRM Essentials and is considered one of CRM's foremost thought leaders. He has a broad range of knowledge in the domain. You could easily make the case, when it comes to small business and CRM, that he is the #1 guy in the world; and he's right up there in the enterprise CRM world, the social networks world, and the video-engagement world. He is also one of the best-loved and best-regarded analysts in the world. And a BFF to me. He is kind and generous, humble and humorous. He has been my partner in a long-running series we've done (whenever we feel like it) called "CRM Playaz," where we deal with the customer-facing universe in a substantial but light-hearted (not light-headed) way.

I know no one more forward-facing than Brent, so I've asked him to tell you about the future of products, services, and tools in service of customer engagement.

So, I'm Paul Greenberg, you're Brent Leary, and we are . . . ready to hear what you have to say, Brent.

* * * * *

TOOLS FOR ENGAGEMENT CHANGE RULES FOR ENGAGEMENT

The way we communicate with each other, both professionally and personally, feels like it's changing by the minute. And they're not just small, incremental changes; they can be big, monumental changes that disrupt what was normal and acceptable in the not-too-distant past.

While many tools and services are playing meaningful roles in changing the way customers and organizations engage each other, below are a few of the areas I think are having some of the most significant impact on building and maintaining customer relationships today and into the foreseeable future.

Chatbots

I have a lot of conversations with industry execs every year, with many of them taking place at vendor conferences. And two conversations stand out about why chatbots will be (and really already are) important to customer engagement now and forever more. Art Papas, CEO and founder of Bullhorn, said during his keynote at the company's annual user conference (Engage) that 65% of millennials would rather communicate with chatbots than with humans for certain interactions with brands. And, when I caught up with him to talk further about that stat, the follow-up to that stat was, "So why not let them talk to the chatbot?" as it's easier to scale responsiveness and deliver consistency via chatbots than with humans. And in certain instances, chatbots actually deliver more empathy than humans because chatbots are way more likely to respond to requests than humans, as even now you may not get a reply to an email, a tweet, or any other kind of channel you may use when looking for answers.

The stat and the rationale reinforced another conversation I had previous to my convo with Art. During his keynote at the big Inbound Conference put on by Hub-Spot, co-founder and CTO Dharmesh Shah stated that conversational interfaces like chatbots may be the most important technologies "in decades." And, when I had the chance to ask him why he felt like that, he said people can express the things they want in direct terms. They don't have to translate it from the words that are in their head. They just have to say the words that are in their head, and that's enough. And, because no translations are needed, conversational interfaces can provide companies with direct, literal pathways to understanding what customers are looking for. Which is what the marketing-intelligence focused chatbot he's created for HubSpot, called Growthbot, has done for the him and the company, along with giving the company more opportunities to interact with customers and prospects.

According to a 2017 study by Opus Research, there were already more than thirty bot platforms on the market for organizations to build their conversational interfaces with, from big enterprises like Microsoft's Bot Framework and Facebook Messenger Platform, to niche startups like Chatfuel and ChattyPeople. Shah built HubSpot's Growthbot using Amazon's conversational interfaces platform Lex, which allows you to build both text and voiced-based interfaces like Amazon Echo's Alexa.

Voice-First Devices

Speaking of Alexa, she and her friends Siri, Cortana, and a bunch of other voice-first services are quickly becoming more ubiquitous in our personal and professional lives. In less than a year's time, the number of Alexa skills built by third-party developers and individual users had grown from fewer than 1,000 to more than 12,000, according to estimates. Meanwhile, Google's entry, Google Home, came out and could recognize up to six different voices. So, for example, six people could ask the same device, "What's my checking account balance?" and the device would be able to tell each person their specific balance. Apple announced the HomePod as their voice-first speaker device to compete with the other two, but it's the public's appetite for these devices—even in these early days—that really shows why they are poised to be important interaction channels.

- With Amazon leading the way, smart speaker sales grew 137 percent from Q3 2017 to Q3 2018, with worldwide shipments expected to reach 75 million for 2018.

- At the beginning of 2018, there were approximately 4,000 Alexa-enabled devices on the market; by September of the year there were over 20,000 devices with Alexa inside—manufactured by 4,500 different brands.

- Midway through 2016 there were approximately 700 Alexa Skills built by third-party developers; by November of 2018 there were over 70,000 skills.

- Google was two years behind Amazon with its Google Home smart speaker hitting the market in 2016, but an RBC analyst estimates Google has sold 52 million Google Home devices worldwide—with 43 million in the U.S.—which are expected to generate $3.4 billion in revenue for 2018.

- The RBC report also suggests annual revenue from Google Home devices is expected to double by 2020.

And, just like other rapidly adopted new technologies, voice-first technologies are quickly changing basic behaviors and expectations. According to a 2018 NPR/Edison Smart Audio report:

- 43% of early mainstream speaker owners bought the device to decrease screen time

- 56% of early mainstream speaker owners say they use their voice assistants on other devices more now

- 42% of early mainstream speaker owners have made at least three purchases in the last three months

While we're still very early days with voice shopping, and the numbers are limited to traditional shopping, the customer journey is definitely being transformed, according to Adobe's State of Voice Assistants survey, where:

- 47% use voice assistants to search for product information
- 43% create shopping lists
- 32% do price comparisons
- 27% check for deals and promotions

As these numbers indicate, once people get their hands on these devices and start using them, it changes behaviors and expectations—quickly. And those changes will happen even more quickly as more of these devices find their way into more homes over the next couple of years. According to research from RBC, by 2020, upwards of 60 million Alexa-powered devices could be sold annually, leading to $5 billion in annual voice-driven sales. All this from a single device that was launched just over four years ago.

Augmented Reality

I'm going to focus on Augmented Reality as opposed to Virtual Reality. Augmented reality is different from virtual reality in that the goal of virtual reality is to make you feel like you are in another physical space. Augmented reality keeps you in your present environment but provides additional information to your line of sight.

Augmented reality superimposes digital content onto a user's view of the real world through mobile devices or headsets. For example, imagine walking down the street and pointing your phone at a store window and seeing a list of today's deals—complete with pictures and videos—pop up without you having to go in.

I'm not looking to diminish VR (or mixed reality) in any way, but I think it's a bit further out in hitting the mainstream because of the more specialized (and expensive) equipment you have to buy for it to work, and the limited content available outside of gaming. But you are already seeing some great examples of how organizations are beginning to incorporate AR into their customer-engagement strategies. And research firm eMarketer estimates 54 million people in the U.S. will use augmented reality in 2019, nearly doubling the 30 million users the study found in 2016.

IKEA unveiled an augmented reality application called Place for smart phones and tablets in late 2017 that let customers visualize how a piece of furniture would look in their house before buying it. Users have a full view of their room through cameras on their iPads or iPhones. Living room furnishings such as coffee tables, couches, floor lamps, and hundreds of other items are available for users to drop into their camera view.

That same year, Gap released a new app called DressingRoom, built on Google's AR platform Tango. The app was created to help customers virtually "try on" clothing through their smartphones. Shoppers choose a Gap style they might be interested in purchasing. After you add information such as height and weight, DressingRoom places a virtual 3D model in front of you and lets you see how different items would fit. And, if they choose to, customers can buy it online without having to step into a store.

The reason The Gap went in this direction is summed up pretty nicely by Gil Krakowsky, VP Global Strategy and Business Development at Gap.

> Technology gives customers incredible autonomy around the shopping experience and it's our responsibility to constantly explore new ways to make the shopping experience effortless and pursue solutions that will add value to the customer experience.

Just like The Gap, retail home improvement chain Lowe's, through its Innovation Labs, created a Tango application that improves in-store navigation. Any customer with a Tango mobile device entering the store can receive live directions to the product they want to buy. If you have more than one product to buy, the app has Waze-like capabilities and can calculate the most efficient route through the store, based on maps generated by 3D scans Loew's has for each store.

Video

Let's face it, it's hard to get and keep people's attention today with all that's coming at them. But one thing that is getting and keeping more people's attention is video, as the following stats illustrate:

- More than 500 million hours of videos are watched on YouTube each day.
- Over half of video content is viewed on mobile.
- 92 percent of mobile video viewers share videos with others.
- Viewers retain 95% of a message when they watch it in a video compared to 10% when reading it in text.
- Video attracts two to three times as many monthly visitors.
- The average user spends 88% more time on a website with video.
  (Source: The WordStream Blog, "37 Staggering Video Marketing Statistics for 2017," March 2017, by Mary Lister)

And, when looking specifically at livestreamed video:

- At just 3 seconds per view, Facebook is generating over 3,000 years' worth of watch time each day.

- Facebook Live videos are watched 3x longer than videos that aren't live anymore.

- Users comment on Facebook Live videos at 10x the rate of regular videos.

- 81% of internet audiences viewed more live content in 2016 than they did in 2015.

- From a branding communications perspective, 80% prefer live videos to blogs, and 82% favor live video to social posts.

   (Source: MediaKix, "The Top 13 Live Facebook Stats You Should Know," July 18, 2017)

So, with estimates of livestreaming becoming a $70 billion industry by 2021, it's easy to see that all forms of video are keys to getting and keeping the attention needed to turn prospects into long-term customers today. And it's also the reason why companies like NewTek—creators of the television industry standard Tricaster (aka the Trickster) video-production series—have created entry-level system that allow companies with SMB budgets to produce professional-level video content on a regular basis. Those who have even more limited purse strings can turn to tools like Livestream's Mevo camera (one of my personal favorites) or DJI's Osmo products to livestream on the go. And if you want to stick to your mobile phone, applications like Switcher Studio allows you to turn your iPhones and iPads into mobile production studios by letting you connect cameras from multiple phones into one multi-view broadcast with the ability switch camera views.

With more of our collective attention going to video, and with means of production and distribution getting more affordable and easier to deliver, video—live or otherwise—has to be a part of pretty much any business' engagement strategy going forward.

Subscriptions

While technology has heightened consumer expectations for better, faster, more consistent experiences, it has also changed their expectations for how products and services are delivered—and how they pay for them. Where traditionally we needed to buy things outright to have access to the things we wanted, more and more we don't have to go the ownership route to use the things we want. In the era of the subscription economy, access trumps ownership, if you want it to.

Just think of all the things we subscribe to that we had to buy outright in the past: music, videos, cars, ties, food, and, of course, software and apps. And companies who have made the transition to offering their customers subscriptions to consume products and services are reaping the benefits of more data on what their customers value and more frequent opportunities to interact with them because they know they have to "show and prove" each month that their product/service is worthy of being kept another month. Companies like Zuora, Aria, Recurly and others have made it relatively easy to create subscription-based business models that are capable of more easily staying aligned with changing customer needs and expectations. And as customers consume more products and services delivered digitally through monthly subscriptions, platforms like Zuora, integrated with customer-success platforms like Totango and Gainsight, can provide key insights into when a customer is susceptible to churning, and they can signal new revenue-stream opportunities.

Even as subscription models and digital disruption seem to go together like peanut butter and jelly, Amazon's hugely successful Prime membership—with its estimated 95 million-plus subscribers—was built on a decidedly "non-digital" foundation: the free 2-day shipping guarantee. So, building a customer base via subscriptions works whether you're selling digital services or offering traditional goods and services that need to be delivered the old-fashioned way. Subscription billing and management platforms can help you administer these services and assist in analyzing the interactions taking place on these platforms. And keep the relationship growing, one month at a time . . .

All Roads Lead to Customer Engagement

The areas above all have impacted or will significantly impact the way people engage each other, which makes it critically important for companies to understand how they should leverage each of them to create and extend mutually beneficial relationships. And as these areas continue transforming and disrupting rules of engagement, as consumers adopt them and adapt their lifestyles to take advantage of what they offer, the ties that bind them are the systems of record, engagement, and analysis that help us see the full picture of what all this engagement means. Which is why customer engagement becomes more important and central to fully understanding where customer needs and expectations are going and how to best meet them.

* * * * *

Thanks, Mr. Leary, for that look into the future and what it means. You rocked it.

Our next guru, Joe Hughes, is going to give us a peek at how ready this stuff really is and what is the best way to think about readiness. Technology is neither simple to understand or implement nor is it optional if you are trying to grow your customer base and still retain your current customers.

Okay, Joe, bring us home.

THOUGHT LEADER: JOE HUGHES

Joe Hughes has an impressive—and long—title: Principal-IT Advisory Digital & Emerging Technology Customer Lead for Ernst and Young Advisory. He also has an impressive—and long—history in the IT industry, having been, prior to his current stint at EY, at Accenture playing a similar role. He is arguably one of the most technology-savvy practitioners I've ever met and, in fact, is as aware, or more aware, of the technology market and what's out there than most of the industry analysts I know—including me. The thing that makes this even better is that he takes the technologies he chooses, and he sees to their implementation—so he has the practical knowledge needed in addition to the market knowledge. Wow. So, Joe, tell us where these engagement technologies are and what we should do. We'll listen. To be clear, these opinions are the opinions of Joe Hughes, not of Ernst & Young Advisory.

* * * * *

THE TOOLS ARE READY—WHAT IS NEEDED IS COURAGE

An overwhelming number of cloud-based tools are now available at a reasonable price, with lower implementation costs, to solve customer experience.

Since the software is so easy to initially implement, CX, CRM, and marketing teams can often set up and run the software with no involvement from traditional IT. Unfortunately, this has led to an unhealthy break between marketing IT and the rest of IT. In many cases, the very tools deployed to help are *actually breaking the customer experience* because they are deployed in silos. Sometimes there were good reasons for separation, like IT being distracted by legacy upgrades, but they need to come together now.

In one depiction of the increasing complexity, Scott Brinker of ChiefMartec.com produces an annual visualization called the Marketing Technology Landscape.

chiefmartec.com/2018/04/marketing-technology-landscape-supergraphic-2018/

The diagram lists all of the software vendors that support the marketing function. In 2011, Scott's chart contained 150 vendors. In 2018, the chart had 6,829 vendors! Astounding!

HOW TO SET THE RIGHT PATH FORWARD

With so many options in the market, we have found the following five themes helpful in choosing technologies that will work together well to help the customer control their experience.

I. Respect All Channels

Customer engagement now needs to accommodate how the customer wants to interact with you. This reality means you can't avoid omnichannel. It is table stakes now to have web, social, mobile coverage—and, yes, even call centers—integrated. We have to be where the customer wants us to be.

A lot of people kept hoping and expecting that call centers would go away because of digital changes, but they will not go away completely. A sample of reasons:

Some experiences provide a human touch by design—Like a higher loyalty class (example a Platinum level with Concierge service).

Inherent conflict in the desire for easy-to-use and price optimization/profit maximization—Too much a la carte is confusing, too little a la carte can be annoying. This turns into a web UI no one is really happy with, and phone calls result.

Third-party integration/agreement failures—Some businesses just won't work together. For example, online travel sites don't allow you to book American and Delta in the same itinerary any longer because they could not come to a code-share agreement.

MVP "Minimal Viable Product" overkill—Everyone is "MVP happy" these days; get the product "out there like a startup" is the mantra. This MVP approach, however, often backfires in existing enterprises. The back office/call center ends up calling the customer back or the customer doesn't get what they want and complains via phone.

Good search and KM still get no respect—Few spend the money they should on Knowledge Management and good search. As a result, customers have to pick up the phone to get their question answered.

If you have to hide the call center phone number, your other channel experiences are broken. We need the *courage* to stand up and say phone calls have a place still, and they are also the canary in the coal mine when we need to invest in our other channels. If balance is achieved, customers will not reach for the phone by default.

Web interfaces, social interfaces, phone, chat, and search all need to get better together—but not at the expense of one or the other.

II. Total Visibility Helps Customers Feel in Control

Cross channel integration or at least visibility is key. We can't just have rearview analytics—how customers responded or campaigns performed—we need to know what is going on as it is happening.

The more control we can give the customer over their experience the better. This control is facilitated when customers can see *all* their past interactions on *all* channels. At first this sounded like a daunting prospect, but now, with cheap cloud MIPS and storage, it is very feasible.

Let's compare the website functionality of the major retailers in 2018. The best one can show every order you ever placed on the web and in the store. This same retailer's account tab also holds every email they have ever sent, and every message and service request. Call records are not on the site yet, but this will be coming soon. Other retailers show only the last couple of years of orders, few show messages sent, and few have in-store purchase records. It is surprising how few retailers realize that historical orders are key to help someone order a replacement. By showing all interactions, you can create more sales!

Showing *my browsing history* is key. The better ecommerce sites show both personalized recommendations and recent browsing history for reference. Sites with just personalized recommendations are thinking old school: "Hey, buy this!"—*push* to customer. *Sites with browsing history are being convenient for the customer.* The incremental cost to do both is minimal.

This is the ideal. While we can't do everything everywhere for the customer, we can help the customer work with us more efficiently in ways *they want to work with us*. Show all historical interactions and look for the tools that give you convenience features for your customer, not just push tools.

We need to face the new reality brought on by text-message support and Facebook Messenger channels—they are "forever." The conversation stream with agents is now kept forever in the hand of our customers anyway on these social channels—we might as well extend this courtesy to all our channels, including call center recordings.

The technology is there. We need the *courage* to harness it.

III. To Know Me Is to Love Me

Customers feel in control of their experience if they feel you know them. And "knowing" means understanding how they use your service and your systems in a non-creepy way, a non-pushy way. Like leveraging recommendation engines to provide browsing history, as mentioned previously. Customers may not want you to know things *beyond the boundary* of their interactions with you, but they do expect you to know everything they have done *within that boundary.*

This requirement means a 360 view of the customer is table stakes. You must have visibility in the call center to all other channel interactions. You must know if the customer is mad at you when they call.

The good news is, this isn't as costly to do anymore because of big data datatype freedom. Force-fitting our data into relational and star schema formats cost too much, and many projects failed. Now we can throw it all in a multi-type big data store with a reference table approach to ID the customer. As long as we have the *courage* to define a common customer ID, we can have the 360 view for a lot less effort.

IV. The Rise of RTIM

We now have technologies to solve the collection and reaction issue as well. In 2015, Rusty Warner of Forrester declared a new Forrester wave called RTIM, for Real Time Interaction Management, which was defined as, "Enterprise Marketing Technology that delivers contextually relevant experiences, value and utility at the appropriate moment in the customer life cycle via preferred customer touchpoints."

Let's unpack that sentence: "Contextually relevant experiences, at the appropriate moment via preferred customer touchpoints." The *customer's preferred touchpoints*—not the *company's preferred touchpoints*. If you know me, it is going to be contextually relevant. If you are doing this in real time, it is at the appropriate moment.

The good news is that this is not impossible any more. Some of the channels are being unified today. There are a number of vendors in the RTIM space now.

Each of the older RTIM vendors is a little biased, based on its roots in a primary channel—some started in the web channel, others in the call center—so you have to be careful which you pick initially. The good news is, all the vendors are investing to give complete coverage.

Consider deploying new sensors on all channels first. A number of CX journey maps in the industry are linear and "happy path." The reality is that journeys are now *non-linear* and *the customer determines their path.* You may think you know the way the customer is using all your channels because you built them a certain way—but do you really?

Deploying RTIM again requires *courage*. You have to first get the channel teams to talk when they all have their own analytics already. You will have to resist the temptation to merge current analytics via reports. The analytics need to be done live, and reactions need to be near-real-time.

V. Courage Is All We Need

So, in summary, we have the technology available to help the customer control their experience for our benefit. We just need the courage to bring call center and web together, the courage to create that universal customer ID, the courage to be transparent with all our interactions, and the courage for marketing IT and regular IT to beat their swords into plowshares—and then we can really achieve better experiences at reasonable cost.

* * * * *

Okay, travelers, we are now on the final stretch of road. We've covered definitions, frameworks, strategies, programs, and even the technologies. To progress on this final leg of the trip, we need to make sure we understand what the outcomes are going to be if we do this the right way. So, next outcomes and measurements.

Let's roll.

SECTION SIX

The Outcomes

U ltimately, we want this all to produce something of value to us. What
are outcomes devoutly to be wished? How do we measure those outcomes? I'll tell you in these two chapters. I swear.

CHAPTER 15

Love Me, Love My Conversation: Satisfaction, Loyalty, Advocacy

I t's interesting. I've written, and you've read, several hundred pages on engagement and self-interest and, everything still comes down to the same already oft-repeated statement.

> *If a customer likes you and continues to like you, they will continue to do business with you. If they don't, they won't.*

But what is different is how that needs to be interpreted at this point. Ultimately, for the customer to continue to do business with you, you have help them achieve the optimal outcomes that they are looking for from you. Continuing to help them with that is what earns you their business and even maybe their loyalty. The next two chapters are going to show what outcomes are possible for you when you help your customers get to theirs via engagement—and how to measure the impact on your business. Fun, huh?

As you've seen, the more that customers are engaged, the more they mean to your company's financial health. But, as stories passed down through the generations that it took to read this book prove, there are other important benefits, too. The absolutely most vanilla way to put it would be that fully engaged customers tend to be happy customers. Given the communications media available to them and how easy it is to purchase things these days, those happy customers—if they are *really* happy—tend to find ways to broadcast that happiness via ongoing purchases and/or letting others know of their happiness.

That is not mere customer satisfaction, a somewhat overrated but still notable outcome. That is either loyalty or, even more desirable, advocacy. But the question is, what is the impact on and by customer engagement for each of them? I'll give you a topic. Does customer satisfaction engender customer engagement? Does a highly engaged customer become a loyal customer or an advocate? What is the value of each, if any, to your company? Discuss.

DISCUSSION: TRUST

In Chapter 9, trust reared its lovely head as one of the most important characteristics of a customer-engaged company. When it comes to establishing satisfaction, loyalty, and advocacy, trust is the single most important requirement, regardless of how great the environment is, how exciting the interactions are, or how fantastic the rewards seem to be. If the customer doesn't trust you, then the rest is meaningless.

This means that to establish any kind of positive relationship the company has to establish and maintain trust. I already spoke to keeping promises as one of the cornerstones of trust; but stoking loyalty or advocacy goes beyond dependably keeping promises. The brand itself has to be credible, meaning that the products and services offered are reliable and the content that the company provides supportable enough for the customer to trust its credibility. There has to be a feeling of intimacy based on the company knowing enough about you to address your needs—something we've been focused on throughout this entire book. To broaden the trust, the company should provide the communications media for the customer to be able share their brand experience with others. That can mean social networks or communities that are sitting behind the firewall, though certainly other communications options are available. Rachel Happe, who you will meet this chapter, will elaborate on how communities engender trust.

If you take all these attributes and apply them liberally, then you have a good chance of capturing the loyalty of your customers and even turning some of them into advocates. But, if you don't, then you'll be lucky to even have rationally satisfied customers. Keep in mind that, in order for the customer to want to do business with the company, he or she has to trust what that company has in store for him or her. Not a complicated idea but complex in its undertaking.

Once you've established trust, then your objective should be clear. Your optimal customer, the one that you are focused on fostering, is the advocate, your active proponent. The customer you settle for is the loyal customer. Earlier strategies called for satisfied customers and some loyal customers who emerged from the pack. No longer good enough. With the availability of social media to both support and malign brands, the brands are more dependent than ever on having their customers as partners, either providing honest feedback or acting as advocates for the brand on social media sites and even, in the most advanced situations, co-creating products.

DISCUSSION: COSTS OF RETENTION VERSUS COSTS OF ACQUISITION

Why is the loyal customer the middle ground, i.e., the most common result you should expect? Aside from loyal customers being fertile ground for your future advocates—your brand ambassadors to use contemporary lingo—they are the customers who are most committed to staying your customers even, on occasion, at their own expense—and certainly at yours. LOL!

I know I've discussed acquisition and retention a couple of other places, but here I'd like to drill a bit deeper into the costs. Forgive me if a bit of the discussion is repetitive.

When you begin to factor in what customer acquisition costs you versus what customer retention costs you, the costs of showing your loyal customers some love begins to make sense.

This has been an ongoing discussion for years. For as long as I have been in the CRM or customer-facing world, the costs of acquisition and retention have been bandied about, but the conclusion is always the same:

> *It costs far more to acquire a customer than to retain a customer—the number that seems to be most popular is five times as much.*

There is an actual calculation for customer acquisition, called the Customer Acquisition Costs (CAC), that is used to measure against the lifetime value of a customer (CLV), which you will hear about more next chapter. The CAC calculation factors in, among other things:

- Costs per lead (CPL), which means marketing costs—demand generation
- Touch cost, which is variable since it covers such areas as sales and sales operations salaries and some marketing salaries as the alignment of sales and marketing continues to evolve
- The costs of conversion at each stage of the sales process

In effect, it's a calculation based on the entirety of marketing and sales costs that go into creating one new customer. This is measured per customer against the projected lifetime value of that customer, although, clearly, given that this is a new customer with a history of a single transaction, so to speak, that's not easy to calculate to any degree of accuracy.

Many businesses simplify both, if they can, into two easy ways to look at it.

- The cost of customer acquisition is the sum of the costs associated with sales and marketing—fixed and variable divided by the number of new customers.

- The lifetime value of the customer is the gross margin expected from a customer, taking into account the costs of overhead in maintaining that customer.

Again, these are simplistic, but they are how you can get a rough approximation of both.

The Numbers

So far, we have one number. The costs of acquisition are five times as great as retention. But there is so much more to consider than just the costs associated with the actual processes. Here's some data from Invesp, experts in marketing and sales conversion (2016), that has been widely circulated. The probability of selling to an existing customer is 60–70 percent, while for a new customer it is 5–20 percent. There is a 50 percent greater likelihood that existing customers will try new products and a 31 percent likelihood they will spend more money. Perhaps most telling, a 5 percent increase in customer retention rates provides a 25-to-95 percent increase in profits.

Ultimately, the level (and type) of satisfaction, the level (and type) of loyalty, and the level of advocacy are the outcome of successful customer engagement with individual customers, and, once these outcomes are established, they can be evolutionary. Emotional satisfaction can turn into loyalty, which can become advocacy if all were wonderful.

But to see how these outcomes are achievable, I think it would be wise to establish the parameters for satisfaction, loyalty, and advocacy, don't you? So, let's.

DISCUSSION: SATISFACTION

As I do a lot, let's start with my definition—or someone else's if they say it better than I do. This one is so easy, it's mine.

> *Customer satisfaction is the degree to which a customer feels positively that a company met or exceeded their expectations when it comes to the company's products and services.*

While simple on the surface, this definition does have some nuance. The American Marketing Association rightfully distinguishes between two types of customer satisfaction: rational satisfaction and emotional satisfaction.

A customer who is fine with the products and services that a company provides him or her but has no particular emotional interest in the company is rationally satisfied. Think of your (or at least, my) typical satisfaction with most credit cards. The product and services associated with them do what you want, so you are fine with that; but a better deal comes alone and, because the cost of switching—which means the total effort it takes to switch—is generally low, then you make the switch to the new card. No muss, no fuss. While you are using the card, you rarely feel any emotional satisfaction. Usually, the card fulfills whatever utilitarian functions you need it to, and that is enough. I say that despite some actual emotional attachment to my American Express Platinum card because of the travel benefits associated with it—throwing my own rationale in my own face.

For a business, emotional satisfaction is much more . . . satisfying. It means that the customer has some sort of emotional involvement with the brand and is willing to go a bit further. This correlates with but is not identical to loyalty. You can be tied to a brand and enjoy your relationship to that brand and still not be loyal to it. For example, think about staying at a hotel that you thoroughly enjoyed, say, a resort in Bali that is not part of a larger chain but a solo operator. The food, the service, the room, the beauty of the island, the enchantment of being away from cares and worries, all led to a wonderful experience. You really were happy with the stay. But, while there might even be a loyalty program for the hotel, the likelihood of you returning on this "affordable-once-in-a-lifetime" vacation to this same place is less than zero, or close to that. You are emotionally satisfied but not loyal—partially because there is nothing to be loyal to and no circumstance that requires or even suggests a second visit. Loyalty requires the behavior for customer retention—continued interactions— and the desire to continue the relationship on the part of the customer. It's not that you wouldn't be loyal if there were a means or reason to continue, but there just is not. Emotional satisfaction has considerably different implications than rational satisfaction.

Satisfaction and Engagement? Are They Related?

Even though satisfaction is seen as a baseline indicator of the customer's relationship to any given company, it stops way short of being an indicator of customer engagement.

Gallup's research in 2017 showed that while half of the customers surveyed deemed themselves satisfied with a brand, only 38 percent identified themselves as engaged. Anson Vuong, Gallup's researcher found, in fact, that there was no correlation between high degrees of satisfaction and high degrees of engagement—meaning one didn't lead to the other. They found that they co-exist and a low degree of one can co-exist and not correlate with, a high degree of the other.

Vuong divided the two most basic levels of satisfaction and the two most basic levels of engagement into quadrants. They are (names his, descriptions mine):

Quadrant I: Low Satisfaction/Low Engagement—Doomed Relationship—Kind of obviously the worst possible place to be. The products, services, tools, and consumable experiences may be overpriced, lower quality, nowhere near frictionless, ugly. In other words, the basic *raison d'etre* of the business suffers by comparison to the expectations of the customer. Additionally, they just don't care enough to provide the outlets to explain the situation. I'd list an example, but it's hard to come up with a company that crass that isn't out of business already.

Quadrant II: High Satisfaction/Low Engagement—Relationship of Convenience—The company offers what the customer needs or wants for the price they want. This is where rational satisfaction resides. This is where the slogan "you get what you pay for" comes to bear. The company offers something. You think it's fine as it stands. You take them up on it. You have no emotional investment in this company, but the convenience or the price or the product quality and features all are of use to you, so you go for it. This is Walmart, Burger King, Ryanair.

Quadrant III: Low Satisfaction/High Engagement—Insulated Relationship—This is where the emotional investment is of a higher order than the fundamentals. For example, the customer could be paying a high premium for something for which the quality is not as exceptional as the price merits, but it has the brand caché. As Vuong puts it here: "The high engagement of their customers creates loyalty through emotion despite the lagging rational aspects of the experience." A significant number of companies in the luxury industry fall into this category. Bling often fits right here. The product isn't all that great, but, hey, I have the product, and it is a (fill in the lux company)! Vertu, the now out-of-business purveyor of luxury mobile devices, fell here. Rarely did a customer like the actual phone, but it costs $10,000 and it's Vertu, and it has diamonds. Caché and carats, people. Though phone quality is still what keeps you in business. Utility trumps caché and carats.

Quadrant IV: High Satisfaction/High Engagement—Dual-Path Relationship—Companies in this quadrant understand that a competitive, rational experience is not enough to attain a market edge. Businesses must also make memorable and meaningful emotional connections, typically through human channels such as great service. Nordstrom and Amazon are great companies that fall into this quadrant. Macys and United Airlines aren't.

Vuong does a great job of not only distinguishing between satisfaction and engagement but also showing that the correlations are not between the two but in how the two work in conjunction. If we assume, and I do, that engagement and satisfaction are not driven by each other, that doesn't mean we don't think about satisfaction. There are reasons to make satisfaction a concern, though not a goal, which I hope become apparent shortly.

Measuring Satisfaction

The biggest problem with customer satisfaction as a "state of interest" to a business is that it, at best, is a foundation for something more, not something that needs to be the epitome of a plan. Rational satisfaction and inertia make little or no differences in how the customer interacts with the company. Both can lead to churn. If inertia is misinterpreted as satisfaction, the churn will be a surprise since the customer seems to have some commitment to the company—a commitment that is not really there. On the other hand, emotional satisfaction is something that does have some meaning because it can lead to other things for a business. A newly acquired customer who has had an emotionally satisfying experience is minimally prone to considering further, hopefully, emotionally satisfying interactions with a company. But as a static condition, it is not something that a company needs to aim for in its planning. It is a passive state that provides no guarantee of anything further at all.

So how valuable is a satisfaction survey and a satisfaction score? Well, I don't want to entirely dismiss them, so I won't; but they are considerably less valuable than they used to be or than they could be.

The Survey

Obviously, understanding how happy a customer is (or isn't) with you has value. Surveys are helpful in assessing a customer's happiness over time with a company or of a single interaction with a company (e.g., the "how was your flight" survey you get from an airline). As I found repeatedly in research for this part of the book, though, one of the problems with surveys now isn't the survey itself, it's the sales person or customer service representative's message to you prior to your receipt of the survey. It goes something like, "Nothing means anything to HQ but a 10, so I would appreciate it if you could consider that." The pressure is on the recipient of the survey to give that 10, or, it's implied, something bad will happen to the sales person. The sad part is that it isn't always the reps who are coming up with the idea on their own. They are parroting what they have been told to say, and they are incentivized to get those 10s.

So, what are the problems here? They are myriad, but two stand out. One is that there are going to be a false amount of 10s because, even if you weren't fully satisfied with the service, the inclination of good people is to help the sales person or CSR. The second, and even worse, part is that the commentary tells you that the home office isn't interested in honest assessments to fix problems but only in good scores. They are trying to control what should be an organic response. A big problem all around.

Surveys like this can be valuable for what they unveil, not for the number they produce. If done well, companies can learn what they are doing right and what they are doing wrong from the results. I'm not saying the bulk of them aren't valuable, but the frequency of complaints calls into question the environments producing them. So, caveat emptor on this. If you are going to produce a customer survey, make sure you not only have the cultural commitment to get better, but that you will let the results speak for themselves rather than try to force the results you want.

The Score

Two of the leading organizations for customer satisfaction scores are the American Customer Satisfaction Institute (ACSI) and JD Powers. They each track satisfaction somewhat differently, with JD Powers tracking the satisfaction of customers with the loyalty programs of the brands involved. The ACSI looks at more traditional benchmarks: product and services satisfaction. They each break down their results by industry, as well as compile a national list. So, for the hospitality industry, the #1 and #2 companies on both lists are Hilton and Marriott. Both of them score exceptionally well. In the ACSI report, Hilton scores 81 and Marriott 80 against an industry average of 76. In JD Powers, they tie at 741, which is exceptional against an industry average of 711.

If you are willing to accept the distinction between rational satisfaction and emotional satisfaction, then those scores present a problem: how do you distinguish between the two types of satisfaction with one general score? The criteria, especially for JD Powers, tend to skew to emotional satisfaction, which makes sense if satisfaction with loyalty programs is the focus. The responders would be members of those programs, who are already, more likely than not, loyal customers.

But, nonetheless, given the differences between types of satisfaction and the low likelihood that the scores reflect that difference, they are still valuable as comparatives. How is the brand doing against the industry as a whole, the country as a whole, against other brands, and other industry-specific brands. There is value in the rankings. For example, it is nice to know that there is a high regard for Hilton and Marriott's programs, who are #1 and #2 in every customer-satisfaction poll that covers hospitality in any way. Plus, their consistently high scores are encouraging to customers who are trying to figure out where to stay; they are a positive factor in decision-making. Think about it this way. Excellent customer-satisfaction scores and good reviews mean I'm going to stay at a Marriott. Or a Hilton.

But, once I do that, for the first or one of a very few times, how do you keep me coming back to the Marriott. I've experienced it, and I like it a lot; but I also like Hilton. And I like Intercontinental. What is it that is going to make me choose Marriott over all others? How is Marriott going to keep me engaged at whatever level it is I need and want to be engaged?

Make me loyal.

DISCUSSION: LOYALTY

Once again, ladies and gents, I bring you the (my) definition of customer loyalty:

> *When a customer is willing to repeatedly purchase a single brand's goods and services over a significant period of time even with equitable competitive offerings easily available.*

This is the middle ground in a manner of speaking—but the distance between loyalty and satisfaction is as substantial as the distance between loyalty and advocacy. Loyalty programs have been premised on the idea of "you scratch my back, I'll scratch yours," which is no longer as effective in business as it once was. (Though if you *actually* scratch *my* back, I'll purr like a kitten.) They have to be a lot more than back scratchers because it's so competitive.

Forrester found in their May 2017 research that 72 percent of the U.S. adults online belonged to at least one loyalty program, but the average number was an insane nine! The largest percentage—74 percent—belonged to a supermarket loyalty program, which, of course, gets you discounts and coupons merely for registered membership. To get them is a matter of just showing your card at the checkout counter—easy. This confirms the 2017 COLLOQUY Loyalty Census data showing that, of those American consumers participating in a loyalty program, the number-one reason for their participation was "easy to use" (53 percent), and the number-two reason was "gives me great discounts" (39 percent)—the exact parameters of a supermarket loyalty program. In case you want to know, number-one reason for abandonment was "it took too long to earn points or miles." What makes this fascinating and shows something of the loyal customer's psyche is that 51 percent of the respondents trusted loyalty programs with their personal information. Even though that's marginally over half, it goes to what I said at the beginning of this chapter. Trust is the factor that drives this kind of emotional commitment. The trust in the programs regarding personal information is just proof of the trust the customer has in the program and especially the brand.

The global loyalty program distribution is very different, but the reasoning is much of the same. The numbers of members globally (with the knowledge that each member of each program is a separate entity here—so you can be in these multiple times if you are a member of multiple programs) is a staggering 3.8 billion, with the largest slice going to retail (1.6 billion) and then travel and hospitality (1.1 billion). What makes this particularly interesting is that, despite the vastly different distribution, the reasons for being in the programs remain pretty much the same—with the biggest driver in retail, for example, being "the program is easy to understand." Being easy and frictionless, from understanding to reward redemption, is clearly what determines the program's success or failure.

The measurement of success for loyalty is on the tricky side. Back in 2002, a man you will hear me speak about at length in the next chapter, Dr. V. Kumar, and the also well-known Werner Reinartz, did a *Harvard Business Review* study of the data from 16,000 customers from a variety of companies that focused on the correlation of loyalty to profitability. In brief, they found that the correlations were weak to none and that whatever correlations were there were (their word) "subtle." Yep. You heard me. Barely there.

"But," you are thinking, "I thought the whole idea of a loyal customer was repeated transactions over time."

It is, but that doesn't assure profitability. It only assures what it sounds like: that they will repeatedly buy from the company.

Kumar and Reinartz found that loyal customers do not cost less to maintain. They ran from roughly the same costs as "not-loyal" customers to—because they were premium customers experienced in the ways of the company— knowing how to game the system, demand more, and get it. This means they actually cost even more than those customers who are not as committed. They also found that loyal customers, over time, paid 5 to 7 percent less for the same goods as the regular customer—again, because they expect something for their loyalty, including significant discounts.

I can attest to that. I have been a super-premium customer of DirecTV for 16 years, spending ungodly amounts of money every month on lots of TV. I stay with DirecTV not due to deep commitment but for a utilitarian reason: they have the premium sports packages I care about, including Extra Innings for Major League Baseball and Sunday Ticket for the National Football League. Extra Innings costs roughly $170 for the baseball season, above and beyond what I pay monthly as a super-premium subscriber. That gets me nearly all of the 162 games of every team. So, assuming 100 percent of games, that's roughly 2,430 games for roughly $170. That's approximately six cents a game. Great deal.

But then you have Sunday Ticket. At last count, it was $300 for the NFL season—again, nearly all the games. For the regular season, that's a total of 256 games at $300, meaning $1.17 a game. Expensive.

Here's the problem. *Every* year, they offer Sunday Ticket as a free incentive for signing up as a new customer. I've been a customer for 16 years at a high premium—probably among their highest lifetime value customers at the consumer level—and they *never* offer me a discount. So, every year, I call them, and then I negotiate anywhere from 25 percent off to a half-price deal. Once I got it for free. But I call them, they never proactively offer me a thing.

Let's look at this from several standpoints—Kumar's and mine.

- I'm expecting that they should do something about this, given my status as a high value customer—anecdotally validating Kumar's research.

- Yet, they do not offer me anything proactively (beyond upsell and cross sell "opportunities"), thus, at best, maintaining my rational commitment to them. (They have the sports packages, so I stick with them.) If they made some proactive offers to show that they value me, then perhaps I would develop some emotional commitment to them, which then lays the foundation for actual loyalty—a real commitment.

- The net result of this expectation, given what has been a rational, utilitarian commitment that has the appearance of loyalty is that I would leave them if someone else carried the sports packages they did, which would mean the best offer wins. I am not loyal, I only appear loyal. I am actually rationally satisfied.

- In late 2017, DirecTV decoupled Sunday Ticket from their general offerings so that anyone, whether they had DirecTV or not, could get the package for roughly $280–$350 a year. That triggered a thought. I already could decouple MLB Baseball because, besides DirecTV's offering, I had MLB.TV, too, a subscription that allowed me access to all Major League Baseball games via the web. With the decoupling of NFL Sunday Ticket, I didn't need DirecTV at all for the two packages, which were the primary reason that I was staying as a rationally satisfied customer devoid of emotional bond.

- I called the Sunday Ticket people, told them that, and the best they could come up with was $17 a month off the package—about 33 percent, no longer enough. They suggested that I call the Loyalty Group at DirecTV.

- I did that and the net result was a free Sunday Ticket and a reduction in my bill by more than 60 percent, driving me to commit to DirecTV and increase my emotional commitment.

- Nonetheless, they didn't do anything proactively, which reflects a poor policy when it comes to retaining long-time and high-premium customers. But I did stay and would say that I've become emotionally satisfied because they did show me some love by doing all that work and giving me a significant financial break.

What does something like this mean in real dollars? I can't speak for the actual impact on DirecTV, but I can give you an example of some data the American Management Association (AMA) produced for an international credit card company over a six-month period.

- Emotionally satisfied customers spent (on the average) $251 per month and used the card 3.1 times per month.

- Rationally satisfied customers spent $136 per month and used the card 2.5 times per month.

- Dissatisfied customers spent $136 per month—the same amount as rationally satisfied customers and used their cards 2.2 times per month—almost indistinguishable from the rationally satisfied customers. Take note, DirecTV.

- Emotionally satisfied customers increased their spending by 67 percent in a 12-month period, while rationally satisfied customers increased theirs by 8 percent.

Revenue is directly impacted by how much someone has emotionally invested in your company. The greater the emotional investment, the more they spend.

Two Types of Loyalty, Too? For Realsies?

It all seems simple, and then the experts get involved. When you take this to a higher plane, the same way you become aware of differences between rational and emotional satisfaction, you find that there are two kinds of loyalty: attitudinal loyalty and behavioral loyalty. An examination of the differences can be handled quickly because of what they are.

Attitudinal loyalty is defined by those who provide positive references for the brand to their peers. In other words, advocates. We'll be talking more about that shortly.

Behavioral loyalty is the loyalty we are still speaking of here. It is characterized by the willingness to repeatedly buy things from the brand. It has a significant economic benefit, including sales of higher-margin products, as well as cost savings since you don't have to constantly market or advertise to these customers. So, it's worth fighting for those customers, even with the costs that Kumar/Reinartz spoke about in their survey. Despite them not being attitudinally loyal, customers like this do have to have enough emotional commitment to keep them buying from you and not someone else.

Okay, I just wanted to clarify that so there is no confusion. Let's move on.

Cultivating Loyalty: Sometimes It's the Little Things . . . and Other Things, Too

Loyalty is peculiar. It is a commitment of a kind when it comes to a business, one that fosters a continued relationship between the customer and the company. But it isn't always programs or tangible rewards that create loyal customers. Sometimes it's the way a business is conducted or the way that individuals associated with the business appear or the obvious attitudes that the business has towards customers. It can be kindness from the business to its customers. It can be attentive behavior by the employees at the business. But what occurs is the overall environment created, and the actions within the environment are what either create or cement the loyalty of those customers.

I'll illustrate that with two personal stories.

THE DENTIST: EMPATHY AND CARE

Due to significant dental issues, I spend a lot of time at my local dentist, Dr. Nadder Hassan, a young, good-looking guy in his early 30s.

What Dr. Hassan has done with his dental practice, acquired from my previous dentist, is eye-opening not just for instilling confidence in his skills and for trust in his judgment, but in how you feel at the office. Let's face it, no one goes to the dentist for fun. No one has a good time. This is necessary health, not entertainment. It is not discretionary, unless you equate your health with a movie or dinner out.

He started by hiring a staff that had quality dental or management skills. He rebuilt the office into an environment that would reduce stress or tension, including TVs with Netflix and whatever else in each room for any adult or child to watch according to what interested them. He made the office itself more inviting, with better lighting and more open spaces. He uses the best possible technology and is a master of the use of every instrument or device in the office. He is courteous and friendly and treats patients and staff with respect. He knows what he's doing, and he is a bit of a perfectionist—so, when you leave the office, even if it took a bit longer than expected, you are certain that you got the job done the right way.

All of this is reflected in his average ratings on various sites, which are between 4.9 and 5.0 in every case.

But, all in all, this doesn't necessarily produce loyalty. Dental work starts negatively, and the best you can do really is reduce the negative to zero. No one wants to return to a dental office for more work—routine or otherwise. But someone who does the work superbly in a great environment will tend to create comfort, which is an optimal condition for emotional satisfaction.

It is, however, the little things that create loyal patients. They work at multiple levels. Some examples:

- Recognizing that dental insurance is horribly inadequate—even the best of it—he created a program for his patients that covers 30 percent of their dental bill for $195 a year. That can be a significant savings if you have anything done beyond just a routine piece of work.

- He created a referral program that, for various numbers of referrals, gets you a $25 gift card, $50 off the next bill, $100 off the next bill, or an iPad.

- He guarantees his work for five years, so that if, say, you have a crown put in and something happens to it in the next five years, you get it replaced for free.

In other words, he's created programs that keep customers willing to come back for more. But there is one more thing that makes a huge difference in how committed a patient can become.

Right before Christmas 2017, I had some serious dental surgery that left me with a very, very sore mouth. My wife was out of town, and I was at home by myself with very little I was able to eat in the house, and I didn't really feel well enough to go out and get anything. On Christmas Day, there was a knock at my door. Who was standing there with a bag full of edible groceries and a Nutribullet to make other things pulpy and thus edible? Dr. Hassan. He had gone out of his way to find me food, knowing I was alone and not able to get around, and he delivered it to me on Christmas Day.

Empathy. A fundamentally kind person. That's the difference-maker in the long run. Remember the characteristics of a customer-engaged culture? Empathy was front and center.

Dr. Hassan's Manassas Smiles, while a small business (but growing fast), is an ideal example of the combination of factors that creates loyalty among customers. Plus, he's just a damned good human being.

It's not the only exceptional business in Manassas, though. Sometimes how the little routine things are handled are just as important.

The Shipper: Logistics and Convenience

As you probably know, when you go to UPS, delight is the least-important thing on your mind. You want to send packages, then get the hell out of there, and that's that. So, the optimal "little thing" is a frictionless experience. The manager of UPS Store 4988 in Manassas, Garrett Sakovich, gets that . . . and takes it from there. He is a young, smart, engaging person who makes sure of two things when you go to his UPS store. First, you are out in a few minutes, and, second, he and the other store employee *help* you get out in a few minutes. Period. From the time you bring in your package to the time you walk out the door is usually no more than a couple of minutes, and you have a receipt to track the package when it goes out. This is such an easy-going and efficient experience that I have no qualms about going out of my way to go to this particular store, even though it adds to the time it takes to do a door-to-door transaction on occasion. But it's smooth. And there is no delight. Just a sense of "done," a sense of accomplishment—and moving on to something else. Which is all you want and need from a UPS outlet.

But, you might be saying, these are small businesses, or, in the case of UPS, a small store within a large business, serving a small geography. What happens to loyalty when you have to scale?

Time for another story before bed. Let's revisit Marriott and its rewards program, which more than 110 million members at the end of 2018. *That's* big.

CASE STUDY: MARRIOTT REWARDS

Marriott is the fastest-growing hotel chain. It has a vast and expanding portfolio of brands—from their own Courtyard Marriott and JW Marriott to major chains like the Ritz Carleton, the Gaylord, Starwood's, and lifestyle brands like Autograph.

It isn't successful for its variety of brands, though that helps, but because ratings for both customer satisfaction and its loyalty program are off the charts.

I'm a Marriott Platinum card holder, devoted to staying at Marriott properties whenever I possibly can, and there are good reasons for that.

What distinguishes the Marriott experience from others is the quality of the day-to-day at the hotel: the ambiance, the courtesy of the staff, the general cleanliness of the rooms, and the management of the property. That will vary from place to place and time to time, but, in general, they are consistently good enough to make me comfortable—which is what I want from a hotel when I'm on a business trip. I might want more when I'm on a vacation, but the bulk of my travel is business travel; I get exactly what I need from Marriott in at least 90 percent of my trips.

But their slogan isn't "Travel Comfortably," it's "Travel Brilliantly."

The loyalty program is designed to take you to the next level, from comfortable to brilliant (though brilliant is probably a bit hyperbolic).

Marriott Rewards, their loyalty program, has been an excellent, loyalty program that is being constantly improved based on customer feedback. That, in itself, fosters loyalty because Marriott is listening to their members. The 2018 merger with SPG set them back with thousands of problems due to the technical integration of the two loyalty programs but their membership loss (to date) has been minimal because of their past history of success.

Like most programs, Marriott Rewards provides you with points for your stay. The points reward is variable based on the amount you spend, the level of hotel you are staying at, and, of course, the length of your stay. Achieving the upper tiers—Gold, Platinum Elite, Premier Platinum Elite and a lifetime Platinum status—isn't easy. For example, Platinum Elite requires that you stay 50 nights at Marriott properties each year (that is nearly 14 percent of your entire year), and it typically means you are traveling far too much. But they try to make it worth your while. As a Platinum member (many of the benefits, though not all, apply to Gold members, too), you get:

- 50 percent point bonus

- No blackout dates on points redemption

- Priority late checkout

- Gift shop discounts

- Guaranteed lounge access/breakfast for you and one guest

- Room upgrades
- Complimentary premium-tiered internet service
- Guaranteed room type
- Platinum arrival gift of 500 points or a boring food or beverage. (Take the points.)

To me, the lounge access along with the points bonuses are the most important perks. Marriott knows that. They learn it by monitoring my activity and gathering the data on it at Marriott hotels across the world. As far back as 2014, they were testing what they called Local Perks, delivering geo-targeted information and offers to interested members during their hotel stay using the member's smartphone and Marriott's mobile app. Rich Toohey, who, at the time, was responsible for these programs as the Vice President of Marriot Rewards, told me:

At the core of Local Perks is a thoughtful digital design that leverages Beacon technology installed at various locations inside the hotel to deliver relevant content and offers. Offers and content are tailored to take advantage of the individual features and outlets available at each hotel.

The pilot for Local Perks was the San Diego Marriott Marquis & Marina. The employees at the hotel spent extra time to make sure that their guests knew of the opportunity and encouraged them to download the app so they could get the offers. The experience, according to the guests who did so, was seamless. Rich again:

The integration of a physical execution component in the form of Marriott's signature service to these digital interactions created a hybrid "digical" program, a holistic hotel experience, and a platform for effective customer engagement.

(Author Note: "digical" means digital and physical combined.)

This was only the beginning for Marriott. They knew that, more and more, their guests, and especially their Rewards members, lived on their mobile devices, so Marriott spent a lot of time honing the application and centralizing their interactions and communications via the app and mobile devices. As of 2018, they are using, among several other technologies, a small company called Chirpify as their loyalty-engagement platform. Members who advocate for the brand and especially the Rewards program via social media channels such as Twitter, Facebook, and Instagram are incentivized with points for their successful engagement—and all of this is in real time. The technology connects Marriott social media accounts with the member database and then broadcasts specific personalized triggers throughout the year that provide the Marriott Rewards members with opportunities to receive points for participation. For example, in 2016 Marriott launched the Reward-a-Friend referral program to get new members who were friends of existing members enrolled. In four days, 7.4 million impressions were recorded.

Marriott integrated its CRM data with the membership database so that they were able to identify whose membership registration anniversary it was and send a personalized "happy anniversary" greeting, and then deposit points in their account in celebration. In the first year, they deposited 4 million anniversary points into member accounts. This is another way that Marriott recognizes the value of the member and makes them feel valued.

The technology has been an especially great enabler of customer engagement for mobile Marriott Rewards members. Between 2016 and 2017, there were 65 million positive earned media impressions and 326,000 social media engagements. This led to the award of 84 million points, which means about 11,000 free nights. Big numbers.

It's not only engagement via direct interactions but convenience that can drive loyalty. Examples include mobile check-in, mobile reservations, and, in more limited release, the use of the mobile device as a room key in some Marriotts. None of these are deeply sexy, nor do they even provide points to the member; but the technology makes things more convenient for the guests, which is a substantial plus when it comes to frictionless customer engagement.

Engagement and loyalty aren't only enabled by technology. Another benefit of the Marriott Rewards program is that it provides access to special experiences, called Marriott Moments, which are only available to Rewards members. The experiences have included a Dwayne Wade personal basketball workshop, snorkeling with a Cousteau, and a series of culinary classes and dining experiences with world-class chefs. Typically, the moment is redeemable by points; but members also have the option of bidding on them to acquire them with a lower points cost. These kinds of consumable experiences give birth to an extensive Marriott partner network, such as the one with the NBA, which not only makes Marriott the hotel of choice for the league but also provides exclusive Marriott Moments at a variety of NBA events and venues.

Marriott has clearly been successful with their rewards program, despite their 2018 glitches with the merger of SPG and Marriott, because they investigate all avenues to make the customer their valued partner by:

- Making membership registration easy
- Being aware of the personalized needs of each member

- Using 21st century technology—meaning they embrace mobile engagement as a strong part of the Marriott offering

- Making sure the basic interactions, such as registration, check-in and check-out, and access to staff, among many others, are frictionless—regardless of whether they are in person, via mobile device, or conducted on the web

- Ensuring that the rewards program is truly special—meaning it provides things you wouldn't otherwise get without it

- Rewarding brand advocacy for the efforts made to broadcast the love—you are valuable *to* us because you have been valuable *for* us

Engagement at all touchpoints that make the members feel valued is how you make sure that your customers come back to you time and time again.

Ah, but wait. I mentioned advocacy as the last point. What is the difference between that and loyalty, if advocacy is rewarded within the loyalty program? Don't be confused by that, brethren. I'll explain.

DISCUSSION: ADVOCACY

Advocacy. The ideal "state of the customer." What is it? How does it impact you? Where does it differ from loyalty? As always, friends of *COSI*, I start with the definition.

> *Customer advocacy is when a customer trusts a brand and is emotionally connected to a sufficient degree to publicly promote their support for the brand to people like them.*

Advocacy requires action by and skin in the game from the customer. While I'm not a big fan of Net Promoter Score (NPS), Fred Reicheld, its creator, has a good definition of an advocate built into the one question that NPS requires you ask of your customers:

> *Would you recommend this to someone you know?*

The key phrase here is "someone you know." It's easy to praise or decry a brand to someone who you don't know because there is no accountability. You'll never see or hear from them again, so you can tell them anything you want. If you know them, however, they probably know you. And that means that you've had some level of repeated interaction with them over some period of time. So, you feel accountability for what you say to them. Think of it this way. If you recommend a chainsaw to a friend that breaks on day one, that friend is going to be upset with you. Hopefully, they don't fix the chainsaw and aren't named Jason.

Brand advocates are those who are speaking to a person like them who more or less trusts their judgment because that person seems to want the same things that they do. So, they listen to the recommendation. Think that's not the case? How many of you use Amazon not just to buy things but also read the reviews about things you are considering buying? I'm guessing the vast majority of you do that. Those reviewers were interested and then purchased the products that you are now considering, so they are "like you" in that regard. You read their reviews because, hey, they already have experience with the product. They can tell you if it was good or bad. But do you know a single one of them? As we have established before, probably not.

Trust in brand advocates is very high—according to Nielsen, 92 percent of us feel that what these advocates say can be trusted. The reason is simple: they are one of us.

This is not a big surprise to companies. They know that the impact advocates can have on a company's product/service sales is potentially enormous.

Come over here and sit down. Storytime.

CASE STUDY: ASOS

ASOS is a UK-based business that focuses on providing customers with more than 900 brands and more than 65,000 fashion-related clothes and accessories that celebrities are seen wearing—thus the name ASOS: As Seen On Screen. This £2 billion enterprise has thousands of brand advocates who, of course, being digital natives and celebrity watchers, are glad to chat up the clothing and accessories on social media. It's what they routinely do. But the benefit of this level of advocacy is that it can be directed to specific things and communicated via explicitly selected channels so that engagement between peers and the company and customers is optimized and remains in the control of the business.

In 2013, they launched an advocacy program, #AccessAllASOS, organized around advocates receiving benefits—ranging from special access to discounts—in return for social media participation—ranging from posting photos on Instagram to Tweeting to writing fashion blogs. They made membership selective. You had to fill out a form that showed that you were a social media "activist." If they "granted" your membership, you became an #AccessAllASOS insider, and this whole new world opened to you. You became a valued "elite" in the world of ASOS.

The tricky part was that being a valued elite didn't mean you got compensated for your advocacy. ASOS had to figure out what they could provide that would encourage outreach from the brand advocates without paying them for it. They were looking for advocates who would be out on the social channels, talking about them positively because they wanted to, not because they were being paid to.

Content was the key. Not only would lifestyle content be of special value to these potential advocates, by giving them content provided by relatable "someone like me" millennial professionals, the potential advocates were increasingly immersed in the ASOS world.

To that end, in the first three months after launch they provided 7,500 pieces of tailored and customized content. But they also launched a YouTube channel devoted to fashion and styling tips, which were provided by little-known professionals who were also relatable millennials themselves. They also sponsored "making it" videos highlighting up-and-coming millennials who were starting to make a name for themselves in areas like fashion design. There were clearly aspirational videos that inspired dreaming about something bigger and led to even further immersion into the ASOS universe. Demographics matter, too. The tips and influencers were made available in specific markets segmented by product and geography.

Not ignoring influencers, either, they incorporated celebrity partners like Ellie Goulding, who was both a brand advocate and an influencer.

Because ASOS already had a strong, loyal following, these kinds of programs weren't the standard loyalty program of the "get stuff in return for buying stuff" variety. Instead, they served as launch pads for advocates. ASOS customers became brand ambassadors, and, due to promotion via social media and video channels, gained influence in the ASOS community and among those who were aware of ASOS but not necessarily committed to the brand. Win-win. ASOS gets trusted advocates with increasing influence, and the advocates get not only discounts and access, but community love and trust. The advocates become immersed in the world of ASOS.

The results were amazing. In the first three months after launch, they had 75,000 positive mentions on social media and, get this, over 21 million views by separate users on the YouTube channel. They also found that, in part because of the power of their social outreach, they were able to reduce marketing costs by16 percent. Additionally, in that first three months, according to technology vendor and ASOS provider Traackr, ASOS increased spontaneous mentions of their brand by 600 percent and exceeded their referral target goal by 26 percent.

This all worked so well, that they followed it up in 2015 with a campaign they called #asseenonme (for those of you who are hashtag blind, that's "As Seen On Me"). Once again, the focus was actions to build brand advocacy, not just loyalty. This one was compensated, though. The idea was that if an Instagram user would post a picture of themselves wearing an ASOS outfit on Instagram, they would get a discount. This ongoing campaign has been so successful for ASOS that 60 percent of all its traffic and 44 percent of all its orders are now mobile—driven by this campaign and other efforts like it.

ASOS understands that advocacy is driven by a deeper emotional commitment to a brand than mere customer loyalty because it involves making your commitment public. Thus, they are not only able to suss out who their brand advocates are but who will *become* an advocate by:

- Knowing what drives their audience—in this case millennials across the globe

- Building out programs to keep them involved in public outreach in an ongoing way

- Providing value (i.e., great content, discounts, insider access) to the individuals willing to be public in their advocacy—something that makes the advocate feel valued

- Immersing those advocates in the ASOS world via the YouTube channel especially

CASE STUDIES

Formal, more traditional approaches are also used that go into more depth than social media conversations. Customer references are a key sign of advocacy. Customers have stories to tell about their problems and issues and how those issues got resolved. They can range from acne to broken sales processes depending on the market and the audience. But the stories resonate because they are customers who are using the products that some company produced and trusting the company that produced them. Potential customers want to hear these existing customer tales because they live in that very same world. So, customer reference programs are a big deal for companies and something they invest time and dollars into. IDC did a study early in 2017 called "The Role of Marketing in Customer Advocacy." It found that the number-one responsibility that the marketing staff of the companies surveyed (90+ percent) had was to secure customer references. The number-two significant Key Performance Indicator (after number of customer advocates) was the number of customer references secured, and the most important advocacy marketing "tactic," even more important than a customer advocacy program, was the presentation and availability of case studies.

Desired outcomes—those related to satisfaction, loyalty, and advocacy—are all based on levels of trust and involvement. There are multiple other aspects that we could discuss, such as the differences between influencers and advocates. (Are there differences? Are they measurable? Are the measures different, and, if they are, do they matter?) We will discuss all that in the next chapter, on measuring customer engagement, so I'll leave you in suspense for now.

Instead, I want to close this chapter the way I opened it, with a discussion on trust—the foundation for all the outcomes that customer engagement can affect (and effect)—including satisfaction, loyalty, and advocacy. The difference is that the voice you will hear is Rachel Happe's, not mine. Rachel is perhaps the foremost expert on communities in the world and a true authority on trust.

THOUGHT LEADER: RACHEL HAPPE

There used to be this expression when I was a kid—around a thousand years ago GPT (Greenberg Perceived Time)—that went, "What's the haps?" It meant "What's up with you?" though "hap" meant "fortune" and "luck" if defined by itself. Okay, I may be stretching the spelling, but Rachel Happe is one of those people I have the good fortune to know. She is arguably the leading thinker and influencer when it comes to communities and engagement, and she's put that leadership to work. She is the CEO of the Community Roundtable, the go-to source for everything that you need to build and manage communities. She is an engaging writer, a real thinker, and a true friend to those she counts as her friends. So, I asked her to write a piece that would show the impact of communities on customer engagement, and, wouldn't you know it, she came up with exactly what you should be hearing, or, in this case, seeing, when it comes to communities focused on trust and engagement. That goes to the heart of what fosters loyalty and advocacy—trust—and, as always, Rachel nails it.

So, Rachel, what's the haps?

. . . . .

FIXING TRUST: USING COMMUNITIES TO INCREASE DIALOGUE, ENGAGEMENT, AND TRANSPARENCY

Trust is in crisis. According to the 2017 and 2018 Edelman Trust Barometer, trust in organizations and leaders is declining across the board and is at a crisis point. Look no further than the rise of fake news, and, while that is often related to media, it is impacting all content. People do not know who and what organizations to trust and ultimately revert to relying only on individuals they know.

Trust underpins both the macro economy and any organization's ability to attract, influence, convert, and support. Because of the current crisis in trust, traditional methods of interacting with markets are also increasingly ineffective. When your market does not trust you, no amount of content and product will change it. Trust is based on people's belief that what an organization says is what it will do. It's believing the intent behind the message.

The best way to fix broken trust is to build relationships through dialogue, engagement, and transparency. No amount of telling will fix trust. The most efficient way to do that is by intentionally supporting a customer community, which *shows* customers that the organization is listening, responding, and working with them to support their needs.

So, What Does a Great Customer Community Look Like?

We often think of customer communities as customer-support communities, and they do indeed often start off that way. If a community is limited to deflecting support tickets and answering product- or service-related issues, however, the organization is missing out on strategic opportunities and the vast benefits that come with them. In an age where trust is in question, all organizations should be implementing community approaches to make their intent, actions, relationships, and interactions transparent.

The best customer communities are more than vehicles to answer product and service questions. They can also be places to:

- Demonstrate an organization's service—and trust—levels to prospects in a credible way by making conversations with existing customers transparent

- Attract prospects by making conversations about similar customer challenges and opportunities discoverable to search engines and giving them a way to connect with current customers

- Capture and prioritize customer needs—and connect customers to the individuals deep within an organization that can use the information to respond, resolve, or innovate

- Allow partners to interact directly and build their own credibility with prospects and customers, efficiently enabling a platform business strategy

- Enable customers to connect with one another in ways that help them learn from each other—saving them time, helping them innovate, and giving them credible resources that can demonstrate the value of your product and services

By consolidating these interactions and making them transparent, the organization can deliver on the following complex strategic goals.

Close the trust gap—Provide customers with credible, trusted support... from other customers. Show customers that the organization is interested in, willing to listen, and responsive to all of their feedback. Demonstrate to prospects that what you say aligns with the experience they will have as a customer.

Increase market alignment—Align messaging in real-time with the way prospects and customers think about and articulate their challenges and opportunities.

Increase innovation—Communities allow product and service teams to see authentic customer conversations in a way and at a scale that was never before possible—providing a much richer and broader understanding of customer needs. At the same time, product teams can also solicit specific ideas and ask the entire spectrum of customers to help prioritize them in a way that was never before possible. Making that process and the trade-offs transparent increases customer trust by helping them see how the organization makes decisions.

Create a customer-centric culture—Communities help the entire organization see, hear from, and understand customers. Traditionally, this exposure was severely limited and fragmented between various customer-facing teams. By giving all employees real-time access to the customer experience, they can better understand how decisions in their domain affect the customer experience—allowing them to make better, faster decisions, using real customer data as their guide.

What Is Required to Cultivate a Successful Community?

An organization's market is also its community. There is no one place their community gathers all the time. By providing a centralized online community hub for congregating, however, they can consolidate many of the conversations and make that information more discoverable, increasing its value to both customers and the organization.

More important than the destination, platform, or channels used by the community, however, is the community strategy, leadership, and management. Community professionals are responsible for ensuring that communities are intentionally cultivated to deliver value to both customers *and* the organization. They do this by engaging, moderating, running programming, facilitating advocacy groups, making information and people easy to find, architecting the technical and data ecosystem, measuring engagement and value, integrating the community into core internal workflows, and reporting back to different areas of the organization the value the community is delivering to them.

Community management is a complex discipline and most organizations don't invest nearly enough in it to see all of the strategic benefits that are possible. Typically, organizations think of community management narrowly, believing it's only responsible for engagement and/or moderation. Because that is only one small aspect of orchestrating strategically valuable communities, it limits the value of the community to the organization. When community teams have the resources to engage in the more strategic responsibilities—building governance, managing internal and external advocate groups, measuring value, and integrating the community into internal workflows—the trust of the community, the breadth and depth of engagement, and value of the community all increase significantly.

Three Essential Questions

Three questions all organizations should ask themselves related to cultivating their community are:

- What areas of the organizations could benefit the most from a community approach?

- How can a community approach both reduce operating costs and increase revenue?

- What is the risk of not investing in community management and how does it compare to other investments being made to increase trust, innovation, and culture change?

◦ ◦ ◦ ◦ ◦

Thank you, Rachel.

Advocacy is an optimal outcome for customer engagement. Loyalty is a valuable outcome. Satisfaction is, at its best, satisfactory. But they are all part of an overall customer strategy. Aim for the advocates, settle for the loyalists, and satisfaction will flow in their wake. There are many other possible specific outcomes, most of which, at one level or another, have been addressed in this book. But that leaves a question open. If you do all this, how do you know that you've been successful? How do you measure it?

CHAPTER 16

The Long Haul Is Nearly Over: Measuring Customer Value

By this time, you're probably ready to get going, either on an engagement effort at your company because you've been so inspired by this book—or else get going, meaning you're ready to quit reading and do something else entirely. It's a lot, I know. Thank you for sticking with me this far. But I also know it's time to let you go. As sad as I am about that, I'm going to wrap it all up—except for the brief summation in the next chapter—with some of the prevailing thinking about measuring the financial value of customer engagement. That is what this ultimately has been about anyway, hasn't it?

I don't like weeds. I prefer flowers. But I'm probably going to get into the weeds a bit in this chapter. Then, when that's done, I'll add some finishing touches and go smell the roses, which are, of course, flowers. I really, really don't like weeds.

I am lucky enough to be on the global advisory committee of SEAT, a consortium of sports business professionals that represents pretty much all of the pro teams and leagues in the U.S., as well as many collegiate and foreign teams and dozens of venues. At a meeting with industry veterans of long standing who were going to be on a panel that I was moderating for SEAT, Bruce Culbert (who you met back in Chapter 7) told me this story of a super fan. He said the fan had never attended a game or bought any merchandise from the team he rooted so hard for and watched nonstop on television; but he was highly active on social networks and in communities.

If you think about the financial impact calculations that have driven things like CRM for years, particularly customer lifetime value (CLV), this particular fan is not important at all. He has very low value by traditional calculations. But with the communications revolution and the ability of customers, particularly advocates, to communicate their passion to others, he could be of immense value. Huh? How? Hold your horses, we'll get there.

What's nice about this is that I don't have to re-invent the wheel when it comes to describing a new measurement—customer engagement value (CEV). Measuring engagement value had been more than competently taken care of by Dr. V. Kumar, who is a pioneer in measuring customer value. His book on this, *Profitable Customer Engagement: Concept, Metrics and Strategies* (2014, SAGE Publications) is by far the best exposition of how to measure customer value in an era where it is no longer determined simply as customer lifetime value—a revenue number associated with the total financial value of a household or single customer over the extent of their relationship to the company. Remember that, first and foremost, this is a book on how to engage customers—so all measurements are those associated with customer engagement, not anything else.

However, be forewarned. This is a tricky chapter. While the central ideas and specific measurements are Dr. Kumar's, what you will read here are my take on those ideas, which may not totally jive with his. Also, the stories and data are taken from my research. I am using my experiences, knowledge, and history along with his knowledge and insights. I'm not, however, altering his formulas in any way, and the elements for measuring the specific valuation are his and only his. I'm not going to show you specific formulas or do any of the calculations. I am, instead, going to tell you what the elements are that go into measuring customer engagement value holistically. If you want the actual formulas to do the calculations or if you want to delve into a lot of detail on any one area, buy his book. The purpose of this chapter is to show how customer engagement applies to financial value.

AT THE FINANCIAL HEART—DR. V. KUMAR AND CUSTOMER ENGAGEMENT VALUE (CEV)

Now it's time to bring in Dr. Kumar's work. I'm going to start by telling you that, as much as I know about engagement, this man knows about value and how it applies to engagement. He is arguably the world's number-one authority on this topic; he is certainly the pioneer who has done the heavy lifting.

Dr. V. Kumar is one of the most recognized professors of marketing in the world. His home base is Georgia State University, where he holds the Richard and Susan Lenny Distinguished Chair and is a Regents Professor of Marketing. He is also the Executive Director of the Center for Excellence in Brand

and Customer Management *and* the Director of the PhD program in Marketing at the J. Mack Robinson College of Business at GSU. As if all this weren't enough—and it actually is more than enough—he is also the first person outside of China to be named Chang Jiang Scholar, Huazhong University of Science and Technology, Wuhan, China, and Lee Kong Chian Fellow, Singapore Management University, Singapore.

He's stockpiled more awards than I have room in this book to describe. He's published over 200 articles in scholarly journals, including the *Harvard Business Review, Sloan Management Review*, and multiple marketing-related journals such as the *Journal of Marketing* (for which he was named the editor-in-chief).

I've met him, and, even with all the accolades, he was as gracious as I had hoped he would be. I actually almost poked his eye out when I met him, but that's a story to be told over a good meal—if you're buying.

WHAT'S IT LOOK LIKE OVERALL?

Why take the time to measure customer engagement, which is very much a behavioral, right-brained set of activities—often with seemingly intangible results?

Here is Dr. Kumar's take on it from his book.

With the vibrant social media climate, engaging with customers has become a key objective of companies. The importance and immediacy of this concept stems from its applicability to a wide range of business types and functions. It applies to firms of various sizes (small, medium, and large), the B2B and B2C industries, the customers in the contractual and noncontractual business settings, companies selling products or services, and firms with transactions that are onetime or continuous in function . . . Customer engagement has been in practice for quite some time, but only by quantifying the value derived from customer engagement can companies justify their efforts.

As I'm sure we're all clear, customer engagement isn't something we concern ourselves with just for the hell of it. It is the best approach to gluing our customers to our company over a long period of time. Optimally, it's about having them as partners who are providing our businesses with value in different ways. Minimally, it's about binding them so that they transact with us again and again.

So, let's quantify, according to Dr. Kumar, but interpreted by me.

Each measurement will be preceded by the definition that Dr. Kumar gives it in *Profitable Customer Engagement.*

STARTING FROM THE TRADITIONAL: CUSTOMER LIFETIME VALUE (CLV)

[Customer Lifetime Value is] the sum of cumulated future cash flows— discounted using the weighted average cost of capital (WACC)—of a customer over their entire lifetime with the company.

When it comes down to it, the best measure of customer engagement is how much was that customer directly worth to you while in the orbit of your company. The formula for measuring that value has been around for years—customer lifetime value (CLV). The concept was simple: over the lifetime of the relationship that a customer has with a company, how much did he spend and, given other factors, how much was that actually worth when it came to net revenue generated for the company. This measurement, given that it anticipates future revenues generated, has been used to figure out who are the likely high-value customers for your company and who are lower-value customers, since it is possible for customer lifetime value to be either less positive or even negative. Of course, the benefit in knowing this estimated number is that it gives you a guidepost for allocating resources to each of the customers you do have. High-value customers get higher degrees of attention than lower-value customers. In other words, it's a way to optimize your resources to best-use. One caveat, though, is that what constitutes the "assets" being valued via CLV calculations can change depending on national cultures. About a decade ago, I was in Singapore, and the discussion of how to value your customers via CLV came up. Several of the Singaporean business leaders in attendance at this meeting seemed to look at lifetime value not as the individual customer's value, but, instead, the value of the household around the individual customer—which could include a spouse and kids and even grandparents who live at home due to the strong family orientation of Singaporean culture.

When developing the calculation, it's important to think through who your calculation is going to include when you are considering the customer in the equation.

ELEMENTS FOR CALCULATING THE MEASUREMENT

- Average lifespan of a customer
- Customer retention rate

- Average profit margin per customer
- Cash flow discount rate—estimated future value of cash flows
- Average gross margin per customer over lifespan
- Period used for the calculation (usually 52 weeks or one year)
- Costs of customer acquisition
- Number of total customers
- Number of customers acquired
- Transactions per year of a customer/customers
- Average size of the order
- Total revenue for the year
- Percentage of the costs of sales
- Cost of sales
- Marketing costs
- Total costs
- Gross profit total or average
- Net present value
- Net present value cumulative profit

That could make for a very complex calculation because, ultimately, you are attempting to determine how much you will realize in profit or revenue from a single customer, customer segment, or group measured against all your other customers. With all those factors baked in, it could get complicated.

But, it's *conceptually* pretty simple. It's the amount of revenue or profit you will make from one customer or household, compared to all your other customers or households over a specific time frame.

The one question that keeps popping up in conversations about CLV is, "How do you know what the length of a lifetime is for a customer?" Starbucks, through the use of extensive customer data and transaction histories, has their caffeinated customer's lifetime estimated at 20 years. A simple way that has been proposed, if you don't have the data to determine it, is to find out your retention and churn rates and divide the churn rate into 1. Thus, if your retention is 70 percent and your churn is 30 percent, then 1 divided by 30 percent indicates an average customer lifespan of 3.3 years. Is this a viable approach to measuring it? Without the specific data to determine it accurately, it will do as well as anything else as a rough estimate. Many companies

I spoke with about this in the course of research said that they do an estimate or a best guess.

CUSTOMER REFERRAL VALUE (CRV)/ BUSINESS REFERENCE VALUE (BRV)

This is probably the one measurement that has a different application in B2C than it does in B2B, which is why, even though they both are referral-related metrics, you see two at the top, the B2C Customer Referral Value and the B2B Business Reference Value. I'll start with CRV.

CRV

The monetary value of a customer associated with the future profits given by each referred prospect, discounted to the present value (PV)

Customer Referral Value (CRV) provides a measure of indirect revenue impact. How much does a customer contribute to the financials of a company via their individual referrals of other customers? These are referrals based on organized programs. Word of mouth (WOM), given the power placed in peer trust, is the most effective way to "do" referrals. What CRV does, though, is take what might have been a word-of-mouth referral from a social media interchange, for example, and move the referral into a formal, incentivized referral program.

In a 2010 academic paper, "Referral Programs and Customer Value" by Philipp Schmitt, Bernd Skiera, and Christophe Van den Bulte, the lifetime value for a referral customer was determined to be 16 percent higher than a non-referral customer due to improved customer engagement, lower churn rates, and higher conversion rates.

An entire form of marketing, called referral marketing, is designed to drive traffic that would ordinarily be ad hoc word of mouth to sites and referral programs. It not only tries to increase awareness of referral programs but also makes sure that there is an organized way for the transmission of what starts out as an unstructured conversation to be converted into part of an incentivized program. The incentives themselves aren't necessarily monetized. In fact, they can be in the form of a credit or discount or even an item, like a bottle of wine. As far back as 2004, a study ("The Benefits of Tangible Non-Monetary Incentives" by Jeffrey Scott, University of Chicago) found that non-cash incentives were 24 percent more effective than cash.

Dropbox's highly successful referral program is a case in point. The referral program is directly embedded into the site almost anywhere you look. The incentive for referrals is more Dropbox real estate for both referrer and referee. In its first 18 months, there were more than 2.8 million direct referrals, and, as of 2016, 35 percent of all signups came from Dropbox's referral program.

This is Dr. Kumar's point. The value of formal referrals is self-evident, and, while its impact is indirect on the corporate bottom line, its value to that bottom line is obvious.

CRV only considers extrinsic motivation—meaning the customers are doing the referrals for some form of reward. While some of the referrals may be for intrinsic motivations—for the good of the people so to speak—they are not identified or considered as anything but extrinsic for the purposes of the measurement. Ultimately, and this is me, not Dr. Kumar, if the person's reference goes to a referral program, the likelihood is that the referrer took the award regardless of motivation, and, thus, for estimating the cost of referrals, extrinsic or intrinsic motivations are no different.

One potentially mission-critical sidebar goes to intent to refer. The "one question" that Net Promoter Score (NPS) asks is, "Would you recommend this company to someone you know?" which reflects intent. The NPS measures that intent. However, in studies done by Kumar early on in this millennium on (among other subjects), the indirect financial impact of influence and referrals, what became apparent was the difference between intent and actual effort. He surveyed 15,000 respondents in financial services and telco. The first question he asked was, "Would you recommend this product to someone you know?" So far, so good . . . that's in line with NPS. Then came question two: "*Did* you recommend this company to someone you know?" Seeing that was both an "aha!" and a "duh!" moment for me—"Of course!" and "How could I not know that?" The answers were telling. Of the 6,700 financial services customers asked, 68 percent said they intended to recommend; but, ultimately, only 33 percent did. Intent isn't much more than an indicator that someone who intends to recommend is more likely to recommend than someone who doesn't. Kind of, "So what?"

ELEMENTS FOR CALCULATING THE MEASUREMENT

- Number of years calculated into the future (projected customer lifetime)
- Number of customers who only join due to a referral
- Gross margin contributed by an individual customer who wouldn't have bought anything without the referral
- Cost of the referral for a particular customer
- Marketing costs needed for the particular customer's retention

- Acquisition cost savings for the referred customer
- Acquisition cost savings for customers who would have joined without the referral
- The (time period) discount rate

How is this different in a B2B environment? In what we have just described, the value is in the indirect revenue impact of a single customer who is engaged with a formal referral program. Clearly that doesn't hold in a B2B "referral." Is it viable to calculate the indirect impact of referrals on revenue when the process for sales is so much more complex, with so many more moving parts?

The answer is yes, it is, but it is different. Thus, we have Business Reference Value (BRV)

BRV

The monetary value associated with future profits as a result of the extent of a client's reference influencing a prospect to purchase

I'm not going to dwell on this one all that long but do want to make a few salient points. Kumar says that B2B purchases are often influenced by customer references. In fact, they play a key role. BRV is the quantification of how key a role customer references play in B2B purchase decisions. While I don't put them as high on the influence chain as their equivalent in the B2C world, there is no question to me that they do play a powerful role as a factor in the decision-making process.

Many companies use testimonials from their customers about how wonderful they have been. They are typically from "customers like me," meaning customer segments that are targeted by the business as most likely to purchase—or at least to be attracted. These aren't the same as celebrity endorsements of a brand. They are from customers who are willing to publicly state that they find the products and services that the company provides to be of great value. As I mentioned earlier, Lattice Engines, a marketing and sales optimization vendor, not only found customers who were willing to specify the explicit value—numbers included—in their short testimonials, but also the personal value that the owner of the projects associated with the technology gained (e.g., got promoted to vice-president), and made it clear that Lattice Engines was the reason for the promotion.

But is that enough to impact the decision-making that adds to CEV? Not necessarily. To remedy that, since the decision-making factors in a B2B purchase have so many moving parts, companies, particularly in the technology sector, have customer reference programs where customers are formally brought into the conversations about the company.

One standout example of a customer reference program that aligns well with BRV is Box. As you probably know, Box is a subscription-based digital storage service that is known for its ease of use, copious amounts of storage for the price, integration with other technology platforms, and mobile accessibility. They have both consumer and business customers. They also have a formal reference program where they use the customers that have agreed to participate in

- Written case studies (this is the bulk of the work)
- Press and analyst calls
- Videos
- Speaking
- Reference calls

Charlotte Lilley, who runs the Box reference program, in a white paper she wrote for the Center for Customer Engagement, estimated that the annual revenue influenced by the customer reference program—their BRV—was $523,970 in 2013.While this publicly available data is old, and there is nothing newer, it makes the point. That's no small chunk of change when it comes to a BRV calculation.

ELEMENTS FOR CALCULATING THE MEASUREMENT

- Degree that references generally impacted the purchase decision
- Degree of influence that a specific reference had on the purchase decision
- CLV of the buyer
- Total number of converted prospects
- Discount rate (in months)
- Time to purchase (month prospect became client after a first month of observation)

CUSTOMER INFLUENCE VALUE (CIV)

The monetary gain or loss realized by a firm that is attributable to a customer (influence) through his/her spread of positive or negative word of mouth

Interestingly, indirect revenue impact doesn't stop with either CRV or BRV but has a further sister-in-arms called Customer Influence Value (CIV). It seems perhaps the most blatantly obvious due to the libraries of documents written on the subject of social media influence and engagement. But it is one of the hardest to calculate since you have to find those influencers on social media who are relevant to both your customers and your prospects, or target segments, and deal with network effects in order to calculate the actual value of the influencer on the purchase of an item or service.

Kumar identifies four drivers of influence that he uses to identify these particular influencers.

> **Activeness compatibility**—This is the number of times that an influencer and his/her network share or see a message. Seeing a message means reading it (and it registers that it was read) and not sharing it.

> **Host clout**—The number of followers that an influencer has. For example, as of December 31, 2018, I have 22,830 followers on Twitter, 2575 friends on Facebook, am linked to 7259 people on LinkedIn, am searched for 1107 times a week on the average on LinkedIn, and had 56,854 views on my most viewed post ever—which, incidentally, was announcing that I finished writing this book to my LinkedIn network, he says, humblebragging. Or just kind of bragging. But the network I have, if I am producing value for a brand, has to be relevant to the brand itself. If I make pronouncements about Ferraris, a few of the people I reach may listen to me because of their general trust in my opinions, but most won't pay any attention. If I recommend a CRM system, however, that comment will have an impact—I think. The primary reasons are that the people who are following me, or I them, have something in common—an interest in CRM or customer-facing systems or technologies and, secondarily, though primary in my heart, the New York Yankees.

> **Talkativeness of the receiver**—How frequently does the influencer get retweeted or shared or, as Dr. Kumar says "hashtagged." Regardless, this is a measure of both influence and potential virality.

> **Generosity**—This is specifically described as "like-mindedness" shared by the influencer and his/her network. This is what I have been calling, "a person like me" or "someone like me" throughout the book. Even though, this is a peculiarly named driver, it is arguably one of the most significant because it is how peer trust impacts buying decisions, among many other things.

Dr. Kumar has a seven-step plan for what passes these days as "influencer marketing," and one of the steps is to incentivize the influencers. That has some merit, but, in terms of the costs of CIV, there is something to be said about organic advocacy, as I mentioned in the last chapter. Influencers can be brand advocates or they can be Katy Perry. But sometimes incentivizing influencers can have a psychic cost that has the potential to create a negative CIV. Several years ago, Walmart started a blogging effort with two so-called brand advocates who traveled the country promoting the company and its products. All seemed good until it was found out that they were actually incentivized promoters—paid actors basically. Now, the content of the blog was authentic; they wrote about what they saw and felt. But the fact that they were basically actors being paid to do this generated a ton of negative publicity and hurt the Walmart brand. Yet, if you had read the content and knew nothing else, it would have seemed fine. Just being paid to say things makes even heartfelt, positive content—which might be organic—look tainted.

Asking how to measure this kind of influence is a fair question because it is complex, it scales, and it has repercussions good and/or bad that aren't always tangible. Often what passes for influence, which is something that can wax or wane over time, is confused with what is actually engagement in a moment of time, i.e., how active you are in a given period, not how influential you are. Klout, which provided a series of algorithms that purportedly measured influence based on activity on social networks, was never measuring influence. It was measuring levels of engagement in a specific time period. Klout's leadership perpetuated the myth that it was influence, and, thus, for a long while, until their acquisition by community platform provider Lithium, having a high Klout score was a badge of honor. And it was remunerative, too, with special privileges, discounts, free "stuff," etc., from brands if your score exceeded whatever level they decided was high enough.

In reality, it wasn't an influence score; it was an engagement activity score. If you were on vacation for two weeks and didn't participate in social networks, your Klout score could drop—sometimes precipitously. Plus, it is hard to put a tangible number on influence given all the factors involved, some of which are offline. I wrote a book on CRM that, for years, was called "the bible of CRM," and, apparently, that made me influential in the CRM world. In fact, my nickname is "The Godfather of CRM," though I think that was an early on typo that stuck. Given my age, I think they meant "The Grandfather of CRM." But, regardless, was I any less influential if I didn't tweet while on vacation? Klout thought so. No one else did.

That's why Dr. Kumar has introduced another measurement needed for the computation of CIV. He calls it the Customer Influence Effect (CIE), which is a measurement of the impact of a single message from a single person. All in all, this shows how influential a message from an influencer can be and introduces virality and relevance into the equation. Clearly a highly influential message from a brand advocate to his/her network is going to be a relevant one.

Tricky Measurement

This is perhaps the most complex of engagement metrics because you are measuring the impact of an influencer and his/her network on purchases. And, due to virality, it can involve a ripple effect that isn't necessary all that tangible or even capable of being made tangible.

The question becomes, is this complex a measurement worth it to a business, given the work needed to gather the data to run the numbers? So that you are not left in suspense, the answer is, yes, it is. If engagement is important to you, and I have to assume it's important enough for you to have gotten all the way through this book, then you realize that it will have an impact on your bottom line. Dr. Kumar is talking about measuring the profitability of an engaged customer directly and indirectly, and, like it or not, digital customers are engaged on digital networks impacting other digital customers.

So, Greenberg, prove it.

In 2014, Ogilvy did a study and found that 74 percent of the respondents looked to social networks for guidance. That means roughly three-quarters of the consumers surveyed go online to find what people are saying about products or services on Facebook, Twitter, and Instagram. It isn't necessarily reactive either. Many people, including me, go to our social networks and ask people about their experiences with products, which products they would they recommend, etc. In fact, Facebook "interest groups" (with no ominous overtones implied) are great places to go to get product guidance from experts, influencers, and brand advocates.

All that's good, but the study that Twitter did in conjunction with Annalect in 2016 provided the rest of the nails needed to drive the point home. They found the following.

- 40 percent say they've purchased an item online after seeing it used by an influencer on Instagram, Twitter, Vine, or YouTube—of course, there is no Vine anymore so that social network is moot.

- 49 percent of people say they rely on recommendations from influencers when making purchase decisions.

- Twitter users report a 5.2X increase in purchase intent when exposed to promotional content from influencers.

One other data point before I move on: Hubspot found that 30 percent of the respondents in one of their numerous studies were likely to respond to a brand offer if reposted by a friend—the power of peer trust.

That data alone supports Dr. Kumar's reasoning for the need for CIV as part of the overall measurement of customer engagement value.

Again, I'm not going to give you the formulae—that's Dr. Kumar's domain—but I will provide you with the rationale and the elements that go into CIV.

ELEMENTS FOR CALCULATING THE MEASUREMENT

Customer Influence Value—This calculates the proportion of the value of the influence of the influencers of the influencer that can be attributed to the decision to purchase. I'm not kidding. This means that, as an influencer, I have a network of people who influence me or who influence others to treat me as an authority. I hang around with sports business professionals and sit on their consortium global advisory board, and, thus, I become an influencer by association. That means those who would be influenced by what sports business professionals say would listen to what I have to say, even though I am not a sports business professional.

Customer Lifetime Value of an individual customer—The same as always.

Hubbell's Influence Value—This is a value defined by network centrality. It looks at an influencer's total connections and assigns a value to each connection according to its distance from the center. The further away the network member is from the center, the less is the value assigned because the connection is weaker.

The reason that this is a complex calculation is because there are networks and ripple effects on the networks involved. Conceptually, it's really pretty straightforward. If I influence my networks to buy something, they will likely (though to a lesser extent) convince some of their networks to buy it, and this continues *ad infinitum*. The further you get from the direct influencer, the weaker the connection, the less likelihood the possibility of a positive result.

Proof of CIV's value rests with stories of course, and the best one is about, not surprisingly, my favorite late-night host—Conan O'Brien.

After he and NBC severed their relationship in early 2010, he began a "One Tweet Campaign," where he started out with a single tweet to 939,000 followers on March 10 about a 32-city comedy tour he was launching.

Hey Internet: I'm headed to your town on a half-assed comedy & music tour. Go to http://TeamCoco.com for tix. I repeat: It's half-assed.

Within two hours of that tweet's publication, before he was able to get out a second tweet about the tour, the entire tour was sold out and he was the number-one event on most ticket vendor sites in the U.S. It was unheard of for a comedy tour.

That is a story that validates CIV, the metric, brought to you by Team Coco. It is a powerful indicator of how social media can impact buyers and how important CIV is to a holistic notion of customer engagement value. So, despite the complexity, which I have barely touched on, it is worth the time and effort you make to include it as part of the valuation of your customer.

But now we move even further into what seems obvious but is actually uncharted territory: how do you measure the revenue impact of feedback and co-creation? This is what Dr. Kumar calls Customer Knowledge Value (CKV). Before I get into CKV, though, I need to speak to you about the framework for it, because it's so very important to understand.

THE FRAMEWORK FOR 21ST CUSTOMER KNOWLEDGE VALUE—SERVICE DOMINANT LOGIC (SDL)

The earlier part of this book was focused on frameworks strategies, and programs. As you may recall, a few key concepts were either continually repeated or constantly implied. Customers

- need to be engaged with companies, not just purchase from companies
- are partners, not the objects of a sale
- are active participants, not just passive "assets"
- need more than great products and services to maintain their engagement with a company over time

Implied throughout this entire set, but not explicit until now, is a theory and framework developed and popularized in 2004 by Stephen Vargo and Robert Lusch, called Service Dominant Logic (SDL). Even though extensive literature on the subject is available, the principal ideas, as espoused by Vargo and Lusch, are simple.

> *The fundamental component of economic exchange is service, not goods. A service is a specialized competency that is applied for the benefit of the company or the customer by the other. True value is co-created by companies and customers and is customer-centric in nature.*

The idea is to find value in the outcomes rather than the technologies used to enable or support the action that leads to the outcome. So, for instance, if you need to drill a hole, the value of the drill is that it supports drilling a hole, not that it's a drill. The drill (the product/good) is used to support the drilling of the hole (the service). The result is that the hole that you wanted to create is now created (the outcome). A company makes only drills when it sees its company mission is to make drills. But if the company realizes that its primary appeal isn't making drills but supporting what it takes to drill a hole, they won't necessarily produce just drills but other faster, cheaper, and/ or frictionless hole-producing devices. They are now in the business of providing—as a service—hole production. Maybe a powerful jet stream of air or a chemical that produces holes would be preferable to some customers. That is the difference between Goods Dominant Logic (GDL) and Service Dominant Logic (SDL). That also goes to the heart of what SDL characterizes as value in use (what I call "use value"). The value of the drill is in its support of the service of producing holes. In GDL, by contrast, it's the price of the drill, determined by the costs of the drill, ascertained from price of the parts needed to produce the drill, the labor needed to manufacture the drill, and the overhead costs that go into logistics (the supply chain, marketing, and distribution), among other things, and the margin thrown in on top . . . to oversimplify.

Even more simply, Goods Dominant Logic says that value is added to products and services during the internal production process. Service Dominant Logic says that value is created by the customer's use of products and services to reach an outcome. The customer's role goes from passive recipient of goods to active participant in service interactions.

I need to warn you about one thing. A trend that shows its face now and then is to associate SDL-related business frameworks with customer-centric (not customer-engaged) behavior. It is possible to say, "Let's focus on the customer," and still not be listening and interacting with that customer around feedback and co-creation, or even being outcomes-focused in your sales and marketing efforts. As I hope I made clear in Chapter 9, it is possible to "do good things" for the customer and still not be building engagement models. Customer-centric activity can be reactive, such as the Ryanair example I gave where the customer-centric efforts were designed to regain revenues and make shareholders happy. SDL requires a customer-engaged culture—at least in the way I'm defining it in this book—one in which the DNA of the company is the cooperative value-exchange, the customer is a partner, and the service interactions are where the value is created.

Lusch identifies three types of roles that the customer plays when it comes to SDL—all of which you will recognize in Dr. Kumar's formulations of customer value.

Ideator—This really means creator. The customer has a job that they do. To do that job they have unique requirements. To date, they have been using existing market offerings to help them accomplish whatever the outcomes they are looking for. They take their specific knowledge and needs and bring it to the company and, given what the company is capable of doing, are able to help design new, previously unconceptualized services that the company can then create.

Designer—This one is more along the lines of the customer looking at what the company's offerings are already, and using the assets available in those offerings to come up with new services. An example would be American Girl, who I mentioned much earlier in this book, adding services like the doll's haircut, theatergoing, or lunch to the overall experience in the store. Those are done using existing assets—the doll, the story, and the accessories—but adding a monetized set of new services that enhance the overall experience.

Intermediary—These are customers with access to social networks and other ecosystems that go beyond their solo capability who can cross-pollinate those networks in not-very-obvious ways with ideas and commentary that will ultimately spark value creation via the networks.

By no means does this cover even the tip of the tip of the iceberg when it comes to understanding Service Dominant Logic. But I needed to give you something of a framework to understand where Customer Knowledge Value plays its role as a measurement. If you are looking to understand more, I would highly recommend all the easily available academic papers by Vargo and Lusch, and the works on innovation and disruption written by Clayton Christensen, especially his most lauded book, *The Innovator's Dilemma* (Harvard Business Review Press, 1997, reprinted many times).

Now to the business of Customer Knowledge Value.

CUSTOMER KNOWLEDGE VALUE (CKV): MEASURING THE IMPACT OF FEEDBACK

The monetary value attributed to a customer by a firm due to the profits generated by implementing an idea/suggestion/feedback from that customer

CUSTOMER COLLABORATIVE VALUE (CCV): MEASURING THE VALUE OF COLLABORATION

The monetary value attributed to a customer by a firm due to the profits generated by the new products/services arising out of the customer's collaborative efforts with the firm

(Note: for the purposes of this chapter, both CKV/feedback and CCV/collaboration are going to be referred to as CKV.)

So far, we've seen directly through the time-honored CLV how referral programs, references, and social-media influencers and their networks impact revenue. These are all the most obvious places to start, but no one has built the models that Dr. K. has. He is far more qualified than I am to explain the calculations, so go spend a few bucks to buy his book and add some lifetime value to the calculation Amazon is doing on you. Then encourage others to buy it and validate CIV.

CKV is, once again, focused on turning an intangible contribution—the ideas that I contribute via feedback or direct collaboration on innovating and inventing new products and/or services—into a measurable financial metric. It is important to know how Customer Engagement Value is measured all in all. That will support the formulation of customer-engagement strategies and programs. It also provides a way to measure the kind of impact that impresses the, let's call it, "capital-oriented" part of the business.

Customer knowledge starts with the identification of feedback "fragments." These are intentional or unintentional and occur in structured and unstructured environments. A feedback fragment could be something like a comment posted in a Marriott customer community—for instance, "The Marriott Marquis Atlanta is very nice, but I wish it had a desk for using a laptop, like every other Marriott I've ever been to." This is a fragment, a piece of product or service advice, and it is communicated outside a formal feedback mechanism.

To measure the value of feedback or of a created product or service, the information provided by the customer needs to be used effectively. That is typically done via a program that captures and then applies the knowledge to product/service improvement or product/service creation. It's not the idea that matters, but the effective use of the idea in improvement or creation. There has to be an institutionalized way of realizing and then measuring the value as part of the overall engagement value provided by the innovator.

The feedback/ideas can be initiated by the business or initiated by the customer. The latter can occur via unsolicited commentary on a social site or by the customer proactively accessing the brand website's comments section. Typically, the feedback is not incentivized via any tangible reward. If the business instigates the collaboration, it can be via incentives (e.g., "If you give us feedback by filling out this survey, we will enter you into a drawing for a $250.00 Amazon gift card"). That's for feedback. If you are co-creating a product with the company, you might get a share of the profits from the sale of the product you were involved with.

Other formal programs could include the voice of the customer programs, customer advisory boards, and user groups with the function that Usenet used to have many moons ago (i.e., a place to brainstorm on solving problems in a particular area) or that the Skype user group Public Mind had to generate ideas on the features that users wanted to see Skype build or adopt. Or, an even better example: Procter and Gamble's Connect + Develop.

CASE STUDY: PROCTER & GAMBLE'S CONNECT + DEVELOP

This program is one of the most epic and long-running examples of customer co-creation. P&G's Connect + Develop has spawned hundreds of products and services—ranging from packaging to oral care to dry-cleaning services—that have launched successfully across the U.S. and the world. To participate, you sign up on the Connect + Develop website. First, you check what kinds of innovation they are looking for in what categories, or, if you have an idea outside their immediate interests, you can submit a form with the details they need to take a look at it.

Their initial criteria:

> We need a clear, concise description that conveys the nature of the innovation and the unique features and benefits it offers relative to existing solutions, and the status of your intellectual property.
>
> Our web portal enables you to attach supporting documents to your submission. If you have a granted patent or published patent application, please attach a copy. It is also helpful to provide the results of any safety, consumer, efficacy, or other relevant testing. Technical illustrations and photos may also be of help.
>
> Remember, all information submitted must be non-confidential. Do not submit confidential information. We will not review any documents that are marked "Confidential" or the equivalent. The documents will be deleted from our portal, and the submission will be declined.

One example of a Connect + Develop product is the little Tide detergent pod that you can throw into your washing machine, creating a far more convenient and accurately measured amount of detergent just dropped straight into the machine. This changed the way that both clothing and dishes are washed and has been a highly imitated standard ever since.

While the incentives with Connect + Develop can vary according to the products co-created, the program has generated hundreds of new businesses for the innovators, and products and services for P&G.

But compensation has to be a part of this, right? How does a company compensate the provision of knowledge that has benefited that company?

When it comes to compensation, incentives are typically quite high. For example, Microsoft, in 2014, developed a program for their software development partners in Europe (ISVs), where, in return for products and solutions built on Microsoft's xRM platform, they received royalties of 60 percent on the product when sold by Microsoft.

I should make a distinction here before I stray too far afield. The 60 percent royalty is a cost when it comes to the calculation of CKV. In fact, the calculation of CKV starts with the computation of the profit after the costs of production and all overheads, including the cost of marketing, etc., are removed.

It is a simple calculation.

ELEMENTS FOR CALCULATING THE MEASUREMENT

- Revenue realized by the products/services improvements or created

- Costs associated with labor, production, and overhead (e.g., marketing)

That's about it.

But what makes this a significant measurement is the SDL framework that defines it because this is an approach that attempts to measure the results of successful innovation in the service of engagement.

Customer Brand Value (CBV)

The net effect of a customer's brand knowledge, brand attitude, brand purchase intention and brand behavior formed due to a prior brand experience and the marketing of a brand

Finally, the last piece, and the most "emotional." You'll note from the definition above a strong parallel to customer experience, i.e., "how a customer feels about a company over time."

This may be the most difficult to quantify. Because ultimately you are quantifying qualitative behavior and tying it to numerous quantitative outcomes. How do you convert all this emotional and behavioral engagement into something that helps define the customer's value to your brand? That is a *really* good and not-easy question to answer, but I'll do the best I can using Dr. Kumar's game plan.

There are eight components that need to be scored and measured for CBV.

- Brand awareness
- Brand image
- Brand trust
- Brand affect
- Brand purchase intention
- Brand loyalty
- Brand advocacy
- Premium price behavior

What makes these interesting is that they are the drivers, in part, and the outcomes, to a large degree, of customer engagement and overall customer experience. But that's what makes them tough to quantify.

To break this down, let's start with a brief description of each of the eight components.

Brand Knowledge: How a Customer Perceives a Brand

Brand awareness—How much is the brand top-of-mind when there is a purchase consideration? If I'm in anywhere in the world, and I say, "Cola," you will answer . . . what? Pepsi? Coke? Shasta? C'mon, I *know* it's not Shasta. Customer purchases are impacted by how aware of a brand a customer might be. Coca Cola (aka Coke) has 100 percent brand awareness worldwide—except in Atlanta, where it is 2 million percent. Kidding. Sort of.

Brand image—This can be brand awareness in context. If your awareness of the brand is negative, that can reduce the likelihood you will purchase that brand. (For example, "Of course I know United Airlines, but they just threw a guy off one of their planes.") But it also can be the conscious positioning or repositioning of a brand. For example, Ritz Carleton has been associated for years with their positioning, metaphorically expressed as "ladies and gentlemen serving ladies and gentlemen." That creates the image of an elegant hotel serving with the utmost courtesy and with exquisite effort and respect for their customers. An example of repositioning a brand is the change that McDonald's has been making to go from a fast food, quick meal, my stomach hurts, purveyor to a healthy food, fresh ingredients easy-to-get-all-the-time provider. They have a long way to go. Just think about how you perceive them right now, and you'll know what I mean.

Brand Attitude: How a Customer Feels About the Brand

Brand trust—This goes to the heart of a customer-engaged culture. This isn't, "I will trust you with my life." This is, "I trust you to keep your promises, such as that the quality of your products will continue to be as good as you say they are or that your services will continue to work as well as you claim." Note that I say "continue" because the trust evolves over time, event after event, with the company supporting that claim. Effectively, it's the company proving to the customer that they can be trusted. It isn't there from the beginning. Minimally, trust would be a driver of rational satisfaction, if not more.

Brand affect—Kumar calls this "a customer's positive emotional response toward a brand." Brand affect can be the emotional commitment someone has to a product or service. Think of the commitment that people have to their iPhones. Or, in a slightly more negative way, think about how an Apple fan responds to a positive view of a Microsoft product. In one of my ZDNet columns, I said something nice about a Microsoft hardware product, and I was trolled by Apple fanboys and fangirls. While that was, let's just say, an immature response to something I wrote, their emotional commitment to Apple is a clear example of a highly positive brand affect. This is the foundation for potential loyalty and advocacy.

Brand Behavior Intention: How Marketing Impacts a Customer's Brand Behavior

Purchase intention—This is the behavioral outcome of customer perception and engagement with the brand. The customer decides either privately or by declaration to purchase a specific product or service or experience in a competitive industry. I bought a Windows 10 touchscreen laptop from Dell after having looked at multiple competitive offers from Acer, Lenovo, Microsoft, Samsung, Toshiba, and some smaller brands. I told a number of people that I intended to buy this particular Dell machine. One of them, who was a Mac convert (fanboys, stay away!), looked at Dell as a result and bought a different Dell machine prior to even my purchase of the one I eventually bought.

Brand Behavior: How a Customer Interacts with a Brand

Brand loyalty—Hopefully, the last chapter is still fresh in your mind so I don't have to repeat what brand loyalty is. Because we are looking to quantify it, as an attribute, the greater the brand loyalty, the greater the brand value.

Brand advocacy—Same here re: last chapter. The greater the brand advocacy, the greater the brand value.

Brand price premium behavior—This one I'll explain. It's the customer's willingness to pay a premium for the products and/or services of similar nature of one brand over another brand. This is the hallmark of many of the products of luxury brands such as Hermès or the more broadly popular Louis Vuitton. There is no question of the quality of the product—and the customers are willing to pay a premium price for that—but they are also paying a premium for the brand caché, which is an emotional cost but still an indicator of the commitment to buy, or if you prefer the more buzzword-laden term, a greater propensity to purchase.

Getting the Score: Measuring CBV

The eight components each have one or more elements that go into the calculation. I'll break them down.

ELEMENTS FOR CALCULATING THE MEASUREMENT

Brand awareness—Measured by how much the customer recognizes the brand; the ability of the customer to recall the brand (author's note: mindshare)

Brand image—Measured by perception of the quality of the brand, its products, services; the customer's expectations of that brand (e.g., "I know I'll love it. Oops, I don't."); company perception (e.g., "They are great corporate givers.")

Brand trust—Measured by trust in the brand (e.g., "They do what they say."); brand honesty (e.g., "We messed up, sorry. We will fix this." And trust is enhanced if they do.); brand reliability (e.g., The 1991 Toyota Corolla never broke down; maintenance was almost nothing.)

Brand affect—Measured by feel-good factor (e.g., "I love those guys and they seem to love me back!"); product satisfaction (e.g., "I've been using this for years and will keep doing it."); brand affinity (e.g., "This brand is so cool and has what I need.")

Brand loyalty—Measured by loyalty (e.g., "I buy their stuff again and again."); brand preference (e.g., "I use Whole Foods 365 for all my cereal purchases.")

Brand advocacy—Measured by customers interactions with other customers on social media (e.g., "I eat Whole Foods 365 cereals all the time, my Facebook friends and Twitter followers."); word-of-mouth communication (e.g., "I need to make sure that at this conference I tell people about this book."); brand advocacy (e.g., "I am committed to this brand and you should be too."), and, yes, this is included separately under the category brand advocacy.

Premium price behavior—Measured by value perception (e.g.. "This is so worth the money I spend on it."); willingness to pay slightly more (e.g., "I know it's five bucks more, but I know I can trust it and count on it."); willingness to pay higher price over competition (e.g., "I know that Brand A costs more than Brand B, but, hey, it's Brand A!")

The category score is calculated by the score of the elements added together, divided by the number of elements. Kumar says that the score can range from 8 to 80, which means that a 1-to-10 scale is used. He also says that the average for a company's CBV score is between 35 and 50.

So, those are the elements.

Here's the "formula" in acronyms:

CLV + CRV + CIV + CKV + CBV = CEV

That's it. Who am I to argue?

CUSTOMER ENGAGEMENT VALUE: THE HOLISTIC VIEW, OR THE ROOM AT THE TOP

Think about contemporary customers for a few minutes. Rather than relegate them to the components that measure them, take a composite customer and think about how they are likely to interact with your company. Then, apply Dr. Kumar's different measurements to see how they fit the customer's real-life activity, and you'll understand why CEV is a more appropriate valuation of a customer than just CLV at this juncture in business history.

The customer . . . we'll call him . . . me, wakes up in the morning and goes online and immediately starts reading. At some juncture, I'm looking at a discussion of PC parts on PCPartPicker.com, and I read great reviews from people like me who are interested in these parts (CIV). I'm looking for a new graphics card for my current gaming PC, and, due to the available content (e.g., performance data) and the reviews, I boil my choices down to cards from MSI or EVGA. A friend of mine, who is a gaming enthusiast, recommends MSI over EVGA for various reasons. If I register on the MSI site and use his name as a member of their community, I will get a 10 percent discount on the card, which, given how pricey they are, is a nice chunk of money. He will get points toward free stuff in the future. I do that (CRV). I love MSI anyway, having used their cards and a number of other accessories and enjoyed my prior interactions with the company, or at least was fine with them most of the time (CBV). In fact, when I order the card (CLV), they recognize that I've had a number of prior interactions with them, in fact, and send me a survey that will take no longer than five minutes to fill out. It enters me into a drawing for a $250.00 Amazon gift card. The survey solicits my feedback on my experience with the company and their products (CKV). All is well in my world and MSI's when this is done.

That, or at least parts of it, are the activities around real-life customer engagement. Something very close to what I'm describing actually happened with me not very long ago, though with a different company and with not-quite as frictionless results, but nearly so. Anyway, I think the point is clear. The value of a customer is no longer in just the transactions with the companies they interact with. It is also determined by the outcomes of the interactions that go beyond the purchase. The advent of social media and communities, and the increased ability for communication between the company and the customer and among the customers themselves, leads businesses to a new way of thinking about those customers, defining their engagement with those customers, meeting customer demands, and measuring the outcomes of that engagement well beyond merely the transaction value.

Okay, that's it. I'm pretty much done. I'm going to run you through a final summary of what I think we've accomplished here, and then I'm taking a break. This was a tough subject because I've attempted to give what is a protoplasmic topic some framework and infrastructure while it changes every day.

I'll meet you at the briefing center. In case you need directions to get there, just turn the page.

SECTION SEVEN

We Reach the End

And now the end is near . . . no, I'm not being apocalyptic, I'm just telling you this is it. The last chapter.

CHAPTER 17

The Beginning of the End of the Beginning

And now the end is near
And so I face the final curtain
My friend I'll say it clear
I stated my case, of which I'm certain
I planned each chapter's course
Each careful step along the byway
And more, ending with this,
I did it my way.

T hank you, Frank Sinatra, for the paraphrase.

Our journey's destination in now in sight. We've managed to outline the basics—at least all the ones I'm aware of—that it takes to become a customer-engaged culture, including the steps that lead to strategies, programs, outcomes, frameworks, results, and measurements once you've committed yourself to customer-engagement as your business priority.

The thing is, though, the landscape is ever-changing. It doesn't stop. You know that old saw, "Time waits for no man." You don't? How can you not know an old saw? Well, no matter. In any case, when it comes to how you interact with your customers, engagement waits for no business. It takes a lot more than a village; it takes a whole urban ecosystem—metaphorically of course—to succeed at customer engagement.

Think about successful companies like Dialog Axiata, who are holistically involved with their customers in a day-to-day way and not ashamed to monetize the engagement and the services associated with that engagement. Think about the Philadelphia Flyers, who empower all their employees to deal with their fans, no matter where and no matter what title they carry, and how the employees are rewarded for their willingness and effort to engage with fans.

Think about Salesforce, who, via their Ignite program, offers free business-transformation services and strategy sessions, not because they are creating an avenue to sell software but because they want to become trusted advisers to their customers. Think about Sal the taxi driver, who goes well above and beyond the required effort to provide a good ride to make sure that his customers are comfortable and well-taken-care-of.

The pressures for these activities and actions are being generated from the bottom up as customers become more demanding and more empowered, and as they have the options to take their business elsewhere if they aren't happy or take their feelings about your brand public if they remain unhappy. Or, they can, of course, say great things about you and buy more things from you if they remain happy. Customers and their control over the conversations about the brand at scale make it impossible for a company to do anything but transform the business that they are in to focus it around customer engagement.

What makes this difficult is that it isn't a cadre of progressive customers who are leading some sort of charge that makes this the effort of a few savvy leaders. I'd call it a global mass phenomenon, except that it isn't phenomenal anymore. Its SOP—standard operating procedure. It's how millions, maybe billions of people operate and interact with each other and with institutions.

Businesses are among the institutions that have been impacted, and, yet, the purpose of businesses—to make money—hasn't changed. How businesses respond to that impact becomes of paramount importance. Changing with the times is now mission-critical, not just something that's nice to do. I hope that's come across throughout this book.

If you've managed to get through all this, you've seen how customer engagement has impacted the customer-facing operations of a business—sales, marketing, and customer service. You've also seen the framework, the strategies, and the programs that could be used to meet the requirements for customer engagement at scale. Most importantly, you've understood the characteristics of the culture that you need to build and secure at your company as you grow and scale your customer base. You've also grasped the idea of value as it pertains to engagement and your business. It is no longer a matter of what do you do for your customers to get value from them for your business. Your very DNA needs to be acculturated to the idea that it is a constant and mutual exchange of value that drives everything. That means that your customers become your partners, not just the object of a sale.

I hope, too, that a few key ideas stuck in your head (in a non-painful way of course). "Keeping the ordinary, ordinary" is one that I hope becomes your daily chant as you make sure that your plans to interact with customers are good enough to keep them coming back. Or maybe the phrase a "company like me" will remind you to make sure that your business is providing the kind of value to the customer that makes them feel valued and feel that you understand who they are as individuals, even as you scale your customer base to the millions. Perhaps, you'll realign your "return on customer" to the creation of advocates, settling for loyalty, and allow for the possibility that you will get a strong back-wash of satisfaction if you are targeting to advocacy as a result, and, thus, the customer as your partner.

I also hope that you see that the Commonwealth of Self-Interest (COSI) is not a fantasy but a real possibility as the PC and video gaming worlds have proven. I didn't write this book to promote a pipe dream.

You might have felt while reading all this, "Maybe you think it can be done, but how realistic is it for me to do it?" Reality is what drives this entire book. This is not about the ideal. This is the baseline for companies that want to grow in the 21st century. Everything in this book has been done already at one level or another. I'm just putting it all together.

The changes that have occurred in how we interact and communicate are both undeniable and irrevocable. It becomes a matter of not whether you want to adjust accordingly, but how you want to handle the change.

Remember, no matter how tough the accomplishment may be, it's still based on the simplest possible principle:

If a customer likes you and continues to like you, they will continue to do business with you. If they don't, they won't.

I trust that you realize that there is a direct business benefit when you do all this. There are dozens of examples throughout the book that, I think, make the point clear. Do all of this or some of this, and reap the whirlwind. If you weren't ready to believe me, you had the word of multiple thought leaders in their respective fields to give you the benefit of their experience and wisdom, whether they agreed with me or not.

What I'm asking you to do here is go forth and build a customer-engaged culture at your company. Doing so will align you with the needs of your current customers and, at the same time, give you the room you need to be fruitful and multiply the benefits to your business. But please, please, understand that in the time it took you to finish reading this book, things have already changed again. Though we approach what feels like the final byway, we didn't get to it before it began to branch into another new road.

That said, thanks for indulging me throughout this book. It's the distilla-tion of what I've been thinking and doing and kind of preaching for the last two decades, but with the changes in the world and the business climate in particular considered as they happened. We may never reach the actual destination, but the journey itself is quite the amazing trip, isn't it? Namaste, and stay engaged.

INDEX

ABOUT THE AUTHOR

Paul Greenberg, often called the "Godfather of CRM," is founder and Managing Principal of The 56 Group, LLC, an advisory firm focused on customer-facing strategic services. His book, *CRM at the Speed of Light,* now in its 4th edition, has been published in nine languages and has been called "the bible of the CRM industry." Paul sits on the Global Advisory Board of the SEAT Consortium as its only non-sports professional. He has been the EVP of the CRM Association, the Chairman of the University of Toronto's Rotman School of Management CRM Centre of Excellence Board of Advisers, a Board of Advisors member of the Baylor University MBA Program for CRM majors, and co-chairman of Rutgers University's CRM Research Center. He was elected to *CRM* magazine's CRM Hall of Fame in 2010—the first non-vendor-related thought leader in its history. Paul is the recipient of numerous awards as a leader in marketing, sales, customer service, social media, and CRM; and he works with customer-facing technology vendors and practitioners to craft go-to-market strategies, engagement programs, product development road maps, marketing/messaging, and outreach. Oh yeah, and he loves his wife Yvonne, the Yankees, and animals—especially cats.